Cult Telefantasy Series

CRITICAL EXPLORATIONS IN SCIENCE FICTION AND FANTASY
(a series edited by Donald E. Palumbo and C.W. Sullivan III)

1 *Worlds Apart? Dualism and Transgression in Contemporary Female Dystopias* (Dunja M. Mohr, 2005)

2 *Tolkien and Shakespeare: Essays on Shared Themes and Language* (ed. Janet Brennan Croft, 2007)

3 *Culture, Identities and Technology in the* Star Wars *Films: Essays on the Two Trilogies* (ed. Carl Silvio, Tony M. Vinci, 2007)

4 *The Influence of* Star Trek *on Television, Film and Culture* (ed. Lincoln Geraghty, 2008)

5 *Hugo Gernsback and the Century of Science Fiction* (Gary Westfahl, 2007)

6 *One Earth, One People: The Mythopoeic Fantasy Series of Ursula K. Le Guin, Lloyd Alexander, Madeleine L'Engle and Orson Scott Card* (Marek Oziewicz, 2008)

7 *The Evolution of Tolkien's Mythology: A Study of the History of Middle-earth* (Elizabeth A. Whittingham, 2008)

8 *H. Beam Piper: A Biography* (John F. Carr, 2008)

9 *Dreams and Nightmares: Science and Technology in Myth and Fiction* (Mordecai Roshwald, 2008)

10 Lilith *in a New Light: Essays on the George MacDonald Fantasy Novel* (ed. Lucas H. Harriman, 2008)

11 *Feminist Narrative and the Supernatural: The Function of Fantastic Devices in Seven Recent Novels* (Katherine J. Weese, 2008)

12 *The Science of Fiction and the Fiction of Science: Collected Essays on SF Storytelling and the Gnostic Imagination* (Frank McConnell, ed. Gary Westfahl, 2009)

13 *Kim Stanley Robinson Maps the Unimaginable: Critical Essays* (ed. William J. Burling, 2009)

14 *The Inter-Galactic Playground: A Critical Study of Children's and Teens' Science Fiction* (Farah Mendlesohn, 2009)

15 *Science Fiction from Québec: A Postcolonial Study* (Amy J. Ransom, 2009)

16 *Science Fiction and the Two Cultures: Essays on Bridging the Gap Between the Sciences and the Humanities* (ed. Gary Westfahl, George Slusser, 2009)

17 *Stephen R. Donaldson and the Modern Epic Vision: A Critical Study of the "Chronicles of Thomas Covenant" Novels* (Christine Barkley, 2009)

18 *Ursula K. Le Guin's Journey to Post-Feminism* (Amy M. Clarke, 2010)

19 *Portals of Power: Magical Agency and Transformation in Literary Fantasy* (Lori M. Campbell, 2010)

20 *The Animal Fable in Science Fiction and Fantasy* (Bruce Shaw, 2010)

21 *Illuminating* Torchwood: *Essays on Narrative, Character and Sexuality in the BBC Series* (ed. Andrew Ireland, 2010)

22 *Comics as a Nexus of Cultures: Essays on the Interplay of Media, Disciplines and International Perspectives* (ed. Mark Berninger, Jochen Ecke, Gideon Haberkorn, 2010)

23 *The Anatomy of Utopia: Narration, Estrangement and Ambiguity in More, Wells, Huxley and Clarke* (Károly Pintér, 2010)

24 *The Anticipation Novelists of 1950s French Science Fiction* (Bradford Lyau, 2010)

25 *The* Twilight *Mystique: Critical Essays on the Novels and Films* (ed. Amy M. Clarke, Marijane Osborn, 2010)

26 *The Mythic Fantasy of Robert Holdstock: Critical Essays on the Fiction* (ed. Donald E. Morse, Kálmán Matolcsy, 2011)

27 *Science Fiction and the Prediction of the Future: Essays on Foresight and Fallacy* (ed. Gary Westfahl, Wong Kin Yuen, Amy Kit-sze Chan, 2011)

28 *Apocalypse in Australian Fiction and Film: A Critical Study* (Roslyn Weaver, 2011)

29 *British Science Fiction Film and Television: Critical Essays.* (ed. Tobias Hochscherf, James Leggott, 2011)

30 *Cult Telefantasy Series: A Critical Analysis of* The Prisoner, Twin Peaks, The X-Files, Buffy the Vampire Slayer, Lost, Heroes, Doctor Who *and* Star Trek (Sue Short, 2011)

31 *The Postnational Fantasy: Postcolonialism, Cosmopolitics and Science Fiction* (ed. Masood Ashraf Raja, Jason W. Ellis, Swaralipi Nandi, 2011)

32 *Heinlein's Juvenile Novels: A Cultural Dictionary* (C.W. Sullivan III, 2011)

33 *Welsh Mythology and Folklore in Popular Culture: Essays on Adaptations in Literature, Film, Television and Digital Media* (ed. Audrey Becker, Kristin Noone, 2011)

Cult Telefantasy Series

A Critical Analysis of *The Prisoner,*
Twin Peaks, The X-Files, Buffy the
Vampire Slayer, Lost, Heroes,
Doctor Who and *Star Trek*

SUE SHORT

CRITICAL EXPLORATIONS IN SCIENCE FICTION AND FANTASY, 30
Donald E. Palumbo *and* C.W. Sullivan III, *series editors*

McFarland & Company, Inc., Publishers
Jefferson, North Carolina, and London

LIBRARY OF CONGRESS CATALOGUING-IN-PUBLICATION DATA

Short, Sue, 1968–
    Cult telefantasy series : a critical analysis of The prisoner, Twin peaks, The X-files, Buffy the vampire slayer, Lost, Heroes, Doctor Who and Star trek / Sue Short.
    [Donald Palumbo and C.W. Sullivan III, series editors]
        p.   cm. — (Critical explorations in science fiction and fantasy ; 30)
    Includes bibliographical references and index.

    ISBN 978-0-7864-4315-4
    softcover : 50# alkaline paper ∞

    1. Fantasy television programs—History and criticism.
    2. Science fiction television programs—History and criticism.
    I. Title.
    PN1992.8.F35S57   2011
    791.45'615—dc22   2011013892

BRITISH LIBRARY CATALOGUING DATA ARE AVAILABLE

© 2011 Sue Short. All rights reserved

No part of this book may be reproduced or transmitted in any form or by any means, electronic or mechanical, including photocopying or recording, or by any information storage and retrieval system, without permission in writing from the publisher.

On the cover: Patrick McGoohan as Number Six from the television series *The Prisoner* (ITV/Photofest)

Manufactured in the United States of America

McFarland & Company, Inc., Publishers
   Box 611, Jefferson, North Carolina 28640
   www.mcfarlandpub.com

For Mr. K

Acknowledgments

Thanks to Donald Palumbo for believing in this project from the start. Your faith meant a lot. Thanks also to my parents, for having the television tuned to the right shows as I grew up, which must have had an impact on inspiring these interests. To Jamie Blake, heaps of gratitude for making those last seasons of *Lost* available to me.

And special thanks to Julian, I hope this is worth the wait.

Contents

Acknowledgments	viii
Introduction	1
1—*The Prisoner*: The Show That Set the Precedents	13
2—*Twin Peaks*: The Death of Laura Palmer—And the Birth of a Phenomenon	33
3—*The X-Files*: Trust, Belief, and Broken Promises	55
4—*Buffy the Vampire Slayer*: Beauty and the "Big Bad"	84
5—How *Lost* Redefined Cult Television: A Mystery Island and a Monster Hit	108
6—Why *Heroes* Failed: The Superpowered Franchise That Fell from Grace	138
7—*Doctor Who* and *Star Trek*: Twenty-First Century Reboots	166
Conclusion	195
An A to Z of Telefantasy Series	207
Bibliography	231
Index	241

Introduction

In an interview with *Alias* and *Lost* creator J.J. Abrams, journalist Steve Rose was prompted to reconsider his assumptions in describing his subject as a geek, affirming that "in an age when the most popular movies and TV series are based on comic books, sci-fi, fantasy and the supernatural, we are all basically geeks now" (Rose 2009). The popularity of recent fantasy-related television is a fundamental motivation behind this book, which asserts a need to revise former assumptions about the likely audience for such material, and questions what has led to this increased interest. Providing an assessment of diverse "telefantasy" series—shows with an SF, fantasy, or supernatural element—it argues that the genre warrants greater critical examination, having produced some of the most innovative series ever made. Although frequently derided as escapist or trivial, notable examples have won industry recognition and critical acclaim, praised for their high production values, complex narratives, and stylistic innovations. Equally significantly, broadcasters have started to recognize telefantasy's value, particularly in generating the kind of interest that is increasingly coveted by the industry. In order to better understand the genre, and how this newfound status has come about, the following assessment provides case studies of *Doctor Who* (1963–89, 2005–), *Star Trek* and its spin-offs (1966–9, 1987–1994, 1993–9, 1995–2001, 2001–5), *The Prisoner* (1966–7), *Twin Peaks* (1990–91), *The X-Files* (1993–2002), *Buffy the Vampire Slayer* (1997–2002), *Lost* (2004–10) and *Heroes* (2006–10). Their production histories are outlined and their aims and intentions noted, a summary is provided of key thematic concerns, and an assessment made of their respective legacies—both in terms of influences on one another and the array of shows they have inspired. In addition, by taking into account the industrial context in which each series emerged, key changes in broadcasting are discussed, including the rise of cable, the effects of deregulation, and the challenges wrought by the digital age. This book is consequently likely to interest anyone studying television or popular culture, as well as fans of fantastic television who would like to understand what such series have in common and what impact they have had within broadcasting.

Over the course of this analysis a number of ideas are challenged, including what constitutes "cult TV." Although the term is generally used to describe shows that elicit intense interest from viewers, it has also generated some discrepancies in its meaning. Reeves, Rogers and Epstein contend that "what distinguishes cult shows from typical fare is that a relatively large percentage of the viewers are avid fans" (1995, 27)—a group they differentiate from "casual viewers" and "devoted viewers" in terms of "enthusiastic viewer engagement," evidenced by activities such as archiving series, using favorite shows as a "major source of self-definition," and joining "interpretive communities" to discuss them (26). Today, with the archiving of series a simple matter of purchasing DVDs, and online discussion boards routinely set up by networks, we might ask whether this distinction still applies, or if the media industry now facilitates activities formerly initiated by fans. Attempting a further qualification, Matt Hills argues that a "cult" series is signaled not only by specific modes of engagement but by "its duration, especially in the absence of 'new' or official material" (Hills 2002, x). However, cult interest is not necessarily conferred in retrospect, but may surround series while they are still in production. Mythology shows—series that have an abundance of narrative detail built up over successive installments, and enigmas designed to foster regular viewing and invite close analysis—can be traced to early examples like *The Prisoner*, which elicited considerable audience engagement and scrutiny as it aired. Later series such as *Twin Peaks* and *The X-Files* were similarly designed to yield intense interest during production, aiming to keep viewers guessing about narrative intrigues (and taking advantage of new media technologies such as the VCR and Internet in encouraging close attention). *Lost* employed a number of mysteries to prompt speculation as it broadcast, as well as planting "clues" in an array of media, and its remarkable success further illustrates why prior assumptions about cult television demand to be reconsidered. Where "cult" was once aligned with an exclusive and marginal interest (generally associated with obscure or rarified tastes, and an identity conferred by fans, rather than a marketing brand), this no longer appears to be the case. The broadcasting industry has proved adept at commodifying cult interest, with many telefantasy series "pre-packaged" as cults prior to transmission. As Sara Gwenllian Jones asserts, "The term 'cult television' has a variety of different meanings" and a diversity of potential audiences. For example, although cult appeal is generally denoted by shows that "accrue substantial active fan cultures"—additionally noting that "such series (though not always) belong to one or other of the fantastic series of science fiction, fantasy, horror, and the supernatural"—this does not necessarily imply that their audience is limited, as Jones points out that "fantastic genre cult television series are very often mainstream programs ... [which] appeal to both a mass general audience and to a dedicated fan base" (Jones 2003, 164–5).

The present work asks why "fantastic series" engender such interest, noting key thematic and stylistic concerns, identifying the methods used to encourage audience engagement, and evaluating how the "crossover cult"— capable of securing mainstream appeal—has transformed telefantasy's fortunes. Where the genre was once relegated to modest budgets, poor timeslots, and a minimum of expectation, recent examples have benefitted from impressive budgets, primetime slots, and a variety of promotional endeavors to secure a mass audience, thanks largely to the surprising success of a fantasy island adventure that pulled in three times its anticipated audience. As Benji Wilson notes:

> When Damon Lindelof and J.J. Abrams sat down to sell *Lost* to America's ABC network ... they envisaged a series of 12 programmes aimed at the niche audience that had embraced Abrams's spy series *Alias*. Abrams and Lindelof found their niche anoraks—it was just that they numbered 25 million people [Wilson 2007].

By blending the fantastic with other generic features, and providing a set of mysteries that would get viewers hunting for clues and engaging in avid speculation, *Lost* combined quintessential cult features with mass appeal, securing unprecedented ratings and radically revising industry assumptions about the potential for "genre" shows. Not only did it inspire network investment in a number of big-budget telefantasy series, we have also seen various cult favorites return to our screens, including a revised series of *Doctor Who* (2005–), a cinematic "reboot" of *Star Trek* (2009), and even a miniseries makeover of *The Prisoner* (2009). The interest taken in shows that first aired over 40 years ago is not simply a matter of nostalgia, but an indication of how the cult telefantasy series has become big business, resulting in shows deliberately constructed to garner crossover appeal, with impressive production values and a number of narrative strategies used to attract high ratings. Viewers are actively pursued through a variety of media and fannish interests—such as paying close attention to texts, discussing plot developments, and archiving and re-viewing series— are no longer considered unusual or excessive, but have become relatively commonplace. However, contemporary developments have not proved unanimously successful. *Lost* may have earned three times its expected audience, but interest diminished as the concept was elaborated, most of the shows that followed have failed to outlast it, and the revisions made to long-standing cult series have all met with criticism from established fans—affirming that the changing fortunes for telefantasy are not necessarily to be championed. In fact, a key question asked in this analysis is whether the heightened status surrounding the genre has proven detrimental to its output, with increased commercial interests becoming more overt and a situation arising in which imitation threatens to efface innovation.

Although the depth of engagement and prolonged audience interest that typically distinguish a cult show are most commonly attached to telefantasy series, this affinity has received little critical discussion—an omission this book aims to redress. The term "telefantasy" originated within fan circles, first appearing in magazines such as *Starburst* in the 1970s (Johnson 2005, 2) as a means of discussing series that involve fantastic elements (whether it be in terms of setting, superhuman abilities, or extraordinary events). Critical use of the term is less common, with the exception of Catherine Johnson's study of the same name, which argues that fantastic television constitutes a discernible genre, a claim this analysis both extends and corroborates in noting shared characteristics and concerns. Despite inherent problems in terms of breadth, particularly given the degree of generic slippage many shows are prone to, it is in identifying their fantastical features that the genre's appeal can be better understood, alongside a propensity at reinvention which has proved crucial to its survival. The series discussed range from 1963 to 2010, mostly concentrating on key developments over the last two decades. A chronological order is followed, with the exception of *Doctor Who* and *Star Trek*, which are assessed in the final chapter to appraise contemporary revisions made in the light of preceding trends. Instead, *The Prisoner* serves as the starting point for analysis, as this maverick series is deemed to have pioneered a number of cult characteristics, evaluating how the innovations of later series emerged via a similar mix of creative endeavor and practical necessity, and highlighting significant industrial developments along the way. A select history of cult telefantasy series is thus provided, revealing how the genre has adapted itself to changing conditions—flourishing when increased competition lead to the pursuit of niche markets, proving able to attract a desired demographic, and acquiring renewed network interest when deregulation resulted in greater media conglomeration and a quest to find shows that could make the most of available assets. Understanding is thus yielded of the factors that have propelled telefantasy's development—including new legislation, new networks and new technologies—all of which would reshape the genre and extend its appeal.

Relatively new territory is explored here. Academic assessments of telefantasy shows tend to fall into three categories: 1) those that confine themselves to a single text (such as the publications edited by Lavery et al. on *Twin Peaks*, *The X-Files*, *Lost* and *Heroes*, as well as the growing number of scholarly collections on *Buffy the Vampire Slayer* and *Battlestar Galactica*); 2) those that situate series within a wider discussion of cult and quality (see Jancovich and Lyons 2003, Bignell and Lacey 2005, Hammond and Mazdon 2005, and McCabe and Akass 2007); or 3) those that focus on surrounding fan cultures (see Jenkins 1992, and Hills 2002). The problem with the first tendency is that it provides limited opportunity to discern shared features between series, which is pivotal to this analysis. Evaluating specific examples as "quality TV" is a notable critical tendency in recent academic work, highlighting respective innovations; yet such an approach tends to obscure their generic identity. While many telefantasy shows share archetypal "quality" characteristics—particularly in terms of high production values and narrative complexity—identifying their generic features is considered to be more revealing (particularly as sit-coms and crime dramas have also been critically assessed as "quality" shows, without yielding the same engagement from viewers). As to the emphasis placed by some critics on fan responses to texts, this has the problem of limiting the area of discussion to reception, and tends to generalize about audiences, often at the expense of getting at the heart of the texts themselves. This study provides a broader analysis of the shows assessed, taking note of how they have been produced as much as consumed, and attempts to acknowledge the diversity of audience reactions in order to offer a more comprehensive account. A similar template is followed for each chapter, discussing the context in which each series emerged, the influences they draw upon, the responses generated, and the legacy they have created. As a result, the reader is able to discern how telefantasy has evolved over the years, note how series have influenced one another, and understand why the industry has made greater use of telefantasy's potential.

Catherine Johnson's *Telefantasy* (2005) is the closest extant work to this in making a case for telefantasy as a genre in its own right, and covers a number of similar series. However, few links are suggested between series, an emphasis on aesthetics tends to elide thematic concerns, and later telefantasy shows are omitted—negating crucial changes that have occurred since *Lost*'s release. By incorporating these developments, the impact of greater industrial investment is demonstrated, including the challenges posed in attempting to cross the niche/mass divide, delivering content in a variety of formats, and aiming to meet increased levels of expectation. Invariably, while this book attempts to offer the most up-to-date appraisal of telefantasy, it is unable to anticipate potential directions taken by the genre. A year ago telefantasy was riding the crest of a wave, and a number of new productions had been commissioned. Most have since been cancelled, and there are signs the genre is falling out of favor—the result of several high profile shows failing to yield the returns sought. As the genre is experiencing a downturn in interest, the hazards of contemporary broadcasting are made clear; yet telefantasy's fate remains open. After all, it has endured such spells before and will do so again, with sufficient flexibility to adapt itself to changing tastes and times, and to engage with audiences in a very particular way.

In appraising the respective innovations and intersections of a number of landmark series, an assessment is offered of a challenging, dynamic, and highly inventive genre. Attention is paid to increased demands: having to reward close attention from viewers (without frustrating them), to offer surprise (yet avoid leaks and spoilers), and to respond to changing viewing patterns through transmedia storytelling (while keeping enough people tuned to their televisions to retain necessary ratings). Series are now made in anticipation of being screened on high definition television (as well as on laptops and mobile phones) and designed to be watched more than once (with DVD extras providing additional incentive for scrutiny)—indicating how cultish levels of engagement have advanced alongside an appetite for shows that reward close attention.

Not all telefantasy shows manage to elicit "cult" interest. Some arrive too soon to find a receptive audience, some are cancelled early, and some simply have something missing. As the following analysis suggests, successful cult shows comprise a number of factors, including an element of good fortune in being in the right place at the right time. The appendix provides production details and descriptions of a variety of series—some famous, others which rapidly disappeared—to show how certain themes have developed and how threads of influence can be discerned. Telefantasy's thematic mutability is thus made clear, complementing the case studies by revealing continued variations on established themes.

Over the course of this analysis a changing industrial attitude towards fans is noted. Where they were once largely negated, the level of interest associated with "cult" appeal is now actively courted by the media industry eager to secure viewers that will regularly watch a given show, potentially purchase related material, and offer virtually instant feedback in online discussions—all of which obviously benefits shows while still in production. From this perspective, fans have become the ideal viewer-consumer, enabling the industry to adapt material to suit their requirements. Viewers are by no means always heard—or always complimentary—yet their willingness to voice criticism has been notably enhanced by the ease and anonymity of the Internet; and it is in regarding television as more than a disposable commodity that has helped create shows with a difference. The standard history for increasingly innovative serialized drama is that this has emerged as an industrial response to increased competition and a need to attract loyal viewing with intricate plots, complex characters, and layers of narrative intrigue—attributes frequently dubbed as markers of "quality." However, these developments obviously require an appreciative and discerning audience—a factor generally omitted from critical discussions, just as the role played by telefantasy series in yielding such an audience and marking out new territory similarly tends to be ignored. As Robert J. Thompson notes, "Quality TV breaks rules," citing its main attributes as an ability to "transform a traditional genre or defy standard generic parameters," a "quality pedigree—involving artists with reputations made in other classier media," an ability to attract an audience with "blue chip demographics—the upscale educated urban dwelling young viewers advertisers so desire to reach," "a large ensemble cast," and the fact that "quality TV has a memory—with examples that tend to refer back to previous events" (1997, 12–13). Cult telefantasy shows are thus quality shows in terms of many of these criteria, particularly this last point. As Matt Hills asserts, "Fans expect adherence to established tenets, characteristics and narrative 'backstories,' which production teams thus revise at their peril" (Hills 2002, 28). Fan investment has often been credited by show runners and writers for intensifying the level of complexity given to select telefantasy shows, inspiring them to make content worthy of avid interest, although this has not prevented many from veering off-course—with *The X-Files* creating an overly intricate mythology that pushed fan loyalty to the limit, *Lost* adding mystery upon mystery and ultimately leaving most by the wayside, and *Battlestar Galactica* seeming to lose the plot entirely by the time its makers opted to end the series. In each case fans enthusiastically participated in their mythologies in attempting to work out respective mysteries, only for frustration to ensue when official denouements failed to satisfy. While cult shows have an unwritten contract with viewers to be worthy of the investment made, and increasingly invite interaction, this does not rule out the likelihood of disappointment. *Heroes* exemplifies a failed cult in this respect and serves as a cogent reminder that despite considerable network investment and an array of "quality" features, success is by no means guaranteed, with an attempt to please different sectors of the audience but one of the hazards faced by contemporary cult shows.

In charting telefantasy's evolution over the last few decades, important developments are discerned, yet challenges are also made to some established critical opinions. For example, although the shows discussed are predominantly American, some British examples are deemed equally significant in the history of cult telefantasy, and are included for this reason. In addition, while critical accounts of the "quality cult" tend to regard its development as being motivated solely by economic factors, this analysis seeks to provide a broader perspective, asserting that considerable creativity has extended beyond practical requirements and continues to make itself felt. Reeves, Rogers and Epstein assert that "the rise of cult TV signals one of the most extreme shifts in American mass communication since TV replaced cinema as the main medium" (1995, 24). As they argue, the dominance of the three networks in the U.S., and their primary appeal to a mass audience, gave way to niche marketing strategies with the rise of cable and satellite television in the late 1970s. An increasingly fragmented climate led to a focus on smaller yet select audiences; and in aiming to interest "quality demographics," a new degree of creativity was fostered because, as they affirm, "the networks' pursuit of sophisticated viewers with money to burn also provided economic incentive for supporting other narrative innovations that are often labeled 'postmodern,' including the blurring of generic boundaries" (30). The implication is that experimentation is pragmatically motivated—a means of creating distinct programming to attract a sought-after market. John Caldwell's notion of "televisuality" is pertinent in this respect, asserting that the 1980s saw greater visual stylization and narrative experimentation as a result of competition and a desire to make shows that stood out (1995). Robert J. Thompson terms this period television's second "golden age," contending that from the birth of *Hill Street Blues* in 1981 to the end of *Twin Peaks* a decade later, a period of innovation made itself felt which quickly gave rise to imitation. Thompson argues that the growth of "quality" characteristics emanated from a desire to reproduce what sells best, asserting that ultimately "'Quality TV' had become a super-genre, a formula unto itself" (2007, xvii). Just as Caldwell considers "televisuality" a stylistic tendency comprised of formerly radical elements rendered mainstream, a similar tone can be detected in Thompson's appraisal, from praising perceived innovations in television to evincing wariness about their mass-production.

Although such misgivings are understandable, unique and challenging series have continued to emerge, a significant number of which are works of telefantasy. Far from innovation ending with *Twin Peaks*, as Thompson contends, a number of interesting shows have followed, often emerging on newer networks, including archetypal "quality cult" series *The X-Files* (which helped make Fox a major network) and *Buffy the Vampire Slayer* (which appeared on fledgling network the WB and similarly found a "quality demographic," launching a flurry of imitators). Hybrid features lent interest to these shows, a degree of sophistication was evident in their writing as much as their looks, and critical acclaim added to telefantasy's growing esteem. While the genre had previously enjoyed periods of popularity (in the late 1950s and '60s, as well as a decade later), it found an increasingly receptive climate as we entered the twenty-first century. If *Twin Peaks* baffled audiences the moment it featured a dream sequence with a dancing dwarf, *Lost* found viewers fourteen years on (and on the very same network) with much greater willingness to be taken on a mystery tour through a strange world. Although sufficient stigma remained around the genre to induce its makers to downplay the fantasy element, it would eventually reveal itself as a full-blown telefantasy show, with a hefty dose of magic and mysticism, and achieve unprecedented success. Why had this change come about? Although Thompson suggests a host of uninspired imitations occurred in the wake of *Twin Peaks*, a steady output of telefantasy series continued to mix and match generic elements, push boundaries, play on the audience's familiarity with popular culture, and occasionally mock themselves with in-jokes that wink at the audience and strategies designed to make the viewing experience far from passive. Numerous postmodern features were thus employed to give each show a new edge, repackaging telefantasy by including elements of murder mystery, soap opera, detective show, and action adventure series. While theorists tend to regard such methods as originating in the 1980s, reiterating a critical tendency to align the evolution of the "quality cult" with specific developments in U.S. broadcasting (even among U.K. scholars), this is far from the case. Many features can be traced back to the '60s cult show *The Prisoner*, which characterized a "spy-fi" series long before the term was coined to describe Abrams' *Alias* (*The Prisoner* has been admitted as a chief influence on his work). *The Prisoner* is consequently discussed as an important pioneer of quality cult features, while *Doctor Who* is also included in this modified history because of its distinction as the longest running telefantasy series of all time. The intent is to revise perceived misconceptions, such as deeming "quality" features to be exclusively American when cross-cultural intersections are a more accurate appraisal. In fact, intertextual elements have been apparent since television began, not only deriving from the pursuit of profit, but through series creators, influenced by their own viewing pleasures, paying homage to shows that have inspired them and displaying similar intentions in their own work. This is not simply a result of industrial cooptation of cult interests, but a more complex situation in which former fans have become involved in the industry and inflected material with a specific sensibility, perpetuating cult interest.

The emergence of new media technologies has also led to increasingly sophisticated fans, enabling them to catch up on cult shows of the past, source information at the touch of a button, and interact with writers and producers. Networks have marked out their digital terrain on the Internet, luring fans to official sites via regular postings from creative staff and an opportunity to ask questions and provide feedback. While *Twin Peaks* was one of the first television series to initiate online discussions, prompting posters to wonder if the show's writers were influenced by their suggestions, this has become an implicit strategy, with writers on many contemporary cult series regularly monitoring fan discussions and occasionally responding to ideas within shows. The last few years have also seen greater use of online resources to stream shows and provide tie-ins such as "webisodes" and "alternate reality" games, further immersing the viewer within the fictional world of a given series. As Sara Gwenllian Jones asserts, "This is world-building for profit" (166)—extending narratives to make the most of available resources and attract a younger affluent demographic that is highly sought by advertisers, yet fans have become equally canny in their use of these resources, as we shall see. Not all genres are suited to having a tie-in website, or liable to attract the kind of viewer that will want to discuss narrative intricacies with fellow fans, speculate on developments with the show's creators, or otherwise extend the fictional world presented onscreen. Telefantasy has a predilection for such engagement, as well as being transposed into various formats (comic, book, game, and film being just a few examples), which is likely to remain a powerful incentive for further investment in the genre, reiterating its critical significance.

Catherine Johnson notes the breadth of themes encompassed by the label telefantasy, describing it as "a broad generic category to describe a wide range of fantasy, science fiction and horror television programs," while also deeming it a "generically unstable category" which often combines elements of other genres (2-3). This is certainly the case in the examples assessed, with hybrid tendencies innovatively reworking established tropes. As a consequence, a standard espionage tale gets an added twist when a kidnapped spy finds himself in a world with impossible technologies, just as a murder mystery is curiously reinvigorated when set in a town populated by strange characters engaged in soapy sub-plots and preyed upon by demonic forces. Aliens, urban myths and human aberrations are taken more seriously when investigated by the FBI; vampires shed their hoary old guise when undercut with sarcastic quips from high school adolescents; and a fantasy island becomes compelling viewing in offering a multitude of genres to explore. Generic instability does not preclude the ability to recognize such shows as works of telefantasy, offering a narrative flexibility that accounts for much of the genre's appeal. Equally important (particularly in aiming to secure crossover success) is the ability to ground its fantasy in some way. Although the fantastic constitutes what is, in basic terms, "unreal," this is often situated in a seemingly ordinary world, juxtaposing the everyday with the extraordinary. Tzvetan Todorov asserts that "the fantastic is that hesitation experienced by a person who knows only the laws of nature, confronting an apparently supernatural event" (1975, 25). Telefantasy hinges upon the suspension of disbelief, asking viewers to withhold their skepticism and take certain plot points as read, yet is most engaging when it utilizes fantastic ideas in the service of good storytelling, with characters and situations that are both intellectually and emotionally satisfying. For the following analysis the term is used to describe series that contain fantastical elements, whether it be specific figures (such as shapeshifters, vampires, or people with superhuman abilities), phenomena (i.e. portals to other dimensions), or technologies not yet known to exist (including machines capable of extensive space travel or time-travel). Whether or not they are supernatural or science fictional in origin, telefantasy encompasses both.

The fantastic can be used for a variety of ends, often adding intrigue and enigma. *The Prisoner* continues to inspire debate about its meaning, with Number 6's entrapment in the Village variously interpreted as death or psychosis, as well as offering a satirical statement about conformity. In the dreamlike logic that propels *Twin Peaks*, the hunt for Laura Palmer's killer is guided by impossible beings that come from Another Place — the origins of which continue to provoke fan discussion. *The X-Files* reveals various monsters in our midst, yet does not allow them to be fully rationalized, while its posited conspiracy plays on the possibility of paranoid delusion, leading several theorists to view it as a symptom of contemporary uncertainty. *Buffy the Vampire Slayer* uses a mythical realm to foreground its rite of passage tale (while generating an audience way beyond adolescence). *Lost* similarly includes a degree of symbolism, its fantasy island ultimately serving as a testing ground for its castaways, aiming for metaphysical depth. In aspiring toward metaphorical significance, such narratives encourage ongoing cult interest, often concluding with oblique finales to foster continued debate. While fans do not demand that events necessarily conform to rational explanation, some internal logic is sought. Characters should therefore be consistent; identifiable motivations must govern their actions; and there are limits in the possibilities allowed. The fantastic does not permit an "anything goes" rationale, even if much of its appeal is centered upon violating established rules.

Rosemary Jackson views fantastic literature as inherently subversive because it "traces the unsaid and the unseen of culture, that which has been silenced, made invisible, covered over and made absent" (1981, 3–4). Kathryn Hume identifies more profound interests, arguing that "fantasy challenges our assumptions about many important issues: the nature of the universe and man's place therein, mortality, morality, corporeal limitation..." while summarizing its appeal as providing the "novelty that circumvents automatic responses and cracks the crust of habitude" (1984, 164 and 167). Televisual fantasy has often sought to question what we take for granted—challenging what may be termed as "consensus reality"—and is celebrated by fans (and a growing number of critics) for this reason. Many of the series discussed in this analysis probe the genre's ability to ask big questions, some of which border on the metaphysical by asking if there is a realm beyond mortal existence and whether our lives are guided in some way. The fact that these concerns have arisen during a time of global political uncertainty is of particular interest, suggesting a form of reassurance has been sought in the most traditional of forms. Older examples of cult telefantasy offer somewhat bleak conclusions in their assessment of humanity—with *The Prisoner* and *Twin Peaks* each foregrounding our intrinsic ambivalence and suggesting corruption is inevitable. *The X-Files* may seem equally cynical, yet in questioning if we are alone in the universe the series is less concerned with little gray men (as many assumed) than an age-old quest for spiritual comfort. *Buffy* may take the unusual step of making a teenage girl humanity's savior, yet affirms that her place in heaven is assured, much like *Lost*'s "survivors." Fantasy may not have to be feel-good to earn cult status, yet this serves as an obvious attraction, and it is perhaps no surprise that the two longest standing SF series to date, *Doctor Who* and *Star Trek*, openly invest an idealized humanity, with representatives who consistently triumph.

While telefantasy has a capacity to be thought-provoking, offering intellectual, philosophical, and occasionally political ideas to bolster enjoyment, its pleasures include a range of factors, such as imaginative diversion (enabling a sense of wonder), visual interest (showcasing special effects as well as displaying cinematic stylishness), a knowing attitude (with in-jokes and allusions), and a heightened mode of engagement (rewarding close attention and often uniting viewers in a common quest). It is a combination of factors that may look formulaic, yet is difficult to get right, as *Heroes* exemplifies. While the show had designs for crossover appeal, aiming to emulate *Lost*'s breakaway success—and initially succeeding—it also proves the fickle nature of the business. Writing in 2007, when the series still evoked admiration, Wilson described it as "a clever pick-and-mix that has succeeded because it offers all the joys of cult viewing to a much bigger cult," further remarking that "at a time when the television audience is becoming ever more fragmented, it suggests that eventually a cult show and a hit show may well become one and the same" (Wilson 2007). Cult interest and commerciality are by no means mutually exclusive, as this study attests, yet the show's floundering fortunes reveal the pursuit of crossover success is a risky endeavor, no matter what parts have been cobbled together from past hits, with numerous other failures in recent years confirming the difficulty of making telefantasy with mainstream appeal. The assertion that "we are all geeks now" is clearly far from true, yet a growing interest in material that is carefully crafted, narratively compelling, and both imaginatively and emotionally rewarding testifies to interesting times for telefantasy. The following analysis explores how such interest has been acquired, noting how landmark shows have wielded their influence on one another and helped create an increasingly receptive audience, while additionally acknowledging that if telefantasy's status has significantly advanced in recent years, the challenges faced by the genre have increased accordingly.

1
The Prisoner: The Show That Set the Precedents

> *It was an attempt—that failed, really—to try a slightly different type of television series and, at the same time, take a stand on something I feel very strongly about: numeralization, mediocrity, this leveling of people by acceptance.*
>
> —Patrick McGoohan

A paradox on many levels, *The Prisoner* (1967–8) remains one of the most experimental and enigmatic series ever made. This chapter evaluates how the circumstances of its production enabled its makers to create a truly unique show, using telefantasy to couch a potent critique against conformity, and involving its audience in a way that had never been attempted before. The following analysis assesses its innovations and considerable influence, contending that, despite McGoohan's initial view of the series as a failed experiment, *The Prisoner* was a landmark achievement. Though it may have frustrated much of its initial audience, it has retrospectively acquired the recognition it deserves, inspiring other attempts to make a "different type of television series" and thereby revolutionizing the medium. While the series was very much a product of its era—borrowing experimental techniques from contemporary theater and cinema, as well as in its anti-establishment views—*The Prisoner* is also shown to be years ahead of its time by devising strategies that would become closely aligned with a cult text, including the level of detail involved in its design and features that invite an unprecedented degree of engagement. An examination is made of its production history, stylistic elements, thematic concerns, and ongoing influence. The miniseries version made in 2009, co-created by U.S. cable channel AMC and U.K. regional broadcaster Granada, is finally contrasted with the original series, noting how changing concerns have impacted on the premise.

The Prisoner has secured a firm place in popular culture, with images and themes (and certain lines of dialogue) that are instantly recognizable and widely referenced. As well as an array of books and websites devoted to the series, allusions have been made to it in a variety of other formats—including music, advertisements, feature films, and later television series—acquiring a level of recognition that is especially significant given that four decades have passed since it was made, particularly considering its initial response. Despite gaining 10–12 million viewers when first broadcast in the U.K., ratings declined amid widening confusion and frustration, production was hastily wrapped after its sponsor withdrew funding, and public uproar followed the finale—all of which partly substantiates McGoohan's view that the show "failed." However, this conclusion was drawn in 1970, relatively soon after *The Prisoner* first aired, and would be significantly revised as appreciation grew. While the majority of viewers were simply baffled by *The Prisoner*, and ultimately outraged by its failure to conform to expectations, a discerning minority noted something special about the series. Within a few years cult interest developed around the show. The creation of the "*Prisoner* Appreciation Society—Six of One" in 1976 led to an organized petitioning of networks to re-screen *The Prisoner* in the U.K., encouraging a reappraisal of its ideas and a growing number of admirers. In the U.S. the series first aired on CBS in 1968, and was shown again, by public demand, a year later. In 1978 it was re-screened on 20 stations across North America, becoming a campus favorite, and even found its way onto the syllabus when it was used as an educational text in Canada. Syndication on various channels around the world, and the release of the series on video and DVD, has enabled it to find new fans, attracting a range of viewers intrigued by its idiosyncrasies and eager to explore its meaning. For these reasons—together with its distinctive look, the themes articulated, and the multitude of innovations heralded—*The Prisoner* constitutes an archetypal example of cult television, eliciting avid interest from fans and clearly indicating extraordinary longevity. In comparison to *Doctor Who* and *Star Trek*, SF series that emerged in the same decade and went on to spawn immensely successful franchises, *The Prisoner* is far more modest, comprising only 17 episodes—barely enough to warrant a single season in contemporary terms. Nonetheless, it contains a wealth of ideas, asks questions that remain the subject of continued speculation, and addresses concerns that have acquired greater relevance as time has passed. Where he once deemed *The Prisoner* to have failed—by dint of its inability to attract mass popularity and understanding—McGoohan revised this assessment, claiming to be "gratified" by the growing response to it, and explicitly complimented its fans in stating the series was intended for "mostly intelligent people" (Troyer 1977). While the statement may seem somewhat elitist, it concedes the fact that *The Prisoner* was not readily conducive to mass appeal, but would reward the interest of select viewers: those prepared to take an active role in deciphering its enigmas and who delighted in its deviations. In many ways it was the first example of "Tease TV," offering a number of "clues" that led nowhere and inciting viewers to watch without providing the anticipated pay-off; yet it also broached serious concerns and would ensure a lasting legacy in simply daring to be difficult. The series established a number of precedents for cult series to come, testing the rules of television SF even as they were being established.

The Prisoner is, ostensibly, a spy series, inasmuch as it focuses on a government agent held captive in a mysterious location; yet it veers towards SF in the fantastical technologies at his captors' disposal and the dystopia they preside over: a society in which indoctrinated inmates are numbered and every attempt at individuality is suppressed. We learn that our protagonist resigned from his job in the secret service and was kidnapped shortly afterwards. He finds himself in a surreal location known as the Village—a place of such extraordinary appearance it invites the feeling he is in a dream. However, a nightmarish reality unfolds as he discovers its residents are routinely brainwashed, and there are no apparent means of escape. The main mystery posed is why our protagonist has been detained in this place and who runs it. His incarceration is allegedly motivated by the desire to know why he resigned, and a different figure appears each week, referred to as "Number 2" and tasked with discovering the reason ("Number 1" remains unknown until the end). Over the course of the series the prisoner states that he resigned as "a matter of conscience" and for "peace of mind," yet precisely what troubled the former agent is never disclosed. The desire to know more about him—and see if he will succeed in either escaping or overthrowing the Village authorities—invites close attention and continued involvement. On occasion we are given information we presume might be useful (encountering former colleagues, for example, or clues about the suggested location of the Village), yet these fail to amount to anything concrete, just as every escape attempt invariably returns our prisoner to where he began, including its oblique ending.

With *The Prisoner*, and arguably for the first time in a television series, audiences were presented with a product that defied their understanding, episodes that added to the central mystery each week, rather than resolving questions, and a protagonist whose name is never divulged (simply being referred to as "Number 6") and whose quest to escape remains unresolved—even by the finale. The fact that it flew in the face of expectation is reason enough for admirers to praise it. As Howard Zimmerman states, "Why bother to watch a show where the action is misleading, the conclusion inconclusive? Because it is provocative, stimulating, thought-provoking" (Zimmerman 1978). It is precisely these traits which have garnered cult interest—demanding ongoing scrutiny and interpretation. Such ambiguity has been deliberately employed in later productions to aid cult appeal, yet it was a daring departure at the time, with the show betraying a pronounced rebellious streak. The fact that the highest paid star in television was willing to stake his career on making such a groundbreaking series foregrounds its exceptional nature—and explains how it was even made. Patrick McGoohan had grown tired of playing John

Drake, the lead in ITC's hit spy series *Danger Man* (1960–1, 1964–7)—known as *Secret Agent* in the U.S.—and was thinking of quitting television altogether when story editor George Markstein conceived the premise for *The Prisoner*. Markstein drew on his former army career in developing the concept, influenced by rumors of a British internment camp where spies were detained after the war. Further inspiration seems to have been drawn from an episode of *Danger Man* ("Colony Three") in which Drake is sent to a mysterious spy school where liberty is curtailed. McGoohan was intrigued by the idea, and thought it would serve as an ideal first venture for his production company, Everyman Films Ltd. In March 1966, only two episodes into *Danger Man*'s fourth season—as his contract at ITC neared its end—he told managing director Lew Grade he was unwilling to make any more but had another project in mind. It was a canny move, calculated to take advantage of his celebrity, and it worked. Keen to retain his star's services, seemingly at any cost, Grade agreed to finance the new series to the tune of £75,000 an episode—an absolute fortune at the time (double that of *The Avengers*, for instance). The high expense was necessitated by the decision to film it in color (a requirement for the U.S. market) and the degree of location shooting involved, as well as costumes, sets, and props that would need to be created. This level of investment—and attention to detail—would make the series an early example of "quality" television. Grade's ability to afford such a budget was made possible by his legendary business acumen, having made a number of series with international (particularly American) appeal from which he had made a good profit. He shook hands with McGoohan without having a clue about *The Prisoner*'s premise yet clearly swayed by the enthusiasm of its co-creator.

Danger Man was integral to *The Prisoner* in various ways, having made McGoohan the household "name" he could capitalize on for his new series, partly influencing its premise with its spy school episode, and inspiring its setting also. Portmeirion, in North Wales, had been used in the very first episode of *Danger Man* ("View from the Villa") and became the main location for *The Prisoner*, lending a surreal quality in its beauty and strangeness. Like the series, it was designed as a unique experiment of undaunted ambition and imagination, combining an incongruous mix of styles and influences that would, according to its creator, Clough Williams-Ellis, almost "steal the show from its human cast" (Hora 1989, 19). McGoohan also assembled much of his crew from *Danger Man* staff, making the most of their production experience, including David Tomblin (who served as a co-executive producer, production manager, and occasional director and scriptwriter), George Markstein (whose role as story editor aimed to maintain coherence), Don Chaffey (the main director on the series, who established its look), Jack Shampan (the artistic director, who created the interior sets at Borehamwood, as well as props such as the cordless phones, signs, and taxis that gave the series such a unique otherworldly feel), and Brendan J. Stafford (the director of photography, who attested to McGoohan's influence in the unusual framing of shots and camera angles). In fact, McGoohan became involved in every area of production, taking the starring role, serving as executive producer, directing a number of episodes, and overseeing its editing and script writing also—inaugurating the role of show runner before the concept was even created. He was given carte blanche in what he wished to do, save for one thing. Prior to bankrolling the project, Grade asked McGoohan to extend the concept from his initial plan of 7 episodes to 13 (on the grounds this would be easier to sell overseas), followed by another season of the same number, depending on how it fared. This expansion would stretch the premise, yet McGoohan and his crew used the opportunity to push the boundaries of television, playing with everything from the associations built around McGoohan's star persona to questioning the function of television itself. ITC may have provided much of the financing, but with McGoohan in charge of the production company he was able to exercise an extraordinary level of freedom, making the series a radical departure from convention.

The promotional material from ITC stressed its originality, stating:

> *The Prisoner* is the most challenging and unusual series ever filmed for television.... It is a series with depth, stories that will make viewers think, and at the same time, will keep them on the edge of their seats with excitement as the Prisoner resists every physical and mental effort to break him [ITC publicity brochure 1967].

Although it was clearly a unique experiment, what is often ignored in discussions of *The Prisoner* are its many commercial aspects, including the combination of allegory and adventure (providing different levels of appeal); the high production values enabled by its budget (making the series look like a prestige product); the fact that it was filmed in color (anticipating new developments in broadcasting and granting long-term appeal); the numerous guest stars who featured as Number 2 (adding variety); the fact that it showcased McGoohan as the main star (capitalizing on his established popularity); the interest shown in the U.S. market (with Grade pre-selling the show to CBS); and the diverse intrigues of its narrative (prompting continued speculation). A bizarre press conference was held just prior to its broadcast, in which journalists were shown the first episode (anticipating the premiere screenings that would become an industry standard), followed by McGoohan asking them questions while he stood inside a cage. Such promotional efforts paid off in raising audience curiosity, and *The Prisoner* sparked intense debate among critics and viewers when it aired, creating an early example of "event television" in the avid discussions that followed each installment. However, ratings declined, production difficulties ensued, the budget over-ran, and with only 13 episodes completed after a year, Grade called time on the experiment, limiting the series to another 4 episodes and prompting much of the crew to leave (with many finding work on *The Saint*). Exhausted yet undeterred, McGoohan managed to complete the series, appearing in the film *Ice Station Zebra* (1967) to bankroll its remaining episodes, and famously writing the finale over 36 hours, just prior to filming and only a few weeks before it was due to air. The extensive production time required to make 17 episodes was seemingly attributable to McGoohan's perfectionism—rewriting scripts and adding various touches in post-production in order to make the program as innovative as possible. He may have abused his position in some ways, by overseeing every area of production and alienating numerous staff (culminating in Markstein's departure), yet McGoohan's determination (and ultimately his creative instincts) also drove the show. It retains the status of a flawed masterpiece; and while it has some relatively weak "filler" episodes, these have to be evaluated alongside the achievements of the entire series. It was audacious, indulgent, and easily the most bizarre experiment television had seen, but it also posed questions that had never been voiced in the medium. McGoohan was undoubtedly ambitious, as well as somewhat egotistical, stretching the crew (and himself) to the breaking point, yet the end result would prove such endeavors were not in vain. In playing with audience expectations, parodying genre conventions, and through its extraordinary creativity, the series would be vastly influential. Later series, such as *Twin Peaks*, *The X-Files* and *Lost*, owe a clear debt to *The Prisoner* in terms of their equivalent experimentation with genre, the surreal world presented, and the intense speculation generated among viewers. Consequently, it is this series that allows us crucial insight into the elements that help define a cult show.

Epitomizing "spy-fi" decades before the likes of *Alias*, *The Prisoner* offered a new twist on the world of espionage, which was a growing interest in broadcasting at the time of its inception. *Danger Man* was the first of the British secret agent series to appear in the 1960s—pre-dating *The Avengers* (1961–9), *The Man from U.N.C.L.E.* (1964–8) and *The Saint* (1962–9), as well as the first Bond film, *Dr. No* (1962)—and differed from its more fantastical contemporaries via storylines that attempted greater realism and a protagonist who was far from typical. At McGoohan's insistence, John Drake was unwilling to kill and avoided romances, asserting that this was inappropriate for a family audience (and rejecting the part of James Bond for the same reason). His ethical code would be inscribed just as firmly on *The Prisoner*, where dalliances with women were eschewed and violence is generally reserved to occasional fistfights with guards. Spy tropes were also given a darker twist in the new series. Gadgets were no longer a means of aiding our hero, but of deceiving and dehumanizing him; far from traveling to various locations—as Drake had—Number 6 is severely restricted in his movements; and, most significantly, the idea of a benign organization working to uphold liberty in the "free West" is utterly confounded by a narrative that insists "freedom" is impossible and considers all forms of officialdom untrustworthy and repressive. Markstein's concept of a secret military base (where former servicemen with sensitive information were required to remain in the interests of state security) had intensely sinister implications, and McGoohan used the idea to question restrictions in society at large. Although he sold the concept to Grade on the basis that it would feature himself as a former secret agent—thus retaining the following built through *Danger Man*—far from serving as a spin-off, *The Prisoner* would take television drama to an unforgettable new realm.

Prior to every episode, the title sequence would recap the premise. A man, physically identical to *Danger Man*'s John Drake, drives under thundery skies through London, angrily hands his notice to a bespectacled man at a desk (played by Markstein) and returns home to pack a suitcase. His photograph is mechanically retrieved from a cabinet and a series of x's typed over his face. Two men, dressed as undertakers, arrive at his front door and pump gas through the letterbox, knocking him out. He wakes in an identical apartment, yet relocated to an extraordinary setting. His first exchange with Number 2, the titular head of this strange society, culminates in the new arrival being termed "Number 6" ("for identification purposes"). He responds with anger: "I am not a number, I am a free man!"—a proclamation that secures laughter as a retort. He soon learns that those in charge—who speak with clipped English accents—are only ostensibly civilized, and that disturbing means are used to maintain order in this society. While it appears to be a cheerful holiday resort, we are alerted to the fact that all is not as it seems by the uniform manner in which "villagers" are dressed, the fearful expressions beneath their smiles, and the mechanical way they halt on command. In the opening episode ("Arrival") a "traitor" is found among them and smothered by "Rover"—a huge white ball that patrols the Village and acts as a mechanical surveillance system. The scene alerts us to the extraordinary power wielded by those in charge, who are able to detect and suppress dissent even before it is visibly manifested. By the episode's end they further prove their power by deliberately toying with the prisoner, allowing him to "escape" by helicopter, only to take over its controls and return him to the Village—affirming his relative powerlessness.

Over the course of the series the prisoner uses every ounce of will to gain the upper hand over his captors, making repeated escape attempts and continually resisting their efforts to "break" him. Compared to others, he is relatively privileged. In trying to obtain the information required, the authorities deploy a number of strategies, yet none that will permanently damage him—as other less fortunate souls are shown to be damaged. As the prisoner explores this strange new world, the thoughtful viewer is invited to speculate on the symbolic nature of the Village and our own lives. It may, as the first episode informs us, have a labor exchange and citizen's advice bureau, but the Village is far removed from the realities of work, or rights. Residents appear to be on a permanent vacation, with an abundance of free time. They are fed and housed and able to pay for goods with credit cards distributed to them on arrival, and thus appear to have virtually all life's necessities provided—aside from individual liberty. Elections are shown to be rigged and unable to create genuine change, as Number 6 discovers when he is voted the new Number 2, only to find someone else is really in charge and the "system" remains unaffected ("Free for All"). There is no distinction, it is implied, between political parties or social systems (or East and West), as Number 2 states in "The Chimes of Big Ben": "Both sides are becoming identical—a perfect blueprint for World Order." When Number 6 seemingly returns to London in the same episode, he pointedly asks his bosses if they are any "different"—only to find that he is still in the Village and his superiors are involved in the ruse. Another episode finds him similarly confronting his former bosses, stating he is unsure "which side" runs the Village, and he is returned to captivity shortly after ("Many Happy Returns"). Repressive forms of social control cut across either "side" of the Iron Curtain, it is suggested, irrespective of ideology, making Cold War distinctions obsolete. Village residents are a cowed population displaying ignorance and apathy (with dissenters either reprogrammed or removed). Number 6's defiance provokes fear among fellow inmates, and he is labeled "unmutual," decried as a "wicked man," and mistaken for a "guard" rather than a prisoner. He continually finds himself either distrusted by others or deceived by them. Even when he joins forces with other rebels in the finale, their ability to make a difference is severely undermined. For an era in which a great deal of optimism reigned about people's collective abilities to foster change, *The Prisoner* tends towards a marked pessimism, with an ending that suggests the entire series is an internal struggle within Number 6 to preserve his integrity—one he is destined to fail.

In its use of experimental, arty camerawork, costumes that stress its theatrical style (and cleverly avoid placing it in any period), intense performance styles, whimsical delivery of obscure dialogue, unusual musical compositions, and use of symbolism, *The Prisoner* presents a rare example of avant garde television. Apparent influences include playwright Samuel Beckett, whose characteristically bleak tone is exemplified in his best-known work, *Waiting for Godot* (1955). Adrian Page notes a similar mood in *The Prisoner*, with a central character imprisoned by unknown forces and unable to escape (Page 2001, 44–6). The penultimate episode, a two-person psychodrama entitled "Once Upon a Time," offers an overt comparison (see Gregory 1997, 38–41), and the finale ("Fall Out") makes its metaphysical leanings manifest. Like the two "tramps" of Beckett's play, whose futile wait for "Godot" represents a life without salvation, Number 6's quest is shown to be unrealizable. Just as Godot will never arrive, our protagonist will never truly find freedom, it is inferred, with the finale revealing his arch nemesis, the mysterious "Number 1," to be himself—the part that seeks conformity and comfort and thus helps to imprison the rebel within. These were abstract, deep, and intensely challenging concepts delivered via a medium that was still struggling to be taken seriously, substantiating the program's legendary status by confounding everyone's expectations.

"Once Upon a Time" concluded with Number 6 seemingly killing Number 2 (Leo McKern) in a psychological battle of wills that induces a heart attack. The finale provides 6's "reward." After being championed by yet another fake figurehead, given a million pounds in traveler's checks, and having his passport and house keys returned, the prisoner is finally taken to meet Number 1. Inside a rocket he finds a masked figure in a white robe. He rips this off and discovers an ape face beneath—the primitive id that makes us all self-satisfied prisoners of our desires; and underneath this is the contorted face of Number 6 himself. At McGoohan's insistence, the unmasking scene was reduced to a one-and-a-half-second shot. As he stated, "I could have held it there for a good two minutes and put a subtitle on it saying 'It's him,' you know. But I thought I wasn't going to pander to a mentality so low that it couldn't perceive what I was trying to say" (Troyer 1977). While these sentiments might be applauded for demanding more of the television audience than convention dictated, the subtlety of the scene, years in advance of VCRs, also ran the risk of being overlooked, and many viewers either missed it completely or simply missed the point. Audiences were expecting a Bond-style villain, not an abstract comment about our complicity in our own coercion, and the brevity of the scene illustrates the extent to which conventions were being pushed, even at the risk of frustrating the majority of the audience. McGoohan encouraged a rapid editing style throughout the series; yet to limit such a big revelation to so short a time was a huge gamble, and rendering the remainder of the finale devoid of any dialogue made it stranger still. Number 6 detonates the rocket (presumably with his alter ego inside) and leads fellow rebels on a violent escape from the Village, returning to London by road. He heads home, yet the final moments assert that he remains a prisoner—with the door to his apartment closing electronically in the same way as those in the Village. Number 6 is last seen behind the wheel of his car, as thunder sounds overhead, inferring that everything has come full circle—a suspicion confirmed by the final shot of prison bars closing over a logo of McGoohan's face, just as they have at the end of every episode.

Prior to the finale's transmission, McGoohan asserted that he fully aimed to be controversial, stating, "I wanted to make people talk about the series. I wanted to make them ask questions, argue and think" (Davis 1968). However, he did not appear to anticipate the uproar "Fall Out" would provoke. Immediately after it aired, audiences jammed the switchboard at broadcasting network ATV (Associated Television), demanding answers. To assuage confusion they took the unprecedented step of distributing a leaflet titled "A Plain Man's Guide to *The Prisoner*," written by an anonymous "ATV correspondent." This decrypted much of the symbolism of the series, stating the Village is a state of mind rather than a real location, and suggesting the rocket scene in "Fall Out" revealed "man shaking off his evil inner self" (a reading which is somewhat unconvincing, given that Number 6 is seemingly doomed to begin the cycle all over again). Nonetheless, for all the apparent insight offered, the "correspondent" appears to understand the frustration felt by viewers, asking

> Was it all hokum? Has Patrick McGoohan taken us all for a ride, or was this the most penetrating study—the most vivid of comments on modern civilization—in the history of British television? The answer, like many aspects of the series, is in the mind [ATC leaflet 1968].

It is in situating events within the prisoner's mind that the finale caused understandable consternation, with viewers (at least those who had noticed the "unveiling" scene) unsure what to make of a villain who is, ultimately, our hero. Far from "shaking off his evil inner self," despite seemingly obliterating his alter ego, blowing up the Village, and returning to London, Number 6 appears to achieve nothing, with the ending suggesting that the struggle to be free and retain our integrity is never truly secured. McGoohan later confessed, "In a way I'm guilty of doing a series like *The Prisoner* without injecting a note of hope into it. The guy should have been victorious against the system" (McGoohan 1977). How Number 6 could claim such victory is a puzzle, however, as the series ultimately asks us to read his imprisonment on a metaphorical rather than literal level. As McGoohan states in the same interview, the finale's point was that "the greatest enemy is ourself. That's who we're prisoners of—ourselves" (ibid); consequently, appearing somewhat uncertain about the show's meaning. After all, if we are the enemy, how is "victory" ever achieved? And what counts as "the system" if the central conflict is finally explained as a metaphysical battle between opposing sides of human nature? Critics tend to overlook such inconsistencies, or explain them as part of the show's allegorical nature, yet McGoohan admitted to only conceiving the finale's revelation at the last minute (Troyer 1977), indicating that Number 1's identity was a mystery even to him. While the twist adds depth, asking us to read the series as a study of humanity's inherent duality, the critique posed against various social institutions—ranging from mass education to the mass media—becomes undermined as a result, along with the possibility of change, creating a finale that ultimately returns us to where we began.

George Markstein publicly expressed bafflement about the conclusion, which is scarcely surprising, given that he departed the show after the thirteenth episode, following protracted disagreements about the direction McGoohan was taking. It is perhaps easy to typecast Markstein as the solid professional writer with a rational concept in mind for the series, while McGoohan takes the role of the difficult but brilliant visionary who steered it away from its conventional spy trappings into an ever more surreal landscape. Yet while Markstein was keen to make the series appear possible, he also understood the metaphysical dimensions of the hero's entrapment, stating that even if Number 6 were to leave the Village, "he would always be a prisoner ... of his circumstances, his situation, his secret, his background ... and THEY would always be there to ensure that his captivity continues" (Markstein 1984). Nonetheless, he largely dismissed the episodes made after his departure as "an absurd pantomime," and the show's coherence undoubtedly suffered as a result—as might be expected in losing virtually all its parameters.

Left to preside over the remainder of the series, McGoohan experimented with other genres and parodied existing formulas, enhancing the tendency to view the series as distinctly postmodern. Marked suspicion is expressed throughout about media power, with televisions used both to spy on residents and indoctrinate them ("The General"). The series also plays on our familiarity with generic conventions, using a hybrid style that veers from action sequences to absurd comedy, as well as episodes that transpose the premise to another genre entirely (as in the Bond parody "The Girl Who Was Death" and the Western episode "Living in Harmony"). Further intertextual references take inspiration from dystopian literature, including Zamyatin's *We* (in featuring an oppressive state where people are numbered) and Orwell's *1984* (particularly the surveillance techniques used and linguistic touches in Village slogans). The entire premise might additionally be described as "Kafkaesque"—articulating a nightmarish world of persecution where sinister agencies deny the protagonist free will, and accusations of treachery are grounds for imprisonment. Several of Kafka's protagonists find themselves transformed (literally, like Gregor Samsa, or geographically, as with Joseph K), and Number 6 is forced to embark on a similar quest to gain control over impossible circumstances, with the paranoia of his situation compounded by continuous betrayal. Displaying self-reflexive tendencies, *The Prisoner* routinely exposes its own artifice—particularly in subverting the usual tropes of the spy series—leading some to claim the series is a "subversive" text that "challenges its audience to see the world in a new light" (Gregory 1997, 24). However, such claims are somewhat undermined by another archetypal "postmodern" trait: an implicit ambiguity which precludes the attempt to determine its true meaning—a factor some have seen as deliberate, rather than arising from a chaotic production, with Mark Bould arguing that "its calculated self-conscious incoherence simultaneously refuses mapping and teases us into thinking we might be cartographers" (Bould 2005, 108).

As Bould deduces, the desire to explore *The Prisoner* is part of its ongoing appeal, and a number of interpretations have resulted from the attempt to make sense of the series. For some, the premise reflects McGoohan's professional dilemma after playing John Drake, providing an "allegory of McGoohan's own frustration at being trapped in the role of a secret agent" (Chapman 2002, 50). Biographical details in "Once Upon a Time" align Number 6 with McGoohan (as does crediting himself as "The Prisoner" at the end of "Fall Out"), and it inevitably reflects many of his personal preoccupations; yet McGoohan has been inconsistent in his assessment of the series, and its potential meaning is open to a range of readings. For some, the entire series is an elaborate delusion—the result of the prisoner experiencing a nervous breakdown (as implied by its cyclical narrative), while others affirm that he is dead (as is indicated by the numerous references made to death). Markstein has suggested that the prisoner was involved in conceiving the Village, which literally makes him a prisoner of his own making, yet this intriguing idea was never developed. For many viewers the preferred candidate for Number 1 was the silent Butler (Angelo Muscat)—one of the few regular characters to appear alongside McGoohan, and who accompanies him "home" in the final scene. His role serves as one of the many red herrings in the series, intended to invite speculation without having any deeper significance. Some have claimed that Number 6 represents an outlawed Christianity (suggested by the greeting used in the Village) or homosexuality (as indicated by his aversion to women). On this last point the series has met with some criticism, particularly as many of its females are portrayed as duplicitous; yet this tendency is equally true of male characters, and the series provides a range of female roles, including several female Number 2s, reflecting an interesting egalitarianism for its time. More explicit political claims are somewhat harder to make, with its satirical elements undermined by the finale. Number 6 is hailed a "supreme individual" by the President (Kenneth Griffith) and given the choice to "Lead us or go." Yet as his "true" identity reveals, the prisoner is already leading them. Page asserts that "the issue of whether social control is maintained by coercion or our own consciousness remains open and relevant" (Page, 46). Yet in targeting ourselves as the enemy the series evades any political affiliations, and with 6 not appearing to have learned very much from his experiences, a bleak conclusion is provided. McGoohan responded to accusations that he made the series too obscure by stating, "There are no subtitles to spell it out. Everyone must answer it for themselves in their own minds" (Older). Although this may dissatisfy those seeking a more explicit "message," it is this openness to interpretation that has maintained a sense of intrigue four decades on.

Perhaps its biggest contribution to cult telefantasy is the level of involvement sought from its audience. From the very first episode the viewer is placed in the same role as Number 2. We also want "information," we want to know why Number 6 resigned, and we watch very closely, looking for clues. Although many leads turn out to be false trails, they provide an intriguing puzzle; and while most viewers were frustrated by its abstract leanings, for fans of *The Prisoner* its appeal lies precisely in its refusal to be easily worked out. Today we are more used to genre mixing, table turning, and unreliable narrators. *The Prisoner* predates such experimentation and helped paved their way. It contains quintessential cult elements because its curiosity value continues beyond the revelation of Number 1's identity, just as its wider implications extend beyond the story of one man's struggle to remain an individual, securing enduring interest. In keeping audiences guessing, in providing details that reward repeated viewing, and in its thematic richness, *The Prisoner* would become a benchmark cult series, inspiring a host of others. Shared features that reoccur in subsequent telefantasy include the subversion of expectation rendered by mixing generic signifiers; high production values; a measure of playfulness (including baroque excesses, dream sequences, and extravagant ruses); allusions made to familiar tropes (referencing other media, fairy tales, and popular culture); a refusal to "pander" to audiences (with complex plotting and unanswered questions); and an insistent ambiguity. That its influence would not be readily apparent in other series for another two decades further proves how far ahead of its time *The Prisoner* was. In a collection published in 1990, commentators claimed no influence could be discerned, with Jacques Sternberg asserting, "*The Prisoner* seems to have inspired no other work of the same kind ... being ahead of one's time does not always lead to being taken up later or caught up with" [Carraze and Oswald 1990, 16].

Ironically, its most immediate successor was launched in the same year that this conclusion was drawn, with *Twin Peaks* (1990–91) similarly born of unique circumstances, and another experiment that would "fail" in commercial terms. As Chapman notes, "*Twin Peaks* ... similarly had a limited lifespan, ended on a note of unresolved narrative ambiguity, and was also largely the brainchild of one guiding intelligence (David Lynch) who enjoyed the sort of creative control that McGoohan did with *The Prisoner*" (Chapman 2002, 51). Like *The Prisoner*, *Twin Peaks* would experiment with the medium, mix genres, horrify and amuse us in the space of a single scene, and take its audience on a journey many were unprepared for. It would also provide an ending that was equally uncompromising, and inspire an equally impressive cult following. Interesting successors, such as *The X-Files*, *Buffy*, and *Lost*, would also emerge over the next few years, similarly melding established formats, boasting good looks, keeping viewers guessing—and crucially finding the receptive audience *The Prisoner* lacked.

Writing in 1977, journalist Mick Ferren assessed the likelihood of another show like *The Prisoner* and claimed that cable television would foster greater experimentation, stating that "competition is probably the only thing that will strong arm the telly giants into raising their sights above the lowest common denominator," and arguing that without such expansion, "shows like *The Prisoner* will continue to be treated as a madman's bastard brainchild, fit only to be used as a sop to some weirdo fringe of the viewing public" (Ferren 1977). In fact, the "weirdo fringe" eventually became associated with a desirable "market." Innovative telefantasy emerged as a lucrative niche as a result of competition a few decades on (as Ferren predicted), proving popular with a coveted demographic and inspiring the established "telly giants" to lavish their resources on shows that stole a trick from *The Prisoner* in terms of stylistic innovation and subversive intent. Increased success would change the nature of cult television, adding a wider range of characters, greater variation in storylines, and narrative arcs designed to extend interest over a number of seasons, and using other media forms to involve audiences. *The Prisoner* did not have these benefits, yet it has been hailed by many series creators as a primary inspiration, including *Twin Peaks* co-creator Mark Frost (who attempted to make a film version of it in 1992) and *Buffy* creator Joss Whedon, who ranks the series among his favorites. *Lost* co-creator J.J. Abrams has also admitted to being a fan, stating, "I loved *The Prisoner*, which was a very odd sort of hybrid of sci-fi, mystery and character, and certainly there are elements of *The Prisoner* in both *Alias* and *Lost*" (Abrams 2006). In encouraging others to similarly blend genres and bend the rules, the series would thus inspire shows that have achieved astonishing success—which is no mean feat for a seemingly failed experiment.

The Prisoner resulted from the tremendous opportunity afforded by an indulgent patron to a charismatic and highly talented individual with obvious ambitions beyond acting. It also benefited from the dedication of a cast and crew willing to try something completely new. Later series would understand the importance of innovative costumes and set design, of varying the cast, of maintaining a mystery for viewers to guess at, of revealing "clues" piecemeal, and of eschewing expectation. Back in the late 1960s no such precedents had been set, and McGoohan sold an avant-garde concept to a commercial network chiefly because Lew Grade was the kind of media impresario famous for going with his gut instinct. As it transpired, *The Prisoner* was too extreme to become the hit Grade anticipated, and it would be their last collaboration. While McGoohan succeeded in making something provocative, this was not without cost. ITC would weather the storm, yet Everyman Films floundered in the wake of the series, and McGoohan's career was eclipsed by the role. Despite Emmy award-winning contributions to *Columbo*, and notable parts in films such as *Braveheart* (Mel Gibson, 1995), he would forever be associated with the character that had no name. McGoohan observed, "Mel Gibson will always be Mad Max, and me, I will always be a number" (Jefferies 2009, 11). Ironically, even in attempting to avoid being typecast as John Drake, he became imprisoned by another role—one of his own making.

Although *The Prisoner* was, in industry terms, a flop—failing to make back the money spent on it, or to acquire more than bafflement from its initial audience—it has influenced some of the biggest hits of recent years. Themes such as the duality of human nature and our tendency toward corruption would be revisited in later cult series. A sense of paranoia is equally prominent (emanating from duplicitous characters and covert experiments), and various forms of rebellion occur (albeit often tempered by a similar fatalism). The level of detail pioneered in *The Prisoner*, which was lost to many on its first airing, would be deliberately incorporated into later series, rewarding repeated viewing via VCR and DVD, and making obscure allusions increasingly notable. A "cultish" propensity to spot details and find links would thus be noted and nurtured—although irrelevancies and absurd departures would prompt speculation that audiences were simply being toyed with. *The Prisoner*'s impressive production values became the norm in key examples of telefantasy, as did the emphasis on stylish filming and editing techniques, and the inventive use of music additionally pioneered in the series. The Internet would play a critical role in shaping subsequent cults and supplementing the onscreen information given—an innovation that might have circumvented the confusion and disgruntlement that followed "Fall Out." Indeed, later cult series would have a number of advantages in terms of newsgroups and forums allowing viewers to share theories and frustrations. Such practices would eventually become orchestrated by broadcasters who recognized their value in promoting discussion (and continued viewing); yet at the time of *The Prisoner*'s inception cult interest was a genuine grassroots concern, emerging through a simple desire by *Prisoner* enthusiasts to discuss and promote the show.

During *The Prisoner*'s first U.K. repeat in 1976, Dave Barrie asked ATV to broadcast his name and address after screening "Fall Out," asking any viewers similarly intrigued by the series to contact him. The response lead to *Six of One*—which initially sought to revive the series and subsequently campaigned to secure repeat transmissions, garnering considerable interest in the press and finding fans in various nations. So it was that an apparent flop came to be recognized as an extraordinary achievement thanks to fans that continue to assemble annually to celebrate and discuss the series, publishing related books, and designing a range of merchandise (including mugs, badges, umbrellas, and even replica costumes). While some attempt was made, when the series first aired, to exploit it as a franchise, this was limited to a few tie-in novels, Dinky toy versions of mini-moke taxis, and a short-lived comic. ITC later realized its cult value, granting *Six of One* a license to manufacture and sell related merchandise, and considering them a joint partner in these pursuits. Despite commonly being deemed somewhat eccentric in their devotion, the Prisoner Appreciation Society should be recognized for their efforts to persuade broadcasters to keep the series on air, and their subsequent aims to extend interest in the show—efforts which helped turn it into an enduring cult. It is partly due to their enthusiasm that *Prisoner* fans have flourished around the world, a factor that would cause their original aim—to extend the series—to eventually be met by a miniseries made in 2009.

Consisting of six installments (one less than McGoohan's original plan), *The Prisoner* was recreated via an Anglo-U.S. co-production deal between American cable company AMC and Granada Television, who responded to continued fan interest by attempting to reinvent the premise for a contemporary audience. The prospect of a remake had been speculated on for years, generally taking the form of a film version, with various directors attached and interesting scriptwriters mooted, including Christopher McQuarrie and David and Janet Peoples. However, talk of another series gained momentum after *Doctor Who* was successfully revised by the BBC in 2005, prompting Granada to announce plans for an updated version of *The Prisoner*. In 2006 Sky One confirmed their involvement yet pulled out after "creative differences" with AMC. Their main point of contention was a feeling the venture strayed too far from its origins, with Sky One's director of programs, Richard Woolfe, citing too many creative compromises with American investors, explaining: "I didn't want to be responsible for taking something that is quintessentially British and adapting it in a way that I didn't feel was reflective of the way people would remember it and the way people would want it to be" (Wilkes 2007).

With Sky gone, any such qualms were seemingly ignored, with the project tellingly described as a "reinvention." Producer Michelle Buck cited the concept's continued relevance, stating, "The conceits for the original series are still absolutely current today ... there's nothing about it that's old-fashioned. It's a modern idea" (Buck 2009). Nonetheless, some changes were clearly deemed vital, with a notable slant toward the American audience. Lew Grade may have had a keen eye on the U.S. market, but *The Prisoner* remained a British production in terms of location, cast and crew, and specific national touches. The miniseries features a number of American actors, including John Caviezel as Number 6, and *Jericho* star Lennie James as his friend, 147, and many of its cultural touchstones are distinctly American. The Swakopmund theme park in Namibia was used to create a Village that resembles a retro notion of U.S. suburbia, with identical A-frame houses and vintage cars, bounded by the ocean and desert, which is reminiscent of *The Truman Show* (Peter Wier 1998) in look and tone. Many changes are exactly what we might expect from a contemporary production with an eye on global (particularly American) appeal. If 6 was a loner in the original series, with a fiancée used to explain his reservations against dalliances, the "reinvention" provides 6 with two love interests in the form of 313 (Ruth Wilson) and 4–15 (Hayley Atwell). We are also given a backstory designed to chime with modern sensibilities. The protagonist's occupation is now in surveillance, and the repeated "mirage" of the twin towers (a symbol of 6's lost world) places the production on a par with other post–9/11 telefantasy, yet has little coherent meaning. At an estimated million dollars an episode the miniseries clearly aims to sell itself as a quality production, and looks ravishing, yet fails in its aspirations to emulate the original, with little to compare the two and still less reason to justify the production.

Having Number 2 played by one actor (Ian McKellan), rather than several, was seemingly intended to provide greater human interest, fleshing out what was initially an interchangeable foil by providing him a family, yet he remains somewhat unfathomable and inconsistent. A troubled relationship with his teenage son, 11–12 (Jamie Campbell Bower), reiterates the "daddy issues" popularized in contemporary telefantasy shows such as *Lost*, yet effaces the former conflict between 6 and 2. The theme of being trapped in a relatively idyllic "prison" is brought home via this figure's outlawed homosexuality imprisoning the young man within his father's expectations, which makes 6 somewhat secondary. While McGoohan's searing performance would be hard to equal, Cavaziel seems to sleepwalk through his part and tends to offer deference instead of defiance, evincing markedly less cynicism than McGoohan's portrayal. This 6 desires connections such as family and romance, allows himself to be fooled into thinking he has a brother, and almost marries a woman selected by the Village dating agency. Still more inconsistently, he elects to work for 2, spying on a "dreamer" who subsequently kills himself (a fate which 11–12 shares, in markedly fatalistic fashion). Seemingly aiming to reassure the wary that the original's oblique ending would not be copied, McKellan told interviewers, "By episode 6 you'll know everything about the Village, where it came from, who created it, and why" (Porter 2009). The finale is true to this claim, with the Village again shown to be a state of mind. Yet far from emanating from 6's own consciousness, it is the product of a fantastical conceit so contrived and ridiculous that it makes "Fall Out" look matter-of-fact. A psychologist, Number 2's wife in the real world, has created the Village in her mind (with the help of psychotropic drugs) to "heal" the troubled citizens of New York, people 6 has identified in his former job in surveillance. This woman is "killed" by her son, 11–12, prior to him taking his own life—despite being revealed as a figment of her imagination—prompting 2 to recruit 6 to take his place, along with 313, in running the Village. In their final scene together, 6 promises a new start, affirming that the Village can be a better place, while a drugged 313 sheds a tear, seemingly lamenting the end of his rebellion. Though this is evidently intended to be a chilling finale, it is deeply unsatisfying. 6's agreement to preside over the Village is too easily secured, with the character offering far less resistance than the original; and although allusions are made to Markstein's original intent (asserting 6's complicity in creating the Village), the story ends just as this prospect begins. Most frustrating of all, however, is the fantastical conceit used to explain the Village. How can real people be situated in the imaginary realm of a person's subconscious? If "Fall Out" reneged on its political inferences, this is ultimately too absurd for words.

Numerous promotional endeavors reveal a desire to create a contemporary cult around this new *Prisoner*. While viewers of the original series were left to themselves to ponder its meaning, the miniseries provides an online forum to discuss theories; and a website, Villagewiki.org, provides an alternate reality game pretending to be a genuine investigation into the Village and its activities—inviting us to think there really is such a place. In addition, iPhone, talk forum and Twitter sites were set up to get viewers talking, exploiting viral marketing techniques to promote the show. These are considerable lengths to go to for a 6-hour miniseries, and are clearly aimed at attracting younger viewers; while established fans were courted with the promise that the remake would "reflect 21st century concerns and anxieties, such as liberty, security and surveillance, yet also showcase the same key elements of paranoia, tense action and socio-political commentary seen in McGoohan's enigmatic original" (AMC website 2009). Additionally promising was the fact that writer and executive producer, Bill Gallagher, attached to it since 2006, was a fan of the original series, attesting:

> I was haunted by *The Prisoner* when I saw it as a boy on its first broadcast. Here was something that was more than television, something I couldn't quite grasp but couldn't let go of. It's a unique opportunity for a writer to be able to go back to the Village and tell some new stories about that strange place and its surreal menace ... we hope to serve up something as beguiling and disturbing as the original was [AMC website 2009].

That the result failed to make a similar impression is attributable to a number of factors. Perhaps the chief obstacle in any such endeavor is that McGoohan was so closely aligned with *The Prisoner* that accepting another person as Number 6 was unthinkable for many fans. He declined to be involved in the production, and his death in January 2009 meant that McGoohan would never know how the successor compared to his own show, yet the changes would doubtless not have surprised him. Back in 1967, at Grade's behest, top CBS executive, Michael Dann, met with McGoohan and listed several factors that would enhance *The Prisoner*'s appeal for a U.S. market. McGoohan responded by commending his ideas and told him to make his own show (Rakoff 1998, 32). In many ways the miniseries makes the compromises McGoohan was unwilling to consider, yet is hamstrung by a conflict between achieving accessibility and aspiring towards more enigmatic intellectual concerns. By airing on a cable network, some artiness was allowed, yet the "beguiling and disturbing" elements of Gallagher's script consist of jarring moments, such as 11–12 stabbing his lover to death, a young child falling down a hole that no one bothers to explore, and 2's grand gesture of retirement by placing a hand grenade in his mouth. While these scenes seem included to provide an edge, they merely result in alienating the viewer and are a long way from the radicalism of the original series. Disturbing scenes, such as jibbering hospital inmates, torture victims committing suicide, or post-op casualties waving a balloon in a lobotomized stupor, remain haunting because they have not been emulated, making the original series impossible to forget. Although the miniseries resulted in an equivalent decline in interest (dropping from 2 to 1 million), it is unlikely to find any champions, particularly among fans of the original who were evidently courted yet had good reason to feel disappointed. Like the "re-imagined" *Star Trek* (2009), the makers of the miniseries sought to avoid direct comparisons with the original while borrowing from its reputation. Describing *The Prisoner* as a concept with "marquee value built in," AMC executive Rob Sorcher added, "This show made an explosion in the genre 40 years ago; to this day, it's loved by so many. This is an opportunity to remake a classic and reinterpret it, and it also gives us a built-in fan base" (Nordyke 2006). Despite the advantages at its disposal, it is a venture that failed, and the original series remains a hard (if not impossible) act to follow in breaking all the rules, playing with convention, and leading us into new territory—attributes the miniseries simply does not share.

That is not to say the original series does not have its flaws. There are episodes where incongruous humor intrudes, such as the ridiculous game of Kosho seen in "Hammer into Anvil" and "It's Your Funeral," labeled by Gregory as "one of McGoohan's jokes at the expense of the viewer" (Gregory 1997, 122), as well as evidence of the premise being unduly stretched in several episodes. "Do Not Forsake Me Oh My Darling" uses a hokey mind transference plot (to explain McGoohan's absence filming *Ice Station Zebra*) and incongruously champions the inventor of a mind-altering power; while "The Girl Who Was Death" is too odd a departure in tone, and its revelation that children reside in the Village makes no sense for the ostensible premise. Further inconsistencies occur in "Fall Out," which counters the pacifist stance taken throughout the series by deploying machine guns and detonating a bomb. These actions may be fantastically treated and prove ineffectual in the end, making a possible statement about the futility of violence, but they seem included simply to create a controversial ending. The conclusion is *The Prisoner*'s most disconcerting feature, delightfully disorienting as it is, because it suggests little point in 6's rebellion, as he ends up exactly where he began. While McGoohan may be praised for opting to end the series in such a strange and unsettling manner, leaving audiences with the suggestion that Number 1 resides in us all, he also leaves us with metaphysical concerns effacing political possibilities, posing problems in how to read the remainder of the series. Bould terms *The Prisoner* a "conundrum that flirts with meaning" (108), and this semantic inscrutability is as much a problem as it is a pleasure. While there is a critical tendency to gloss over its inconsistencies in an urge to commend its innovations, we would do well to remember that *The Prisoner* was—like any other television series— created in specific circumstances. Born of conflicting intentions (between Marstein and McGoohan's differing aims, and Grade's simple desire for a hit), it added oblique elements to preserve its mystique and keep viewers watching, with much of it made up as they went along, including a conclusion that, by McGoohan's own admission, was only conceived at the eleventh hour. While it remains undoubtedly daring in urging audiences to look more closely at their lives, and reminding us of our essential duality, the finale is pessimistic about what we can accomplish, suggesting resistance is within us, yet always accompanied by the figure in the ape mask, who prefers to opt for an easy life—our true enemy, despite many suggested targets, finally proving to be conformity and complacency.

Elements of the series can be seen in a variety of films that hinge upon themes of indoctrination and conspiracy, including *Videodrome* (David Cronenberg, 1983), *The Truman Show* (Peter Weir, 1998), *Dark City* (Alex Proyas, 1998), and *Cube* (Vincenzo Natali, 1997); while rebellious secret agents are interestingly reworked in *Cypher* (Vincenzo Natali, 2002) and the *Bourne* trilogy (Doug Liman, 2002, Paul Greengrass, 2004 and 2007). *The Matrix* (Larry and Andy Wachowski, 1999) borrows the freeze-frame scene from "Arrival"— yet makes the power responsible more abstract; while *Fight Club* (David Fincher, 1999) parallels the series' finale in revealing Tyler Durden (Brad Pitt) and the narrator (Edward Norton) to be the same person—although it notably allows the conformist to eliminate the rebel within. *The Prisoner* additionally casts its shadow over a variety of telefantasy series that play with expectation and bend formulas out of shape—many of which have proven that viewers can be receptive to the unconventional and strange. As the remainder of this book makes clear, *The Prisoner* hovers in the background of most of the major cult shows of the last two decades, undiminished by the years that have passed since its initial transmission, eternal and inspiring proof of what telefantasy is capable of. The next chapter evaluates one of its most identifiable successors, the product of equivalent creative freedom and a similar desire to make unusual television, taking us across the Atlantic to Twin Peaks, USA.

2

Twin Peaks: The Death of Laura Palmer—And the Birth of a Phenomenon

> *It's impossible to remember who wrote what or who did what, but David liked coffee and I liked pie, I know that much.*
> —Mark Frost

Twin Peaks (ABC, 1990-91) became one of the most unusual television series ever made, largely due to the irreverent attitude shared by its creators. As Mark Frost has asserted, he and fellow collaborator David Lynch had an "outsider's mentality" that influenced their approach, recalling "we both had some wild ideas about how to shake things up.... We demanded and received complete creative control. *Twin Peaks* came out of that. It was two guys going off, creating their own studio, owning their own show" (Frost 2002). Their "ownership" was somewhat compromised by ABC's interventions and eventual decision to cancel *Twin Peaks*, yet the show remains a landmark in terms of its artistry, subject matter, oddball humor, and the reaction generated by it. This chapter explains how the series was conceived and evaluates why the murder of a homecoming queen in a fictional northwest town seized the public's imagination in the way it did, assessing the contrasting response to its second season—after the killer was revealed at ABC's insistence—and the legacy it has left. Emerging two decades after *The Prisoner*, *Twin Peaks* serves as the next stop on our journey through cult telefantasy because it was the first series to experiment in quite so innovative a manner. It caused an equivalent sensation when it aired, and it promotes continued debate among fans to this day. While *The Prisoner* set a new benchmark for telefantasy in the late 1960s, *Twin Peaks* realized its potential at the start of the 1990s, inaugurating a new degree of experimentation and serving as a key inspiration for subsequent television. If a cult series is distinguished by the level of interest it provokes, and the way it becomes the focus of conversation and critical inquiry, *Twin Peaks* achieved cult status from the outset. In debates in "water-cooler" conversations at work, magazine and newspaper articles, talk shows, and newly formed Internet sites, enthusiasts pored over episode details in attempting to unravel the show's central puzzle: the question of who killed Laura Palmer. The same kind of fevered speculation had accompanied *The Prisoner*, yet *Twin Peaks* achieved this response with a new generation of viewers—and in a very different context.

The series developed as key changes occurred in U.S. television, often dubbed the "post-network" era. Industrial expansion in the 1980s threatened the former dominance of the "big three" networks (ABC, CBS and NBC), and they responded by aiming to set themselves apart from emerging cable channels, creating what Caldwell has described as an era of "televisuality" in which "stylistic showcases, high production value programming, and Hollywood stylishness can all be seen as tactics by which the networks and their primetime producers tried to protect their market share" (Caldwell 1995, 10). An accompanying development was a tendency towards "narrowcasting" in which networks concentrated on finding the "right" audience—typically, the demographic considered most attractive to sponsors, neatly summarized by Roberta Pearson as "those with disposable incomes and inclined to spend it" (Pearson 2005, 15). In attempting to lure such an audience, programs were specifically designed to stand out in the schedules via a distinct visual style and an innovative attitude, aiming to grant credibility and increased commerciality to the networks. The development of so-called "quality" television thus had very pragmatic origins: to give a specific segment of the audience something on terrestrial television worth watching, and upping the stakes in terms of style and delivery to achieve this aim. Notable precursors had appeared a decade earlier, with CBS generally attributed with inaugurating "quality" shows through smart sit-coms such as *The Mary Tyler Moore Show* (1970–77) and *M*A*S*H* (1972–83). Irreverent, adult, and particularly appealing to an educated and relatively affluent audience, these paved the way for later innovations by setting the bar higher than their counterparts (see Feur). Robert J. Thompson dates television's "second golden age" from 1981—coinciding with NBC's groundbreaking police drama *Hill Street Blues* (1981–7)—asserting that a new type of programming became apparent which was "better, more sophisticated, and more artistic than the usual fare" (Thompson 1996, 12). ABC followed suit with the comic detective series *Moonlighting* (1985–9) and the ensemble drama *thirtysomething* (1987–9), yet by the close of the decade it was trailing in third place among the "big three" and keen to find a new hit. The commissioning of *Twin Peaks* would provide a dramatic turnaround. As Caldwell states, "The strategic placement and promotion of *Twin Peaks* in primetime spring programming was a major factor in the financial re-ascendance of ABC as a programming force" (Caldwell, 286–7). Nonetheless, despite initial commercial success and critical praise, the network failed to treat the show particularly well, forcing its makers to reveal Laura's killer, moving it around in the schedules, and cancelling it by the following spring. Lynch has openly blamed them for its demise, arguing:

> The question of what happened to Laura Palmer was the goose that laid the golden egg. Then ABC asked us to snip the goose's head off, and it killed the goose. And there went everything [Jensen 2007].

While the series combined cinematic good looks and a unique style to attract attention, seemingly epitomizing prestige programming, network interference drastically affected the show's appeal. Yet while it may have been deemed a commercial failure in terms of declining ratings, it remains a groundbreaking achievement within television, using the medium in highly inventive ways. A combination of murder mystery and melodrama served to elicit intense audience engagement, but fantastical means were used to "solve" the crime, making the series a frequently overlooked example of telefantasy. Just as *The Prisoner* created a puzzle for viewers, *Twin Peaks* offered various "clues" in tracing Laura's killer, involving audiences on both an intellectual and emotional level as the entire town became the subject of investigation. If *The Prisoner* took everyone by surprise in subverting the traditional spy series, *Twin Peaks* achieved the same result by combining a detective thriller with a surreal soap opera, and adding the supernatural to the mix—with the killer eventually revealed to be an evil presence emanating from the woods. An ever more convoluted story juxtaposed stark reality with extraordinary conceits, including subject matter within its dark fictional world that had not been explored before in primetime drama. As Colin Odell and Michelle Le Blanc state, its content—at its grimmest—includes

> the shadier side of human sexuality ... incestuous rape, prostitution and sexual slavery through heroin addiction ... themes that television executives would usually run a mile from, particularly in relation to a teenage girl. Somehow *Twin Peaks*' combination of quirky surrealism and high production values managed to get such unlikely material past television's moral guardians [Odell and Le Blanc 2007, 75].

Network publicity surrounding the show pre-sold it as something out of the ordinary. Although this created a buzz around the series, there was little indication of the stir *Twin Peaks* would cause. It took hold of people's imaginations because we had not seen anything like it, because it permitted a level of intelligence among its audience (rather than offering patronizing or predictable material), and because it had a hook that grabbed us. Yet why should an ostensible murder mystery make such a deep impression? The answer is as varied as the potential suspects lined up as Laura's killer. It was new, it was unusual, everyone was talking about it. All the criteria that have become firmly associated with a cult product, and which were established with *The Prisoner*, were there—and taken by *Twin Peaks* into entirely new territory.

The series is often critically aligned with the creative work of David

Lynch, who secured a reputation among cineastes for strange and unsettling films—from his disturbing horror debut, *Eraserhead* (1978), to the skewed melodrama of *Blue Velvet* (1986)—yet Mark Frost's input is equally important to note. Having worked on *The Six Million Dollar Man* (ABC, 1974–8), as well as serving as writer and story editor on *Hill Street Blues*, Frost had considerable television experience, wrote a significant number of *Twin Peaks* episodes (writing or co-writing eleven, to Lynch's three), revised most of the scripts, and was responsible for many of its mystical motifs—with similar ideas explored in his later novels *The List of Seven* (1993) and its sequel *The Six Messiahs* (1995)—factors which demand that he take joint honors, at least, in the creative shaping of *Twin Peaks*. He and Lynch met through their mutual agent, Tony Krantz, in 1986. Initially collaborating on an aborted adaptation of Anthony Summers biography *Goddess—The Secret Lives of Marilyn Monroe*, they established an easy rapport and developed a number of ideas together, including an off-beat comedy entitled *One Saliva Bubble*, which was similarly shelved. Krantz inspired their next venture at a meeting with Lynch in 1988, encouraging him to make something for television along the lines of *Blue Velvet*. Lynch and Frost developed *Twin Peaks* between them (initially titled *Northwest Passage*), conceiving the setting way ahead of its characters. As Lynch recalls, "In my mind was a place surrounded by trees. That's important. For as long as I can remember, woods have been mysterious places. So they were a character in my mind. And then other characters came to our minds" (Rodley 2005, 161). Chief among such characters is Laura Palmer. As Frost asserts, "This notion that the girl next door was leading a rather desperate double life that was going to end in murder came center stage. As we figured out who she was, and realized that she was dead, everything flowed from there" (Patterson and Jensen 2000). They pitched their ideas to ABC's Chad Hoffman with the scantiest of premises: a body of a young woman discovered in a small town, and an investigation that delves into the lives of its residents, mixing a detective plot with elements of soap opera. Hoffman's response is akin to the leap of faith taken by Lew Grade with *The Prisoner*: "I figured what the hell? You've got to take a chance on something like this," reasoning, "this will either be an incredibly terrific success or it will be very cool and no one will get it. But it will not be boring" (Patterson and Jensen 2000).

Emerging, as Patterson and Jensen assert, through a combination of "art, commerce, intuition and chance" (2000), *Twin Peaks* evinced a degree of synchronicity as filming for the pilot commenced. Snoqualmie Falls in Washington served as the ideal location, eerily mirroring the town Frost and Lynch had imagined—even down to its saw mill. Equally fortuitous was the agreement made with distributors Warner Home Video, who requested a version with a "closed ending" for potential sale in Europe in the event of a series not being commissioned. This motivated Frost and Lynch to find a way to wrap things up, and an accident on the set provided odd inspiration. The sight of set dresser

Frank Silva unwittingly caught on film during a take inspired Lynch to cast him as Laura's killer. The closed version culminates with Laura's murderer being killed by a one-armed man and ends with a strange dream sequence that came to Lynch one afternoon during editing. This celebrated scene, complete with jazz score and dancing midget, meant little at the time, yet it would be re-used and elaborated upon within the series. Consequently, while the closed version deviates considerably from the eventual denouement, and was simply a rapidly devised solution to a puzzle they hadn't yet planned out, it contains many seeds that would be sown in the series proper. Such impromptu additions reveal the level of experimentation, intuition, and general serendipity that affected production, and which would later become incorporated within the series' mythology (with the "European" pilot becoming a much coveted artifact for *Peaks* fans).

The version presented to ABC executives denied any such closure, anticipating a series that was designed to sustain long-term interest. Yet despite the lack of dancing midgets and crazed killers, it announced itself as something out of the ordinary. Lynch only directed three of the eventual thirty episodes in the series, but the pilot is one of the most memorable, locating us in a town that is both familiar and unsettling. A body is found and identified as a local girl, and a dramatic score by Angelo Badalamenti emphasizes the pathos of her discovery. The police deputy who arrives at the scene is too overcome with emotion to take the required photos—affirming that this is no ordinary police procedural. Similarly expressive performances follow from other characters, undercut with bizarre humor. Just as the policeman is incongruously "soft" for his job, the squeaky-voiced secretary at the police station (later shown to be his girlfriend) is used to rupture the somber mood, wrong-footing viewer expectations. In addition, a number of secrets are divulged about the dead girl. The discovery of her diary (or, rather, the first version found, in a text replete with doubles and doppelgängers) provides a clue about a potential suspect ("J"), while traces of cocaine and a hidden key to a safety deposit box prompt further investigation about the deceased. The box contains $10,000 in cash and a porn magazine, indicating a shady double life, and so begins a highly convoluted journey to find out exactly what happened to Laura Palmer—and who she really was. Noir undertones are evidenced by allusions to a world of vice; locations linked to 50s Americana, such as a diner and a biker club, serve as settings for various trysts; and elements of a buddy/cop format also feature, as a federal agent arrives in town to help the local sheriff trace the killer. Familiar motifs are thus melded together in a strange introduction to an even stranger town, providing the unsettling feeling of having been here before, largely through film and television clichés. While the standalone version concludes with a sinister looking man killed in the basement of a hospital, leaving us none the wiser about his identity, the standard version ends with various narrative threads dangling, aiming to involve us on a number of levels.

Although the pilot is often recalled as one of the most intriguing ever made, some debate followed test screenings before ABC decided to purchase the series, eventually scheduling it for broadcast in the spring of 1990. Any qualms were soon allayed via an astonishing reception, with the first installment garnering an estimated 35 million viewers. *Twin Peaks* became ABC's biggest success of 1990, earning the highest ratings the network had seen for four years. It no doubt benefited from heavy promotion, as well as being a mid-term season replacement, with the first season comprised of only seven episodes—enough to whet the audience's appetite without risk of overindulgence. A talented production team was evident, from set and costume design and the moving score by Badalamenti (a long-time collaborator of Lynch's), to the many stand-out performances among a cast that combined newcomers with familiar faces. While Lynch and Frost created the narrative world and its main characters, other key contributors include Harley Peyton and Robert Engels (who were responsible for a significant number of writing credits), while a host of directors (many emerging from the "indie" scene) helmed individual episodes, each contributing to a very cinematic look and an innovative feel. Many have since commented (in recollections assembled in the Definitive Gold Box DVD Set released in 2007) that a rare degree of ownership over their input provided an impetus for creativity. Just as *The Prisoner* acquired a reputation during production for endeavoring something new, directors sought to get involved in *Twin Peaks* due to its reputation as a one-off in television that was willing to reward individual artistry. The fact that the series earned an astonishing fourteen Emmy award nominations (the most for any series that year) is testimony to its recognition as a breakthrough show (even if it only won two). As the first season ended with a host of cliffhangers, speculation went into overdrive during the summer of 1990 about what the next season would bring.

It is in extending the premise for its second season that problems began, with ABC insisting that the series reveal the identity of Laura's killer—an edict that is generally viewed as sounding the death-knell for the series. Disclosing its central mystery diminished the incentive for many viewers to continue watching, and new narrative directions failed to compensate. As Lynch focused on a new film, *Wild at Heart* (1990), Frost was left in charge of a production that splintered its focus and increasingly lost its appeal. A scheduling move from a Thursday to a Saturday night slot did not help declining ratings, and it was put on hiatus midway through the second season—an ominous sign that often indicates imminent cancellation. Fans organized a campaign to save the show, entitled COOP (Citizens Opposed to the Offing of *Peaks*), which followed in the footsteps of the "Save *Star Trek*" campaign of the late 1960s. It involved letters, local rallies, and online petitioning of producers and advertisers (Jenkins 1995, 78). This moved the studio to allow another six episodes to tie various narrative threads together, and Lynch returned to direct the concluding segment. Far from wrapping everything up, however, the fate of various characters was left uncertain, and the final scene left us with the ultimate in open endings. Closely paralleling *The Prisoner*'s revelation scene in "Fall Out," the ending posed unsettling questions about the duality of human nature, with a hero who proves to be as fallible as Number 6, a quest that is similarly unfulfilled, and a killer who is still at large—and potentially more dangerous than ever.

As soon became evident, no third season would follow, and although Lynch made a tie-in film, *Fire Walk with Me* (1992), he conceived this as a prequel and thus failed to resolve the show's many loose ends (a cause of conflict with Frost, who opted out of the film project). Admirers have subsequently been left to perpetuate the series via their own imaginative efforts and continue to discuss its enigmas—just as they did when *Twin Peaks* was first broadcast. The series benefited from the emergence of the Internet when it aired, enabling "*Peaks* freaks" to find one another, while the VCR afforded the opportunity to record and re-view each episode in the quest for "clues." Such technologies remain a key factor in its continued cult status. Now that the entire series is finally available as a "complete" DVD box set (with the second season, and the two pilots, having previously been notoriously difficult to obtain), not only have established fans been able to see it again, but a new generation of admirers has been created. Two decades after its initial broadcast, *Twin Peaks* has found a new audience, often led by personal recommendation—sometimes parents, according to online testimonials, as well as series creators who frequently cite *Twin Peaks* as a formative influence. The series would fulfill the network's aim by delivering the kind of audience they wanted (deeply engaged and eager to take part in the mystery), but they lost the majority when they meddled with its formula and prized open its secrets. Nonetheless, ABC provided the opportunity that would enable *Twin Peaks* to become an exemplary cult show, rewriting expectations—for viewers and industry alike—about what was achievable in a primetime drama series.

Subversion of expectation is the show's primary delight, and evident from the start. A body is washed up on the riverbed of Twin Peaks, Washington, and identified as local homecoming queen Laura Palmer (Sheryl Lee). Soon after this discovery, a second girl, Ronette Pulaski (Phoebe Augustine), is found wandering along the highway, just across the state line—leading local sheriff Harry S. Truman (Michael Ontkean) to be joined in the ensuing investigation by FBI Special Agent Dale Cooper (Kyle MacLachlan). While all the genre conventions are in place to expect an arrogant cityslicker, the agent who arrives flouts such clichéd expectation. Cooper's first scene shows him driving towards Twin Peaks, animatedly discussing his journey with "Diane" on his dictaphone, providing exacting detail on the weather report, his last meal, and the need to find a motel that's both "clean and inexpensive." Upon arrival, he is courteous, keen to listen and understand, and anything but the by-the-book federal agent we may have expected, and we are quickly alerted to the fact that any assumptions are to be deliberately confounded. Viewers waiting to see the murderer revealed via a steady process of deduction would soon be frustrated by the meandering technique adopted, with the investigation into Laura's death leading into various peripheral stories among the townfolk. This was partly influenced by Dickensian literature (according to Frost), as well as drawing from *Blue Velvet* by investigating a community that is, on the surface, quaint and homely, yet shown to have decidedly sinister qualities. MacLachlan largely reprises his role of Jeffrey in *Blue Velvet*, who finds a severed human ear on his way home one day, which prompts him to explore the seamy underside of Lumberton (a literal "lumber town"—just like Twin Peaks). Cooper may have some added quirks, yet is similarly "tested" during his investigation. Described by one critic as looking like "a young demented Robert Vaughn" (Tucker 1990), he seems at first to be a goofball, yet he quickly proves himself to have a remarkable eye for detail, finding a "clue" in the freeze-frame of a home video tape owned by Laura (prompting fans to watch equally closely). Nonetheless, despite giving the impression of a highly organized individual who will soon have matters resolved, he makes clear in the pilot in a speech to the town's leaders that the investigation is likely to take "weeks and months." Each episode is intended as a day in narrative time, making the entire series only one month since the discovery of Laura Palmer's body; yet the need for continued deferment derails the investigation as different subplots are explored, and various supernatural twists render Cooper's task as wayward and eccentric as Twin Peaks itself.

Cooper interviews virtually every resident in endeavoring to understand what happened to Laura, yet seems equally interested in apparently trivial details, such as the quality of fare served up in the Double R diner (which is routinely commented on, both to fellow diners and the unseen "Diane"). With eccentricities of his own, including his delight in coffee and pie, he fits right into Twin Peaks, is sufficiently intuitive to give locals like the "Log Lady" (Catherine E. Coulson) credence (a woman who carries a piece of wood like a babe in arms and speaks in gnomic riddles communicated by the said piece of wood), and uses a variety of unorthodox approaches to solve the case. This includes ideas derived from Tibetan Buddhist belief, suggesting his subconscious holds the answer, with the rock throwing exercise (in an effort to find "J") proving particularly memorable. The more time he spends in Twin Peaks the more he becomes part of an increasingly odd soap opera—just as we become immersed in its residents' lives. As in *The Prisoner*, a heightened sense of the absurd is combined with a discernible mix of genres and moods. The tone shifts abruptly from one scene to the next—from the comic affair between ditzy secretary Lucy (Kimmie Robertson) and equally childlike police deputy Andy (Harry Goaz), to the sense of dread that pervades the lives of other characters, including the threat of domestic violence faced by waitress Shelly

Johnson (Madchen Amick) at the hands of her husband Leo (Eric Da Re). There are also moments so off-the-wall they can only be described as surreal. Chief among these are visits from the various spirit guides that help Cooper find the killer, one taking the form of a dwarf, credited as "Man from Another Place" (played by Michael J. Anderson), who appears to him in a dream early in season one, and "The Giant" (Carel Struycken), who offers oblique clues in the second season.

The first such encounter occurs in the celebrated "Red Room" scene that concludes episode two (and was first conceived for the "closed" version of the pilot). We witness Agent Cooper's dream, which finds him sitting in a red-curtained room with the aforementioned "Man from Another Place" and Laura Palmer herself, who whispers the name of her killer in his ear. Needless to say, Cooper cannot recall this vital piece of information when conscious. Just as delving into Number 6's mind in "A, B and C" will not reveal why he resigned, so Cooper's dream can only tease us with the identity of Laura's killer, adding the fantastic to the mix of genres already in place. The next morning Cooper affirms, "My dream is a code waiting to be broken"; and the fact that the local police team are prepared to grant such methods credibility places us in an entirely new world, demanding an equivalent suspension of disbelief on our part.

While this surreal departure delighted emergent fans of the series, these twists — together with the growing number of potential suspects involved in Laura's death — started to convince some viewers there was no resolution in sight. Those who felt frustrated by this seem to have misunderstood the point of the series, for beneath the veneer of a murder mystery lies an intent to confound us at every turn. The series' tagline itself — "Where everyone knows everyone, and nothing is as it seems" — explicitly invites viewers to question appearances. The production design and shooting methods further underscore the lack of realism, for like *The Prisoner*'s use of canted angles and quick edits, a similar stylization is present here, with expressive camerawork not only adding a cinematic quality, but reinforcing the dreamlike nature of the series. Unlike a conventional detective thriller, the series has an emotional resonance that aims to involve us in the most basic of ways: by tugging at our heartstrings. As Rodley notes, "The series is remarkable for its many scenes of naked pain and despair, often expressed in uncontrollable sobbing" (156). This is particularly evident in the pilot, where the impact of Laura's death is confirmed via the shock and grief exhibited among various townspeople, and is most painfully shown in the searing scene where Laura's parents learn the tragic news — on either end of a telephone — and respond with an emotional honesty that would grip many viewers and keep them watching. Lest the point is forgotten, on the morning of Laura's funeral (in episode 3) Cooper reminds (and reprimands) his FBI colleague Albert Rosenfield (Miguel Ferrer) — the outrageously rude citysclicker we might have had in his place — that Twin Peaks is different from the world he is used to, pointing out that "murder is not a faceless event here. It is not a statistic to be tallied up at the end of the day. Laura's death has meaning here to everyone. That's a way of living I thought had vanished forever from the earth." It takes more than this speech to chasten Albert, yet the point is to assert a community that cares—about this particular girl at least, a homecoming queen who offers their most positive self-image.

However, as we learn through Cooper's investigation, Laura was a great deal more complex. She did not simply deliver meals to the needy, or tutor select residents in her spare time, but had a secret drug habit, worked at a brothel, and had affairs with a number of men—including Shelly Johnson's violent husband, Leo, and the town bigwig, Benjamin Horne (Richard Beymer). Both men are implicated as her potential killers, among others, yet the real culprit is revealed in episode 14—the moment of revelation ABC insisted upon. However, far from offering closure to the case, the rug was pulled from under our feet. We see Laura's apparently doting and grief-stricken father, Leland (Ray Wise), violently kill her lookalike cousin, Maddie (Sheryl Lee); yet the scene intercuts another figure in Leland's place. This is revealed to be "BOB" (Frank Silva), of whom Laura's mother had a "vision" in her bedroom (replicating Lynch's first sighting of Silva), and who is described in Laura's secret diary as having molested her since the age of 12. The horrific idea of paternal incest is thus revealed to viewers, ahead of the police. They catch up in episode 16, when Cooper's memory of his dream is jolted by the offer of gum(!), and he finally recalls Laura's dream whisper to him (from episode two): "My father killed me." Even this does not provide the whole "truth," however, with BOB presented as an evil spirit who has possessed Leland since childhood, leading him to sexually abuse his own daughter from early adolescence before eventually killing her. This is Laura's closely guarded secret, used to explain her darker side—taking drugs and selling herself to deal with the damage—with BOB manipulating a seemingly unwitting Leland.

The revelation is both shocking and sad. Even in a town full of strange folk, Leland Palmer is one of the strangest—yet also one of the most sympathetic. Prone to dancing and singing at odd moments, as well as breaking down in public, his behavior is seemingly explicable as a symptom of grief; yet specific scenes infer more sinister connotations, such as when he fights with his wife over Laura's photograph, cuts himself on the smashed glass, and smears his blood over her image. A similar tendency to exceed boundaries with his daughter occurs at her funeral when he flings himself on Laura's coffin, which abruptly malfunctions, indecently going up and down as he lies on top and his wife curiously rails at him: "Don't spoil this too!" Such details affirm that Frost and Lynch knew all along who the killer would be and provide uncomfortable hints from the outset. That they managed to dissuade us from suspecting Leland is partly due to the secretive production methods used on set, only telling Ray Wise the truth when the network forced the disclosure. The actor had played him as a father driven almost insane with grief, and was very upset to discover otherwise. Leland's apparent delusion is evidenced by the fact that he kills another man, Jacques Renault (Walter Olewicz), when he learns he is a suspect in Laura's murder, and Wise provides such a moving performance when interrogated over this (in episode 11) that he commands total sympathy. "Have you ever experienced absolute loss?" he asks Truman and Cooper. "It's deep down. Inside, every cell screams. You can hear nothing else." Because these are (seemingly) the words of a devoted and loving father, and conveyed with such conviction, Leland achieves considerable pathos, and to have him revealed as the killer was a cruel surprise, even if nagging doubts had been suggested at times.

Like *The Prisoner*'s startling conclusion, *Twin Peaks* similarly confounds expectation by dispensing with a conventional villain; and in dropping a bombshell of this kind in a primetime U.S. drama series it proved equally incendiary. If *The Prisoner* suggests that we are all fundamentally prisoners, and questions the oppressive nature of living in an apparent democracy, *Twin Peaks* potentially unsettles its audience still further by looking beyond Laura's happy homecoming photo (a repeated motif throughout the series) and revealing the twisted truth behind the smile, insinuating that carefully preserved myths are precisely that, including the idea that home is necessarily a safe and nurturing environment. However, strange means are employed to make the truth more palatable for viewers, using BOB to explain Leland's actions, as well as attempting to perpetuate a sense of mystique. Lynch did not intend the murder to be resolved until much later, if at all, pointing out that *The Fugitive* (1963)— which is referenced in the inclusion of a "one-armed man" in *Twin Peaks*— managed to preserve its enigma until the end, and blaming network pressure for not allowing the mystery to continue:

> The way we pitched this thing was as a murder mystery, but that murder mystery was to eventually become the background story. Then there would be a middle ground of all the characters we stay with for the series. And the foreground would be the main characters that particular week.... We're not going to solve the murder for a long time. This they did not like. This they did *not* like ... and the pressure was just so great that the murder mystery couldn't be a background thing any more ... but the mystery was the magical ingredient [Rodley, 180].

If mystery was the magic ingredient, audiences were roughly disenchanted. By making the killer Laura's father, albeit inhabited by an "evil" spirit, Lynch and Frost acceded to network demands—yet via a plot twist that introduced the most disturbing of ideas. Randi Davenport has stated, "If *Twin Peaks* is 'about' the horrors of incest, it is equally about the horror of the secret life of the American family" (Davenport 1993, 264). While I would not go so far as to claim that *Twin Peaks* is primarily "about" the horrors of incest, broaching this taboo subject would highlight many of the series' concerns:

subverting conventional ideas of normality, foregrounding duality, and taking the soap's "dysfunctional family" theme to its most extreme conclusion.

The two worlds of Twin Peaks—its wholesome all-American façade and its shadowy interiors—are literally embodied by Laura, creating an intensely conflicted identity. Unlike Teresa Banks, the first of BOB's victims who, we are told, had no one to mourn her, or Ronette Pulaski, whose blue-collar parentage is mocked in their matching plaid shirts, Laura Palmer comes from a seemingly loving middle-class family—yet the demonic BOB has been head of this household for years. The inference is that it is precisely because no one expects such horrors to happen amid such apparent normality that they are allowed to continue. Laura is, as the "Man from Another Place" informs us, "filled with secrets." She is a case for repression if ever there was one, and the community that mourns her appears equally in denial. During her brief life, no one seems able to assist her—making her plight a matter of wider culpability than the man (or demon) who killed her. Although she saw a psychiatrist, Laura withheld her abuse from Dr. Jakoby (Russ Tamblyn), whose flirtatious interest in his patient sets him up as a suspect. Her boyfriend, Bobby Briggs (Dana Ashbrook), was aware of her self-destructive side yet similarly ignorant of its cause, and uses anger to assuage his apparent guilt, railing at her funeral:

> You damn hypocrites—you make me sick! Everybody knew she was in trouble. But we didn't do anything. All you good people—you wanna know who killed Laura? You did. You all did. And pretty words aren't gonna bring her back.

Although Bobby's outburst is attention-seeking and immature, his comments appear increasingly accurate. Harold Smith (Lenny Von Dohlen), the recluse Laura charged with keeping her secret diary safe, does not seem at all moved by her situation; her mother, Sarah (Grace Zabriskie), claims psychic powers yet fails to protect her daughter from abuse (with Leland's drugging of his wife unconvincing); and even her best friend, Donna (Lara Flynn Boyle), and secret boyfriend, James (James Marshall), despite claiming to be the only ones who really loved her, cannot conceal their disappointment in her or their greater desire to be together. This is a community that prefers comforting illusions to unpleasant truths, and we might venture to speculate whether much of the audience stopped watching after Laura's secret is exposed due to a similar reluctance to venture into such murky territory. Invariably, as Lynch predicted, once this revelation was made, the impetus to continue watching diminished—even if the unmasking of Leland failed to tell us much about BOB.

The peaking of interest in *Twin Peaks* seems inevitable. Linda Ruth Williams suggests that the "generic undecidability" of the series produced a fundamental schism, noting the extent to which "the uneasy line between investigation and involvement is crossed and recrossed, as is that between humor and melodrama" (Williams 2005, 39). This "slippage" may have been a primary source of its novelty, yet created an irresolvable tension, and she concludes that "there is a sense that *Twin Peaks had* to self-destruct, given that it was pitched across such unsettling and perhaps incompatible generic demands" (49). The series seems to have fundamentally misjudged its audience, as its murder mystery, far from receding into a "background story" (as intended), became the central concern for many viewers. Laura's death may have been designed as a catalyst for the ensuing melodrama—a way into its various intrigues—yet we were led to care more about Laura (arguably) than the figures that mourn her. The truth of her pitiable life, and violent death at the hands of an incestuous father, thus struck viewers an uneasy blow, and having a demonic entity added to an already complex mix was an ingredient too far for some.

The idea of an "unnatural father" was apparently intended from the outset, with Lynch and Frost telling Ray Wise it had been him all along. In making BOB the evil force behind his actions, the series has interesting resonances with the folk tale "The Maiden with No Hands," which also centers on an incestuous relationship between father and daughter—and disingenuously attempts to explain the father's actions as the work of the devil (which is essentially how BOB is represented). The result is discomfiting not only because incest is such a repugnant idea, but because of its treatment. Does the fact that BOB possesses Laura's father (leading him to abuse and kill his daughter) really mean that Leland is innocent of these crimes? Clearly, if BOB had the same appearance as Leland, rather than being played by a different actor, this "explanation" would be much less convincing; and even as it is, the use of a clichéd "the devil made me do it" plea remains unsatisfying. Furthermore, unlike the original tale's heroine, who leaves home and starts a family of her own, a life beyond Twin Peaks seems impossible for Laura, who welcomes death (in her final secret diary entry) as the only way to evade "BOB." The fact that she continues to haunt the community even in death (as well as Cooper's subconscious) adds further folk tale motifs, returning from a watery grave because her story demands to be known, although an attempt to provide a happy ending remains deeply frustrating.

In episode 16, having finally recalled Laura's whispered words, Cooper tricks Leland into a jail cell and converses with BOB. Asking if Leland was aware of his actions, he is told, "Oh, Leland's a babe in the woods—with a large hole where his conscience used to be." Perplexingly, because he is apparently unaware of his crimes, he cannot be deemed guilty of them, and a contrived return to innocence results when BOB causes him to fatally injure himself. As he vacates Leland's dying body, BOB also returns his memory—enabling a redemption scene written primarily to appease Ray Wise, as much as to reassure audiences that a happy ending for this family was still possible. However, in seeing "the light" as he dies, together with Laura's smiling face (securing her apparent forgiveness), the scene resembles the fake happy ending to *Blue Velvet*, with its ersatz robin and waving firemen. If the sentiment is unconvincing, so is any sense of closure, with no one to punish for Laura's death and BOB still unnervingly at large.

The next episode begins with a shot of the woods, followed by the camera panning from Laura's photo on the mantelpiece to Leland's portrait beside it, disconcertingly uniting father and daughter. At Leland's surprisingly well-attended wake, Cooper reassures Sarah Palmer that while "there are things dark and heinous in this world ... Leland did not do these things, not the Leland that you knew," and tells her of his daughter's apparent forgiveness. We were then expected to turn our attention to other intrigues, yet doing so was difficult, particularly with Laura's death unsatisfactorily resolved; and this is the moment the series "jumps the shark"—dramatically veering from its initial quality. Two geriatric brothers have a spat among the sandwiches, announcing a new subplot but appearing inappropriate and off-key, and when Cooper responds with the line, "Harry, I'm really gonna miss this place," the perfect parting shot was delivered. However, far from ending here, the series goes on, constructing a host of subplots to explain Cooper's continued presence in town.

Odell and Le Blanc have tried to argue, against the general consensus, that far from losing its way after the Leland revelation, this is the moment the series "hit its stride as the ne plus ultra of soap operas, the perfect dissection of conventional soaps, extended plotting cranked into overdrive for absurdist effect" (Odell and LeBlanc 2007, 74). This is a commendable effort to reclaim the series, yet we might ask if reading the series as a pastiche soap opera is any better than as a murder mystery. Various plot intrigues, from illicit affairs to underhanded business deals, clearly resemble the sensationalist soap opera plotting of shows like *Dallas* and *Dynasty*, and a parodic intent was also illustrated in "soap-within-soap" *Invitation to Love* (watched avidly by Twin Peaks residents, with plots that parallel events in season one), while Cooper's shooting by an unknown assailant in the first season finale obviously plays on the infamous "who shot JR?" cliffhanger. Nonetheless, while these traits may be "cranked into overdrive" in the second season, as Odell and Le Blanc aver, they do not have adequate dramatic ballast, and the remainder of the series is too removed from its compelling origins to make anyone seem worth caring about. Given the extent to which Laura herself involved us from the very beginning, it was difficult to simply "move on"—as is necessary for any soap opera—leaving a void the writers struggled to fill. Various strategies were deployed, yet they lacked the depth of emotion Laura's death evoked, and many misfires occurred in trying to extend the show's narrative horizons. James leaves town and becomes involved with a duplicitous older woman (negating his apparent love for Donna). A young woman—accused of being a witch—entrances the town's men-folk in an attempt at comedy that falls flat, as does the paternal rivalry that ensues over Lucy's unexpected pregnancy. The false belief the would-be fathers have that an orphan boy, "Little Nicky" (Joshua

Harris), is cursed provides another misfire, seeming to ridicule the demonic denouement to Laura's murder. A more successful comic twist came in the form of middle-aged housewife Nadine (Wendy Robie), who acquires super strength after a blow to the head, as well as amnesia. In reliving her high school days (under medical advice) and gaining the adoration of a former knuckleheaded jock, Nadine confounds the pitiable figure she was initially portrayed as, and interestingly prefigures Buffy Summers in demonstrating her superior strength at cheerleading practice (an idea later revisited in *Heroes* also). Moments of continued delight were also provided in David Duchovny's brief turn as transvestite DEA agent Denis/Denise Bryson, as well as David Lynch's standout role as Cooper's stone deaf boss, Gordon Cole; yet too many inconsistencies in plot development and characterization suggested the series' labyrinthine contortions were beginning to unravel.

With the writers having lost sight of BOB, another villain was created via a former colleague of Cooper's, Windom Earle (Kenneth Welsh), who arrives in town seeking revenge against him. The grudge is explained by Cooper having had an affair with his wife, Caroline, and subsequently surviving an attack by Earle in which she was fatally injured—resulting in Earle being committed to an asylum until his recent escape. Hiding out in the woods, occasionally venturing into town in a succession of disguises, he plays a deadly game of chess with Cooper (taking a real victim for every piece lost). Cooper faces an additional problem in being investigated by internal affairs, questioning a raid he took part in across the Canadian border (and his suspected involvement in drug trafficking). He clears his name by involving Denis(e) in a sting, and uncovers another vendetta against him—a bereaved criminal, the third of the Renault brothers, who blames Cooper for his brothers' deaths and attempts to kill him. Windom Earle is more intent on making him suffer, and as Cooper falls in love with a new arrival in town, Annie Blackburn (Heather Graham), in a few hastily contrived scenes, he gives Earle a suitable weapon with which to exact his revenge. Despite a commendable performance by Welsh, Windom Earle was a pantomime villain compared to BOB, and giving Cooper a questionable past seemed like a mistake—removing the innocence that was key to his appeal. As the season dragged on, various eccentric additions went into overdrive.

Air Force officer Major Garland Briggs (Don Davis), formerly connected to Windom Earle via their work together on real-life UFO investigation Project Blue Book, infers a sinister connection between Twin Peaks and the U.S. government, with allusions made to contemporary abduction theories promoted by Whitley Streiber, suggesting that Cooper was summoned to the town by unknown forces. These ideas seemed to be increasingly outlandish attempts to keep audiences interested in a floundering show. Retrospective comments from cast and crew offer various reasons for the resulting backlash, with many viewing Lynch's absence during the second season as integral to its failings, as

Sherilyn Fenn suggests in claiming the show became strange for its own sake, without Lynch's insistence on a "bottom of truth" (Fenn 2007). However, Lynch is equally fond of strangeness for its own sake—his entire oeuvre containing elements that border on incomprehensibility—and *Twin Peaks* is arguably his most popular, and accessible, work because it is a collaborative endeavor (not to mention the constraints imposed by the medium). Describing his working relationship with Frost, Lynch has suggested, "Maybe he helped bring me into more of a real world" (Rodley 161)—an idea that parallels McGoohan's relationship with Markstein—and it seems fair to say that tempering Lynchian weirdness was intrinsic to making the series—at its best—so intriguing.

Attempting to discern a precise reason for *Twin Peaks*' appeal remains a difficult task. As Lynch has stated, "What made *Twin Peaks* Twin Peaks is hard to talk about. I don't think even we knew what it was" (Rodley 158). Nonetheless, many have attempted to fathom the answer, with critics often citing the postmodern aspects of the series, including intertextual allusions (in the choice of characters' names, familiar actors cast, and the recycling of specific plots); generic hybridity (in its mix of soap opera, detective series, film noir, 1950s youth films, comedy, horror, SF and fantasy); a sense of parody (evidenced by overdetermined plot intrigues and excessive performance styles); and various examples of self-reflexivity (as occurs during moments where characters express an awareness of their contrived existence, such as when "Big Ed" Hurley [Everett McGill], kept from his true love by various twists of fate, asserts that their world "feels like its designed to keep us apart"). However, citing its postmodern traits only goes so far in summing up *Twin Peaks*. The collection of essays *Full of Secrets* offers a number of critical approaches to the series, including a discussion of its gender roles, the innovative use of diegetic music, and a pronounced preoccupation with its postmodern features; yet it also tends to veer into abstraction. Henry Jenkins' contribution makes an interesting contrast in questioning what involved viewers to such an extraordinary degree, appraising fan responses to the series by focusing on newsgroup alt.tv. twin-peaks, which emerged within a few weeks of the series' first broadcast. This provides a fascinating insight into this newsgroup and their collaborative attempts to solve the mystery of Laura's killer. The sheer density of the show was clearly a primary attraction for a specific segment of the audience. Like *The Prisoner*, it gave viewers work to do in spotting references, making connections, and working out the significance of its symbolism—from traffic lights and ceiling fans to the obscure poetry used at certain points. The series evidently benefited from the availability of VCRs, enabling fans to re-watch episodes for clues and exchange tapes, while access to the Internet enabled them to trade observations and speculate on likely developments. Some commentators among the group point out that suggestions made about narrative prospects seem to anticipate actual plot lines, and query if the show's makers were getting ideas from their discussions—with one poster asking, "I wonder how much we are writing our own show?" Yet Lynch's reputation as a "trickster author" caused others to wonder if they were being duped by the series, speculating that it might all be revealed as Cooper's dream (Jenkins 1995, 62). These concerns illustrate the hesitance engendered among cult fans: expressing a desire to deeply explore specific texts yet obviously wanting to believe such investment is not in vain. *Lost* would similarly promote endless speculation, as well as prompting nagging doubts that its creators might, as many speculated of *Twin Peaks*, simply "be making it up as they go along" (64). Jenkins emphasizes the investigative role played by *Twin Peaks*' "reception community" and asserts that "for some, the revelation of a supernatural or science fiction dimension in the series made their previous efforts futile and destroyed the pleasure of the game" (66). However, while this may have alienated many viewers by negating attempts to solve the mystery in a rational manner, the supernatural constitutes a significant part of *Twin Peaks* mythology among continued fans of the series, reiterating incompatible elements at work in the show and prompting very different reactions. Although some newsgroup members cited a reluctance to have any mysteries resolved, wanting to perpetuate the magic of the series, others reacted with frustration in realizing it could go on indefinitely, with the "solution" to Laura's murder creating further enigmas relating to BOB, other fantastical figures, and the origins of evil in the town. Freeze-framing scenes, and exploring close-ups and cutaways, would offer no help in making sense of these deeper enigmas, undermining "viewer mastery" of the text and thus becoming a cause of frustration. Invariably, its success was fleeting not only because of scheduling problems, the diverse nature of audience interests, and the anti-climax that followed the forced revelation of Laura's killer, but because this fundamentally changed the nature of the show. BOB would impact on the remainder of the series by taking us into a mystical realm, and it is in identifying itself as a work of telefantasy that *Twin Peaks* would arguably prove most challenging to viewers, many of whom rejected the move as a contrivance.

For a select minority, however, these elements provide an enduring point of intrigue, and the series is most interesting when the divide between the supernatural realm and reality is breached. A key source of pleasure for such fans is the way fantastical ideas are inserted within the narrative, combining the extraordinary with the everyday. Various characters are evidently not "real," including Mrs. Tremond (Frances Bay) and her grandson Pierre (Austin Jack Lynch—often referred to as "the corned cream kid"), the geriatric bellhop (Hank Worden), and other magical figures. This is a world where dreams afford vital clues, characters come from "Another Place," and events do not fit rational explanations. The series consequently has some affinity with "surrealism"—a movement that explored the world of dreams to provide some insight into the subconscious. Lynch deeply admired its most famous cinematic example, *Un Chien Andalou* (Bunuel and Dali, 1920), and *Twin Peaks* shares a number of elements, particularly the "Red Room," which provides a location for the subconscious (like *The Prisoner*'s Village), taking Cooper's investigation beyond the town, into the woods, and, ultimately, further within his own self. Although such departures would help to affirm its cult status among fans, the show's fantastic elements alienated more "mainstream" viewers and left many at a loss about how to view the series. Too off-beat and unfocused to work as a thriller, too unsettling to amuse as an exaggerated soap, its strange juxtapositions may have elicited curiosity; yet the further it deviated from a recognizable format, the more it divided its audience, particularly in how seriously we were expected to take it.

As is inferred in the repeated motif of playing cards, chess games, domino pieces, and casino chips, the series continually plays with its audience, frequently leading viewers astray. For example, Benjamin Horne is primarily shown as a figure of "evil" in *Twin Peaks*—the epitome of a greedy capitalist, whose business interests include not only land development but prostitution, and whose lack of concern about his kidnapped daughter, Audrey (Sherilyn Fenn), is satirized by his expressing greater relief at the ransom money's safe return. If the series was "Dallas with an IQ," as one reviewer dubbed it, Horne was its "JR"; yet he has nothing to do with Laura's death. Instead, the demonic BOB provides an image of evil that is much harder to identify because it is seemingly all-pervasive. Arcane powers are said to reside in the woods surrounding Twin Peaks, within Black and White Lodges located near a clearing known as "Glastonbury Grove." This is where Major Briggs communes with unknown forces and where Windom Earle heads with the abducted Annie, hoping to acquire an infernal power. The Lodges are a means of explaining where BOB, the Giant, the "Man from Another Place," and other fantastical beings reside, yet additionally symbolizes the duality within us all. Good and evil, and our propensity toward either disposition, are, as the Giant hints, "one and the same," a fact made evident in the final episode when Cooper gains entry to the Lodges and encounters a number of doppelgangers, including his own. He meets Earle and offers to trade his soul to save Annie, whereupon an incensed BOB destroys Earle, claiming he has no right to make such a deal. Cooper is found, with Annie, on the ground at Glastonbury Grove, yet the final scene reveals that BOB has taken his form. He wakes at the Great Northern, hits his head against the bathroom mirror, and we see BOB's reflection grinning back at us. Like the finale in "Fall Out," the plot has come full circle, rendering our hero's efforts inconsequential, with an unspeakable evil still at large.

The series drew upon American Indian mythology, according to Frost, in the notion of spirits lurking in the woods; and the fact that the Log Lady's husband died in a fire adds to the idea, repeated through close-ups of flames, fireplaces, red traffic lights, and cigarette smoke, that danger pervades the community. Some have contended that the log holds the spirit of her dead husband—an idea that hinges on easily the strangest scene in the entire series, when Josie Packard (Joan Chen) is killed by BOB and her spirit is trapped in a wooden drawer-knob. If Kosho was McGoohan's joke at our expense, such departures take absurdity to new levels, causing us to question if the entire series was, like the puzzle box that infuriates Catherine Martell (Piper Laurie), a series of intrigues intended simply to divert us. As the central mystery veers from seeking to identify Laura's murderer to attempting some explanation for BOB, potential interest would understandably narrow; yet enduring obliqueness has also helped to secure its cult status, extending the series way beyond the thirty episodes to which *Twin Peaks* finally amounted. Do we ever really find out who killed Laura Palmer? The answer becomes ever more abstract and ephemeral the more one looks into it.

David Lavery summarizes the detective work involved in watching the series and the intellectual pay-off this yields, arguing that much of its appeal lies in

> tracking its intertextual, allusionary quotations: the many actors and actresses reborn from the never-never land of old TV and movies, the red herring evocations of old movies, allusions to previous Lynch films, numerous inside jokes, cameos by Lynch (as Gordon Cole), Frost (as a newscaster in the first episode of the second season), and even Lynch's son Austin (as Mrs. Tremmond's magical grandson Pierre). These and many other facets of *Twin Peaks* invited fanatic cultic participation [Lavery 1995, 6–7].

Its principal pleasure is thus aligned with the opportunity it offered viewers to test their observational skills and flaunt their knowledge. If *The Prisoner* was best appreciated by "mostly intelligent people" (in McGoohan's words), a similar attempt was made with *Twin Peaks* to appeal to a select audience. As Helen Wheatley notes, "This niche audience was assumed to have a good deal of cultural capital and a high level of media literacy, in order to make sense of the program's dizzying network of allusions and complex plotting, a select, but lucrative, viewer group in the eyes of advertisers" (Wheatley 2006, 167). However, the fan base that stayed with it was clearly too "select" to make ABC's investment worthwhile, proving that even with niche audiences in mind, the numbers still count.

The anxieties expressed by some posters on the alt.tv.twin-peaks site were ultimately proven to be accurate: the show's makers *were* making it up as they went, as the most prolific of the writers, Harley Peyton, subsequently admitted to the newsgroup, with many plot points created with an attitude of "set them up, figure them out later"—much like the "Red Room" scene that Lynch installed and later elaborated upon. This includes the finale, with Cooper's possession in the final scene "only decided in the last weeks of production" (much like *The Prisoner*'s final twist); Peyton cites the "chaotic state of the creative process" to explain little opportunity to plan such developments in advance. Invariably, *Twin Peaks* suffered the same problems and pressures of any other series in terms of limited production time, advancing deadlines, a diverse group of writers with a large cast to write for, staff leaving to work on other projects, and the sheer number of installments required for its second season, with twenty-two episodes pushing its ideas to the limit. In hindsight, the series would have benefited from a limited run of episodes, and ABC's insistence that they reveal their trump card ahead of the finale clearly didn't help matters; but *Twin Peaks* has secured its legacy both in terms of the shows it has inspired and the continued interest it holds for fans.

Fans continue to celebrate the series, holding an annual festival in Snoqualmie, much as *Prisoner* fans return to Portmerion. The fanzine *Wrapped in Plastic* (1992–2002) ran for a decade after *Twin Peaks* ended, affirming the level of detail used to interpret the series: providing a timeline of events, analyzing the Windom Earle/Dale Cooper chess game, and critically comparing the series to folklore, Arthurian legend, and Kafka, as well as exhibiting interest in UFOlogy and *The X-Files* in later issues. As to official *Twin Peaks* merchandise, some inventive efforts were made to cash in on its success—and extend its fictional world—including a CD soundtrack featuring Badalamenti's score and singer, Julee Cruise; *The Secret Diary of Laura Palmer*, written by Jennifer Lynch and replicating a key prop from the series; and the similar *Diane: The Twin Peaks Tapes of Agent Cooper*. The latter's follow-up, *The Autobiography of FBI Special Agent Dale Cooper: My Life, My Tapes*, would extend the detective's backstory, while Lynch and Frost's *Access Guide to the Town* promotes the idea that Twin Peaks is a real place (a conceit later cults would emulate via such means as alternate reality games). *Fire Walk with Me* might be seen as another *Twin Peaks* tie-in, but it attracted criticism for being much darker in tone. Given that it covers the last seven days of Laura Palmer's life, it is scarcely any wonder the mood would be bleak, yet why Lynch opted to detail her end remains odd. The film was badly received (it was even booed at Cannes), and Lynch has since claimed that problems with its running time (rumored at five hours initially) necessitated omitting considerable footage. The rights over releasing a director's cut currently remains in legal limbo; but while fans have long anticipated its release, it is unlikely to provide any answers to the series, largely because *Twin Peaks* is not solely attributable to Lynch, and because a desire to preserve its enigma is apparent. As it is, *Fire Walk with Me* adds little to the series other than to infer that the "good Cooper" is still in the Black Lodge, while confirming, in an odd temporal twist, that Annie is dead. As is the nature of any mythology, many questions remain. Is Cooper deliberately sent to Twin Peaks to discover its secrets, or to ensure his corruption? Are the FBI/Washington connected to occult practices at the Black Lodge? The show's makers have opted to leave such questions open, leaving our hero's fate similarly unresolved. Like Number 6, Cooper has been construed as mad (with some claiming "Diane" is a figment of his imagination). Twin Peaks, like the Village, serves as a metaphysical testing ground rather than an actual location, and audiences are similarly left to make of it what they will.

Having watched *The Prisoner* in his youth, Mark Frost has admitted the impact it had on him, stating, "It just blew my little mind to pieces," and he even considered making a film version (Jackson 1992). *Twin Peaks* continues the legacy achieved by *The Prisoner* in pushing the envelope still further for television and has proved to be an equally hard act for its creators to follow. Lynch subsequently sought to interest ABC in a spin-off series following the exploits of Audrey Horne in L.A., but the network declined, and the concept eventually became *Mulholland Drive* (2001). A further collaboration with Frost, on radio show spoof *On the Air* (1992), failed to secure the same appeal and was cancelled in its first season. Despite calls for a follow-up to *Twin Peaks*, Lynch has demurred, arguing that the Internet has replaced television today, while Frost has jettisoned broadcasting for writing novels, scathingly asserting, "It is now blatantly what it has always been surreptitiously—an advertising medium. The programming is a viral cover for the real message—advertising" (Frost 2002). Ironically, it is their mutual lack of interest in television that enabled Lynch and Frost to create such an off-beat series. Like *The Prisoner*, *Twin Peaks* tested the boundaries of television and has inspired countless others to do the same, with those directly citing its influence including Joss Whedon, Bryan Fuller, David Chase, and Damon Lindelof. It would tempt other directors to work in television, including Oliver Stone (*Wild Palms*, Fox, 1993), Steven Spielberg (*Band of Brothers*, HBO, 2000), and Lars Von Trier (*Kingdom Hospital*, ABC, 2004), and, as Wheatley contends, the series marked a shift towards "stylish, intelligent, 'knowing' drama" during a period of intensifying competition (166–175). Although Thompson affirms that the "revolution" deemed as television's second golden age lasted only a decade, claiming that its end was signaled by *Twin Peaks*—and dismissively describes it as "a series that made no sense" (1996, 150), he also admits that it "changed the face of television" (153). Its cinematic features and challenging departures would reappear in later programming, confirming the existence of a more discerning viewer—rarely recognized by the networks up until this point—who would be increasingly targeted, helping to confirm greater audience acceptance for the strange and unsettling, together with an appetite for complex plotting. This paved the way for series we may never have seen otherwise. Emerging simultaneously, its manifestly White Lodge counterpart, *Northern Exposure* (CBS, 1990–5), provides a cozy flip-side to *Twin Peaks* in its quirky Alaskan community, while darker suburban intrigues appear in *Picket Fences* (CBS, 1992–6) and *American Gothic* (CBS, 1995–6). *Desperate Housewives* (ABC, 2004–) also owes a debt to *Twin Peaks* in lampooning melodramatic excesses among the residents of Wisteria Drive, one of whom is played by Kyle MacLachlan. Similarly indicating a smart bit of intertextual casting, Ray Wise has graduated from playing a character possessed by a demon to playing Satan himself in the cult horror comedy *Reaper* (ABC, 2007–)—albeit one who is happy to concede eventual defeat to Christianity, reassuring his newest reluctant recruit: "Don't worry. I know how it all ends. God wins." *Twin Peaks* would offer no such comforting homilies in the dark moral universe inhabited by its fictional community, all of whom are prey to an insurmountable evil, reiterating fundamental unease. Later takes on the quirky community have continued to this day, including *Happy Town* (ABC, 2010) which presents an oddball town (and hints at the fantastic) in a manner that clearly references *Twin Peaks*, and was treated just as churlishly by the network, with fans having to go online after its abrupt cancellation to see the last few episodes.

Among an array of strange relations, *Twin Peaks*' most direct descendent is *The X-Files* (Fox, 1993–2002), which features an equally unorthodox FBI agent whose past—like Cooper's—comes back to haunt him, and whose investigations uncover a bizarre world of mutations, strange powers, and clandestine experiments, ultimately implicating the government itself. The mix of paranoia and high production values initiated by *The Prisoner*, and which *Twin Peaks* further endorsed, would be elaborated via a show that combined a signature look with ongoing intrigue—and would additionally achieve unprecedented success. Accordingly, it is to *The X-Files* that the next chapter turns, taking us on the journey Cooper never made: from Twin Peaks back to the FBI's HQ in Washington.

3

The X-Files: Trust, Belief, and Broken Promises

> *I don't think* X-Files *jumped the shark.... I think it was good till the end and I think that while it changed with the exit of David Duchovny, I believe that during that period there was excellent work done, excellent storytelling, and I'll stand by all nine years of the show.*
> —Chris Carter

Although cult appeal is not necessarily determined by production length, the longer a show goes on, the higher the risk of a wane in quality. When a series is cancelled early, fans can at least console themselves with knowing that it didn't suffer the alternative fate of going on too long, losing what it had, and letting them down. This prospect is evidenced wherever a production exceeds its original tenets, makes obvious concessions to commercialism, and basically takes the wrong turn that is popularly described as "jumping the shark"—a fate *The X-Files* (Fox, 1993–2002) exemplifies all too clearly. Series creator Chris Carter may contest this view, yet his personal investment in the series detracts from his ability to offer an impartial critical appraisal, and his decision to prolong *The X-Files* over nine years—after many of the original cast and crew had departed—suggests a degree of devotion that was ultimately detrimental to the series. This chapter evaluates the show's considerable achievements and undeniable influence, yet argues that it "jumped the shark" long before one of its leads decided to leave, asserting that Carter's unwillingness to admit the premise was exhausted smacks of the same kind of denial that serves as a central trope in his conspiracy thriller-cum-monster show. It additionally asks whether fan investment in the show—attempting to follow an increasingly complex mythology in the hope that it would yield a worthwhile resolution—was invariably a broken promise. While the series earned a reputation for being "radical" in its distrust of officialdom, in conflating actual events within its fiction, and in its suggested probing of state secrets, it would eventually reveal the most cynical of motives: aiming to satisfy the needs of a continual series format and the demands of an ambitious network—at the expense of its audience.

The X-Files was a surprise success that had immense ramifications within the industry. In securing mass ratings it confirmed telefantasy's interest beyond a niche audience and changed the way "cult" series would subsequently be evaluated. The series aligned itself with "quality" television in terms of its visual style, narrative complexity, references made to an amalgam of influences, and an intriguing ambiguity. Although many thought it would be cancelled in its first season, it was eventually commissioned for another eight, spawning a host of imitators and making the paranormal detective show into a winning formula. Nonetheless, although its premise was extended, in marked contrast to *The Prisoner* and *Twin Peaks*, it would incur comparable criticism for baffling, infuriating, and ultimately disappointing a large sector of its audience. Originating from Carter's long-held desire to make a "scary show," *The X-Files* uncovered various monsters in our midst—and implicated the government as the most dangerous of all. It also stemmed from Carter's personal interest in spiritual matters—he described himself as a "nonreligious person looking for a religious experience" (Patterson 2008) and inflected the series mythology with this concern by exploring what lies beyond "rational" understanding. Appearing to catch the pre-millennial zeitgeist, the series became the network's biggest hit, yet the pursuit of profit appeared to take precedence, and, despite coping with a tireless production schedule for an extraordinary length of time, its originality waned and narrative coherence dwindled. Carter had acquired a reputation as a perfectionist, motivated by a commitment to making a unique and challenging series, yet as other projects divided his time, cast and crew members left, filming moved from Vancouver to L.A., and the show's tortuous mythology was stretched to the breaking point, it became harder to perceive the result as anything more than self-indulgence. The attempt to infuse the paranormal with a degree of credibility became jettisoned via a plot arc that was ever more unbelievable, and by the time the series ended it had lost much of its audience, failing to fulfill the promise that kept many watching for the best part of a decade.

Carter's reasons for persisting with the series are partly explained by the fact that other creative ventures, *Millennium* (1996–9), *Harsh Realm* (1999), and attempted *X-Files* spin-off *The Lone Gunmen* (2001), had each failed—forcing him to focus on the concept that had worked. When *The X-Files* finally ended, he planned to adapt the franchise into a series of films—an idea stalled by a legal dispute with Fox that took several years to resolve. When it did, Carter was reminded of his film plan and agreed to co-write and direct a second feature film, *I Want to Believe*, in 2008—despite the network offering a limited window for production just prior to the writers' strike. In the six years since the series had concluded, erstwhile admirers had continued to fan flames of interest, posting fan fiction and video mash-ups online, as well as placing ads in the trade papers asking for the franchise to be revived—all of which convinced Fox there was an audience out there for another film. By contrast, in interviews given during its release, Carter said he'd spent the last six years largely forgetting about the series. He also stated that he had "come closer to faith" over this time than ever before, and concerns with spirituality weigh heavily in the film (Patterson 2008). Despite fan-pleasing efforts such as referencing classic episodes, including cameos by Carter and other staff, and reuniting its original leads, the film smacked of an attempt to cash in on a faded franchise rather than an effort to revitalize it, and the disappointing response (barely recouping its production costs in the U.S.) indicates the degree to which Carter and his team failed to reconnect with the show's fan-base. While some critics opined that the post–9/11 world no longer needed fabricated fears, the real reason behind the film's failure seems to be its hasty execution and poor plot, suggesting Carter had succumbed to integrity failure in simply jumping when Fox told him to. A contributory factor is that the movie ignores the government/alien plot that underpinned the series (put simply: aliens are due to take over the planet in a plan government officials have secretly endorsed). The decision was explained as a wish to avoid the complexity of the alien arc, yet a story involving a psychic pedophile and an illegal organ trade lacked the necessary X factor and left many fans feeling cheated.

The feeling was far from new, particularly for those who had devoted years to following a trail that looked increasingly likely to lead nowhere—and ultimately found these suspicions confirmed. Having conceived a hook to keep viewers watching—a quest, undertaken by the series' leads, to uncover an insidious plot against humanity—the show focused on continually frustrating, rather than fulfilling, their mission. Just as Lynch described the mystery of Laura Palmer's killer as a "golden goose that kept laying these beautiful eggs" ("A Slice of Lynch" 2007), Carter pursued the same strategy in a show that endlessly denied closure. Still more perplexingly, the political ideas within the series' mythology lost their radicalism as blame shifted from shady government operatives to a villainous alien species holding them ransom. Carter may have posed as a cynic, citing the Watergate scandal as "the most formative event" of his youth, and describing the series' tagline—"Trust No One"—as a summary of his own "personal philosophy" (Lowry 1995, 12), yet fans were ill-advised to read much into this. The show's paranoid premise was simply a means of adding intrigue. Inspired by the fact that a sizable number of American citizens believed they had been abducted by aliens, it originated as a joke at the expense of those who believed we were victims of an ongoing campaign of exploitation and disinformation. Some critics realized this a while back, with Bruce Headlam asserting, "*The X-Files* isn't paranoia—it's paranoia camp, Carter's grim parody of conspiracy theories" (Headlam 1995). Many fans took its ideas seriously, however. Like the "*Peaks* Freaks" who pored over obscure details, even as some feared the show's makers were simply playing with them, self-termed

"X-Philes" got hung up on the trivia and only realized, relatively late in the day, that its mysteries were being spun out without any promise of resolution. Celebrity fan Stephen King went from penning a guest script for the show to lambasting its demise through overkill. Deeming the show guilty of adhering to the "Prime Network Directive: Thou Shalt Not Kill the Cash Cow," King affirms that "minus the continuing presence of David Duchovny, *X-Files* blundered off into a swamp of black oil, and in that swamp it died. I could have throttled the executives at Fox for doing that, and Chris Carter for letting it happen" (King 2005). Carter is thus accused of betraying the show (and its viewers) by pushing the premise to its limits, a contention most would agree with. In failing to offer any closure, even at its end, he left many feeling they'd been taken for a ride—a feeling that was simply compounded when he resurrected it on the big screen.

Having proved itself to be a show with a difference—turning polemical slogans into catchphrases, and adding subversive potential to the scare factor—*The X-Files* ultimately seemed to lead fans a merry dance. Yet despite such disappointment, its influence on the genre is undeniable, securing a level of success that would reignite network interest in "genre shows" of its kind. *The X-Files* would serve as a landmark in telefantasy by demonstrating that there was a sizeable audience for a contemporary SF/horror show—as well as a taste for convoluted mystery—leaving an indelible mark on later television and rewriting the definition of "cult" television. While *The Prisoner* and *Twin Peaks* were considered relative failures (in industrial terms) when they first aired (due to declining ratings), *The X-Files* would prove that a cult show could secure mainstream appeal and last a considerable distance. Unlike these earlier series, its creator was unknown, and the show received little promotion, yet it managed to overcome these limitations and cause a sensation. In its distinctive look, mix of influences, the ideas explored, and the interest cultivated, the series serves as a crucial stepping stone between cult shows of the past and the "blockbusters" that would follow. If *The Prisoner* and *Twin Peaks* each "inform" *The X-Files* by exploring themes of conspiracy and corruption, as well as pioneering a new level of experimentation, *The X-Files* would show that a comparatively humble series with a modest budget and little fanfare could perform relative miracles. In its subject matter, narrative strategies, and engagement with fans, it would establish elements franchises such as *Lost* and *Heroes* would readily borrow from, as well as initiate a host of imitators with a focus on aliens or the paranormal. Efforts to revive the franchise may have failed, yet the show's legacy is proven in the diverse series it continues to inspire—while additionally warning of the consequences in taking a mythology too far.

The X-Files emerged during a period of intense change in U.S. broadcasting. From the late 1950s up until the late 1980s, ABC, CBS, and NBC dominated production. The trinity was finally challenged by competition from cable and satellite stations, and the arrival of Rupert Murdoch's Fox network.

Launched in 1986, Fox began as a rank outsider yet built itself up from scratch to become one of the most successful networks in U.S. television, and quality telefantasy would play a key role in its ascent. Fox shrewdly invested in in-house productions to conserve costs, and targeted content at the 18–49 demographic, tending to focus on comedies and teen dramas. It aimed to extend this range in the early 1990s, commissioning pilots for potential hour-long drama series that would add prestige to the network and keep sponsors happy. Few would have believed—from the score of ideas produced as pilots in 1993— that a series in which two FBI agents investigate unexplained phenomena would become such a hit, yet *The X-Files* exceeded expectations and became a huge franchise. Earning industrial plaudits, as well as high ratings, the series confirmed Fox's place amid the established oligarchy and restored a sense of gravitas to SF within television—a medium in which the genre had been virtually absent for years. As Catherine Johnson states, the achievement wrought by *The X-Files* was thus two-fold: "securing Fox's position as the fourth major network in American television broadcasting and reinvigorating the science fiction genre during the 1990s" (Johnson 2001, 30).

Given that Chris Carter had previously written comedy and family-oriented series, *The X-Files* seems a radical departure, yet he had long nurtured the idea of making something "truly frightening." In 1992, he became a producer at Twentieth Century–Fox Television, with the task of developing potential series, and used the opportunity to explore this idea further. Carter pitched his concept to president of television production Peter Roth, who took it to Bob Greenblatt at sister company Fox Broadcasting. His main influence was cited as *Kolchak the Night Stalker* (Universal TV/ABC, 1974–5), a series that explored paranormal phenomena in a modern setting, as Gary Gerani's description illustrates:

> The premise of *Kolchak the Night Stalker* is that ancient fabled monsters stalk twentieth century America. In the dark corners of our nation's cities, in alleyways and abandoned buildings, in scientific research centers, on college campuses, aboard luxury liners, within sewers, sports arenas, high-rise buildings and hospitals they lurk, waiting to pounce on their next unsuspecting victim [Gerani 1977, 135].

As Carter saw it, *Kolchak the Night Stalker* was hamstrung by the fact that middle-aged newspaper reporter Carl Kolchak (Darren McGavin) simply happens upon supernatural entities during the course of his work. Two decades on, his show would provide an array of "monsters" to both frighten and fascinate audiences, yet situated their discovery in a more realistic premise. Carter hit on a framing device that elevated the series beyond potential schlock value by conceiving a special unit within the FBI to provide an explanation for regular encounters with the strange and supernatural. Two detectives—a believer and a skeptic—investigate seemingly inexplicable cases. Not only would their opposing views provide interest, their differing genders added a new spin to the buddy-cop format, and Carter additionally gave his "believer" a personal motivation: a search for his missing sister, taken at the age of eight, who he claims was abducted by aliens. The alien angle put Greenblatt off, yet attracted his successor, Sandy Grushow. A pilot was commissioned, with the aim of potentially replacing an existing Fox show, *Sightings* (1992–7), which reported on paranormal phenomena such as alleged UFOs. Popular interest in aliens thus played a crucial role in the development of *The X-Files* (and would, in turn, become intensified via the show). Carter's pilot script introduces the detectives and provides an alien encounter as their first investigation, adding intrigue by suggesting an official cover-up. From the outset the intent was to make the concept work as innovative drama, with a central relationship between its main characters that was as compelling as their quest. Carter set up Ten Thirteen Productions to make the pilot and soon found himself battling to retain creative control.

Carter was fortunate in finding actors with a ready chemistry, but had to fight to keep them both in the show. While David Duchovny was unanimously approved for the male lead, Fox Mulder, Carter met resistance in wanting Gillian Anderson to play his partner, Dr. Dana Scully. The fact that there was considerable negativity towards Anderson, with executives desiring "more of a bombshell" (Lowry 1995, 15), says much about the climate in which the series was born and how groundbreaking it was—not only in choosing an actress on the strength of her performance (rather than obvious sex appeal) but in creating a female character whose intellect is contrasted against her more intuitive male partner. Carter took a risk by insisting on Anderson, as well as in this role reversal, and insisted their relationship remained platonic (a decision he felt very strongly about in the beginning). His willingness to challenge Fox executives played a huge role, yet while Carter additionally wrote a number of key episodes and was very involved in all levels of production, the show equally depended on a host of fine actors making regular and guest appearances, as well as benefiting from an extraordinary creative team. This included writers James Wong and Glen Morgan (prior to leaving for *Space: Above and Beyond* in the second season), and memorable contributions from Glen's brother, Darin Morgan (before he left to work on *Millennium*); regular directors David Nutter, Rob Bowman and Kim Manners; producer Paul Rabwin; story editor Frank Spotnitz; creative consultant Vince Gilligan; and writer and co-executive producer Howard Gordon, who later devised the similarly themed *Strange World* (1995) with *Heroes* creator Tim Kring. *The X-Files*' artistic aspirations were established in the pilot, with Robert Mandel directing, and cinematographer Tom Del Ruth achieving a distinct cinematic look that would subsequently be emulated by John Bartley (who would distinguish himself further with *Lost*) and his successors. As with *The Prisoner* and *Twin Peaks*, the soundtrack played an equally important role as the visual techniques used, with Mark Snow lending a particular mood to the pilot (and subsequently creating the distinctive theme for the show). The decision to shoot the pilot in Canada would prove additionally significant, with the eventual series settling on the same location to enable a modest budget to be used to maximum effect. Back in 1993, however, few expectations existed when a hastily assembled crew gathered in Vancouver, working alongside several other units shooting pilots, each hoping to be commissioned for the upcoming Fall season.

The decision to shoot the pilot in Vancouver was partly dictated by the story and a need to "go where the good forests are" (Lowry 1995, 17). In using this location—and situating its action in mysterious woods—the pilot bore an obvious resemblance to *Twin Peaks*, a series which Carter admired. The vortex of leaves shown in the pre-title sequence elaborates on the allusion (calling to mind Glastonbury Grove), and the story opens with a young woman's body identified by a small town official in a manner that was very similar to the discovery of Laura Palmer. Her murder prompts an investigation by the FBI, with mysterious marks on her body enlisting the attention of Special Agent Fox Mulder, who has a particular interest, we are told, in cases "outside the bureau mainstream." The fact that Duchovny had a small but memorable part in *Twin Peaks* (as transvestite DEA agent Denis/Denise) underscores an additional link between both series, and a number of *Twin Peaks* alumni would appear in *The X-Files*, with the first season including Michael Horse ("Shapes"), Michael Anderson ("Humbug"), Don Davis ("Beyond the Sea" and "One Breath"), and Jan D'Arcy ("Tooms"), while Frances Bay, Kenneth Welsh, and Richard Bymer are seen later in the series. Certain thematic parallels can also be discerned. Alien encounters had been intimated in *Twin Peaks*' second season, with Major Garland Briggs monitoring deep space transmissions and formerly working (with Windom Earle) on Project Blue Book—a genuine investigation into UFO sightings conducted by the U.S. Air Force. One can only surmise where the writers planned to take this idea, but *The X-Files* would make alien lore central to its mythology. Nicknamed "Spooky" by his colleagues, Mulder's openness to extreme possibility and penchant for the paranormal is very reminiscent of Agent Cooper, and from the moment we see him using a compass and spray paint to chart missing time we recognize a kindred spirit. He asks Scully soon after meeting her, "When convention and science offer us no answers, might we not finally turn to the fantastic as a plausibility?" Like Cooper, Mulder's methods and beliefs are unorthodox, yet Scully's scientific training imposes some rigor on their inquiries into the paranormal, granting the fantastic greater veracity. Furthermore, while *Twin Peaks* confines itself to a particular locale in the Pacific Northwest, *The X-Files* pilot infers that equally strange phenomena are apparently occurring throughout America, deploying thriller conventions to elicit interest, and evidently hoping to attract *Peaks* freaks, as well as viewers who'd become disillusioned with its excesses.

The inexplicable deaths of local teenagers creates our first mystery, yet wry humor offsets the darker elements of the story, and intrigue is added in learning more about our leads. From her initial appearance at the FBI's headquarters, summoned to a meeting with a group of sinister men, Dana Scully is very reminiscent of Clarice Starling (Jodie Foster) in *Silence of the Lambs* (1990), yet reveals herself to be more than a promising cadet. Having trained as a doctor, she opted to teach at Quantico, we are informed, because she perceives the FBI as a means to distinguish herself. This explains why she has been selected for new duties—working alongside the infamous Fox Mulder to make a "proper scientific evaluation" of "the X files" (his one-man mission to pursue paranormal phenomena within the bureau). Despite distinguishing himself as a brilliant criminal profiler early in his career, Mulder describes himself in his opening line as "the FBI's most unwanted," and his basement office indicates his evident fall from grace. Far from expressing reticence in having Scully assigned as a partner, he welcomes her perspective, and their first case provides a taste of what to expect, with a series of mysterious deaths, what appears to be an alien corpse in a coffin (with an implant lodged in its skull), and teenagers consigned to the local psychiatric hospital after an alleged alien encounter in the woods. They all have the same mysterious marks on their bodies, and one routinely returns to this location at night, despite apparently being in a coma. He later states that he has been routinely summoned to "the testing place" by something in the woods and seemingly killed his friends there while "possessed" by an alien force. The truth remains obscure, however, as the agents are treated with suspicion by local officials, moved on from the murder scene, and find their corpse stolen from the forensics lab. A fire in their hotel wipes out all their remaining evidence—or nearly all. When Scully is finally debriefed by her superiors and rebuked for the lack of substantiation in her report, she produces the implant from the corpse, constructed from material, she coolly informs them, that she has been unable to identify. This affirms that her role will be more complex than they imagined. Mulder calls that evening to inform her that all their paperwork on the case has disappeared, and so begins an intriguing partnership, indicating conflict in their opposing beliefs, while establishing a degree of trust between them. The last shot provides a compelling cliffhanger featuring a mysterious man—previously seen smoking in the background of Scully's initial interview and after she has been debriefed by her bosses—placing the implant (among others) in a vast storage unit in the Pentagon. So begins a plot arc that would take viewers through nine years of suggestion and secrecy, corroborating the suspicions of existing conspiracy theorists, luring others into its mysteries, and working its way into the national consciousness.

The progression from pilot to popular cultural phenomenon was by no means certain, however, and the series did not get the go-ahead until the pilot was screen-tested with a number of Fox executives. Even then, faith in the project was muted, with higher hopes placed on the off-beat Western *The*

Adventures of Brisco County, Jr., which was broadcast just ahead of *The X-Files* on a Friday night (Lowry 1995, 19). The time slot was unlikely to yield much of an audience, but the show was allowed time to establish itself and became an example of "appointment viewing." Against expectation, the tongue-in-cheek Western found itself cancelled (creator Carlton Cuse would later find success writing and producing *Lost*), while *The X-Files* became the flagship series Fox had been looking for. Although the first season's ratings were relatively low, the show scored highly with the urban, educated, 18–34 sector, and by the second season it was Fox's biggest hit. The reasons were evident enough. It featured two charismatic leads and pioneered a format that rewarded regular viewing, via a developing mythology, while self-contained episodes encouraged casual viewers. It also had a central conceit that allowed a sense of wonder without feeling silly, and included political connotations that resonated with its audience. As the pilot's closing cliffhanger made clear, aliens and the U.S. government were explicitly linked, and the series would further explore this connection—often blurring the boundaries between fact and fiction. The pilot even went so far as to claim, in the opening credits, that events were based on "documented evidence"—a ploy used to add a dubious sense of authenticity (Lowry 1995, 13). Although such claims would be replaced in the series proper with the opening line, "The Truth Is Out There" (and occasional variations), and episodes would encompass a variety of strange phenomena, the sinister relationship between aliens and the U.S. government would make up the wider narrative arc of the series, cleverly drawing on a growing field of popular inquiry to make the drama seem grounded in fact. So-called "monster-of-the-week" episodes incorporated a number of subjects, including human mutations, serial killers, sinister communities, and various parasites and predators, yet each case remained unresolved to perpetuate intrigue and corroborate Mulder's "paranoia." The alien episodes affirm that the government has a vested interest in keeping the population ignorant, while our agents' ability to gather proof is consistently undermined, epitomizing Todorov's definition of the fantastic in its continual hesitance about the events shown.

Like other cult programs numerous references were made to other texts, with *The X-Files* by no means the first SF series to explore the possibility of extraterrestrial existence on Earth. The BBC's *Quatermass* serials (1953–9) had similarly suggested that aliens are intent on colonization and in cahoots with politicians (a link Carter appears to have acknowledged by asking *Quatermass* creator Nigel Kneale to write for the show—although this sadly never materialized). Alien infiltration was further explored in a variety of series, including *The Invaders* (1967–8), which featured one man's struggle to convince others of an alien plot (lead actor Roy Thinnes would later be cast as a fugitive alien in *The X-Files*), while *UFO* (1970–3) broached similarly disturbing possibilities surrounding alien/human hybrids. Another important thematic precursor is *Project UFO* (1978–9). As popular interest in real-life encounters increased in the U.S. after World War II, an official inquiry was set up to assess them, resulting in Project Blue Book (the government-authorized investigation into sightings that took place from 1952 to 1969, and which was previously name-checked in *Twin Peaks*). *Project UFO* was directly inspired by this inquiry, as its opening pointed out, with each episode investigating a particular "case." However, while the official verdict attributed most sightings to natural phenomena, *Project UFO* suggested that many were genuine. *The X-Files* distils a number of these ideas, incorporating ufology and military history to lend weight to its premise. The alien myth arc was elaborated upon each season and provided a hook to keep viewers watching: questioning whether our detectives would succeed in exposing a cover-up involving extraterrestrials and learn the truth about Mulder's missing sister. This quest dramatically anchored the show, providing character interest while cleverly feeding into popular interest in aliens—as well as a growing distrust of officialdom.

From the end of World War II, tales of alien encounters had proliferated, and an alleged incident at Roswell, New Mexico, intensified speculation that the U.S. government had engaged in a cover-up. In 1947 a saucer-shaped object is said to have shattered above a ranch in the New Mexican desert. A military base in the area allegedly recovered extraterrestrial beings and their craft—which was used, according to popular myth, in clandestine military operations, enabling the development of experimental aircraft. Despite state secrecy surrounding the event, it has fuelled decades of debate, and *The X-Files* both references the incident and substantiates it. Carter was particularly drawn to the fact that over 2 million Americans (3 percent of the population) claimed to be abductees—a conviction he wanted to explore (Lowry 1995, 11). The 1990s saw a widening of beliefs, often included under the "new age" banner, yet it was also a time of manifest ambivalence, with optimism about the future nestling cheek-by-jowl with a sense of pessimism about our prospects. The perception of aliens within the popular imagination reflected the same uncertainty—from messianic innocents (vividly symbolized by E.T. and his remarkable capacity to feel and heal) to sinister ideas about ruthless invaders. While some looked to the skies in the hope that we were not alone, others affirmed that extraterrestrials existed, but were anything but benign. Abductee accounts featured a recurring theme of citizens removed from their home, being experimented on, and returning to face yet another ordeal, with many such tales culminating in sinister government agents (popularly termed "Men in Black") visiting their homes, debriefing them, and attempting to silence them via a number of techniques. Such testimonies suggested the government had not only lied to the American public for decades (using "black ops" agents to enforce these lies), but that members of the public were routinely being experimented on. Carter researched these beliefs, connected them to post–Watergate paranoia, and helped corroborate them. If *Project UFO* tended to side with public accounts by challenging official claims, *The X-Files* went a step further in aligning itself with "extreme" conspiracy theorists and actively implicating the U.S. government, thereby acquiring "subversive" appeal.

A popular claim within alien-related conspiracy theory, promoted at the height of *The X-Files*' popularity, was that Steven Spielberg had been commissioned by the U.S. government to "prepare" the population for contact with aliens, with friendly examples featured in *Close Encounters of the Third Kind* (1977) and *E.T.: The Extra-Terrestrial* (1983). In contrast, *The X-Files* purports to reveal "the Truth." Abductee testimonies featuring painful biological experiments increased during the late 1980s and '90s, and thanks to writer Whitley Strieber, who wrote about his experiences, Harvard psychology professor John Mack, who took abductee accounts seriously, and the opportunity provided by the Internet to exchange information, more people began to tell their stories. *The X-Files* legitimizes these alleged encounters by offering an explanation of governmental collusion and denial, and linking the "incident" at Roswell with references to "radiation experiments on terminal patients, Watergate, Iran Contra, and the Tuskagee experiments"—all of which are cited by Mulder to indicate the heinous acts the state has proved capable of ("EBE"). This is the closest the series gets to a political statement, affirming that we cannot trust what we are told because we have continually been deceived. Carter and his team researched the abduction experience, attended UFO conventions, and weaved together various theories, adding credence to the possibility of a coverup. The series contended that the government not only knew of extraterrestrial life, but were actively colluding with aliens, leaving citizens the unfortunate victims of both seemingly dispassionate forces. While these efforts turned many viewers into believers, the show's accusations became increasingly outlandish. Cloning experiments, hybrid humans, and shape-shifting aliens took us further away from a carefully rendered plausibility. Mulder's attempts to find his lost sister were continually stalled, and evidence was routinely commandeered by figures we would only know through monikers such as the Cigarette Smoking Man/Cancer Man (William B. Davis), the Well Manicured Man (John Neville), and the cronies they oversaw. Terming this group the "Shadow Syndicate" summed up their amorphous nature, and Watergate is clearly referenced in their efforts to preserve state secrets (with Mulder's sister notably taken as they watch the Nixon hearings together on television; while naming an informer "Deep Throat" (Jerry Hardin) provides another reference to this event). However, the series suggests that illegal phone tapping is fairly innocuous compared to the atrocities the Syndicate are capable of, activities traced from Fascist alliances at the end of the Second World War to a deal struck with extraterrestrials at humanity's expense. *The X-Files*, even to its most ardent fans, made a number of mistakes in going on too long, resolving too little, and making speculations that were too extreme; but perhaps its biggest flaw was the alien mythology used to underpin its premise, which ended up undermining it instead.

Over the course of nine seasons we discover a complex history in which aliens mutate dramatically. There are innocent victims, iconic large-eyed "grays" who are captured by the military and experimented on, their technologies exploited, as well as aliens (of human appearance) that have gained the upper hand over humanity, forcing the Syndicate to agree to a breeding program to extend their race. Various "hybrids" further muddy the waters, with benign clones such as Jeremiah Smith (Roy Thinnes) denied the right to exist; a hostile alien entity which resides in Black Oil and takes over humans before killing them; and a breed of "supersoldiers" created from combined human and alien DNA. Aliens are variously presented as merciless abductors ("Fallen Angel"), the victims of genocide ("EBE," "Anaszasi"/"The Blessing Way"/ "Paperclip"), and shape-shifting bounty hunters used by the Syndicate as assassins ("End Game"). They are ultimately so contradictory as to confound any attempt to determine their meaning, much like the Truth our agents seek to establish. The Syndicate is equally ambivalent. Despite being set up as villains, informants rank among them, and even their most sinister actions are ultimately defended as a desire to protect the human race. Hence, although we are shown cloning experiments which deny their "subjects" any rights ("Herrenvolk") the series suggests that humanity's survival rests with such techniques. Mulder's family history becomes interlinked with this plot. He discovers his father was involved in his sister's disappearance, having overseen an alien/human breeding program while working for the Syndicate and sacrificing his daughter to serve its end. As with *Twin Peaks*, however, paternal guilt is evaded, with Bill Mulder's actions oddly legitimized by an ulterior motive to preserve the human race, indicating the contorted logic of the mythology.

Ironically, the series established itself through the very ambiguities that would ultimately infuriate its following, with fans and critics applauding the show's complex plotting and refusal to explain matters. Despite Fox's demand that greater closure be provided, Carter retorted that you "can't put aliens in handcuffs" and insisted on retaining a sense of mystery. In giving the fantastical a semblance of veracity, various possibilities were extrapolated. If the U.S. government was powerful enough to conceal the existence of extraterrestrials, so the logic went, the show could freely speculate on what else might be possible, including humans with strange powers, primeval creatures, and various other phenomena. Certain storylines may have strained our ability to suspend disbelief, particularly those which seemed to be directly inspired by the *National Inquirer* or *Fortean Times* (with Bigfoot and a U.S. equivalent of the Loch Ness monster investigated), yet an edge was provided in suggesting the world was not only a great deal stranger than we knew, but that the real monsters to be fearful of were the forces that aimed to keep us docile and dumb.

The series incorporated strands of folklore, urban myth, scientific extrapolation, and conspiracy theory, filtering a range of popular cultural interests with references to films and obscure historical facts. In naming an episode

"Paperclip," for example, the series referenced the codename for an actual operation in which German scientists worked at White Sands Proving Grounds after World War II—the base attached to the Roswell "incident" and where experimental aircraft were allegedly tested. Those unfamiliar with alien lore, or secret military history, could google "paperclip" and discover that underneath the fiction of the series lay an unnerving grounding in fact. The series would routinely play with such distinctions and become identified as quintessentially postmodern in doing so: reworking contemporary anxieties via metaphorical monsters while challenging the concept of a singular objective reality. Over the course of nine seasons we would witness a host of bizarre menaces endanger our agents, see them become separated when Duchovny left the series, accommodate new recruits in their place, and eventually find Mulder and Scully reunited, yet with no real resolution. If *Twin Peaks* surmised that "evil" is insurmountable, a shape-shifting chimera that can never be conquered, *The X-Files* would concur with this appraisal, leaving fans to wonder if the extended time taken to arrive at this conclusion had been worth the wait.

Season one introduces the main characters and indicates the variety of cases that might be labeled an "X file." This includes humans with amazing powers, such as telekinesis ("Shadows"), pyromania ("Fire"), or the ability to live an extraordinary lifespan by eating human livers ("Squeeze")—as well as man-made monsters such as an artificial intelligence ("Ghost in the Machine") or psychotic clones created by government experiments ("Eve"). The show's "myth arc" is also initiated when Mulder tells Scully about his sister's disappearance and his belief that she was abducted, eliciting her sympathy—without corroborating his account ("Pilot"). Ensuing episodes further test their contrasting beliefs. They encounter Max Fenig (Scott Bellis) who attests to being a regular victim of abduction yet is also, as Scully notes, a diagnosed schizophrenic ("Fallen Angel"). The episode questions Mulder's potential delusion—only to confirm his beliefs when Max is abducted before our eyes. After discovering Max has "disappeared" again, at the end of the episode Mulder exclaims, "How can I hope to dispel lies that are stamped with an official seal?" and this mix of anger, frustration and despair increasingly come to define him. By contrast, Scully's cynicism may be intended to win over doubters in the audience, yet her rational perspective fails to account for the phenomena encountered and becomes gradually undermined. A belief in aliens seemingly contradicts Scully's scientific training, but so does the cross she wears, suggesting a conflict in her beliefs. A number of episodes question what lies beyond death, one of which shows Scully experience a vision of her father the moment he dies ("Beyond the Sea"). The fact that he is played by Don Davis, who played Garland Briggs, adds to the *Twin Peaks* feeling of the scene, and her grief permits a rare view into her psyche as she questions whether her father was proud of her. Scully even considers allowing psychic serial killer Luther Lee Boggs (Brad Dourif) access to these doubts, yet refuses to open herself to extreme possibilities. Mulder's convictions provide comparative comfort, but we also see how his beliefs endanger their lives and blind him to "the Truth." A faked photograph of a UFO, given by his informer Deep Throat, is intended to send him on a false trail and provide a cover story for a downed Iraqi jet, seemingly using aliens as a smokescreen and leaving Mulder uncertain "which lie to believe" ("EBE"). The same episode introduces the Lone Gunmen—three figures who publish a newsletter on conspiracies and serve as important allies. After describing them as the "most paranoid men" she has ever met, Scully finds a bug in her pen, making her think again. The season ends with Mulder kidnapped and evidence of extraterrestrials secured, only to be immediately relinquished to ensure his return ("The Erlenmeyer Flask"). Deep Throat helps Scully steal a preserved alien fetus, but pays with his life during the exchange, removing a charismatic figure from the show. Confirming they had ruffled some feathers, the season ends with the news that the X files is to be shut down and the agents reassigned to other duties. The series secured an average of 8 million viewers in the Nielsens, ensuring a second season.

Season two sees Mulder continue his mission to prove the existence of aliens, and further indicates the dangers of this pursuit. Scully's skepticism is compromised by her own abduction ("Duane Barry")—a storyline (motivated by Anderson's unexpected pregnancy) which reveals the strength of Mulder's feelings towards her and further tests what lies beyond this realm. Scully's return, in a coma, and uncertain prospects for her survival, provide a standout episode in which her consciousness wavers in the dreamlike image of her sitting in a rowboat, loosely moored to a jetty, urged to remain by a "Nurse Owens" who, she later discovers, there is no record of at the hospital ("One Breath"). It is an episode from out of *The Twilight Zone*, suggesting she has been visited by an angel (as her hand closing over her cross implies). Elsewhere the season revealed various secrets underlying small-town America, including a Satanic cult among members of a PTA ("Die Hand Die Verletzt"), cannibalism at a fast food chicken processing plant ("Our Town"), and alien experiments carried out on children ("Red Museum"). It also provides a rightly adored deviation from the usual route when Mulder and Scully investigate the deaths of former circus freaks in the trailer park they now call home ("Humbug"). The first of several memorable contributions written by Darin Morgan, the episode even includes *Twin Peaks*' "Man from Another Place" (Michael Anderson) to add to its quirky delights, and amusingly plays with distorted perceptions, like Morgan's other work. Seeds were also sown for later exploration, with Mulder temporarily assigned with another agent, Alex Krycek (Nicholas Lea), to investigate the consequences of sleep deprivation experiments on Vietnam vets ("Blood"). Krycek is later revealed to be working for Cancer Man, and kills Scully's abductor to cover the Syndicate's part in her disappearance ("Ascension"). The mythology is deepened in a mid-season two-parter ("Colony"/"End Game") which reunites Mulder with his long-lost sister, only to reveal her to be a part-alien clone who is killed by an alien bounty hunter (Brian Thompson). The season ends with the first installment of a triple episode storyline that uncovers various suppressed secrets, including Mulder's personal links to the alien plot. An earthquake in New Mexico reveals a buried chamber and coincides with a hacker's retrieval of files from the Defense Department collating information on UFOs since the war. Reference is made to an international agreement (referencing the fabled "Majestic 12") in which several nations pledge to prevent the threat of alien invasion by summary execution at first contact. Mulder's father is on the point of telling his son about his past when he is executed by Krycek. The finale culminates with Mulder discovering the buried chamber is full of deformed corpses, and he is apparently killed when it is blown up ("Anasazi").

Season three charts Mulder's recovery after a group of Native Americans perform a healing ceremony. The strange corpses are linked to Operation Paperclip, carried out by Nazi scientists on U.S. soil after the war. Mulder discovers a photograph of his father, taken in the early 1970s, with one of these scientists—who is killed before he can provide further information. Scully's sister, Melissa, is mistakenly shot after a warning is issued to Scully by the Well Manicured Man. Somewhat illogically, given the efforts made to silence witnesses, he reveals the truth about Bill Mulder, telling Mulder his sister was taken to force his father's silence about alien/human hybrids, created with the help of known war criminals. The Lone Gunmen additionally inform us that the U.S. granted immunity to Nazi scientists to capitalize on their expertise in testing the limits of the human body, which is said to have helped America win the space race. Aliens are thus aligned with Holocaust victims, and the U.S. military with Fascists, and we further discover that Japanese scientists were also given refuge by the government ("731"), deepening the idea of sinister collusions. Krycek recovers the hacked UFO data for Cancer Man—only to escape execution—confirming the ruthlessness of the Syndicate; and their danger is further indicated when Scully meets other "abductees" and realizes they all have cancer ("Nisei"). Another menace is introduced as Krycek becomes infected by the Black Oil—a substance emanating from a meteorite that has been lurking at the bottom of the sea since the end of the war ("Piper Maru"/ "Apochrypha"). Despite the murders of Mulder's father and Scully's sister over a tape they eventually forfeit, the pair remain determined to uncover the Truth and opt to stay in the FBI ("The Blessing Way"/"Paper Clip"). The season's stand-alone episodes reprise established themes, including gifted individuals such as a boy who can control lightning ("DPO") and a man who knows how people will die ("Clyde Bruckman's Final Repose"); the dead returning to exact revenge ("The List"); a native curse brought to life ("Tesos Dos Bichos"); and strange contagions ("War of the Cocraphages," "Piper Maru"). The most memorable episodes come at the end of the season. A story about a Chinese racket, gambling on human body parts, was terrifying because it seemed all too possible ("Hell Money"); an episode focusing on their boss, Assistant Director Walter Skinner (Mitch Pileggi), provided interesting insights into the character ("Avatar"). But the standouts for many were two episodes that parodied the show's premise. "Jose Chung's *From Outer Space*" includes experimental pilots, dressed as grays, menacing Men in Black who admit to using aliens as a state smokescreen, and various conflicting testimonies of abductees and alien worshippers which are used to show that even one alleged encounter is open to a host of interpretations. Darin Morgan's script thus threatens to undermine the entire series by suggesting there is no definitive Truth. "Quagmire" (which Morgan also contributed to) achieves a similar end as Mulder and Scully go in search of a mythical lake monster, dubbed Big Blue, and end up stranded on a tiny rock, discussing whether Mulder's search for the Truth is the same as Ahab's quest for an elusive whale. When they realize they were never as stranded as they believed, and that the rock is only a few yards from the shore, the point is readily made: they are victims of their own distorted perceptions. While a rational explanation concludes the episode (and a giant alligator is blamed for local deaths), they leave the scene before the "Truth" is confirmed—a ravishing shot of the mythical monster swimming by in the distance. The season finale ("Talitha Cumi") provides a mythology cliffhanger, yet a series of dubious coincidences undermine any logic and make it a strong contender for the moment the series jumped the shark. Cancer Man meets with Mulder's mother, intimating a secret relationship, and the ensuing dismay puts her in a coma. Mulder manages to interpret a "clue" her damaged mental faculties provide him with, and finds an alien "stiletto" in his parents' summer house—a weapon, we are told, which is needed to kill aliens (the bounty hunter type, rather than the "innocents" that expire with a simple bullet). He inexplicably concludes that colonization is planned in a poorly plotted finale which makes no sense. The fact that Carter created *Millennium* in the same year may have contributed to these lapses. A shady conspiracy thriller with a more adult edge, it repeated much the same formula yet divided his attention—with problematic consequences.

The fourth season took a darker turn, seemingly in response to Carter's concern that *The X-Files* had become a "mainstream show" (Lowry 1996, xvi). It opens by extending the cloning plot—with a smallpox eradication program used to "catalogue" the U.S. population. Mulder finds a whole batch of his lost sister, the same age as when she was lost; yet none is able to speak, and the facility disappears ("Herrenvolk"). Elsewhere we were treated to a full-on horror show via the deformed results of an inbred family ("Home"), a terrifying serial killer who lobotomizes his female victims ("Unmhe"), and a look at the Black Oil's effects in Russia, where people cut their own arms off (as well as those of their children) to save them from being tested by the state ("Terma"). A rare moment of light relief comes with a biography of Cancer Man, which reveals him to be the assassin of both JFK and Martin Luther King; yet he also cuts a sad and lonely figure as a failed writer who has only stayed in his occupation due to a succession of rejection slips ("Musings of a Cigarette Smoking Man"). Otherwise, the season revealed a number of inconsistencies. A contribution to an established theme (Mulder reencountering a man he helped convict) finds Mulder admit the possibility that his sister was a pedophile's victim rather than an abductee ("Paper Hearts"). Like "Quagmire" and "Jose Chung's *From Outer Space*," the effect undermines our heroes' quest, as well as our faith in the story being told (offering an alternative fate for Samantha Mulder that plays on the idea of aliens as a "screen memory"). Adding to the morose tone of the season, Scully learns she has terminal cancer as a result of her "abduction," and Mulder discovers she had ova extracted by government operatives ("Memento Mori"). Some humor is offered when a shape-shifter (played by Darin Morgan) takes Mulder's form to romance Scully—and proves how self-centered Mulder is by comparison ("Small Potatoes"). The finale teases us with a fake alien and leaves Mulder apparently dead ("Gethsemane").

By its fifth season, attempts at melodrama were becoming increasingly repetitive. Mulder seemingly dies (again), yet this is shown to be a feint ("Redux"). He meets his sister (again) but can no longer trust it's her ("Redux II"). We also encounter Melissa's secret daughter ("Christmas Carol"); and Scully meets a little girl she believes is her own daughter, but who dies of cancer before she can prove this ("Emily"). Juxtaposing this increasingly fraught personal life are cases involving variations on Frankenstein, vampire, and zombie tales; and a two-parter ("Patient X"/"The Red and the Black") continues the saga of Krycek and the Black Oil. The season ends with a 12-year-old boy said to be living proof of a link between aliens and humans. As ever, nothing comes of their attempt to use him to expose the Truth ("The End"). Ratings were at their height, gaining an audience of 15 million, with lucrative syndication rights sold, and efforts were made to further exploit the franchise with a summer movie. Released between the fifth and sixth seasons, the feature film *The X-Files: Fight the Future* (Rob Bowman, 1998) reworked the same alien tropes and featured a much-hyped kiss between the pair—which may have provided a good return at the box office yet remained a mistake to many fans. Although the series brought cinematic qualities to television, transferring the concept to the big screen added scale and spectacle without getting any closer to resolving their quest. For many fans, *The X-Files* should have ended here, particularly as Duchovny announced he was not prepared to return to Vancouver to continue the series. Carter opted to move production to L.A., to accommodate his star, and lost much of the established crew, including R.W. Goodwin, special effects man Toby Lindala, and directors Kim Manners and Rob Bowman. He justified the decision by stating there were more stories to tell. The remains of the series suggest otherwise.

The sixth season tried to shake things up by introducing a new director in charge of the X files in the form of Deputy Director Kersh (James Pickens,

Jr.)—who is far more involved with the Syndicate than Walter Skinner. We also learn more about the alien colonizers and the deal the Syndicate made with them (agreeing to assist their plans in return for saving their families). Bill Mulder is posthumously redeemed as a man who may have endangered the human race but worked on a vaccine to save them ("Two Fathers," "One Son"). Other cases include body switches, sea monsters, the Bermuda Triangle, and a prisoner able to pass through solid objects ("Trevor")—an idea later reprised in *Heroes*. The season ends with a story that further mixes the counterculture and conspiracy theory with "cosmic galactic radiation" created in a Sandoz lab ("Biogenesis").

A sense of repetition was evident from the beginning of the seventh season, with an opening story about a fast food worker who eats human brains ("Hungry"), and a number of episodes similarly refer to past cases, with Mulder apparently dying (again) from something contracted in "Tunguska"—only to make another miraculous recovery. His mother commits suicide as an odd response to learning she has a fatal illness, convincing Mulder his sister is no longer alive ("Closure"). Mulder is taken ill (again) towards the end of the season, and stories about genies, werewolves, and poltergeists add the supernatural to the soap. The season ends with Mulder kidnapped by the alien bounty hunter and Scully discovering she is pregnant. Given that we have only seen a kiss between her and Mulder, and that her abduction apparently made her infertile, the conception is suspicious, but her pregnancy continues to full term, with her child becoming the new hook for the remainder of the series.

Season eight assigned a new partner to Scully in the form of John Doggett (Robert Patrick), played by an actor best known as the liquid metal man in *Terminator 2*—providing an in-joke when supersoldiers are unveiled as part of the government's genetics research ("Salvage"). Roles are reversed as Doggett plays the skeptic to Scully's believer, and another female agent, Monica Reyes (Annabeth Gish), assumes Scully's role as her pregnancy advances. Scully realizes she has the same obstetrician as another pregnant abductee ("Per Manum"), inferring her child is part of an experiment. Mulder is found dead (again) and even buried this time, only to be exhumed, alive, 3 months later. Audiences were beginning to tire of such twists, and although Doggett and Reyes created an interesting partnership, the sheer improbability of events was now too much. The finale provides another chance to see Mulder and Scully kiss, when her child is born—an event filled with nativity references, with the Lone Gunmen serving as the Magi and Mulder following a bright light to find the child ("Evidence"). His paternity is suggested by the fact that Scully opts to call her son William, telling Mulder this is after his father.

The ninth and final season centers on the new family in peril. Mulder goes on the run in New Mexico, seemingly to protect them (enabling Duchovny to further abscond from the series), and the baby is threatened in various ways. Scully meets another new mother, who had a baby supersoldier yet lost her child. William is abducted by an alien-worshipping cult, claiming him to be the future savior of an alien race, but he is eventually recovered ("Providence"). The baby is shown to have strange powers (moving a mobile above his crib with his mind), yet Scully seems untroubled by this and continues teaching at Quantico while Reyes and Doggett remain in charge of the X files. An anticipated spin-off, *The Lone Gunmen*, was cancelled, and the sidekicks return to the main series to assist with babysitting duties and are given a heroic exit ("Jump the Shark"). The very last installment concludes the series with an unbelievable turn of events. Mulder returns, after an entire season away, and is framed for murder, creating a dramatic excuse for a trial in which various witnesses are called. Found guilty and sentenced to death (despite no body for his alleged victim), he is sprung from jail by Skinner and Doggett and meets with Scully. We learn that she has given their son to a Christian couple to raise, believing he will be safer. Cancer Man is killed, somewhat pointlessly, and Mulder and Scully ponder if their efforts were for nothing (no doubt reflecting the thoughts of many fans). Mulder's final speech reveals that the subtext of the series had nothing to do with the government, or "Truth," but a desire to make life meaningful in the face of our mortality:

> I want to believe that the dead are not lost to us. That they speak to us as part of something greater than us—greater than any alien force. And if you and I are powerless now, I want to believe that, if we listen to what's speaking, it can give us the power to save ourselves ["The Truth"].

It is ultimately an oblique reference to God that we are left with. Having forfeited their son, due to an apparent inability to protect him, and seemingly subject to continued persecution, Mulder concludes the series with a suggestion that belief in a higher power is their last refuge.

Audiences who had watched from the outset had also wanted to believe ... that the years invested in the series would prove to be worthwhile, but its ending failed to repay this investment. Many suspected they would never get the answers sought, with ratings declining after its fifth season, and the reasons are evident enough. The series became increasingly depressing viewing as family members were killed off and little chance of personal happiness seemed possible for our protagonists. If *The Prisoner* and *Twin Peaks* end with somewhat dour conclusions, *The X-Files* continues the trend, affirming that Earth will be invaded by aliens in 2012 (a date that coincides with Mayan prophecy), and that nothing can be done to prevent this. For some, the series lost its way as the alien storyline took greater priority. Certainly, after the biggest tease was revealed in the seventh season, with hope for Mulder's sister finally gone, it was difficult to justify the series continuing. For many, it "jumped the shark" when Mulder and Scully became romantically involved—a move that went against Carter's original instincts. Ultimately, after nine years of waiting for answers, the show simply exhausted our interest, its final spiritual concerns providing a very muted pay-off.

In broaching existential questions surrounding "the Truth," and its refusal to accept official explanations, *The X-Files* attracted a young, educated, and fairly cynical audience. By mixing its alien material with odd killings, strange creatures, and other tall tales, its format emphasized diversity, enabling casual viewers to watch at random, while devotees had the additional draw of episodes which developed the alien/government plotline, as well as being able to trace the changing relationship between Mulder and Scully. The show created a new subgenre in the paranormal detective series, investigating threats posed by special powers, possessions, and clandestine experiments. One of the show's most celebrated monsters, Eugene Victor Toombs (Doug Hutchison), who can squeeze into the smallest of spaces to prey on unsuspecting humans, was intended to signify the worst in us all, with a former sheriff stating, "It's like all the horrible acts humans are capable of somehow gave birth to some kind of human monster" ("Squeeze"). Many of the show's monsters similarly epitomize an evolutionary will to survive (the same impetus instigating colonization in the myth arc), and the series suggests they are beyond either legal or moral restraint, creating a certain thrill. By situating monsters in the everyday, using the FBI to investigate them, and employing techniques like autopsies and forensic examinations, as well as typed dates and locations placed onscreen (resembling dossier entries we had privileged access to), a new spin was placed on the supernatural—taking strange creatures and odd occurrences beyond the world of make-believe, and making us key witnesses.

Equally important is the relationship between its lead characters, providing its own narrative strand to follow. The gender politics of the series, featuring an assertive young woman with a sharpness of intellect that often proved superior to her partner, would attract many female fans. Mulder may have been in charge of the cases, delegating tasks to Scully, but she proved capable of working on her own initiative (and Anderson showed she could carry the show when Duchovny largely disappeared for the last two seasons). Making a refreshing change from conventional female roles, Scully was as driven and focused as her partner, commanding equivalent respect. Referring to one another by their surnames implied a lack of consequence about gender, which was reinforced as they took turns saving one another from peril, yet they also had a mutual affection that was clearly designed to keep audiences guessing. In presenting them as occasionally sparring, sometimes joking, with contrasting personalities and strengths, *The X-Files* appeared to borrow from another unusual detective series of the period, playing on unresolved sexual tension in a similar way to the investigative duo in *Moonlighting* (ABC, 1985–9)—and, much like the relationship between Maddie (Cybil Shepherd) and David (Bruce Willis), their progression from a platonic relationship proved similarly unwise. The series may have had a breadth of appeal, yet for some the overarching question was not whether our protagonists would ever be able to prove that a government conspiracy existed, but whether they would ever become an item. A sensational cover of the Australian *Rolling Stone*, featuring the actors in bed together, played on the romantic interest in their characters, yet Carter announced on several occasions that this would never happen, despite the network's wish to extend a romance, explaining his decision by stating:

> As soon as you have them looking googly-eyed at each other, they're not going to want to go out and chase these aliens. The relationship is going to supplant or subvert what's going to make the show great, which is the pursuit of these cases [Lowry 1995, 16].

He reneged on this resolution after the fifth season, coinciding their first kiss with the first film in what appears to be a canny marketing move. Drawn closer by various separations, near-death experiences, and personal tragedies, Mulder and Scully eventually conceive a child together, and while the series falls short of creating a happy family, a number of fans viewed their romance as a wrong turn. Many of those initially drawn to Scully were disappointed by her character's development, and although Carter deserves to be commended for creating such an interesting female figure, the greater narrative interest taken in Mulder remains notable. While an interesting gender reversal occurred in the series, some conflict went on behind the scenes, with Duchovny petitioning Carter to dramatically develop his character, and actively contributing to the series mythology to this end, while Anderson campaigned simply to achieve equal pay. The result of this unequal input is that Mulder (and his backstory) remains our focus, even when he is present only through Scully's references. Despite proving herself as an impressive federal agent, there was an evident need to "feminize" Scully by showing her as a grieving daughter, a worried partner, and an increasingly frequent victim. Various psychos menace her, and her "abduction" by the Syndicate reinforces the idea of an avaricious patriarchy intent on exploiting her. Rendered barren as a result of their experiments, and seemingly condemned to die, the fact that she is miraculously "cured"—with Mulder fathering her child—seemed more than a little trite, and although fulfilling a suggested romance between the pair would satisfy the "shipper" contingent of the audience, for others the tension was gone.

As their personal and professional lives began to coalesce, the show's popularity waned. This was perhaps inevitable. After so many seasons without getting any nearer to pinning Cancer Man down, audiences were beginning to choke with frustration at the relative lack of development. The ability to suspend disbelief was also becoming harder as both Mulder and Scully lost practically every family member yet continued to work for an organization that was patently corrupt. Their devotion to duty seemed less credible, or commendable, as time went on, particularly as the FBI seemed largely motivated to suppress the information they gathered, making them complicit in the very cover-ups they were working to expose. As the alien myth arc advanced, the focus shifted from shady government agents to extraterrestrials that were impossible to confront, affirming one commentator's point that, far from the radicalism claimed in some quarters, "*The X-Files* promotes the very powerlessness it pretends to challenge" (Lyttle 1996). If the two *Washington Post* journalists, Woodward and Bernstein, were the inspiration for Mulder and Scully in their quest to uncover the Truth, our fictional investigators are never able to disclose what they know, and as evidence was regularly lost, and events became ever more extreme, it was clear the audience was being unduly toyed with. Samantha returned, only to be revealed as a clone, mysteries were spun out with no resolution in sight, and the series gravitated towards a fatalism that was ill-equipped to see us into the next millennium, with an implied futility regarding our heroes' mission. While they struggled to discern the Truth from the spin, they never had enough to build a case, and although they form alliances with certain fringe groups, Mulder and Scully believed they were better able to change things from within. However, they failed to be more than an annoyance to their masters—and might even be seen to collude with them by amassing evidence that could then be neatly disposed of, alerting them to the whereabouts of wanted individuals and helping to legitimize their smokescreen. Scully may not "debunk the X files," as originally intended, but as she and Mulder expose others targeted by the Syndicate, they become complicit in its machinations, their efforts at defiance proving ineffectual. After years of tireless commitment to their jobs, far from informing the world about how they have been misled, Mulder and Scully cannot even protect their families, and eventually resemble dupes because they continue to work for a questionable organization. Even with the help of sympathetic bosses and contacts in Congress, their work never amounts to more than a collection of tabloid tales, without the required evidence to support them, creating an overwhelming sense of defeatism.

While a fitting conclusion to such a long-running series would always be difficult, it seemed to fizzle out rather than finish, and results in a similar sense of despondency as its predecessors. *The Prisoner* repeatedly returns Number 6 to the Village, after every escape attempt, and simply widens his "cell" in the finale, implying that genuine freedom is illusory. *Twin Peaks* also left many dissatisfied by continuous deferment, and depressed by the suggestion that "evil" is insurmountable. Such series fly in the face of conventional entertainment in daring to end unhappily. In fact, as Adrian Page has commented of *Twin Peaks*, "The notion of truth itself is questioned and the conclusive revelations of other drama series may seem far too glib by comparison" (Page, 44). *The X-Files* also questions "the notion of truth itself." Yet while it introduced itself each week by affirming "The truth is out there," the series never brought us any closer to understanding what this entails. Indeed, it ran the risk of diminishing the veracity of real-life government scandals, such as Watergate, by conflating them with Roswell, alien autopsies, and the like, and might even be seen to use UFOs and other phenomena in the same way as the U.S. government is alleged to—as a way of diverting interest from events that are altogether more sinister. While the myth arc may foster a sense of cynicism, it might equally influence a willingness to believe practically anything, or potentially obscure more mundane workaday forms of corruption that don't have the same exoticism as alien cover-ups. Although it obviously touched a nerve as the millennium approached, the political implications of conspiracy theory were made prone to ridicule through the sheer extraordinariness of the alien plot. Carter may have garnered greater credibility for ufology in the 1990s, but this was arguably at the cost of discrediting serious political concerns, which is perhaps the show's greatest irony.

Far from providing closure to any case, each episode tends to culminate with a monster that has survived, clues that remain undetected, or evidence that has disappeared. Borrowing from horror and SF, yet also veering between serious drama and humor, the series continues the generic experimentation used by its cult precursors and references various sources, from Scully's obvious allusion to Clarice Starling in *Silence of the Lambs* to motifs taken from films such as *The Boys from Brazil* (1978), *The Thing* (1982) and *Coma* (1978), as well as thrillers such as *Marathon Man* (1976) and *All the President's Men* (1978). A number of recognizable actors appear, and cross-references and allusions appeal to a "knowing" audience in a similar manner to *Twin Peaks*. Moments of self-parody are also provided—sometimes in entire episodes, such as "Jose Chung's *From Outer Space*," which not only ridicules the alien lore that the show usually takes seriously, but additionally mocks the "alien autopsy" broadcast by Fox in 1995 (itself influenced by *The X-Files*). Its cynicism is another archetypal postmodern element, suggesting that everything is worthy of scrutiny—although whether this is progressive remains moot.

What is perhaps most interesting about the show is the relationship formed with the audience. The Internet provided a growing fan base with a place to discuss events, and Carter has acknowledged the part played by the alt.tv.x-files site in rallying early interest in the show, echoing the alt.tv.twin-peaks forum set up a few years earlier. The official Delphi website may have been launched in 1995 (the same year as the first *X-Files* convention), but the series benefited from online discussions in its first season, which helped to promote viewing. Although it was consequently galling to see these "unofficial sites" ruthlessly pursued by Fox's legal team, by encouraging the show's writers to contribute to the Delphi site, and thereby tempting fans to use this forum, the network elicited the kind of interaction *Peaks* fans had hoped for. Fans were additionally encouraged to visit the site by placing episode titles online rather than on television, and some were rewarded by being referenced in certain episodes (with the passenger manifest in "Little Green Men," two characters in "Die Hand Die Verletzt," and a figure in "Within" all named after prominent X-Philes). The writers also extended characters, such as Skinner, in response to fan interest, and used feedback to convince the network of desired changes, methods later shows like *Lost* would similarly apply, incorporating fan ideas within the texts and taking advantage of growing Internet use in extending its fictional universe.

When *The X-Files* finally ended, M.S. Mason invited a number of critics to ponder its impact on television. Timothy Burke asserts that its "mythology of conspiracy" was "unprecedented in television. We are surrounded by invisible powers. Nothing is as it seems. Democracy is always under threat"; while Doug Mann claims, "It was one of the few cases of television commenting indirectly, but intelligently, on the present social and cultural landscape, specifically the postmodern condition" (Mason 2002). Such contentions were a common means of intellectually defending the show, yet its dictate "to trust no one" leaves little to believe in, and the series ultimately subscribes to the same fatalism as the abductee accounts that partly inspired it. There may be liberal critiques formed about the "military industrial complex," and an attempt to side with various fringe groups, but *The X-Files* evades any solution to millennial anxieties with its catch-all nihilism. Carter would later admit, "I've never really been a conspiracy theorist. I mean, I love all the JFK conspiracy theories. I love the theories about 9/11. But only because they're so imaginative" (Ivan-Zadeh 2008). Anyone who saw the show as politically grounded might be accused of being equally imaginative. For Carter, the government was no more than an "all-purpose bad guy," invariably replaced by aliens to let them off the hook.

With the passage of time, and continued syndication and DVD releases providing the opportunity to reappraise the series, *The X-Files* has managed to rise above the disappointments of its last few seasons and is generally remembered as a trend-setting example of quality television, with references in recent shows encouraging new interest in the series that inspired them. Admittedly, the series was most interesting in its first few seasons, with surreal and beautiful meditations on life (and death) when Scully loses her father in "Beyond the Sea" and fights to wake from a coma in "One Breath"; quirky and amusing stories like "Humbug" and the oddly moving "Clyde Bruckman's Final Repose"; and numerous terrifying human mutations and infestations. If many felt cheated by the fact that an exposé never occurs, they might be accused of taking the show too seriously, with a number of clues (particularly in episodes written by Darin Morgan) affirming its status as a pastiche cobbled together from various parts simply to entertain, like the Fijian Mermaid in "Humbug."

In contrast to their subsequent ruthlessness towards new shows, Fox were remarkably indulgent with *The X-Files*, giving it time to prove itself, capitalizing on audience interest with an array of merchandise, and only cancelling it after ratings severely declined, with the series becoming the longest-running SF show in North American television (until *Stargate SG1* surpassed its record). Fox never forgot the show that put it on the map, and the success of subsequent telefantasy series, as well as continual fan activity, led them to finance another feature film, testing the waters for a potential revival. The transition from a regular series to occasional films was proven by *Star Trek* to be a dicey endeavor, and the film ran the risk of burying the good memories many fans still had of the series.

I Want to Believe features Mulder and Scully on a case involving a murder, a missing federal agent, and an alleged psychic—whose abilities Mulder is asked to confirm. It caters to established fans in referencing elements from the series and attempts to fill in some gaps about the intervening years. Although Anderson and Duchovny expressed reticence towards a romantic relationship, arguing this had proven problematic in the series, they are portrayed as live-in lovers (Hilton 2007). Scully has returned to her former career as a doctor, and Mulder, still officially at large after evading military imprisonment, spends his time at their home archiving strange stories from the papers. The FBI seek him out, stating they are prepared to drop charges against him in return for his help, and Mulder heeds Scully's advice that this will be good for him. However, his response, when asked by the alleged psychic what makes him an expert in assessing his authenticity, underlines the dismal feel of the film: "I once investigated a series of cases on unexplained phenomena for the FBI." The inference is that the driven young man we once cheered on for so many years is now burnt out. His former drive, motivated by the search for his sister, has dissipated after giving her up as a lost cause; and in no longer working for the FBI another vital aspect of his identity is lost, suggesting the X files was all that separated him from the likes of Max Fenig (who shared the same beliefs without his relative privileges). Neither does his relationship with Scully offer much comfort, which is perhaps the worst thing the writers could have done in taking audiences down this path. Pillow talk involves fretting about work and discussing their lost son (as if he is dead rather than adopted). An attempt to add depth, with a theme about faith, seems somewhat pretentious, and its weak story would make for a disappointing episode, much less a full feature.

If this was an opportunity to see Mulder and Scully again, older and wiser but still figures to root for, it fails to deliver, with Mulder overly-dependent on Scully and still somewhat immature, visibly sulking when she prioritizes her job—tending to a sickly young boy—over helping with his assignment. Scully's reticence about his continued involvement with the case appears uncharacteristically selfish, saying, "We are the people who come home at night, to a happy home. I don't want that darkness in our home." Her difficulty coming to terms with the prospect of her patient not surviving also seems inconsistent with working as a doctor, and the fact that she manages to perform radical stem-cell surgery after googling a few articles off the Internet indicates risible writing. If Scully was always in Mulder's shadow in the series, she has at least succeeded in making a new career for herself; but like in the old days, she returns to the role of trusty sidekick, saving the impetuous Mulder from danger, with help from Skinner in a surprise cameo that fails to compensate for a poor film. While the story raids features from various episodes (a serial killer on the loose, a psychic used to trace murder victims, and an illegal trade in body parts), it is absurdly plotted and estranges the pair when they should be working together. The film ends with the paranormal aspects of the case overlooked by the papers, which Mulder naively expresses annoyance about, and the reconciled couple looking forward to getting away from the "darkness"—after she has performed some miracle surgery.

Just why the film is so very bad is difficult to fathom. Despite being written by the first movie's writers, Frank Spotnitz and Chris Carter, *I Want to Believe* left most viewers bitterly disappointed. A rare commendation came from newspaper critic David Cox, who states that while the series aimed "to titillate the comfortable by conjuring up fanciful perils," the post–9/11 world needed no such diversions: "Nowadays we have no more need of fictional chimera. We face real threats aplenty" (Cox 2008). Having disparaged the series as escapist nonsense, the film's religious concerns are deemed better suited to troubled times, yet its appeal to a higher power (emulating the end of the series) might cause us to reconsider what the show was about, particularly as Carter has amended the usual origin story behind the series, stating, "The idea itself came out of my religious background" (Rhodes 2008). Did *The X-Files* undermine our faith in the government and attempt to elicit greater credulity in the paranormal simply to affirm a belief in God? Was Carter pushing his own religious agenda or simply making a buck? Matthew Gilbert describes *The X-Files* as "a failed mythology show" because of its inability to offer audiences the payoff promised, and accuses Carter of the basest of motives, asserting that he "extended the mythology beyond any possibility of cohesion in order to keep making money on it" (Gilbert 2004). The conclusion is hard to refute, and the fact that Carter opted to coincide the second film with a new book, *The Complete X-Files: Behind the Scenes, the Myths and the Movies* (2008), suggests a further aim to cash in on his best-loved work. Seemingly resigned to the fact that this is his only creation likely to be a hit, he seems intent on simply turning the handle on the franchise, irrespective of what comes out. The sequel's poor ratings may have caused plans for a third film, intended to coincide with the predicted Mayan D-Day of 2012, to be put on hold (a decision that may have also been influenced by the fact that Roland Emmerich's film on the same theme left audienced nonplussed), leaving the future of the franchise uncertain.

Although there remains a risk of detrimentally affecting the show's reputation with examples such as the second feature, its legacy is assured, particularly in the host of shows it has inspired. The extraordinary success *The X-Files* achieved in its heyday led to a host of imitators. Investigations into paranormal phenomena include *Burning Zone* (1996–7), *Strange World* (1999), *Mysterious Ways* (2000), *PSI Factor: Chronicles of the Paranormal* (1996–2000), *Special Unit 2* (2001), and *Freaky Links* (2000–2001). Shows that focused more specifically on alien encounters can also be traced to its influence, such as *Dark*

Skies (1996–7), *The Visitor* (1997–8), *Taken* (2002), *4400* (2004–7) and *Invasion* (2005), as well as more recent series such as *The Event* (2010–11) and *V* (2009–11), although none have equaled the success of the parent series. Programs like *Jericho* (2006–8) take conspiracy theory to a new level, implicating government operatives duping U.S. citizens with a nuclear attack on home soil, and equivalent paranoia about the excesses of Homeland Security have appeared in a range of series, suggesting that 9/11 has merely intensified distrust against the state. Another aspect of *The X-Files'* appeal—the relationship between Mulder and Scully—would be interestingly paralleled in series such as crime drama *Bones* (2005–), with a sensitive male FBI Agent, Seeley Booth (David Boreanaz), working alongside female forensics expert Dr. Temperance "Bones" Brennan (Emily Deschanel) to solve murders in L.A. The SyFy channel's biggest hit to date, *Warehouse 13* (2010–), also reworks the "intuitive" male/ "intelligent" female dynamic via two agents exploring a host of paranormal phenomena, all played in a much lighter tone than Carter's series. Just as ABC has toyed with variations of *Twin Peaks* over the years, the Fox Network has aimed to find a comparable hit to the show that secured its status, regularly offering space on its schedules for SF programs (albeit with greater interference, heightened expectation, and much less patience than they gave *The X-Files*). The closest they have come to finding a replacement is paranormal detective series *Fringe* (2008–). Devised by J.J. Abrams, Roberto Orci, and Alex Kurtzman, the series follows a female FBI agent and two male boffins who investigate paranormal phenomena and uncover a vast conspiracy. Abrams has been wary of direct comparisons, arguing, "It wasn't, like, 'OK, let's do *The X-Files* again.' It was, 'What kind of show is something we would tune in to see?'" (Brownfield 2008). Nonetheless, as he and fellow executives brainstormed their favorite shows for inspiration, *The X-Files* and its precursor, *Kolchak the Night Stalker*, featured prominently, and it is *The X-Files* that *Fringe* is most reminiscent of, indicating its continued influence.

The range of series that have referenced *The X-Files* proves how extensive its legacy is, but whether its themes have the same resonance today is another matter. As the last century drew to a close, it is tempting to consign *The X-Files* to a time when crop circles and UFO sightings were taken more seriously, interpreted as signs from above rather than pranks or tricks of the light. Having found our way through the millennium, the series' original context is necessarily altered. We have no less reason to think the government may be lying. On the contrary, this idea has made the transition from sounding fantastical or alarmist to being fairly commonplace, particularly in the aftermath of 9/11 and alleged Weapons of Mass Destruction. Yet while audiences might have a greater readiness to believe in cover-ups, they also seemingly prefer greater optimism in their fiction, which is partly why a series like *Heroes* was initially such a hit. It may have similar elements to *The X-Files* (with a covert organization, experimental research, and people with superhuman powers), but it allowed its "heroes" to triumph at the end of each season. By contrast, Mulder and Scully failed to bring down the Syndicate (or thwart the planned colonization looming in front of us), leaving audiences with little to invest in. Carter's aims appear somewhat confused—wanting to scare audiences but also to amuse, and to imbue a sense of cynicism while also provoking a degree of faith. With hindsight, religious concerns always hovered beneath the surface, questioning if there is a life beyond this realm and if we have someone to watch over us. Spiritual concerns would become more overt in series such as *Touched by an Angel* (1994–2003) and *Joan of Arcadia* (2003–5), and the question of a higher power is revisited in a number of later telefantasy shows, including *Lost*. Angels and demons—and the idea of sin and redemption—add a metaphysical dimension to numerous series that followed, with supernatural forces often guiding or empowering humans, providing a sense of comfort that was manifestly absent from Carter's series. Furthermore, while Mulder and Scully were always thwarted in some way, we would see protagonists enjoy greater freedom— including characters who don't file reports, claim expenses, or have bosses to answer to. *Supernatural* (2005–) ups the ante on modern-day monster-hunting, with two brothers who use credit card scams to finance their travels around the USA. Sam and Dean Winchester (Jared Padelecki and Jensen Ackles) explore similar myths to *The X-Files*, with an emphasis on the demonic. Their fraternal relationship provides a sense of intimacy and friction that is very reminiscent of Mulder and Scully, counterpointing the sensitive and intuitive Sam against his cynical wise-cracking sibling. Series creator Eric Kripke has acknowledged his source material as Neil Gaiman comics and Joseph Campbell's studies of heroic quests, yet it is difficult to imagine the series without Carter's show. Many of *The X-Files* crew have worked on the series, including Kim Manners and David Nutter. In typical postmodern fashion, *Supernatural* explicitly references *The X-Files* (the brothers introduce themselves as "Agents Mulder and Scully" in the pilot), as well as making various allusions to popular film and television. It similarly employs humor to make light of itself, and uses the Internet to entice viewers into its fictional universe. However, to cite *The X-Files* as *Supernatural*'s main inspiration is not the whole story—even if it might also be classified as a paranormal detective series with a wider plot arc (the Winchester family history, and a battle between heaven and hell, being unveiled over successive seasons). An equivalent influence is another series which features demon-hunting as a catalyst for maturity, offers another variation on Campbell's heroic quest, and came out of nowhere to cause a sensation.

As we shall see in the next chapter, *Buffy the Vampire Slayer* was no less surprising in its popularity than *The X-Files*, and would prove to be equally innovative in the differing genres, references, and moods combined within its premise. It would also be notable in having a female lead—a character who, far from being an imperiled victim or loyal sidekick, is nothing less than a superhero (albeit one who is also appropriately "feminized" over the course of the show). The series would similarly feature paranormal phenomena and provide an array of fantastical beings, such as werewolves, vampires, and witches, yet placed in a context that would combine believable drama with a sense of wit and wonder, granting us even stranger encounters with supernatural forces. To Sunnydale, California, then—home of the Hellmouth.

4

Buffy the Vampire Slayer: Beauty and the "Big Bad"

> Buffy *came about from the very simple idea of a beautiful blonde girl who walks into an alley, a monster attacks her, and she's not only ready for him, she trounces him.*
>
> —Joss Whedon

Buffy the Vampire Slayer may have started out as a simple idea, but it became a cult hit through subverting expectation, using an adolescent girl with magical powers to rewrite established rules. Launched on new network the WB in 1997, the series looked, on the surface, to be of little likely interest beyond teenage girls, but its audience would soon learn that there was more to *Buffy* than meets the eye. Although it attained only moderate ratings, averaging 4.8m over its seven-year run, the series came to epitomize a high point in innovation, earning admiration from industry insiders, intense devotion from fans, and notable attention from academics. Although a number of telefantasy series have attracted scholarly interest, this phenomenon reached new heights with *Buffy*, as is indicated by the number of publications generated in response to the series—proving that its fan base extended way beyond the expected teen audience. This chapter considers the factors behind *Buffy*'s appeal, evaluates its innovations, and examines the phenomenal influence it has had (including the proliferation of supernatural teen dramas that have followed; shows focusing on paranormally "gifted" females; and the range of telefantasy series that have referenced *Buffy* in some way, including the revised *Doctor Who* and *Heroes*). The show's combination of well-crafted dialogue, carefully constructed characters, metaphorical richness, and a sufficient degree of change to keep viewers interested, would elicit the kind of devotion that remains the hallmark of any cult, and its ongoing influence indicates the extent to which Whedon's seemingly simple idea has, like its unlikely hero, evidenced an exceptional ability to survive.

From its very title, *Buffy the Vampire Slayer* set out to confound assumptions. It is a show which initially seemed to be a joke, yet has since been taken very seriously; which appeared to set expectations low, yet has achieved high praise—from fans and critics alike; and which may have been principally targeted at adolescent females, yet found a much wider audience. The premise concerns an adolescent young woman given the responsibility of protecting her community (and often the world itself) by slaying the various demonic forces that enter the fictional suburb of Sunnydale, California, and equipped with superhuman strength and healing abilities to help her fulfill these duties. While the show's title immediately invites amusement, viewers would soon learn not to be fooled by appearances. In fact, this might be the ultimate "mission statement" of the series, not only in terms of its incongruously named hero, but the depth of meaning derived from her experiences. Although it originated as a television spin-off of a somewhat lackluster film, the series managed to trump its source material by adding a degree of seriousness to its scenario and in its continual ability to surprise. *Buffy* may remain a teen drama series by dint of its protagonist's age, but other features made it compulsive viewing, both for its target demographic and others who became drawn to the series, combining a degree of irreverence with heartfelt drama and juxtaposing a world of fantasy with the all-too-familiar. Like the other series discussed, *Buffy* dared to tread new ground and would equally benefit from the talents of a cast and crew that took great pains to render its premise with conviction and creativity. It also took full advantage of the contemporary media-literate audience by referencing a number of motifs from popular culture and using humor to offset taking too serious a tone. Diversity was a key element of its success, providing audiences with different sources of interest: the visual appeal of lavishly designed set-pieces and the excitement of skillfully choreographed action sequences; the fascination of demonic rituals steeped in arcane lore; monstrous figures that were suitably multi-faceted; characters we cared about; the melodrama of relationships in turmoil; and a steady stream of comic lines used to inject some levity while tracking its protagonist between high school, home and the graveyard—charting a key transitional period of her life from adolescence to adulthood.

In the original film, *Buffy the Vampire Slayer* (Fran Rubel Kuzui, 1992), the incongruity of a Valley girl vampire killer sets the main tone of the narrative, which details how a seemingly vacuous blonde discovers, rejects, and finally comes to terms with her identity as a "Slayer"—the latest in a succession of females given the task of saving humanity from evil. A world that seems to revolve around cheerleading practice and shopping is interrupted one day when Buffy Summers (Kristy Swanson) is visited by a mysterious man who claims to be her "Watcher" and explains that she has a supernatural gift to locate and destroy vampires. Reluctant to believe such a fantastical idea, it is only when vampires take over her high school prom that she realizes her abilities and comes to accept her calling. With stars such as Donald Sutherland and Rutger

Hauer involved, viewers might have been forgiven for expecting more from the film, yet it was squarely pitched as a summer movie—to be watched, enjoyed, and forgotten—and audiences and critics had no problem with the last of these. Poor features rarely serve as the catalyst for a landmark television show, yet the eventual series had a number of differences. In particular, it would develop the character much further over seven seasons, providing a rite-of-passage tale relating the difficulties of growing up, while also extending its appeal beyond the adolescent audience. In fact, the show is no more reducible to being considered a teen drama, or even a teen comedy-horror, as *The Prisoner* is a spy series, *Twin Peaks* a murder mystery, or *The X-Files* a detective series. *Buffy* similarly evades easy assessment in the range of themes and moods assembled within its format, belying its schlocky title in various unexpected ways. In addition, much like these other shows, it might never have existed without a level of good fortune and timing, as well as having the right people involved.

The film would have been the end of *Buffy* had it not been for Gail Berman, an executive at Sandollar Television who saw Whedon's original script in the early 1990s and considered its potential as a series. She remained convinced, even after the movie's uninspiring reception, that there was a market for the concept and promoted the idea of adapting it for television. Sandollar was contractually obliged to contact Whedon beforehand, and, against expectation, he not only gave his approval but committed himself to the project, becoming the eventual show runner for the series—a decision which would be integral to its success. Equally important was a willingness to respect his vision. During the making of the film, Whedon had been treated as a writer for hire, with the director, Fran Rubel Kuzui, asking him to reshape his original script by reducing the horror and increasing the humor. Kuzui served as an executive producer on the series but took a backseat in the creative proceedings—a decision she describes as "having the grace to say to Joss, 'This is yours now.' The grace to say to Joss, 'I know you had an original vision. Let's go back to that, and let's make this TV show along the lines of what you want to do'" (Golden and Holder 1998, 248). It is a measure of Whedon's own graciousness that he was willing to overlook the way his idea had been handled and start again. This was of no small consequence, given that the inspiration for *Buffy* was extremely personal. As he has put it, "I was raised by an extremely strong woman—uncompromising, fun and funny—and I wanted to make a somewhat low-key, fun, and feminist horror movie" ("Television with a Bite" 2002). Despite frustration with the treatment his script underwent for the film, Whedon jumped at the chance to helm a series inspired by the concept and would stamp his mark on the show not only in terms of dialogue and humor, but in basing much of it on his own unhappy school days.

The main obstacle was in finding an interested broadcaster. As Berman has stated, "There were no young women in television at the time. Certainly, not young empowered women, and that was basically the pitch for the television show, to take this young woman and turn her into a kind of a superhero" ("Television with a Bite" 2002). Despite being a time when "girl power" became a new buzz word, it was a pitch the major networks rejected, deterred by the idea of a female lead. It was a relatively new organization, keen to establish itself among the existing order, that would make the required leap and express interest. The WB was Warner Brothers' fledgling network, launched in January 1995 within a few days of rival network UPN (United Paramount Network). Both "netlets" emerged in response to Fox's success and recent media deregulation, but they struggled to secure regular viewers and would find their destinies interestingly shaped by *Buffy*, with the WB the first to take a chance on the show. Two years old, yet without an established audience, the WB wondered if *Buffy* would attract a potential niche market of young female viewers. A short "presentation" version of a pilot was initially ordered, and *Buffy* was commissioned four months later as a mid-season replacement for the soap opera *Savannah* (1996–7). The same situation had occurred with *Twin Peaks*, and a brief opening season would similarly have its benefits in concentrating creative efforts without exhausting them. As Anne Billsun notes, the 12 episodes that constituted *Buffy*'s first season provided enough "time to establish the characters, format, and ground rules ... without needing to pad the concept out to a quality-sapping twenty-two episodes" (Billsun 2005, 31).

The series was set to debut in the Spring of 1997, and Sandollar combined with Whedon's newly formed production company, Mutant Enemy, and Twentieth Century–Fox Television to produce it (with Mutant Enemy situated in the offices formerly used for Carter's Ten Thirteen Productions on the Fox lot). The production team Whedon assembled would prove integral to *Buffy*'s consistently high quality, with a small group of directors used throughout the series, including David Solomon, David Grossman, James A. Contner, and occasionally Whedon himself, as well as regular writers such as Marti Noxon, Jane Espenson, Davids Greenwalt and Fury, and Douglas Petrie—a team who took note of fan feedback in developing characters, seemed to care about these characters as much as viewers, and helped to make the series a unique experience. For the most part they were given a great deal of freedom, yet the WB insisted on some initial changes, including recasting Willow (a sidekick to the main protagonist) and adding a male love interest—a stipulation that would create Angel (David Boreanaz), a brooding vampire who subverts intentions, in typical Whedonesque fashion, when a romance with Buffy is shown to be unrealizable. As Whedon reasoned, in response to fan disappointment over this matter, "What people want is not what they need," asserting that the fulfillment of this romance would have been less dramatically satisfying (Pearson, 25). Citing Whedon's decision to withhold audience pleasure in this way, Roberta Pearson asserts that an unprecedented degree of freedom exists among today's "hyphenates," who, she argues, "can now dare to be different because of the transformations of the television industry that have fundamentally altered their relationships with the networks and with the audience" (Pearson, 25). This contention is partly corroborated by the fact that *Buffy* was relatively indulged by the WB (allowing Whedon to disappoint the "shipper" contingent of the audience), yet a dispute over funding also saw *Buffy* move to UPN after its fifth season. In the very public feud that resulted, the WB appeared to negate the worth of the show, infuriating its creator. Whedon has acknowledged the debt owed to the WB, noting, "There's no other place where *Buffy* could have happened," yet he considered this debt paid by the show's reception. Indeed, while the WB's CEO, Jamie Kellner, made much of the fact that they gave *Buffy* a home when no one else was prepared to, stating, "No one else wanted the show ... but we stuck with it" (Rice 2001), he failed to acknowledge what the network received in return.

Buffy debuted with the highest Monday night rating in the WB's history, and the show became the network's first standout success. Ratings for the first season averaged 3.7m — a very respectable sum for a new network struggling to make a dent in the industry. It also attracted an audience advertisers were interested in, helping to boost network revenue as the price for commercial "spots" increased. Critical interest helped promote the show, ratings climbed, and the WB's confidence was such that they moved its airdate from Mondays to Tuesdays for season two — an event timed to coincide with Buffy and Angel finally consummating their relationship. The narrative result would prove to be dramatically riveting, with Angel turning "bad," being killed by Buffy at the end of the second season, returning from a hell dimension (in suitably reformed state) at the start of season three, and leaving the series altogether by the end of the season for his own spin-off series, *Angel* (1999–2004), in which he heads a paranormal detective agency in L.A. Inventively making use of the emerging franchise, with both series running in tandem, characters from the original show made guest appearances on *Angel*, and vice versa. This tactic had successfully been deployed with *The Six Million Dollar Man* (1974–8) and its spin-off, *The Bionic Woman* (1976–8), and was seen a few years prior to *Buffy* with *Millennium* and *The X-Files*; but a greater level of sophistication occurred with the *Buffy*/*Angel* crossovers, adding complexity to the material. This largely ended after UPN took over *Buffy* in 2001, while the WB retained *Angel*, yet an ambition to push the boundaries of the medium was clear, and similar experimentation would be illustrated in terms of content.

Like any other writer, Whedon was influenced by past shows — in terms of what he wanted both to achieve and avoid — professing an admiration for *The Prisoner* and *Twin Peaks*, while deriding *The X-Files* for its lack of development. As he has stated:

> One of the reasons why *The X-Files* started to leave me cold was that, after five years, I just started yelling at Scully, "You're an idiot. It's a monster," and I couldn't take it anymore. I need people to grow, I need them to change, I need them to learn and explore, you know, and die, and do all of the things

that people do in real life. And so [on *Buffy the Vampire Slayer*] we're very, very strict about making sure that things track, that they're presented in the right way. Because, ultimately—and this is one of the things that I did find out after we had aired—the soap opera, the characters, the interaction between them is really what people respond to more than anything else. And although we came out of it as a sort of monster-of-the-week format, it was clear that the interaction was the thing that people were latching onto [Whedon, NPR Fresh Air, 2002].

Whedon's frustrations with *The X-Files* echoed those of many fans, with characters placed in various extreme situations without significantly changing as a result. Transition was considered vital for Whedon's series, providing a sense of dynamism and enabling emotional authenticity. As to *Buffy*'s "monster-of-the-week" format, the series would emulate *The X-Files* in combining standalone episodes with a wider plot arc, yet it avoided a similarly drawn-out tease by creating seasonal threats to overcome. Buffy's adversaries are colloquially termed "the Big Bad"—an abbreviation of the "Big Bad Wolf"—the kind of breezy colloquialism that was typical of the series, mocking the sense of jeopardy faced by its protagonist. Seasonal variations provided a new thematic focus, yet the ensemble cast was equally important in maintaining interest. Indeed, while it may be named after its lead, the show's heart, its "soap opera" quality, lies in Buffy's interactions with those around her.

The series announces its subversion of expectation in the opening moments of the pilot ("Welcome to the Hellmouth"). A pre-credit scene shows a young couple breaking into a high school at night, apparently intent on making out. The boy informs his date that he once attended the school and boasts about the view from the roof. The girl, a blonde in school uniform, behaves with the kind of fey innocence that marks her out as an impending victim, yet after asking if what they are doing is a good idea, and if they are really alone, she suddenly reveals her vampire status and attacks the boy. Cue music, opening titles, and the kind of table-turning that is but a small indication of things to come. If this is an unlikely shape for a "monster" to take, our hero assumes equally improbable form as another petite blonde who has recently arrived in Sunnydale. Day breaks with Buffy Summers (Sarah Michelle Gellar) waking in a bedroom surrounded by boxes to start her first day at a new school. Buffy has relocated with her mother to make a new start in Sunnydale, yet soon realizes her past will not be easy to shake off. In a departure from the film (emulating Whedon's original script), we learn, during her welcome talk with the school principal, that she burned down the gym at her previous school. Having torn her school record up in a gesture of purported fairness, Principal Flutie (Ken Lerner) promptly staples it back together when he realizes the severity of this misdemeanor, thereby summing up the hypocrisy of the adult world. She may have acted to save fellow students, but the principal is not interested in the circumstances, and what she was saving them *from* is clearly beyond his understanding—as it will be to most of the adults around her. Neither is she able to evade her responsibilities as "the Slayer," as another Watcher is encountered in the school library, Rupert Giles (Anthony Head), who again invokes her mythical duties. This elicits some dismay on Buffy's part, declaring she has "resigned" and disclosing her reasons, stating that the realities of her destiny as a Slayer can only constitute a troubled and lonely life. By lunchtime a dead body is found at school (the break-in boy from the pre-title sequence) with puncture wounds on his neck, and Buffy returns to the library to learn about the Hellmouth that lies directly beneath them. Giles tries to instill the new facts of life: "Werewolves, zombies, succubae, incubi: everything you ever dreaded was under your bed and told yourself couldn't be real by the light of day, they're all *real*." Unfazed, Buffy undercuts him with a sarcastic quip, a strategy that will become a mainstay of their relationship, yet it doesn't mean she isn't taking him seriously. She knows these entities are real, she just doesn't know the scale of the impending disaster when the divide between both worlds is breached. To make this clear to viewers, we are treated to a vertical descent shot into the domain underlying this small town: an elaborate fantasy world with all the gothic trappings of a candlelit hell dimension where the Nosferatu-like "Master" wakes from his slumbers, and minions promise to get him something "young" to eat. Like the opening shot in *Blue Velvet*—where the camera zooms in beyond the well-manicured lawn to reveal insects feeding on each other—this is our first glimpse of a world that will increasingly encroach upon our protagonist's life, threatening to destroy her world unless she elects to do her duty.

Buffy's reticence in accepting her Slayer responsibilities emanate from the same conflict she has in deciding who to hang out with at her new school—evincing a desire for normalcy that is also a denial of who she is. In-crowd status is offered by Cordelia Chase (Charisma Carpenter), a cutting rich bitch (albeit with attendant insecurities, including a bed-ridden mother condemned for not having an acceptably cool "condition"). Buffy easily passes Cordelia's taste test, yet has too much empathy for those she scorns to take her advice about fitting in. In fact, she takes the proffered advice—"know your losers"—literally, and soon attracts derision for her "downward mobility" when she is seen with the school geeks at lunchtime. Although Buffy approaches shy bookworm, Willow Rosenberg (Alyson Hannigan), to get help with her studies, their quick friendship underpins why Buffy endears herself to us—because she has a heart, is similarly misunderstood, and values those overlooked by the school hierarchy. She even creates a gang for them. That evening, at local nightclub The Bronze, Buffy begins to take her responsibilities more seriously after Willow unwittingly leaves with a vampire, enlisting fellow misfit, Xander Harris (Nicholas Brendon), to help find her. By the end of the concluding two-part episode ("The Harvest"), Buffy not only manages to prevent the Master and his cronies from feeding on her classmates at The Bronze, but utilizes the help of Willow, Giles, and Xander to do so. These will become the "core four," the main members of the self-titled "Scooby Gang" who work together to fight the various demonic entities that will regularly come their way. Although she is supposed to work alone, Buffy's duties are considerably lessened by the camaraderie the other "Scoobies" provide, and their oddball status—and commitment to one another—help to explain the show's appeal. As Whedon affirms, "The core of this series, emotionally, is a very safe place. These are people who care about one another, and when their world is upset, *you* care about it" (Golden and Holder, 241). *Buffy*'s misfits were unlike those seen in previous teen dramas, and with a combination of wit and empathy the show effectively made us part of the gang. The remainder of season one reveals more about the main characters and their world, indicating Buffy's struggle with her duty, some friction with her mother, and her growing attraction to Angel. Adolescent metaphors are elaborated in stories that include a girl who becomes invisible because no one notices her, a competitive mother who tries to live through her daughter by inhabiting her body, and a playground pecking order that goes into overdrive when some youths become demonically infected after a field trip to the zoo. In each case Buffy manages to put things right, yet the Big Bad of the season is the Master, who wants to open the Hellmouth and thus end humanity. Prophecies predict Buffy's death, and she is drowned in the finale; but Xander revives her with CPR—reminding audiences how much she needs her friends, and reiterating that nothing is certain in this world.

Season two introduces a number of new characters, including vampire couple Spike (James Marsters) and Drusilla (Juliet Landau). Another Slayer, Kendra (Bianca Lawson), also arrives, intended to replace Buffy after her brief "death" (despite her protest that she was "only gone for a minute"). Xander and Cordelia become an item, Willow finds herself a boyfriend, Oz (Seth Green), and Giles begins a relationship with IT teacher (and gypsy techno-pagan) Jenny Calendar (Robia La Morte). Buffy and Angel celebrate her 17th birthday by getting intimate; but after experiencing a moment of true happiness, a gypsy curse causes him to resume his former evil state. The resulting alter ego, "Angelus," torments Buffy, kills Jenny, and joins former cronies Spike and Dru to end the world. Willow finds Jenny's computer disc and casts a spell to restore Angel's soul—at the very moment Buffy gathers the strength to plunge a sword into him. The Big Bad of the season, very evidently, is Angelus, the version of Buffy's boyfriend she has heard about but tried to deny, who shows himself capable of vast cruelty. He also proves Buffy's courage, selflessness, and heroism when she dispatches him.

Season three returns Angel, after centuries of torment, from a hell dimension, and shows Buffy's willingness to forgive him as he is slowly rehabilitated. A new Slayer also arrives, with Faith (Eliza Dushku) replacing Kendra (who was killed by Drusilla in season two). Buffy's 18th birthday is marked by another trial, as the Watchers' Council drug her and pit her against a mad vampire to see how she fares. They also fire Giles, claiming he is too close to her, and replace him with stuffed shirt, Wesley Wyndham Price (Alexis Denisof). Vengeance demon Anyanka (Emma Caulfield) is transformed into a mortal and becomes a regular character, adding some humor, and Faith turns bad after crossing the line, killing a human and refusing to show remorse. She elects to work for the Big Bad of the season, the town Mayor and fledgling demon Richard Wilkins III (Harry Groener). Faith wounds Angel with a poisoned crossbow and is put in a coma by Buffy, who saves Angel with her own blood. The season finale is graduation day, commemorated by the Mayor's transformation into a giant snake demon, and the school unites, under Buffy's tutelage, to defeat him. Angel informs Buffy he is leaving town and heads to L.A.

Season four signals a difficult transition period from school to college. The series survives Angel's loss, but a new setting and situation take some time to get used to. Willow discovers her magic powers with new friend Tara (Amber Benson), who becomes her lover. Buffy finds another boyfriend, Riley Finn (Marc Blucas), whose troubled ego provides further relationship difficulties. She is recruited into the Initiative—a military taskforce located beneath the campus at Sunnydale College and run by Professor Maggie Walsh (Lindsay Crouse), who Buffy soon falls foul of. The Big Bad is Walsh's monstrous creation, Adam (George Hertzberg)—part vampire, part demon, and seemingly partly inspired by the "supersoldiers" plot from *The X-Files*. The Initiative HQ looks like a leftover Bond set, Walsh is killed in traditional *Frankenstein* style by her creation, and further familiarity sees Spike get a chip in his brain, courtesy of the Initiative, which serves as the equivalent of Angel's soul restoration, setting him up as a potential ally.

Season five introduces Buffy's younger "sister," using a spell to convince the regular characters she has always been present in their lives. Dawn (Michelle Trachtenberg) is revealed to have been supernaturally created to protect a mystical portal from being opened by the season's Big Bad, a god called Glorificus (Clare Kramer) who, like her predecessors, wants to bring about the end of the world. Although intended to protect the key to this portal, Dawn is also designed to test Buffy in new ways, and her artificial origins are ultimately deemed immaterial, as Buffy's feelings towards her make her human (and she behaves in a convincingly brattish manner for us to also forget where she came from). The fan response to this new development was one of reservation, particularly as it seemed motivated by the network's desire to attract younger viewers. However, Whedon explained the decision on a dramatic level, arguing:

> It's about accepting that family's a part of your life, even when you think of yourself as independent, and it's about the extraordinary love that a family can bring you, and we very much said Buffy's love interest is going to be her sister for the season ["The Story of Season 5," 2002].

In giving Buffy a sister to take care of (and killing her mother off), further change was instigated, yet the most dramatic transitions were going on behind the scenes as contractual difficulties ensued between the show's producers, Twentieth Century–Fox, and the WB. In almost doubling purchasing costs to $2 million per episode, arguing this was needed to cover the show's production expenses, Twentieth Century–Fox made financial demands the WB were unwilling to meet. Jamie Kellner dismissively told *Entertainment Weekly*, "It's not our number 1 show. It's not a show, like *ER*, that stands above the pack," further contending that *Buffy* was attracting an older audience than the network desired (its teen demographic having dropped by a third by 2001). Whedon responded by pointing out that *Buffy* was the second highest-rated show on the network (with religious family drama *7th Heaven* [1996–2007] coming first); that its audience's average age (26–29) was already known to the network; and that it had "put the WB on the map critically" (Rice 2001). *Buffy* had also cemented the network's identity, influencing them to commission a host of supernatural teen dramas that would prove pivotal to their success. Nonetheless, the WB balked at paying more, arguing that audience interest had peaked, with the fifth season dropping from the 5.2 million average of the last few seasons to 4.5. Kellner even hinted at cancelling the show, stating, "Maybe what we should be doing is to not stay with the same show for many years, and refresh our lineup" (Rice 2001). He abruptly reconsidered when UPN countered his offer, protesting that their acquisition of *Buffy* would set a poor precedent for the industry, asserting the network was a Fox affiliate. The furor represented an important test case by which to assess the consequences of deregulation, and Kellner made the most of surrounding media coverage, attempting to win sympathy. Fox was accused of "self-dealing," having vested interests in UPN through News Corporation's purchase of station affiliates Chris-Craft/United Television, and the WB was presented as an underdog. Many commentators saw this as strategizing from Kellner, yet Sarah Michelle Gellar vowed to quit the series unless it remained with the WB (a comment she quickly retracted after being reminded of her contractual obligations). Twentieth Century–Fox chairman Sandy Grushow maintained that Kellner's lower offer was insufficient to cover production costs, and Whedon issued a number of statements protesting against Kellner's low opinion of his show, all of which resulted, after a year of wrangling, in *Buffy* moving to UPN. It is a testimony to Whedon's understanding of the industry (a third generation writer, with several years in Hollywood having doubtless given him ample reason to be cynical) that he had a clause in *Buffy*'s contract that allowed him to move it to another network; and its relocation seemed inevitable, although *Angel* would remain with the WB in a messy custody battle. *Buffy*'s fifth season finale was the show's 100th episode, and the last to air on the WB, concluding with a dramatic cliffhanger as Buffy sacrifices herself to save her sister, closing the portal between dimensions—and leaving the audience on tenterhooks—

while allowing UPN trailers to declare that the Slayer would be "reborn" on their channel for the next season.

Season six would be the most controversial of the series, criticized by many because of its darker tone. The premiere episode attracted a remarkable 7.7 million viewers, yet ratings fell to an average 4.6 over the season, and negative feedback emerged as problems intensified among the gang. Buffy is resurrected through a spell cast by Willow and has trouble adjusting. She embarks on a secret relationship with Spike, revealing a disconcerting masochistic streak, and real life intervenes in having to work to support Dawn (although the idea that her salary at the Doublemeat Palace would keep the impressive roof over their heads preserves an element of fantasy). Willow loses Tara when a bullet meant for Buffy hits her girlfriend instead, and Willow turns bad after failing to revive her, flaying the perpetrator, Warren (Adam Busch), alive. As the ringleader of a trio of nerds who have been dabbling with magic, Warren proves that humans pose an equivalent danger to any demon, exposing a narrative loophole in how to deal with such figures. Given the morality upheld in the series (which prohibits murdering humans, no matter what they've done), we are meant to deplore Willow's vengeance; but as Dark Willow becomes the Big Bad of the season by killing Warren (and subsequently wanting to end the world), established "rules" become muddled. Many characters behave badly and—for many fans—somewhat inexplicably. The lovable Xander cruelly dumps fiancée Anya at the altar (returning her to vengeance demon mode), and Spike responds to Buffy's attempt to end their relationship by trying to rape her—an act which is especially troubling in Buffy's consequent forgiveness (and unmitigated trust). The finale ends with the world about to be destroyed by Willow; but when all else fails—including Buffy's might—Xander tells her a story about a crayon she once broke, reiterating his unconditional love, and manages to find the human beneath the grieving witch.

The last season brings Buffy's journey to a conclusion. The Big Bad is a force dubbed "the First Evil," which takes possession of an evil preacher, Caleb (Nathan Fillion), whose minions murder various "Potentials" (Slayers-in-waiting) around the world. This results in a group of girls seeking refuge at Buffy's house, Faith returning to help with their training (and dividing their loyalties), and a redeemed Anya and Willow also pitching in (neither of whom have to do any jail time, like Faith, prior to readmission to the gang). Another apparent inconsistency is shown in the fact that another of the nerds, Andrew (Tom Lenk), who was led by the First to kill his friend, Jonathan (Danny Strong), is also recruited to the cause without any need for penance. Buffy continues to rely on Spike (despite everyone's understandable antipathy—reworking the illicit Angel period of season three) and conceives a plan to help them win their seemingly hopeless battle. She decides to break the established rule about successive Slayers and enlists Willow's help to share her and Faith's powers with the Potentials, giving them the strength to fight demonic hordes. Her belief in Spike is also corroborated when he uses an amulet to close the Hellmouth, destroying Sunnydale in the process. Buffy's journey thus comes full circle, from first arriving in town as the chasm is about to open to finally ensuring it is sealed again, and although Giles mentions "another Hellmouth in Cleveland," we are allowed a sense of closure as the survivors survey the wreckage of their former town.

Whedon intended the series to be a celebration of female empowerment, saying, "The one thing I hoped to take part in was a shift in popular culture in the sense of people accepting the idea of a female hero—not just a heroine, but a hero—in a way that hadn't been done really since Sarah Connor or Ripley" (Whedon, "The Last Sundown," 2003). To aim for a "shift in popular culture" is a high ambition, and promoting a female *hero* is equally notable. By definition, a hero leads the narrative and propels the action. The term "heroine" is not only a linguistic diminutive of the word, but of the concept also—with heroines tending to play a secondary supportive role, often as damsels in distress. The hero's journey, as Joseph Campbell's study of this theme affirms, involves various tests of character and has been used as the source material for many stories, from the earliest oral traditions to various references onscreen. Putting aside childish things, leaving home, having to endure tragedy or torment, and finally accepting and fulfilling one's duties are not only key features of the traditional "coming-of-age" narrative, but offer a dramatic exploration of humanity itself. However, contemporary variations have tended to focus on male experiences, and telefantasy is no exception. Elements of the hero's journey can be seen in all the series here assessed, with Number 6, Dale Cooper, and Fox Mulder each undergoing specific trials, yet in each case their journey is not completed, as they fail to fulfill their respective quests. Buffy Summers provides an interesting contrast by vanquishing various foes, overcoming personal difficulties, and completing her journey. She was by no means the only female hero we had seen. As Whedon notes, the leads of the *Terminator* and *Alien* franchises staked out this territory years earlier, but Buffy is considerably younger and (importantly) somewhat easier to identify with.

Buffy's superhuman powers may help her combat danger, yet the show's writers continually sought to retain her humanity, thereby enabling the connection forged with viewers. As Whedon comments, "If they're not feeling it, if her relationship to what's going on isn't personal ... then it's just guys with horns running around, and some good jokes, but it's not going to resonate" (Golden and Holder 1998, 241). In placing an adolescent female at the forefront of the narrative, and championing her strength and skills, Whedon provided a new kind of role model to a new generation of viewers. She may be dressed in the latest outfits and express more concern about dating or having "last month's hair" than in saving humanity (initially at least), but it is her ordinariness and accessibility that make her a powerful icon. *The Prisoner* may have given us assertive females serving as Number Two, *Twin Peaks* may have commended the strength of its tragic central figure (as well as providing transgressive figures such as Nadine), and *The X-Files* may have taken a courageous leap in promoting a smart female scientist as a main character, but the travails of a supernaturally enhanced adolescent girl embarking on nothing less than the hero's journey would take the telefantasy series to a new level. Whedon's stated influences include female action heroes, comic characters such as *The X-Men*'s Kitty Pryde, and a reaction against horror film clichés—particularly "that blonde girl who would always get herself killed. I started feeling bad for her. I thought, y'know, it's time she had a chance to take back the night" ("Welcome to the Hellmouth" 1999). In this last respect, Buffy's precursors include what Carol Clover refers to as the "Final Girl"—a figure who manages to withstand attack in the "slasher" subgenre and makes it to the end credits (Clover 1992). Indeed, Buffy Summers is the ultimate Final Girl in being fantastically equipped to defend herself. She may look and sound more like a generic "victim," her miniskirts and mannerisms more readily associated with the kind of female character who is often attacked and annihilated in horror; yet it is in forcing us to revise our assumptions that the series derives much of its power and pleasure.

The show generated a keen sense of affinity with Buffy and her gang as they battled a host of menaces and struggled through puberty. As television critic Matt Roush has commented, the series had a particular attraction for those "who like to live out our childhood through television, which happens so rarely, that we can express that sense of wonder" ("Buffy 101: Studying the Slayer" 2003). Viewers were not only offered the imaginative thrills of a world of magic, but given the chance to re-live their adolescence through characters they could identify with. These weren't sneery, impossibly good-looking teens like those featured in the likes of *Beverley Hills 90210*; they were likeable, down-to-earth, smart, and endearingly maladjusted. Willow Rosenberg was the archetypal geek whose transformation into a powerful witch was a joy to behold, even as the series expressed caution when she is seen to abuse these powers. Xander Harris was similarly self-effacing. Funny yet vulnerable, he presented an interesting departure from the conventional depiction of male characters his age, often stating his sense of inadequacy in attempting to live up to masculine archetypes, and openly expressing his affection and admiration for his female friends. Cordelia Chase reminded us that even those in the "in-crowd" had their insecurities, and was refreshingly unconcerned about stating her opinions—crass and ill-considered as they often were—making an effective contrast to the frequent yearnings for normality expressed by Buffy, whose blonde good looks and apparent ordinariness are contrasted with the weight of expectation placed upon her. As the series progressed, other characters joined the Scooby Gang, and some switched "sides," adding an important sense of development. Willow undergoes some of the most dramatic changes via an exploration of sexuality that presented another interesting departure from the norm (even if Tara's dullness threatened to undermine any progressive intentions), as well as in gravitating to Big Bad status for a season. Former vengeance demon Anya effectively replaced Cordelia (after the latter moved to L.A. and *Angel*), providing amusement in her tactlessness and some empathy as she attempted to deal with her human form and accompanying emotions, similarly turning bad for a spell when Xander breaks her heart. The motif first explored with Angel is reiterated throughout the remainder of the series when various characters serve as both antagonist and accomplice, adding to the show's emotional complexity as Buffy is "tested" in various ways, providing conflict (as well as companionship) as she attempts to balance her Slayer responsibilities with being a good daughter, sister, and friend.

While *The X-Files* proved reluctant to alter its format, lest this detract from its success, *Buffy*'s makers had no such hesitation, challenging their hero (and audience) to accommodate continual transformation. Over the course of the series, Buffy embarks on a number of unhappy affairs; meets her nemesis in the form of rogue slayer Faith; acquires a supernaturally created sister; loses her mother; and battles a succession of enemies in a bid to save the world. She also grows up. Having graduated high school, gone to college, and dropped out in order to look after Dawn, Buffy's life veers close to being depressingly realistic by season six, as she takes a job in a hamburger joint to pay the bills. Work prospects seemingly improve in the last season when the new school principal (who also moonlights as a demon hunter) offers Buffy a job as a counselor at the rebuilt Sunnydale High, but by this point she was also a mother figure, back at a school she had clearly grown out of. If the entire premise was intended as a metaphoric rite-of-passage, it appeared to have run its course once Buffy acquired parental responsibilities—experiencing evident conflict in trying to protect the world and also take care of Dawn. The series gets around the problem in breaking the rule that makes her the Chosen One, recruiting others to the cause. By closing the portal to the underworld and sharing her powers with a group of Slayers-in-waiting, she no longer has to bear the weight of the world on her shoulders, but can inspire a younger generation while sealing the source of danger—as optimistic an ending as one could imagine (bar being reunited with Angel in the closing moments). Seven eventful years thus conclude with Buffy watching Sunnydale's destruction when the Hellmouth is finally closed, leaving nothing but a vast crater and the familiar "Welcome to Sunnydale" sign hanging on its hinges. The Scooby Gang are left to contemplate what they will do next—and then break the moment, in typical style, by suggesting they head for the nearest mall.

It is this mixture of the everyday and the extraordinary that gave the show a level of credibility amid incredulous proceedings. Although Buffy's preternatural strength and Slayer instincts are vital skills in thwarting a host of adversaries, her wit and the friendship of an endearing group of misfits kept her (and the series) grounded. While it could be argued that the traumas faced are treated too lightly, missing the opportunity to provide her with greater depth and interest, a decision was clearly made to keep Buffy intact as a hero. Rare exceptions include such episodes as "When She was Bad" (after her first brush with death distances her from her friends) and "Bargaining" (when she reveals that she was taken from heaven—after her second death—and is clearly shell-shocked by her return), as well as two interesting episodes, "Out of my Mind" and "Normal Again," in which Buffy briefly bails on reality because she is unable to cope. For the most part, however, she retains an astonishing ability to deal with the problems thrown at her. On a moral level her integrity is unsullied; she uses her powers responsibly, and although she is allowed to joke as she slays she is never allowed to enjoy her calling, as Faith does. Many "vices" are transferred to the "rogue Slayer," from a sense of arrogance about her calling to an open admission of sexual pleasure, so as to retain Buffy's virtue; and it is a credit to the show's writers that Faith remains sympathetic. She is even used to undercut the show's credo in the "body-switch" episode "Who Are You?"—parodying Buffy's sanctimonious tendencies by repeatedly stating: "You can't do that, because it's wrong." However, even as it appears to mock its own simple sermonizing, the episode gives Faith a new understanding about the need to toe a heroic line, and she leaves town with her body restored yet her brash confidence severely ruptured, starting her on a path to redemption.

If *The X-Files* toys with religious concerns about an afterlife and a higher power, *Buffy* also has a Christian subtext—not simply in confirming that heaven exists, but in its continuous Catholic exploration of guilt, sin, and redemption (which are repeated motifs, despite Whedon's stated atheism). If forgiveness is divine, it is also heroic within the series' morality. Hence, even when Spike attempts to rape Buffy he is forgiven when he shows contrition; and as he sacrifices himself in the finale, Buffy even holds Spike's hand and tells him she loves him. Her actions may seemingly undermine the feminism of the series, recalling Laura Palmer's "forgiveness" of her abusive father as he dies, but the intent is to suggest that redemption is always possible and that everything (and everyone) is open to change. The Slayer's relationship with Spike was criticized by many fans as a corruption of the Buffy/Angel romance, and seemed to affirm a central flaw in her choice of men; yet in giving Spike a way to redeem himself, Buffy's belief in him is ultimately affirmed. Renegade Faith and "evil" Willow are similarly chastened by the end of the series, their roles focused on assisting Buffy in fighting the good fight rather than serving as rivals; yet even as these darker alter egos are outlawed, the series allows multiple readings and affiliations, aware that the least "heroic" figures are frequently the most interesting. Nonetheless, while Buffy is occasionally questioned, it remains her show, and the forces of good triumph in a spectacular and moving finale. The characters may seem a little lost in their last scene, uncertain what to do now that their mission is complete, yet greater closure is provided than in the other series discussed. Buffy extricates herself from the role assigned to her and becomes a free agent—which is more than our previous protagonists achieve, and more than we tend to manage in real life, yet the ending is obviously intended as a wish-fulfillment fantasy—the ultimate Scooby Doo ending where wrongs are put right, even if there are a few casualties.

For all the deaths and disappointments Buffy has had to face, for all its scares and traumas, the main plot arc has been about getting through life's adversities, and she proves herself the ultimate Final Girl in making it all the way to end, defying numerous prophecies that said otherwise. The show ended, much as it began, by breaking established rules, and a major source of its appeal lay not only in the mix of tones and storylines, but a skillfully rendered fictional world in which almost anything could happen. The series never allowed its material to become predictable or familiar, and despite the risk of displeasing fans, it stayed true to its imperative towards continuous innovation, extending the narrative path laid by previous cult hits.

Buffy shares Number 6's rebellious nature in questioning the Watcher's Council, as well as the Initiative, yet proves better able to master her destiny in "resigning" from each organization, forming powerful alliances with others, and charting her own course. On a generic level, just as *The Prisoner* parodies Western and Bond themes, *Buffy* engages in equally radical experimentation. "Hush" dispenses with dialogue to emulate a silent horror classic; "Restless" enters the inner world of its characters' dreams; and the musical episode "Once More with Feeling" renders every line of dialogue in song. *Twin Peaks'* influence is also apparent in the importance placed on dreams, abrupt mood changes, and the idea of a demonic realm that borders a small town; yet the morality of the Buffyverse favors the White Lodge, with human life deemed sacred, vengeance outlawed, and good finally triumphing over evil. While Laura Palmer welcomes death as her only means of escape, Buffy's powers enable her to avoid becoming another tragic blonde, conceived by Whedon as a born survivor who ultimately vanquishes demonic forces (even if she destroys her hometown to do so). Unlike *The X-Files*, sinister organizations are overcome. The government-financed Initiative project implodes with Walsh's destruction, the Watcher's Council is destroyed by Caleb, and the supernatural threat to humanity is exorcised via the Hellmouth's closure. While Mulder and Scully fail to defeat the Shadow Syndicate (and the aliens they have struck a deal with), *Buffy* refuses such fatalism and allows its leads far greater agency in overcoming the forces that threaten them. As we have seen, Whedon wanted to avoid the sense of intractability apparent in Carter's show, yet some interesting links are apparent. *X-Files* episode "Die Hand Die Verletzt" anticipates much of *Buffy*'s premise, with its demonic science teacher summoned by a Satanic PTA. As we discover, Sunnydale was founded by a demon-worshipping Mayor—and the fact that he has a meeting with the PTA on his "to do" list exemplifies the sort of witty intertextual allusion frequently seen in the series. In addition, Mulder and Scully often engage in the kind of banter that is typical of "Buffyspeak," as occurs when Mulder suggests telekinesis during an investigation and Scully replies, "You mean how Carrie got even at the prom?" ("Shadows")—situating the characters in the same world as ourselves, as consumers of pop culture—a motif which reappears throughout Whedon's series. Feminist impulses are also extended. Like Scully, Buffy offers an assertive and unusual female character, yet one who is central to the tale rather than playing a supporting role; and although Buffy is similarly "feminized" via maternal duties, and has some problematic relationships, the series concludes with an empowering affirmation of female strength.

In creating a compelling and intricate mythology, the show consistently made inventive use of the television medium. Certain episodes recreate a period drama, extending backstories to explain how an Irish drifter became the demonic Angelus, and how a bad Victorian poet nicknamed "William the Bloody" became Spike. Episodes such as "Storyteller" adopt the perspective of a minor character, and parallel universes create interesting flipsides and flashforwards. For example, an "evil Willow" is first encountered in the season three episode "The Wish." Later that season, in "Doppelgangland," regular Willow meets her alter ego and describes her as "skanky ... and kind of gay"; yet far from being a throwaway witticism, this turns out to be a prescient line, anticipating later events (including her realization about her sexuality in season four and her subsequent turn to "evil" in six). Further indicating how much planning went into the series (in marked contrast to other cult shows), Buffy and Faith's dreams often foretell future events. While Faith lies in a coma in season three, we are allowed to enter her mind (just as we entered Scully's in "One Breath") and hear dialogue that only makes sense two seasons later. Making a bed with Buffy, within her unconscious state, Faith refers to "little sister" coming in "703"—an oblique reference to Dawn's arrival. Such detail adds a level of complexity that would reward those taking a keen interest in events, or watching the series again, anticipating techniques later used in *Lost*. Another interesting element is the use of music, not only in terms of the score accompanying the action, or the notorious musical episode, but diegetic elements, such as guitar solos Giles performs in a local café and the various unsigned bands showcased at The Bronze. A CD release of this music would provide an interesting crossover between the fictional world and the real world (as occurred when singer Julee Cruise "performed" at The Roadhouse in *Twin Peaks*, as well as on the accompanying soundtrack and in live gigs during its initial broadcast), and many featured bands later gained some prominence. Other merchandise includes an official magazine, collectible figures, tie-in novels and games, and various DVD box-sets; yet *Buffy*'s unofficial contributions are perhaps more significant, including scholarly collections published long after the series ended, affirming that the show's audience were clearly more than high school kids.

As can be seen from the host of books surrounding the show, it has been read on a number of levels, generating concerns that include analysis of its moral universe, its depiction of gender roles (often cited as an example of Third Wave feminism), and its significance as a contemporary television text—particularly in its postmodern features. *Buffy*'s extensive critical appeal affirms that the interest given to cult shows is no longer limited to fanzines and websites, but includes scholarly speculation; and it is notable that, even for seasoned critics, the series stood out. Ann Billsun was in her fifties when the series aired and explains its appeal by affirming that Buffy was "the kind of heroine for whom I'd been searching all my life" (Billsun 2005, 16). Another fan-scholar, Vivian Sobchack, invited to comment on a DVD feature analyzing *Buffy*'s critical appreciation ("Slayer 101: Studying the Slayer"), notes its feminist credentials yet argues that its appeal is equally explained by providing audiences with an ideal community—a view that echoes Henry Jenkins' summary of the impetus behind many cult shows, asserting that fans are drawn to "a utopian dimension" found in examples of "affiliation, friendship, community" (Jenkins 1992, 282). Some critics have attested to television's bardic role—its ability to tell stories that become incorporated into the audience's lives—and *Buffy* appears to be an ideal example. As Mark Roush comments, "*Buffy the Vampire Slayer* is a form of TV literature. It's something that can be studied, and that can be fruitfully analyzed, the way any good allegory can be" ("Slayer 101," 2003). Academics and critics have readily admitted their pleasure in such analysis, which has lent esteem to the series; yet fans have been equally motivated by an interest in deconstruction, and the official website The Bronze provided a forum to share their views and interact with *Buffy*'s writers. *The X-Files* was one of the first series to encourage such interaction, with Carter admitting that fan interest made him take its ideas more seriously, and *Buffy*'s writing team have also commended fans for making them raise their game. As story editor Douglas Petrie states:

> If we can really lead our audience in one direction, and then make a radical left hand turn that they didn't see coming, that's great ... and it's a tremendous amount of work because they're always ahead of us. They're just the smartest fans that I know of [Petrie 2001].

It is in raising the bar in terms of audience expectations that the show would achieve an enviable reputation, inspiring a host of imitators. *Buffy* may have ended in 2003, yet elements have reappeared in subsequent series. Its spin-off, *Angel*, would extend *Buffy*'s universe for an older audience as well as reworking a similar concept as the cult show, *Forever Knight* (1989–96), with its reluctant vampire turned detective. Angel is the show's hero (assisted by a similar team of helpers), and the "Big Bad" is the legal firm Wolfram & Hart, who have made a pact with demons to secure their power. However, the satire is offset by soapier elements, such as Angel's emerging feelings for Cordelia, the return of ex-lover Darla (Julie Benz), and the discovery of a son. Its more accomplished episodes invariably seem to be crossovers with the original series, including the heartbreaking "I Will Remember You," in which Angel is finally granted the mortality that will make his love for Buffy realizable—yet sacrifices his humanity to protect her (leaving her with no memory of their brief time together as lovers). The series would also welcome guest appearances from Faith, who risks her life to restore Angel's soul, as well as Spike (proving that some characters simply cannot be killed off). *Angel* would only survive *Buffy* by a year, with the WB cancelling it, despite consistent ratings of 4 million, but shows such as *Blood Ties* (2006–) and *Moonlight* (2007) provide variations on the same theme, combining the Buffy/Angel romance with paranormal investigations. More direct *Buffy* influences include the high school settings of *Vampire High* (2001) and *Hex* (2004–5), while adaptations of similarly themed books have sparked a resurgence of interest in vampires. *True Blood* (2008–), inspired by the "Southern Vampire Mysteries" books by Charlaine Harris, offers a more adult take on *Buffy*'s premise, adopting a risqué tone with depictions of violence, drug-taking and sexuality deployed in a Southern Gothic twist. The series' creator, Alan Ball, was previously responsible for *Six Feet Under*, and the show is an archetypal "quality cult," from its marketing to its reception. Far costlier than *Buffy*, averaging three to four million dollars per episode, it debuted with a 1.4 rating and has since snowballed in popularity, becoming HBO's most successful drama (eclipsing their previous hit *The Sopranos*), attracting an average audience of 12 million, winning awards and securing additional revenue through high DVD sales. Like *Buffy*, it features a young woman with a special ability, a thing for vampires, and a best friend with witchy skills, yet Sookie Stackhouse (Anna Paquin), somewhat disappointingly, is also chiefly defined by her romantic entanglements. Vampire romances have become big business since the hit film *Twilight* (2008), based on a series of novels by Stephanie Meyer, was released. The tale of a misunderstood teenage girl and her tortuous relationship with a vampire obviously plays on the Buffy/Angel dynamic, even if the author claims to have been inspired by a dream. Tapping the same market, *The Vampire Diaries* (2009–) is similarly adapted from a series of books (by Lisa Jane Smith) and focuses on a teenage girl caught in a love triangle with two vampires. Produced by former *Dawson's Creek* creator Kevin Williamson, the result is a pubescent variant of *True Blood*, with another female protagonist whose relationship difficulties take precedence, her chief characteristic being continual forgiveness and forbearance. In fact, all these examples provide questionable female role models who ultimately play second fiddle to their brooding boyfriends, affirming how exceptional *Buffy* was by comparison. That is not to say that its legacy is safe, however. The current vampire craze has caused Fran Rubel Kuzui to express an interest in making another *Buffy* film—with her company (Kuzui Enterprises) having retained the rights to the concept since her first less-than-inspiring feature. Little has been heard since discussions were publicized in 2009, yet the fact that a new "Buffy" movie does not require Whedon's approval or involvement is a reminder of his relative powerlessness. Marketing for the potential film described it as a "darker event-sized movie" with franchise potential, and stressed that it would have no connection to the original series' characters, thereby side-stepping seven years of an intricately constructed universe. While *Buffy* fans would no doubt declare it "non-canon" and stay away, *Twilight* lovers are another matter.

The exploitation of Whedon's concept is far from new, of course. The WB hosted a number of supernatural dramas after *Buffy*'s success, launching *Charmed* (1998–2006), a comedy about three witch sisters, a year after *Buffy* first aired; acquiring *Sabrina the Teenage Witch* (1996–2003) from ABC in 2000; and commissioning *Roswell* (1999–2002) and *Smallville* (2001–2011), which similarly play on the supernatural teen motif, while *Supernatural* (2005–) offers an equally irreverent mix of comedy and horror via its demon-hunting brothers. The most successful products in their line-up, in other words, all echo *Buffy the Vampire Slayer*—the series Kellner took a chance on yet subsequently failed to acknowledge. Other commentators have more readily noted its importance. Bryan Fuller has created a number of series with supernatural females in the lead, including *Wonderfalls* (2004), *Dead Like Me* (2003–4), and *Pushing Daisies* (2007–8), and cites *Buffy* as a pioneering example for both himself and the industry, stating, "*Buffy* showed that young women could be in situations that were both fantastic and relatable, and instead of shunting women off to the side it put them at the center" (Salem 2003). Although some caution should be voiced, given that Fuller's shows have all been cancelled—with *Dead Like Me* seemingly re-made as *Reaper* (2007–) with a gender switch—it remains the case that before *Buffy* it was hard to imagine a female character heading a series (the reason most networks passed on the premise). This situation changed after it aired, particularly as a young female audience became targeted. UPN were only too pleased to acquire *Buffy* on the strength of its female following, and president Dawn Ostroff credits the series with showing the network "the kind of audience we could attract: young, female and cutting edge" (James 2006). Thanks to *Buffy*, female-led supernatural shows increased, not only on the netlets but the major networks also. Immediately after *Buffy* ended, an interesting offshoot of the paranormal detective series emerged, featuring women supernaturally able to connect with the dead to solve crimes and protect the living. In *Tru Calling* (2003–5), *Medium* (2005–11), and *Ghost Whisperer* (2005–10) female protagonists attempt, like Buffy, to juggle their personal lives with their "gifts," mixing strands of soap with the supernatural. The fact that all three appeared on major networks (Fox, NBC and CBS), with the last two shows earning double figures in their prime, signals an interesting development for telefantasy. In proving popular among female audiences these shows intensified network interest in a market *Buffy* helped to identify, although attempts to appeal to female viewers would not remain a priority if ratings failed to hit the desired mark, as their eventual cancellation affirms. The point is further exemplified with *Eastwick* (2009). Focusing on three supernaturally gifted women, the premise was conceived by Maggie Friedman as a show about female empowerment and achieved a high percentage of female viewers, as well as favorable reviews, yet was cancelled by ABC when ratings dropped below 5 million, affirming that major networks will only offer very conditional support to such shows.

Although *Buffy*'s legacy is indicated by discernible efforts to create telefantasy aimed at a female audience, the results have tended to be disappointing. The "reimagined" *Bionic Woman* (NBC, 2007–8) has a number of similar features, with a young woman, Jaime Sommers (Michelle Ryan), who has extraordinary strength, a little sister to take care of, and a nemesis, Sarah Corvus (Katee Sackhoff), serving as an unpredictable alter ego. The Sommers sisters also have a similar background to their virtual namesakes, with a dead mother and a father described as a "flake." BERKUT, an organization designed to counteract terrorist threat, resembles the Initiative—particularly in cyborg experiments which create Jaime's bionic implants, yet their sinister features are never interrogated, woefully little is made of Sackhoff's intriguing character, and the show was cancelled after one season. A super-strong girl also appears in *The Sarah Connor Chronicles* (Fox, 2008–9)—a television spin-off of *The Terminator* franchise in which the adolescent John Connor (Thomas Dekker) attempts to save mankind from annihilation, assisted by his mother (Lena Heady) and female cyborg Cameron (Summer Glau). Looking like a sullen teenager, Cameron's immense strength belies her slight build, and scenes at high school, early in the first season, are very reminiscent of *Buffy*, particularly when she is counseled after the suicide of a classmate and gives the appearance of an emotionally disturbed adolescent. Disappointingly, the second season failed to build on its potential, and the series was cancelled after losing two-thirds of its viewers. Neither example advances the notion of female empowerment, with Jaime and Cameron deferring to male authority figures and providing little more than eye candy that kicks ass, affirming that shows that draw upon *Buffy* are not necessarily faithful to the same concerns, and reiterating how extraordinary it remains. Russell T. Davies has credited *Buffy* for making the revised *Doctor Who* possible (its "Whedonesque" influences including numerous pop culture references and its use of a seasonal plot arc), while the inclusion of an indestructible blonde schoolgirl in *Heroes* further indicates the *Buffy* factor—while offering another pale comparison.

Despite the show's reputation, Whedon has experienced considerable difficulties with other projects, demonstrating that a series creator's position, even one responsible for such a remarkable achievement as *Buffy*, is always precarious. When his next venture, *Firefly* (2004), was cancelled by Fox after 13 episodes, Whedon commented, "There will always be shows the networks don't get. My only hope is that one day I'll understand what it is the networks want" (Pearson 2005, 21). In contrast to Pearson's view of Whedon as the "hyphenate" par excellence who can do as he pleases, this comment confirms that pleasing the networks is the ultimate priority—an aim that corresponds with drawing sufficient numbers. *Firefly* averaged 4.7 million viewers per episode, roughly the same as *Buffy* in its last two seasons, and the question of whether Whedon's work can attain mass appeal has continued to dog him. After plans to revise *Wonder Woman* stalled, Whedon forswore television, only to surprise many fans by creating another Fox series, *Dollhouse* (2009–10). He did so as a favor to Faith actress Eliza Dushku, who serves as its star, yet the result is scarcely recognizable as a Whedon project. The premise involves an illicit organization which manipulates humans to perform specific assignments and subsequently wipes their memories, focusing on a young woman called Echo who gradually recovers her identity. With its spy-fi elements and a female lead who adopts various personas, *Alias* (2001–6) seems to be an obvious antecedent, as well as suggesting a journey of self-discovery akin to *Buffy*, yet a distasteful scenario involving the sexual exploitation of "dolls" alienated many viewers, and a confused narrative stood in contrast to the intricate plotting of its predecessor. The first season attracted 4.6 million, apparently inheriting *Buffy*'s audience, and Whedon fans, seemingly driven by loyalty rather than the intrinsic merits of the show, successfully petitioned Fox to renew it. Whedon sought to convince executives that fans would nurture the series, stating, "I don't make hit shows, I make shows that stick around. There's a market there that exists beyond Nielsen numbers" (Surette 2009). However, despite drafting in Alexis Denisof and Summer Glau for the second season, it attracted barely 2 million viewers and was duly cancelled, its many disappointments making the decision hard to view as anything other than a relief. Although certain ideas recall *The Prisoner* (with the dollhouse symbolizing an artificial life based on manipulation and delusion), the series was poorly written, providing little incentive to care about the characters—in marked contrast to *Buffy*—with scant involvement from its creator. Whedon responded to *Dollhouse*'s cancellation by stating he would focus on "online pursuits"—seemingly intending to bypass network television—and continues to involve himself in other media such as comics and film; yet whether his subsequent career will ever eclipse *Buffy* remains to be seen.

Buffy appeared during a decisive moment in broadcasting, in which competition intensified via the growth of cable and smaller networks specializing in what established broadcasters would not show. While Fox aimed at an older audience in making its ascent, newer broadcasters emerged to fill the resulting vacuum. Smaller netlets, the WB and UPN, had a remit to experiment, making shows that were, as Emily Nussbaum notes, "too risky, wonky, or downright weird for the other networks; they *had* to take chances to survive" (Nussbaum 2006). The WB may have taken a relative risk with a vampire show, but it was one they would greatly benefit from, as would the UPN, although their battle over *Buffy* had greater consequences than who got to air its last two seasons.

Born virtually simultaneously, having experienced mutual difficulty establishing an identity, they eventually became carbon copies of one another—post-*Buffy*—pursuing the same audience, splitting their potential viewers, and proving unable to survive in an increasingly ruthless climate. Far from expanding opportunities within broadcasting and providing an alternative to the majors, deregulation in 1996 appeared to consolidate their advantage, and smaller networks struggled to compete—finding themselves continually outbid in their effort to secure hit shows, less willing to take risks, and increasingly reliant on mergers and acquisitions to survive. Ironically, *Buffy*'s two competing networks had to join forces in the end. As Meg James argues, "The WB's loss of *Buffy*—which breathed new life into the struggling UPN—set in motion a pitched battle for the coveted youth market that would eventually doom both networks" (James 2006). With difficulty finding new hits, and rising debts, they realized it made greater sense to merge, and the WB and UPN became the CW Television Network in 2006. Jointly owned by CBS and Time-Warner, the network has attempted to retain the same identity as its forebears, airing youth-oriented telefantasy hits such as *Smallville* and *Supernatural*, and further drawing upon *Buffy*'s legacy via *The Vampire Diaries*. Like its predecessor, the show premiered as the network's biggest hit, securing 4.8 million viewers; yet ratings have declined, and there is little indication that it will have the same legacy or resonance.

Challenging expectations, revising assumptions, and making female-led telefantasy a viable proposition, *Buffy*'s impact on the industry is all the more significant because it was so improbable. As David Greenwalt describes it, "*Buffy* is the little show that could. *Buffy* started with that silly title and flew under the radar" (O'Hare 2001), making its name by defying expectation and taking advantage of the opportunity afforded by the WB. However, the series remained subject to various difficulties, with its timeslot and target market imposing restrictions on its material; having to produce a grueling 22 episodes per season; and requiring sets and effects that entailed considerable expense (more than the WB were ultimately willing to provide). Although UPN threw it a lifeline, they would eventually cancel *Buffy* after two seasons because it remained a "little show" in terms of viewing figures. Nonetheless, while it did not yield the kind of ratings that would secure it a place among the established networks, *Buffy* influenced what they would subsequently show. Character-driven plots, seasonal arcs, tongue-in-cheek humor, and intertextual references would all be redeployed in later series, and an emphasis on continuous change would similarly signal attempts to stay one step ahead of the audience—with characters that go bad or find redemption. Rule-breaking would become the order of the day in ensemble dramas that mixed supernatural elements with an ongoing soap, utilizing various narrative strategies and a host of generic features to invite regular viewing, and taking advantage of new media platforms to cultivate a cult audience.

New technologies would usher in another era as networks, chasing the lucrative youth audience, found much of their demographic were no longer watching television. As Nussbaum notes, the need for "niche TV" was effaced by "DVDs, BitTorrent, the video i-Pod, video-on-demand, TiVo, not to mention the whole tangled Wild West of the Web" (Nussbaum 2006). Anticipating such developments, the WB created a host of interactive features on homepages for hit shows, their pursuit of the adolescent market influencing the network, as Eric Freedman asserts, "to consider online space as a critical address point for its viewership of internet-savvy teens" (Freedman 2005, 178). The major networks would similarly focus their resources on upgrading for the digital age, incorporating new technologies in marketing shows, and creating new variations on telefantasy that would confirm a continued capacity to surprise. Back in 1997, as Nussbaum reminds us, *Buffy the Vampire Slayer* was "considered an oddball gamble for a network, a goofily named TV series based on a flop movie" (Nussbaum 2006). A decade on, with most networks owned by major corporations, and any exceptions tending to emulate their strategies, we might presume the time for "oddball gambles" was over; yet as our next example proves, risks would still be taken in the business, and spectacular success would change the stakes for telefantasy. A fantasy island with an invisible monster would be no less improbable a pitch than a teenage girl with a mission to slay vampires, yet *Lost* similarly defied expectation and became the first definitive cult series of the 21st century. Borrowing features from a number of predecessors—including *Buffy*—characterization was key, guilt and redemption feature as prominent themes, pop cultural references added fun, metaphysical speculation provided depth, and a series of ongoing mysteries would help to secure the kind of ratings that would make it a network dream, taking telefantasy, and audiences, into uncharted territory.

5

How *Lost* Redefined Cult Television: A Mystery Island and a Monster Hit

It can't be a normal island. If I do it, it will be a weird borderline sci-fi show.

—J.J. Abrams

    Lost (2004–10) originated as a pitch along the lines of "*Cast Away*—the Series," yet J.J. Abrams' insistence on changing the concept from a reality-based drama to a "weird borderline sci-fi show" created a sense of enigma that would prove integral to its success, fundamentally altering broadcasting attitudes towards telefantasy. Aligning cult interest with commercial appeal, various means were used to attract a contemporary audience, and the following evaluation notes both the timeliness of the series and the methods used to promote it. As we entered the 21st century, broadcasting faced a number of challenges, with a proliferation of channels splintering audiences and alternative entertainment forms taking them elsewhere. The lifting of FCC restrictions on cross media ownership a decade earlier enabled multimedia conglomerates to extend their share of the market, acquiring channels to promote in-house productions and investing in online resources in response to changing audience preferences. Nonetheless, even the biggest networks, with a number of affiliates, were party to the usual risks in selecting what to invest in—as was proven by the fact that ABC trailed fourth among the majors in 2003, when the idea for an island adventure series was first conceived. *Lost*'s anticipated financial expense prompted huge misgivings at ABC's parent company, Disney, leading to the sacking of its commissioning executive before the pilot even aired; yet despite minimal expectations, the series became a breakaway hit, earning three times its anticipated audience. With its desert island setting and mix of supernatural phenomena, soap opera, and conspiracy, *Lost* combined various modes of appeal to become a hugely successful "crossover cult," a feat that is at least partly attributable to the fannish enthusiasms of its creators—individuals with a host of influences they wished to draw upon, the opportunity to innovate to their heart's content, and an audience that delighted in the puzzle placed before them (for some time at least). In attempting to prolong interest, *Lost* inevitably lost its way, frustrating many viewers when the concept seemed to be interminably drawn out. While such criticism eventually prompted the studio to set an end-date, with the promise of a "highly anticipated and shocking finale" (Adalian 2007), *Lost*'s conclusion left a number of its central mysteries unresolved, causing many to wonder, six years and 121 episodes on, if they had been caught in the longest of cons. Although the show's long-term standing is uncertain, particularly given the critical response to its ending, it remains the case that from the moment it first aired *Lost* rewrote the rules for telefantasy, attracting unprecedented numbers, utilizing new methods to sustain curiosity, and redefining our understanding of cult television.

The commissioning of a big-budget SF drama was a risky venture for a network experiencing difficulties, but *Lost* provided returns that served as a game-changer for the industry. Network interest in telefantasy had petered off during the 1980s, and by the 1990s, after the "quirky community" cycle initiated by *Twin Peaks* had run its course, new examples of the genre were generally consigned to newer networks, tending to be regarded as a niche interest. The ability to attract intense fan interest and critical acclaim, as well as a demographic seen as increasingly important, would help revise these attitudes, yet *Lost* additionally offered the kind of blockbuster ratings no one had thought possible. It did so by eliciting a cultish level of engagement, making the most of online resources to extend its narrative universe and enhance viewer interest. Its makers understood that for a series to achieve success today it needs to have more than an interesting idea, the right team overseeing production, adequate financial support, or a place in the schedules that will net the required audience; it must additionally exploit the technologies that are overtaking broadcasting and give viewers further incentive to get involved. The series combined a number of generic elements to maximize interest, and provided a number of questions to provoke discussion, taking evident inspiration from past cult shows, particularly in making the most of the Internet. *Twin Peaks* was one of the first series to attract online interest, with the twin-peaks.alt site set up by fans to exchange ideas about an increasingly baffling series. *The X-Files* withheld onscreen episode titles to direct fans to the official Fox website, its writers making them increasingly obscure to see if viewers could work out their meaning. *Buffy*'s writers would regularly canvas online opinion to try and maintain an element of surprise. *Lost*'s makers deployed still more innovative ways to involve their audience (and keep them guessing), pioneering the use of new media in both its marketing and delivery, and scattering a range of clues to plot intrigues throughout its extended universe, thereby epitomizing the changing shape of the contemporary cult.

The series earned unprecedented ratings for a telefantasy show, attracting 20 million viewers at its height, regularly positioning itself in the Nielsen top 10, and becoming a global phenomenon. Key to fostering such interest was an attempt to determine what the show was about. Originally conceived as a realist drama, its premise was dramatically reconceived to incorporate elements of the supernatural and science fictional—including spatiotemporal travel and figures capable of conversing with the dead—combining an escapist adventure with an array of fantastical features to create an angst-ridden meditation on fate, guilt, and redemption. Originating as a simple outline about a group of castaways, derived from a corporate hunch at ABC Entertainment, and shaped (in part) by quirky young writer/director/producer J.J. Abrams (who only agreed to become involved if he could add a monster), *Lost* would eventually reveal itself as a fully fledged SF/fantasy show—overcoming initial concerns that this might put viewers off, and proving to be its biggest draw. Displaying a shrewd appreciation of the elements needed to attain cult interest, *Lost* created the perfect hit formula, from costly production values flaunted onscreen to the interactive features written into its ongoing mystery, taking full advantage of Disney's assets to sell itself to the audience, and amply repaying investment via lucrative advertising deals and high DVD sales.

The role played by the Internet in *Lost*'s marketing, and the relationship it has had with its audience, has earned considerable critical interest. Henry Jenkins modified his appraisal of fan activities from the "participatory culture" claimed in the early 1990s (perceiving fans as a beleaguered faction of the audience fighting corporate claims of ownership) to the "convergence culture" he views as the situation today, and uses *Lost* (and its interactions with fans) to illustrate. Whether the series was as "democratic" as he asserts (in encouraging viewers to research sites, find hidden clues, and exchange ideas), or simply a canny marketing ploy designed to augment interest, increase revenue, and modify material to improve its "hit ratio," is a question that demands some consideration. The series clearly made the most of teasing the audience, with narrative hooks designed to keep us watching and an arc that became increasingly abstract. Ironically, for a network that was responsible for *Twin Peaks*—and demanded that its central mystery be revealed in its second season—ABC favored the opposite strategy with *Lost*, aware that its mystery kept viewers tuned in and evidently wanting to milk their hit for as long as possible. What is still more ironic, however, is the fact that the biggest hit the network had seen in years almost never happened.

The series originated when Lloyd Braun, head of ABC Television Entertainment, floated the idea of an island drama during an annual brainstorm for new projects in the Summer of 2003. Inspired by the film *Cast Away* (2000) and the mammoth success of reality television show *Survivor* (2000–), the idea snowballed when a contact at Spelling Productions recommended writer Jeffrey Lieber, who drafted a storyline (titled *Nowhere*) in which the victims of a plane crash learn survival skills on an island. With the approval of ABC president Susan Lyne, Braun opted to develop the concept and commissioned Lieber to write a pilot. Disliking the result, as well as Lieber's subsequent rewrite, Braun then contacted J.J. Abrams, a producer responsible for the established ABC hit *Alias*, sending him Lieber's script to canvas his opinion. The decision may seem curious, given the realist brief Lieber had been sent was in marked contrast to *Alias* (a spy-fi drama with an intensely convoluted plot that played with time travel, clandestine organizations, duplicitous characters, and predestination), but *Alias*' ratings of 9 million and a solid audience of younger viewers helps explain why Abrams' view was sought. It is at this point that issues of ownership become complicated with regard to *Lost*'s origins (and why so many figures share co-creator billing for the series). Although he was fired from the ensuing production, Lieber's contribution was sufficient to merit official accreditation, including key characters in his script such as "a doctor, a fugitive, a pregnant woman, a drug addicted man, a military officer, and a spoiled rich girl" (Bernstein 2007). Where it differed to the show we know is its realist approach—a factor ABC initially insisted on, yet which Braun was clearly open to persuasion about, particularly in seeking additional mileage from the concept.

Although Abrams is often credited with adding the supernatural element, it was fellow producer, Bryan Burk, who inspired him to rework the island adventure with an SF angle. Lieber's concept did not, according to Burk, have sufficient scope to make an entire series: "It was just about people stuck on an island and, from what I read, seemed very generic. You'd definitely run out of steam" (Vaz 2005, 21). A conversation with Burk about his desire to make a science fiction series caused Abrams to rethink the script he'd been handed and wonder if these ideas could be combined. He worked with *Alias* writers Jesse Alexander and Jeff Pinkner to develop the idea of a mysterious island where strange things happen, and contacted Braun with his take on the concept. The response was unmitigated enthusiasm; but since Abrams balked at having another production to helm, Braun contracted writer-producer Damon Lindelof to work alongside him. Lindelof was working on the Tim Kring drama *Crossing Jordan* (2001–7) at the time and appeared to be the ideal collaborator for Abrams, sharing a love of the same cult shows, as well as being avid *Star Wars* fans. They developed the main characters and co-wrote the pilot together; but when Abrams focused on other projects during the first season, Carlton Cuse was drafted in, sharing show-runner duties with Lindelof for the remainder of the series. Although Abrams subsequently had limited involvement in production, it is in developing *Lost*—and ensuring it made it beyond the pilot stage—that his influence is marked. It was his direction, and the crew he put together to film the pilot, that made it so arresting; and with Braun fired midway through its filming, Abrams served as the drama's most passionate defendant.

Creating a cult series with potentially broad interest was a matter of combining the right elements. Like *Survivor*, the premise focuses on a group of strangers who attempt to co-exist on an island—and are also "tested" in certain ways. The cast are mostly young, good-looking, and dressed to suit their tropical location (providing obvious mainstream appeal); yet the premise also questions the circumstances behind their situation, adding a touch of conspiracy theory as well as supernatural elements. Our protagonists arrive on their deserted island location not as knowing contestants but as the victims of an airplane crash. A series of flashbacks reveal that their lives are intricately connected, creating a mystery that elevates the series above a simple island adventure. *Lost* would re-write the rules for television drama, yet its anticipated costs—with an ensemble cast and location shooting in Hawaii—added to the risk factor. Knowing it would have to have sufficient impact to grab as many viewers as possible, Braun agreed to back the pilot to the tune of $12 million—making it the most expensive pilot in television history. His enthusiasm was clear, yet the top brass at Disney were appalled. Given that ABC ranked fourth in the ratings—behind NBC, CBS, and Fox—and had not seen a profit for 7 years, it is perhaps easy to see why then-chairman Michael Eisner saw Braun's decision to green-light the series as the equivalent of buying some magic beans. It was a belief he simply didn't share, describing *Lost*'s premise as "a crazy project that's never going to work" (Craig 2005). Braun was fired, along with Susan Lyne, while the pilot was in production, and Stephen McPherson became the new president of ABC Entertainment. The decision was made to finish the pilot, due to the level of investment already committed, but Abrams had to battle ABC's request to provide a closed ending in order to make it work as a standalone film (Vaz 30). As with *Twin Peaks* and the "European" version of the pilot, this would give the network the option of selling the pilot by itself, thereby offsetting their investment while also curtailing the possibility of any future installments. Abrams successfully argued that such closure was impossible, and thus helped to secure *Lost*'s future.

The pilot presents a dramatic opening to an intriguing series. Oceanic Flight 815 crashes en route from Sydney to L.A. on a tropical island of unknown location, and we watch as its dazed passengers struggle in the immediate aftermath. A smartly dressed man called Jack (Matthew Fox) immediately takes control, caring for wounded passengers and delegating responsibilities to others. After taking care of the injured as best he can, he enlists a young woman called Kate (Evangeline Lilly) to stitch his own wound—an act that inaugurates an intimacy between the pair that would be teased over successive seasons. As night descends, the survivors gather around camp fires on the beach, yet the disaster scenario shifts gears when a "monster" announces itself with a strange sound and the tramping of trees in the distance. The next day Jack goes in search of the cockpit section of the plane, accompanied by Kate and the furtive Charlie (Dominic Monaghan), whose wit counterpoints the tension. They find the pilot alive, but he tells them the radio went dead during the flight and that they were a thousand miles off course when the turbulence hit, limiting their chances of being found. The monstrous sounds reappear, the pilot is pulled from the cockpit, and they flee as the wreckage is shaken by a gargantuan force. The episode ends with the noise abated and the three characters looking up at the pilot's bloodied corpse hanging yards above them in the trees. Charlie asks, "Guys, how does something like this happen?" and the *Lost* logo announces the first of many cliffhangers.

An intensive advertising campaign was launched prior to the pilot's transmission, with online ads, advance cable screenings, a thousand message-in-a-bottle ads placed along the U.S. coastline, and a highly original television trailer. The cast, dressed in formal evening attire, slowly dance by the broken fuselage of a downed plane, with captions asking us to spot the "murderer," "thief," "drug addict," etc.—suggesting that assigning labels to characters might not be any easier than reducing the series' premise to a simple airplane crash. These promotional endeavors created the desired effect: the pilot netted 18.6 million viewers, and Braun's instincts were proven to be right.

The first season focuses on 14 individuals (of the 48 known to have survived at this point). Where Jack (a doctor by profession) is concerned for others and a natural leader, a man of more disheveled appearance, Sawyer (Josh Holloway), is shown to be a crook, chiefly motivated by self-interest, as well as serving as a rival for Kate's affections. She is also shown to have a shady past, and was in the process of being returned to the United States, under arrest, prior to the crash. Jack tells her that who they were before doesn't matter, but this seems far from the case, with various secrets disclosed—via flashback—as the characters reflect on their lives. We are also presented with various conflicts and rivalries. Jack not only has to watch Sawyer closely, he has a contender for leadership in the form of an enigmatic older man called John Locke (Terry O'Quinn), who frequently undermines his decisions and leads younger male characters to serve his uncertain ends, including a naïve young man called Boone (Ian Somerhalder) who incurs fatal injuries while investigating a crashed Beechcraft plane at Locke's behest. He may have worked for a box company back home, yet Locke believes he has a higher purpose on the island—and matters of faith, destiny, and questionable leadership are further articulated throughout the series. Interesting casting decisions are evident, with very different characters to those usually seen in conventional U.S. series, such as the overweight yet amiable Hurley (Jorge Garcia) who surprises us by the fact he is a multimillionaire lottery winner—and because he is so down-to-earth; an African American man, Michael (Harold Perrineau), who is not cast as the usual criminal or police officer, but as a construction expert and devoted father to son Walt (Malcolm David Kelley); a former Iraqi soldier, Sayid (Naveen Andrews), who provides technological expertise; and a Korean couple, Sun (Yunjin Kim) and Jin (Daniel Dae Kim), who offer an outsider's perspective (with subtitles signifying their estrangement from the rest of the group) as well as providing surprises of their own.

Season one allows us to get to know the characters and presents some supernatural features of the island, including the fact it has polar bears—despite its tropical climate—and is home to the mysterious "monster." Various characters experience inexplicable visions: Kate sees a horse, paralleling Sarah Palmer's vision in *Twin Peaks*; and Jack follows what appears to be his dead father into the jungle, leading him to a cave that provides shelter and a vital supply of fresh water for the survivors (as well as revealing his father's empty coffin and two skeletons—dubbed "Adam and Eve"—whose identity sets up a long-term mystery). A mystical quality to their location is further implied by the fact that Locke has acquired a miraculous ability to walk while on the island, yet it also offers less welcome gifts, including a cargo of heroin found soon after Charlie's addiction is revealed. Over the course of the season it becomes clear the survivors are not randomly assembled from a chance flight, and they are not alone. In attempting to send a radio signal, the survivors discover an existing distress call and trace it to a French woman called Danielle Rousseau (Mira Furlan), who sent the SOS 16 years previously—suggesting their efforts to contact the outside world will prove equally futile. She attests to having been part of an expedition crew that crashed after following certain coordinates (the same sequence of numbers Hurley used to win his millions and which will reappear at various points in the narrative). A virus is alluded to, and Rousseau confesses to killing her colleagues when they became infected. She also claims that her child was abducted a week after she gave birth, and warns against predators in their midst. Further intrigue is added when a fellow survivor, Ethan Rom (William Mapother), is exposed as a fraud, his name not appearing in the passenger manifest. It is inferred that he is one of the "Others"—the term used to describe other island inhabitants who have only been vaguely sensed up until this point, and revealed only by barely audible whispers. The discovery comes too late for expectant mother Claire (Emilie de Ravin), who is kidnapped by Ethan. She is eventually found, albeit with no memory of what has happened, and Ethan is shot dead by Charlie during a second attempt before we can learn anything about his group. The baby is born safely but is taken by Rousseau, hoping to make a trade with the Others for her lost child. She is persuaded to return the boy, yet these events motivate certain members of the community to work more intensively at trying to leave. Michael builds a raft, with a plan to set sail with Walt, Jin and Sawyer. The season ends with its launch, yet hope is soon dashed when a boat comes alongside them and its occupants open fire, taking Walt and leaving the other rafters at sea. A further cliffhanger is provided as the lid to a mysterious "Hatch" in the jungle is blown off—despite Hurley's misgivings when he sees it has been printed with his winning lottery numbers, convinced this is a bad omen.

Season two reveals the contents of the Hatch and introduces new characters. Michael, Jin and Sawyer make it back to land and discover other crashed passengers (from the tail section of the plane) have settled on a different part of the island. In contrast to the community under Jack's leadership, the "Tailies" have been picked on more ferociously by the Others, and their leaders, Mr. Eko (Adewale Akkinnuoye-Agbaje) and Ana Lucia (Michelle Rodriguez), employ much tougher forms of command. As they join the established camp, the paranoid Ana Lucia mistakenly shoots one of the survivors, Shannon (Maggie Grace); yet despite these inauspicious beginnings, the new group is quickly assimilated into the collective. Over a number of flashbacks the histories of various characters are tied together in improbable ways. A complicated story arc goes further into the past, serving as a novel way to take viewers off the island, extending the range of locations used and deepening our understanding of individual characters; yet their situation remains a mystery, adding intrigue for some viewers and fueling frustration in others. The discovery of an underground bunker located beneath the "Hatch" provides new clues. A training video for a project termed "the Dharma Initiative" indicates an experiment on the island—which may be ongoing. The bunker's sole occupant, a Scottish man called Desmond (Henry Ian Cusick), leaves soon after the Hatch is opened, relieved he has someone to take over his duties (inputting a series of numbers in a computer every 108 minutes to avoid an unspoken calamity— the same numbers we have come across before). The computer appears to be useless for any other function (such as alerting the world of their whereabouts), although Michael believes Walt is using it to contact him. Desmond is shown to have met Jack in the past, further tangling the storylines without telling us anything. By this point a growing sense of implausibility began to manifest itself, with too many connections made, too much time spent going over characters' pasts, and some figures abruptly removed. Ana Lucia was killed off (seemingly in response to intense online dislike, as well as possible "retribution" for killing an established character), and although Hurley acquires a touching love interest in former clinical psychologist Libby (Cynthia Watros), who knew him when he was committed to an asylum after misfortunes following his lottery win, she is also shot dead. Michael is shown to be responsible for both deaths, secretly working for the Others in a bid to get off the island. His assigned mission is to rescue a man who calls himself Henry Gale (Michael Emerson), a figure who has been held captive in the Hatch since Ana Lucia found him in the jungle. After freeing him, Michael and Walt finally leave by sail boat. The season ends with some of the survivors captured by the Others and still no idea why any of them are there.

Season three promised to provide some answers, responding to increased frustration from viewers. Henry's real name is revealed to be Ben Linus, and he is shown to be in a position of command among the Others. New characters were introduced among this group, as well as the survivors, including crook couple Nikki (Kiele Sanchez) and Paulo (Rodrigo Santoro), who were so disliked by Internet posters they were killed off mid-season by being buried alive! While these character exits suggest some responsiveness to audience criticism, the continued build-up of mysteries fueled suspicion that the writers had no clear direction and were simply piling everything into the mix. Supernatural elements increased. Desmond is revealed to have precognitive powers, Locke experiences visions of Boone, and the monster returns (after an entire season away) to kill Mr. Eko. The relationship between the survivors and Others becomes complicated as characters switch sides. Jack befriends an Other called Juliet (Elizabeth Mitchell), who tries to persuade him to kill Ben; yet he refuses. Locke's father (previously seen conning him out of a kidney and further revealed to be responsible for paralyzing his son) also appears—to test Locke's willingness to be a killer. He also refuses, and Sawyer does the deed instead, his own backstory conveniently providing necessary motivation. A mysterious figure called Jacob is revealed as the leader of the Others, but he remains unseen, using Ben to do his bidding. A woman called Naomi (Marsha Thomason) parachutes in from the outside world, hired by Desmond's former girlfriend, Penny (Sonya Walger), and the survivors learn that a freighter is anchored 80 miles offshore. The possibility of escape is compromised by Locke's conviction that the freighter is a threat. Charlie dies trying to find out, and attempts to warn Locke's group as he dies that the boat poses danger. The most interesting backstory revelation is Ben's prior affiliation with the Dharma project. Underlining a father/son subtext that was growing increasingly evident, Ben is revealed to have been a member of this group; but he became embittered, killing his father (and other members of the Initiative) in 1992 in a massacre dubbed "the Purge." As a consequence of the toxin used, the island's birthrate is destroyed, which explains why children have been abducted by the Others. The season ends with the survivors intensely divided in their assessment of the freighter and its implications.

Season four was hit by the Writers Guild strike and restricted to 14 episodes, yet it responded to criticisms by shaking up the formula. The plot gains momentum by finally focusing on characters leaving the island. Jack and his party try to contact the freighter, while Locke and his allies join forces with Ben to prevent this. A number of new characters arrive by helicopter, including the pilot Frank (Jeff Fahey), who should have been on their doomed flight; Charlotte (Rebecca Mader), an anthropologist; Daniel Faraday (Jeremy Davies), a physicist who is aware of the island's special properties; and Miles (Ken Leung), a "ghost whisperer." They reveal that they have been hired to find the island by Charles Widmore (Alan Dale), a wealthy businessman formerly seen in Desmond's backstory as the disapproving father of his girlfriend, Penny, and who sent him to the island years earlier via sailboat. Jack's deceased father, Christian Shephard (John Terry), also makes a reappearance, leading Claire to a mysterious cabin. A sense of cosmic retribution becomes evident when we learn that Michael managed to get back to civilization after his deal with the Others, yet became estranged from Walt after admitting what he did to secure their freedom. After repeated suicide attempts fail, he returns to the island via the freighter and dies in an explosion. A strike team attacks Ben's HQ, and Locke seeks advice from a figure believed to be Jacob, leading to the biggest leap imaginable (even in such a far-fetched narrative) when Ben turns a giant wheel to move the island and is thrust into the future. Six survivors are rescued by helicopter and make it back to the outside world: Sayid, Hurley, Sun, Kate, Jack, and Claire's baby, Aaron, who Kate pretends is hers. They are dubbed "the Oceanic 6" by the press, and agree to cover up the island's existence (to protect fellow survivors from Widmore). We realize they have also jumped forward three years; yet far from offering escape, the writers appear intent on punishing them. Sayid marries his childhood love Nadia (Andrea Gabriel), but her murder leads him to work for Ben as an assassin, killing a number of Widmore's people. Hurley becomes convinced the curse of "the numbers" is back, gets involved in a car chase with the police, and is readmitted to the mental hospital he was in before the crash. Sun is consumed by grief for Jin (who she believes is dead), gives birth to their daughter and takes over her father's business (Paik Heavy Industries), becoming involved with Widmore. Kate is tried for her past crimes but saved from a jail term after Jack testifies on her behalf. She is ordered to remain in California for ten years, and continues to pretend Aaron is her son. Jack returns to working as a surgeon, becomes romantically involved with Kate, and finally holds a funeral for his father (despite Christian's body having disappeared on the island). However, when Claire's mother attends the service he is devastated to learn that Claire was his half-sister and guiltily distances himself from Kate and his secret nephew. After continued visions of his father, Jack becomes an alcoholic; and when Locke (now going by the name of Jeremy Bentham) somehow makes it off the island, tells Jack what a terrible state he left it in, and seemingly commits suicide, Jack adds drug abuse to his problems. Ben convinces him they must all return to the island, with Locke's body, to put things right.

In showing characters managing to get off the island, the writers debunked certain theories circulated by fans (including the possibility the island is a giant spaceship—or a figment of one character's imagination) while additionally dissuading viewers from thinking about the characters' eventual escape. However, far from enabling the Oceanic 6 to rebuild their lives after leaving the island, events initiate their ineluctable return. As with *The Prisoner* (and the number of escapees is an obvious allusion), the outside world offers no real solace—and little difference to the one that held them captive. Improbable coincidences occur, fate continues to intervene in their lives, and the past will not let them be, with the suggestion that they were never truly lost on the island but found themselves there instead. Some critics asserted, early in the show, that "the irony of *Lost* is that as the survivors' probability of being rescued decreases each day, their likelihood of finding themselves, and starting a new life, increases" (Porter and Lavery 2006, 47). Season four affirms that "a new life" cannot be found elsewhere; and while the Oceanic 6 receive financial settlements from the airline, they fail to prosper in the real world. Kate appears to be the sole exception. Acquitted for past crimes, and seeming happy acting as a mother to Aaron, a decade in sunny California hardly looks like a sentence, and she even secures a proposal from Jack. However, Kate is compromised by a promise to Sawyer (whispered to her in season three's finale), and her relationship with Jack deteriorates when he learns about his kinship to Claire. The escapees all remain prisoners of the past, burdened with guilt and grief, losing their sense of self. After her husband's apparent death back on the island, Sun affiliates herself with an unscrupulous organization. Sayid loses the love of his life and becomes coldly exploited by Ben. Hurley has another breakdown; and as visits from dead people are misconstrued as madness, he seems unable to escape the label placed on him. Most frustratingly, the character who proved to be such a capable and caring hero succumbs to despair after learning about his half-sister. Jack began the series burdened with remorse about his father and ends the fourth season still haunted by him. Flashbacks reveal Christian Shephard to be another poor father figure, like many in the series. It is suggested that he had an affair with his son's wife, and even tried to blame Jack for a patient's death caused by his own negligence. Jack helped convict him of professional misconduct after realizing that he operated while under the influence of alcohol—leading to his father being struck off, drinking heavily, and dying of a heart attack in Australia before they could resolve their differences. His inability to bury his father seems increasingly significant, creating the impression that Christian has been revived by the island to enable Jack to confront issues with his father in order to lay him to rest. In fact, all the Oceanic 6 seem to have unfinished business there, even if few are willing to return.

Season five alternates between on-island and off-island events, as well as various points in time. We learn of the difficulties facing those who remained on the island after it moved, with many killed in an attack, and the island subsequently skips through various periods, prompting Locke to go down a well! He encounters "Christian" there, who tells him he should have moved the island previously, and not Ben, and that he will have to die to return again. Locke turns another wheel and is transported off-island to the same time as the Oceanic 6. Widmore finances him to find his fellow survivors and elicit their return to the island, but after repeated failures and discovering that his former girlfriend is dead, Locke becomes suicidal. Ben prevents him from hanging himself—only to inexplicably strangle him and make it look like suicide. Jack is led to Daniel Faraday's mother, Eloise Hawking (Fionnula Flanagan), who has a contraption that pinpoints the island's whereabouts, and calculates a specific flight to Guam (Ajira Flight 316) as their way back. Jack echoes the feelings of many viewers by this point in stating how ridiculous the idea is, but is told to make a leap of faith. Showing the extent to which he has become a follower, he even complies with the directive to take something of his father's with him on the flight, putting a pair of his father's shoes on Locke's corpse. Despite their stated reluctance, the other escapees all find their way onto the same flight (flown by Frank), which duly crashes, and subsequently become separated in time after landing on two different islands. Those on "our" island have gone back thirty years. Flashbacks reveal that after Locke's wheel-turn, the time-skipping stopped in 1974, during which Sawyer, Miles and Juliet were recruited into the Dharma Initiative and subsequently joined by Jin after a group of French explorers find him at sea (one of whom is revealed to be a young Danielle Rousseau). Hurley, Jack, and Kate arrive three years later and pretend to be new Dharma recruits—realizing how suspicious the group is of potential infiltrators. Sayid is found separately, accused of being a "hostile," and threatened with execution. While his fellow survivors do little to help, a young Ben Linus (Sterling Beaumon) secures Sayid's escape—only to be shot by him in return when Sayid realizes who he is. However, Sayid fails to kill Ben, implying that they are trapped in a time-loop and unable to alter their apparent destiny. Daniel Faraday repeatedly asserts that established events cannot be changed, yet becomes convinced, by the season finale, that the opposite is true, trumping wheel-turning as a ludicrous plot device by asserting that the detonation of a hydrogen bomb will negate a dangerous build-up of electro-magnetic energy—and the circumstances leading to their first flight crashing will never have occurred. Daniel is unwittingly killed by his own mother (who is pregnant with him at the time), yet Jack becomes intent on fulfilling his plan. He explains his motives to Sawyer as heartbreak over losing Kate's love (seeming happier with the knowledge she will be on her way to jail if the last three years are obliterated). The fact the other survivors are willing to support him (including Kate) is equally bizarre, repudiating the idea that the island is where they have each "found" themselves, and seemingly jettisoning any sense of continuity or credibility for the season to end with a bang—literally. The last scene ends as the bomb detonates, followed by an unprecedented fade to white, and no idea whether they will all be killed, back on their original flight, or any number of possibilities.

By this point little incentive is given to view proceedings logically. Although a vast conspiracy was suggested in attempting to explain why a specific group of individuals have been brought together on the island, this ultimately evades rational explanation. The mysterious Hanso Foundation may have financed the Dharma experiment, but they have nothing to do with our survivors; and although Charles Widmore is clearly very wealthy, the ability to ensure all the "right" passengers were on the same flight in 2004 suggests a greater power at work. Providing a fantastical answer to this question, the fifth season finale includes a startling revelation. We are finally given a face for the mysterious Jacob (Mark Pellegrino) and learn, through a variety of flashbacks, that he hand-picked each of the survivors to join him on the island.

The pre-credit sequence shows him at odds with another figure, billed as "Man #2" (Titus Welliver), who declares how much he wishes to kill him if only he could find a "loophole." They appear to be engaged in an eternal conflict, with their respective black and white shirts implying that they represent good and evil, and their few lines of conversation suggest that Jacob has routinely invited people to the island to prove his rival wrong about humanity. A number of fans dubbed this figure "Esau"—Jacob's biblical brother—and he espouses profound cynicism about human nature, declaring that each visit always ends the same way, with fighting, corruption and destruction. He is revealed to be capable of shape-shifting, adopting Locke's image, and eventually secures the desired "loophole" by influencing Ben to kill Jacob. A turn to the mystical is thus shown via godlike adversaries, with long-term island resident Richard Alpert (Nestor Carbonell) claiming Jacob made him immortal, and the reborn "Locke" fueling further mystery about what these figures are capable of. Like the aftermath of the bomb, these revelations were designed to keep viewers enthralled and intensify speculation. Does the fade to white indicate death or a new epoch? And what was implied by Jacob's final words: "They are coming"?

With only 17 episodes to answer a host of questions, the final season had a lot to live up to. Carlton Cuse promised:

> The end of the show will be a combination of trying to answer mysteries the audience still cares about, such as the statue and the Smoke Monster. We'll also be answering the skeletons in the cave question. We will answer the questions we feel are important and central to the plot. At the same time we will be trying to tell redemption stories about the characters. These characters do indeed have a destiny [Cuse 2009].

The statement refers to mysteries speculated on from the beginning, including the skeletons found in season one (which many believed were the remains of crash survivors, generally thought to be Rose [L. Scott Caldwell] and Bernard [Sam Anderson]), and the Smoke Monster (which had been rarely seen yet was frequently discussed). Having taken so long to reach a conclusion, *Lost*'s makers had an unenviable task in providing a satisfying and coherent end. By introducing a cosmic conflict between godlike beings, Lindelof and Cuse provided a fantastic framing device in which anything was possible, yet their biggest challenge was in making the series seem more than a monumental tease. Having taken fans on an increasingly circuitous route, they needed to ensure that the journey felt worthwhile.

The sixth and final season opens with Jack gazing out of the window onboard Oceanic Flight 815, which only experiences turbulence after hitting an air pocket, suggesting that Faraday's idea worked and negated the original crash. However, we are also shown events back on the island, after the explosion, with the characters standing around the scene, indicating two timelines. The alternate universe/"flash sideways" begins on the plane and charts what happens to each character after reaching L.A., noting some interesting changes. On arrival, Jack learns that his father's coffin is missing, goes home to deal with his father's estate, and confronts problems with an emotionally estranged son (a figure never mentioned before). Kate manages to evade custody and hijacks a cab—only to find a pregnant Claire in the back, on her way to give her baby up for adoption. Instead, events conspire to have Claire meet her half-brother and his family after being mentioned in Christian's will, priming the wary viewer to reel at the coincidences emerging. In a similar vein, Sayid visits Nadia (now married to his brother) and gets caught up in a gangster scenario that also involves Jin and Sun. Jack's hospital provides a key meeting place for several characters, and a school finds Locke (in a wheelchair once more) and Ben working together as teachers, both of whom now have very different relationships with their fathers than previously seen. Hurley is no longer subject to a "curse" due to his lottery win and becomes a rich philanthropist. He even meets Libby, now a mental patient, who convinces him they have met before. Desmond works for Widmore, with no mention of Penny, and is seemingly content with his career until he encounters Charlie and starts remembering another life. These are engaging departures from what we have seen before, exploring the flip-side to many characters (including Sawyer now working as a cop), and the reappearance of figures we have previously seen die adds to the appeal. Back on the island, however, the usual series of improbable events occur. Hurley sees a vision of Jacob, who directs the "lostees" to a temple to get help for the wounded Sayid—only for him to be killed by its residents and mysteriously resurrected. Claire is discovered in a near feral state, driven mad by the loss of her child, much like Rousseau, and in thrall to the entity now masquerading as "Locke," who reveals his true form as the Smoke Monster. Fan speculation that he is Jacob's twin brother is proven to be correct (although he remains unnamed), with the mythology episode "Across the Sea" revealing their origins and illustrating how Jacob made his brother into a monster, as well as disclosing the identities of "Adam and Eve." The episode establishes the cause of their conflict, yet undermines efforts to demonize "Locke" (aka Esau/Flocke/Man in Black) and cast Jacob as a figure of virtue, with the "bad twin" a great deal more sympathetic in many ways. To fuel further intrigue, we are shown structures such as a lighthouse with a compass and numbers that correspond to the survivors' names, as well as a cave with numerous names crossed out on the ceiling. After a rigged submarine kills Sayid, Jin and Sun, only a handful of survivors remain. They eventually meet with Jacob and learn that they are all candidates to be caretakers of the island, chosen because they were each unhappy with their former lives. Jack elects to replace Jacob—yet works alongside his brother (bafflingly), lowering Desmond into a sacred spring, where a magical light serves as the source of the island's powers. Desmond is instructed to remove a magical plug, the apparent aim being for "Locke" to destroy the island that has held him captive for eons, but an unforeseen consequence is the removal of his powers also. Jack has a showdown with his nemesis in a cliff-top fight in which he is mortally wounded. Kate arrives in the nick of time to help kill "Locke" and manages to leave with Sawyer, Frank, Ben and Claire on the Ajira plane, leaving Jack endeavoring to protect the island by replacing the magic plug. Aware he is dying, he confers his custodian powers to Hurley before performing this final heroic act, despite Desmond being uniquely equipped to survive this. Over in the alternate universe, events moved toward an ending that had been speculated on for years. The characters' lives begin to coalesce, each recalling flashes of their past on the island, and eventually making their way first to a concert and finally a chapel. Jack discovers his father's empty coffin inside and learns that not only is he himself dead, but a number of his fellow islanders are gathered in the building, having also passed away. His dead father appears and handily explains that while they all died at different times (disputing the popular fan theory that they died in the initial crash), they created this place in order to "move on" together, their time on the island being the most significant part of their lives, and Christian finally opens the church door to bathe them all in light. Interspersed with this big reveal are scenes of a wounded Jack, back on the island, who makes his way out of the pool, lies down in a familiar looking bamboo grove, watches the plane fly overhead, and closes his eyes—an almost exact reversal of the pilot's opening scene.

Lost's creators warned, in advance, that the conclusion might be inconclusive, with Lindelof asserting, "I don't think it would be *Lost* if there wasn't an ongoing and active debate," and admitting that some might view it as "the worst finale in the history of TV" (Lindelof 2010). Opinion was divided between those who felt suitably warm and fuzzy at seeing everyone reunited in the great beyond and those who expected to have a great deal more answered. Disappointment was exacerbated by the fact that Lindelof and Cuse had proven to be somewhat dishonest, repeatedly misdirecting fans who had guessed, virtually from day one, that the island was some kind of purgatory or limbo. The alternate universe, in which the plane makes it to L.A. and everyone's lives seem happier than they had been, ultimately substitutes for this idea—a place the characters go to after their deaths to wait for one another—yet this seems clumsily contrived to side-step the fact that their big twist was anticipated from the start. Christian Shephard—whose name now serves as a corny indication of his true purpose—tells Jack all the events on the island were real, in a line seemingly intended to assuage viewer frustration, yet such assurances failed to dissuade a significant number of viewers from feeling they had wasted their time following events that don't really matter. Lindelof has suggested there will be an immediate reaction to the series and a "legacy reaction," one that will come "six months, a year down the road, looking at the show as a whole" (Hibberd 2010), and ultimately this will be the measure of its true cult status—whether it is capable of sustaining enduring interest, even after its ending has been revealed. The planned release of new DVDs with extra scenes suggests an intention to continue milking the series for as long as possible; yet while some may be motivated to watch the series again, with the benefit of hindsight, whether this would be a rewarding experience is far from certain. After all, despite two seasons' notice, and the fact its creators told fans countless times they knew how it would conclude, there was a rushed feeling to *Lost*'s ending. Trading a great deal on nostalgia and sentiment, the conclusion seemed to affirm long-held suspicions that the writers really had been making it up as they went. The mixed reaction to *Lost*'s finale suggests an interesting division of priorities. Those who loved it tended to assert that its emotional impact was more important than providing answers to the show's mysteries. For detractors, the show's main puzzle — what they were all doing on the island — was the bait that had lured them into *Lost*'s world, and no amount of sentiment could substitute for a denouement that left the island as enigmatic as it began. Right up to the end, Lindelof and Cuse appear to have played a canny game with viewers, knowing that it is by keeping things vague that they will keep people talking about their show, and refusing to elaborate on the finale in order to retain its mystique.

Although *Lost*'s ultimate legacy is still to be decided, the scale of its appeal has secured its place in broadcasting history. From its opening pilot, imaginations were fired, and *Lost* became part of everyday discussion — in the same manner as other cult series — earning critical admiration and winning a number of awards, as well as becoming a quintessential example of "blockbuster TV." The reasons are apparent enough, with a format that provides escapism via an attractive cast in an exotic location; drama as the detailed histories of each character and their relationships with one another unfolds; mystery in terms of their whereabouts; and certain SF and quasi-mystical features as the crash that caused them to be stranded together is implied to be more than an accident, just as their prior connections, laboriously detailed over successive seasons, are shown to be far from coincidental. The look of the series, the strength of its performances, and its unusual combination of features would make *Lost* compelling viewing, yet its lack of resolution would prove to be a poisoned chalice. As time went on, and the plot seemed to be unduly attenuated, admiration lead to intense frustration from fans. Accused of layering one enigma on top of another to compensate for a lack of narrative direction, it only appeared to find its way again after the end-date was confirmed, the action took us off-island, and we finally began investigating the island's past. For many viewers this was all somewhat belated, particularly as the crucial question — what the survivors are doing on the island — remained unanswered. Waning interest was confirmed by a drop in ratings, yet the show was still a big hit, in relative terms, when ABC agreed to end it, making this an unprecedented move. While Fox seemed reluctant to ever call time on *The X-Files* — largely because Carter doggedly persisted with the show — ABC was faced with show-runners who, having spent years building up *Lost*'s enigmas, leading audiences down various false routes and bluffing a good deal, were reluctant to spin it out any further, partly prompted by audience response to the show. While *Lost* intrigued viewers, it also tested their patience. Delaying the survivors' rescue was perhaps understandable, yet by the end of the second season the story didn't seem to be going anywhere either. Message boards were filled with commentators attesting to feeling hoodwinked by a series that failed to yield any concrete explanations and seemed set to go on indefinitely. Its makers responded by affirming they had an ending planned, and let ABC know they wanted to start winding the series up. Seeking to protect their reputations, as much as their product, Lindelof and Cuse used the Television Critics Association tour in January 2007 to let the network know how they felt. Lindelof told reporters, "The underlying anxiety is that this is not going to end well [if they don't pick a finale date]. None of us wants to be on a stalling show." Cuse added, "We look at *The X-Files* as a bit of a cautionary tale. That was a great show that probably ran two seasons too long. *Lost* has a much shorter shelf life" (Rice 2007). As a result of this public expression of their qualms, ABC agreed to set an end-date; but they divided the show's final episodes into two short seasons (much as they split seasonal box-sets in half), crassly aiming to make the most of their hit. They were also keen to retain their producers' services, aware their contracts were due to expire, and doubtless influenced by the fact that J.J. Abrams had signed a deal with Warner Brothers the previous year. While the network technically owned *Lost*, Lindelof and Cuse had proven integral to it, sharing show-runner duties, writing the majority of episodes, and contributing to regular podcasts, all of which enhanced their negotiating position. ABC Entertainment chief Stephen McPherson may have claimed the decision to end the series was motivated by a desire "to give the audience the payoff they deserve," but fellow executive Mark Pedowitz cites a less selfless motive in wanting "to make sure we had the team responsible for its success in place for not only the run of the show, but so that each of their future series creations have a home at the studio after *Lost*" (Adalian 2007). As Lindelof has affirmed, the network could have continued the show without them, yet they recognized its worth was implicitly tied to its creative team—and ultimately determined by its fans (Goldman 2009). Although many cult series are prematurely canceled, leaving fans battling with broadcasters to secure some closure, *Lost*'s audience helped advance its end through continued criticism. Does this indicate a greater level of power on their part? Or did ABC decide their golden goose would no longer be forced to lay any more eggs to ensure a higher yield over the last few seasons of its run? Announcing an end-date was clearly a calculated risk, knowing interest was likely to intensify as a result, and was therefore consistent with the game-plan adopted from the start: motivate interest by whatever means necessary.

The show's relationship with its audience played an integral role in its success, and while some felt manipulated by its ongoing mysteries, others delighted in *Lost*'s fragmented narrative and ability to prompt continued speculation. As we have seen, a cult text invites a particular form of engagement, and piecing "clues" together provides a fundamental pleasure. Whether it is identifying why a secret agent resigned or tracing a homecoming queen's killer via increasingly surreal clues, viewers are asked to pay close attention to detail in order to solve a given mystery. Shows like *The Prisoner* and *Twin Peaks* may lead us along a wayward path, confounding closure, but they yield greater long-term interest and deeper philosophizing because of their enigmatic qualities. *Lost* clearly aimed to emulate such forerunners by asking viewers to do some investigative work, yet it involved the audience on a wider level. In its first week of airing, a Flash game (I-am-lost.com) appeared online, providing further information about each character; and an official website, The Fuselage, was set up to enable fans to ask questions of its creators (devised by former *Buffy* writer David Fury and modeled after the official *Buffy* website, The Bronze). *Lost*'s producers regularly responded to fan theories on this site, yet also mislead fans by refuting ideas that later proved accurate. Like the insertion of numerous meaningless "clues" in the show (i.e. the Dharma logo on the shark), this was generally viewed as part of the "game" by fans, many of whom were led to explore a variety of media in their quest for answers, finding extra clues in jigsaws, games and interview statements, revealing the extent to which the show tapped into fannish pursuits.

Intriguing strategies were used to promote the series. "Alternative reality" game The Lost Experience was first launched in 2006, between the second and third seasons, and described by ABC as "midway between content and marketing." The "game" was played on three continents (USA, the U.K., and Australia) using websites, voice-mail, television and newspaper ads to extend the fictional world of the series. A novel was published, entitled *Bad Twin*, supposedly written by a passenger from Oceanic 815, and quarter-page ads were placed in newspapers by the Hanso Foundation, seeking to discredit the book's references to their organization. The fact that the author's name is Gary Troup—an anagram of "purgatory"—alludes to a popular fan theory about the show (that the survivors are all dead and thus compelled to go over past misdeeds), suggesting either a joke at their expense or a possible corroboration. Such tactics revolutionize traditional advertising methods, blurring the distinction between fact and fiction. The Hanso Foundation website contained Easter eggs offering further information about the organization; Apollo chocolate bars (which feature in the series) were sold from select outlets—with additional clues printed on their wrappers; and the soft drink manufacturer Sprite paid for a number of television and Internet ads, citing the company as a "sponsor" of the Hanso Foundation, cleverly aiming to profit by association. A new phase of the Experience began in 2008 with the launch of the website The Dharma Initiative. The homepage featured a statement by fictional founder

Alvar Hanso. Alluding to regrettable developments by former colleague Thomas Werner Mittelwerk, and his own recent imprisonment, Hanso sounds sinisterly cult-like in welcoming "a second chance to build a future that can support, enrich, and cradle us all in peace and joy." The site's appeal, like the ads and candy bars, lies in making the fictional world more authentic, updating the likes of *Twin Peaks: Access Guide to the Town* via the worldwide web. Click a tab labeled "research" and you discover the Initiative's objectives on the island, with interests that include "meteorology, psychology, parapsychology, zoology, electromagnetism, sonic weapons, telekinesis and remote viewing." The "jobs" tab includes postings for laboratory assistants and researchers (and invites applicants to leave their e-mail address); while the "merchandise" section offers the opportunity to buy a 100 percent cotton Fruit of the Loom t-shirt printed with the Dharma logo. Like *Prisoner* fans who opt to wear a Village badge (outside of conventions), such attire not only signals appreciation of the show, but makes the wearer a willing "recruit" within its fictional world—with attendant ironies of its own.

These extra-textual directions are, in some ways, more interesting than the series, particularly in attracting "maverick" responses. The "gaming" may fall short of any creative input (in being designed to be followed rather than contributed to), yet some fans posted fake additions to the Experience—including initiation videos and maps falsely detailing the location of other Hatches on the island—beating *Lost*'s marketing team at their own game. While these contributions frustrate the attempt to make sense of the official mythology, they might also be applauded as an attempt to "deprogram" the easily duped segments of the *Lost* fan base. Unsolicited additions are an obvious temptation, particularly when authorized versions appear to make elaborate jokes at the fans' expense, or are simply a let-down. The official meaning of "the numbers," for example, a puzzle set up from the first season, indicates that when "canonical" answers were eventually forthcoming, they did not necessarily make much sense. For those who had speculated on the meaning of the numbers that reappear throughout the series (4, 8, 15, 16, 23, 42)—including suggestions they were coordinates, a mathematical puzzle, or held Gnostic significance—the official explanation is a long-awaited disappointment. The Lost Experience describes the numbers as representing the Valenzetti Equation (which was claimed on Amazon to be the subject of the first book written by fictional author Gary Troup). Each number symbolizes a potential means for humanity to destroy itself—either by global warming, chemical warfare, overpopulation, or other likely methods—and the equation is designed to calculate our eventual doomsday (and allegedly delay it). Audiences are given a pseudo-scientific piece of nonsense, in other words, as the reason for the code. An electromagnetic anomaly, housed directly beneath the Hatch, is said to require release every 108 minutes (the sum of the "equation") to avoid a catastrophic buildup—and the cause of Oceanic 815's crash is cited as a direct consequence of failing to comply with this rule. The explanation is what television writers refer to as "phlebotinin"—techno-babble designed to explain away a plot point—and is so "out there" it not only defies logic but severely undermines the level of attention certain viewers had given the show. In fact, as the series advanced, and we were given increasingly outlandish information about the island's possibilities, *Lost* abandoned any rational attempt to explain events by substituting mystical hokum for "pseudo-science"—confirming it was never really a show about airplane survivors, but one that had entered another realm entirely.

A notable sector of the audience anticipated such developments early on, and it is interesting to note how the show's makers altered their reactions to popular explanations for *Lost*'s mysteries, shifting from outright denial about fantastical leanings to tacit incorporation. For example, off-island action in season four may have been designed to refute "fake world" theories (i.e. suggestions that events are taking place on a vast spaceship), yet even if the real world is shown to exist, the island refutes rational explanation and may as well be presided over by aliens when it comes to figures like Jacob and his brother. Another intriguing idea, promoted by fans, was that the island is the setting for a covert reality television show (with the survivors serving as an unwitting cast). Although this was also officially dismissed, Jacob's selection of survivors on the island—and the fact he and his adversary manipulate their "cast"—adds a new dimension to the concept. Many fan theories were thus worked into the show in some way, despite ostensible rejection, including time travel (which was decisively ruled out by its producers, only to feature heavily in the narrative). The persistence of debunked theories marks an admirable unwillingness (like the fake contributions made to *Lost*'s mythology) to simply be followers, yet official dismissal suggests marked unease about fan speculations, particularly in anticipating future plot points, exposing continuity flaws, or challenging the creators' claims. This reveals an interesting stress point in the relationship between *Lost*'s producers and the fan community, encouraging involvement while seeking to retain creative ownership—a dilemma that became particularly evident when fans realized, virtually from the outset, what the show's big mystery was. Speculation that the survivors are experiencing a form of purgatory was persistently voiced by fans—and officially refuted countless times—but the anagram reference in The Lost Experience, and prevalent themes of guilt and redemption, suggested otherwise. In the end, this theory was largely corroborated. Christian Shephard tells Jack that he and his fellow survivors are in the equivalent of a limbo—a place without time where their souls have waited so they can "move on" together; yet he additionally asserts that the island itself—and the events that took place there—were real, implying that fans were close in their guesswork but not quite right. The fact that this information is delivered by a less-than-trustworthy figure does little to substantiate it, even if Christian now appears to be the kindliest of patriarchs; and the ending left many fans feeling unduly deceived. Given a tendency toward duplicity from *Lost*'s creators since the series began, viewers should have perhaps grown accustomed to feeling hoodwinked, with Lindelof and Cuse regularly seeking to disprove certain assumptions, either because they pre-empted future developments or because they affirmed a generic identity the network initially wished to conceal. In doing so, they increasingly contradicted themselves, particularly in making realist claims that failed to correspond with the show.

The reluctance to reveal the series as a work of telefantasy derived from corporate concerns at ABC, with Braun's successors aiming to downplay this angle and *Lost*'s show-runners conspiring in the ruse. Early in season one, for example, in response to the "alien abduction" theory, Lindelof told the Sci-Fi Channel, "I don't think we've shown anything on the show yet ... that has no explanation in the real world we all function within," adding, "There are no spaceships. There isn't any time travel" (Wilkes 2005). This is a baffling statement, as any realist intent is immediately undermined by the vast monster introduced in the pilot, characters with special powers, and an island that can move in space and time. If the aim was to affirm *Lost* as a plausible drama, it was clearly misleading to anyone watching. David Fury, who worked on *Lost* in its first season (along with other Whedon alumni), cited ABC's reluctance to disclose its fantastical leanings in explaining the many holes in *Lost*'s plot, stating, "Those answers were resting in the field of sci-fi and that's where we had to draw the line" (Porter and Lavery, 20). Lindelof's statement about "real world" constraints may attempt to uphold this "line," but it didn't fool many fans; and although Fury denies characterizing the series as "a sci-fi show in the closet coming out," a degree of repression was clearly in evidence. It took four seasons before *Lost* eventually "came out," with Lindelof stating, prior to the penultimate season, that the series had always been a "time travel show," arguing, "We're just making it more apparent in the storytelling now. You'll realize that time travel has been in the DNA of the show for quite some time—but we think the audience is now prepared to go on that journey with us" (Tanswell 2009). In fact, fan speculations indicated a readiness to suspend disbelief from the start, determinedly subscribing to fantastical theories, whatever Lindelof and Cuse maintained. Denying its true identity may have arisen out of a desire to avoid spoilers and potentially harness a wider audience, but as events departed from "the real world we all function within," there were serious consequences in how we should define *Lost* and what we could reasonably expect from it.

From the outset, *Lost* aimed to combine mass appeal with cult interest. Seemingly to avoid limiting prospective viewers, its telefantasy leanings were only tentatively suggested and its premise sold as an escapist drama in which an attractive ensemble cast attempt to survive on a desert island. However, another strand of interest was also provided. The incongruous presence of a polar bear and monster affirm that this is no ordinary island, which is further hinted at by the visions experienced by characters, and the "gifts" they receive, recalling shows such as *Fantasy Island* (where dreams come true for guests) as well as a classic episode of *Star Trek* ("Shore Leave") in which a planet conjures up whatever inhabitants are thinking. These features remained fairly covert, with greater interest in detailing the backstories of each character (taking us to familiar scenarios in a host of locations), yet contrasting elements resulted in confused cues. The discovery of the Hatch and the existence of the Dharma Initiative intimated a conspiracy at work, recruiting new "participants" to the island, yet how (and, more particularly, why) our survivors have been brought together remained uncertain. Improbable connections between passengers, and mystical features on the island, undermined any rational explanation, and with a vast corporate plot proving implausible, the show finally veered toward the patently fantastical, with Jacob serving as a figurative stand-in for Fate, bringing survivors to the island on a mystical recruitment drive to find a new protector. A new explanation was also given for the numbers, corresponding with the names of specific survivors, underlining the destiny motif yet appearing somewhat contrived and ridiculous.

Although mystery is integral to a mythology show, this comes with attendant risks, as *Twin Peaks* notoriously proved. Just as viewers wanted to establish Laura's killer, irrespective of the show's various subplots, *Lost*'s continued efforts at circumlocution merely increased demands to get to the point: what the survivors are doing there in the first place. This eventually yielded an answer that failed to dramatically satisfy. In many ways *Lost* repeats the same experiment as *Twin Peaks* by testing the limits of serialized drama, including a range of characters, incorporating a number of generic themes, and aiming to prolong its mystery for as long as possible. Indicating key changes in industrial attitudes over the last two decades, ABC exhibited much greater tolerance towards *Lost* than was afforded to *Twin Peaks*, encouraging the withholding of information where they had previously demanded answers. The success of ongoing mysteries in series such as *Alias* no doubt helped to persuade them that *Lost* could profitably be built up as a slow-burner, and high ratings evidently eased any doubts about alienating viewers, allowing the show's makers to chart their own narrative course. However, despite a more favorable climate for experimentation, *Lost* repeats the same mistake as *Twin Peaks* in combining elements that create impossible inconsistencies. If *Twin Peaks*' mix of murder mystery and surreal soap opera were fundamentally incompatible—with the killer question preventing many from enjoying its other features—*Lost*'s combination of escapist adventure, conspiracy thriller, poorly explained SF, and mystical fantasy are even more at odds with one another. Like its predecessor, many supernatural elements appear motivated simply to fuel intrigue (emulating the second season of *Twin Peaks* in embracing gratuitous weirdness), playing numerous games with its audience while simultaneously asking to be taken seriously.

A key metaphysical concern in *Lost* asks if humanity can transcend its limitations. The Dharma project was seemingly motivated by this desire, yet any progressive intent is undermined by their regimented social order and questionable ethics, problems shared by the Others also. Although Jack's group set a more positive example, they are also prey to conflict and corruption, affirming the same ambivalence represented by *Twin Peaks*' Black and White Lodges, and striving for similar symbolism. Significantly, the Dharma logo, like that of the Hanso Foundation, is a variant of the yin-yang symbol, underscoring the duality of human nature (a theme in all the shows assessed). By examining our flawed natures and contrasting dispositions, *Lost* questions if we are capable of change, reworking longstanding literary and philosophical concerns in an attempt to distinguish itself as a quality cult series. In examples ranging from Jules Verne's *Mysterious Island* (1874) and H.G. Wells' *Island of Dr. Moreau* (1896) to more recent variants such as Aldous Huxley's *The Island* (1962) and Alex Garland's *The Beach* (1996), attempts to build a better world usually end in catastrophe, with humanity proving to be essentially flawed. *The Beach* provides a caustic examination of a community based on a remote island in South East Asia (close to where *Lost*'s island is initially located), and shows how far people can fall from their ideals. An attempt to lead an "alternative" lifestyle proves just as oppressive, dogmatic and dangerous as anything the world outside has to offer. Far from enabling a democracy to flourish, a murderous dictatorship ensues to "protect" the island community, emulating the very tendencies they wished to transcend. The book has acquired a reputation it scarcely deserves, basically updating William Golding's *Lord of the Flies* (1954) for gap-year travelers, yet it appears to be an "ancestor text" for *Lost* (to adopt Lavery's term) in many respects. *Lord of the Flies* offers another apparent influence. A powerful allegory of human nature, using children stranded on an island to stress the primitive within us all, it offers a number of parallels with *Lost*, including the contest for leadership and divergent responses to their predicament. A "monster" in their midst propels fear and superstition, and the boys devise a primitive religion to protect them from the unseen menace surrounding them, finally proving how fragile civilization is when the majority opt to become savages and set upon weaker members of the group. *Lost* presents a similar scenario, yet injects far greater optimism. The Oceanic survivors quickly settle into a peaceful community, with hostilities mostly transposed to outsiders. A murderous monster may appear, but human predators outside the group present a greater threat. Moreover, while *Lord of the Flies* provides a chilling inquiry into human nature, staged in a godless world without any moral compunction towards virtue, *Lost* survivors are deemed worthier representatives, each having been chosen by the island's equivalent of god. Some may stray from the path of righteousness, but they are either soundly punished for their crimes (i.e., Michael) or manage to redeem themselves (as Ben appears to by the end), affirming a moral universe absent from Golding's allegory.

The survivors are relatively indulged in this "testing ground"—with mysterious food drops, ample shelter, and a seemingly endless supply of clean clothes—and they remain improbably well-groomed, well-fed, and generally well-disposed to one another, even as any chance of rescue decreases over successive weeks and the Others are revealed—resulting in a scenario that never strays too close to reality. If it did, of course, it would be harder to enjoy. A baby born on the island would not necessarily have such an easy birth; Walt's pet dog, Vincent, might well have been eaten; medication retrieved from the plane would not be sufficient to cover virtually all ailments; and the suntan lotion would run out as rapidly as the general sense of bonhomie exhibited by the survivors. *Lost*'s makers try to have it both ways, creating an island with some threatening elements, yet not at the expense of spoiling its otherwise idyllic appearance. Admittedly, some characters die, the baby is stolen (albeit returned unharmed), and continued threat motivates the desire to leave; but despite some conflict, a model community is forged. Unlike the ruthless leadership followed by the "Tailies," or Ben's repressive command, Jack's egalitarian methods are approved, and everyone works together to make their society function. This is where *Lost* loses narrative coherence—being too idealistic in its portrait of the survivors to provide a realistic study of human nature, while fantastic departures undermine the attempt to take it seriously (with the rationale behind the input code, like wheels that can move the island and propel time fluctuations, presenting examples of bad SF used simply as a plot device). Audiences were asked to overlook such weaknesses and focus on various mysteries—whether it is the meaning of the numbers, the different languages spoken, or an increasingly convoluted timeline—and, for a remarkable length of time, the strategy worked. Like the scene in the pilot when Jack instructs Boone to find a pen—simply to keep him occupied—many fans enthusiastically embraced their given quests without realizing their true purpose.

In attempting to decipher *Lost*'s mysteries, fans participated in various online discussions, resulting in a pooling of knowledge that Henry Jenkins deems inherently progressive. According to Jenkins, media consumers acquire power as they "learn to cooperate within the knowledge cultures emerging within a networked society," and he cites fan attempts to make sense of *Lost* as a positive example of interaction, arguing that "it is designed in a way to generate constant secrets which we want to uncover ... providing fuel for the participation of large-scale knowledge communities" (Big Shiny Thing 2006). Jenkins thus attributes the same idealist connotations to *Lost*'s audience as he has to fan culture in general. If we are encouraged to share our differing expertise, the logic goes, we become a functioning community, able to work together for the benefit of the entire group. We might even liken ourselves to the show's survivors, who, under Jack's leadership, bring their individual talents to the mix. This is an encouraging view of audience interaction, moderating his earlier view of fandom as a "participatory culture" only insofar as the industry is viewed as less hostile to such pursuits, with both groups benefiting from a mutually beneficial relationship. The truth of the matter is a little more complex. As any *Lost* message board indicates, viewers don't feel the same way about the series or its characters, and individual interpretations are not necessarily accepted, but sometimes unequivocally dismissed. Furthermore, while some viewers studied *Lost* in extraordinary detail, the series did not seem to fully deserve such attention, particularly given developments that appear somewhat ad hoc.

As with many other shows, *Lost* emerged through chance as much as design, considerably altering from its original intentions. Jack only survived the pilot at the network's instance, with Kate originally intended to serve as leader after his demise, which would have made *Lost* akin to the female-led series (*Felicity* and *Alias*) previously created by Abrams. Intriguing as it is to speculate on Kate as the show's lead, the decision to retain Jack had huge ramifications in terms of *Lost*'s concerns (including its father/son motif and focus on troubled male leaders) reprising some notable *Star Wars* themes. Without Matthew Fox's nuanced rendering of Jack, or the expansion of Ben's role after Michael Emerson's impressive performance, the result would have been another series entirely, and we can only wonder if it would have had the same impact. Various roles were conceived on the fly to create parts for actors who stood out during auditions, leading to a wider cast than anticipated (and additional pressure in developing their characters). Characterization suffered as the series progressed, partly due to the number of parts to write for, as well as in having to service the needs of a twisty plot. In fact, while some fans argued, post finale, that *Lost* is better understood as a character drama than a mystery series, it caused criticism even on this level, with the neat pairing up of the congregation belying the many love triangles that occurred in the series, and proving especially frustrating, given the host of contrivances used to separate Kate and Jack over six seasons, to see their only chance at happiness together to be in death. As for our hero, despite only surviving due to network pressure, Jack is made to suffer to an inordinate degree—only to die in the end, sacrificing himself for what is, at best, an over-extended metaphor.

Prior to the finale's broadcast, Lindelof asserted:

> The only thing that's ever mattered to us is what is going to happen to those people? What is the character resolution?... All the crazy island mythology stuff, we love it, but it's like terrorists attacking Jack Bauer, it's stuff that happens in order to tell cool character stories [Hibberd 2010].

A great deal of *Lost*'s audience became overwhelmingly focused on this "stuff that happens," never realizing it was a low priority for its makers, which explains why its supernatural and science fictional elements are ultimately so unsatisfying (simply being used to further intrigue or to advance incredible proceedings). For example, in explaining the cause of the plane crash as a consequence of the "inputting" having been missed—and the electromagnetic shockwave that resulted—a "solution" is provided which fails to explain why the passengers have so much in common. A few seasons on, Jacob's involvement offers the "real" answer to this enigma—one that demands a still greater suspension of disbelief. Just as *Twin Peaks* attempted to preserve its central mystery by making a demon responsible for Laura's death, *Lost* uses Jacob and his brother in the same way, allowing the writers to take a huge flight of fancy. Noting its predecessor's importance in influencing television creators to "think outside the box," Porter and Lavery contend that "it is hard to imagine ABC allowing J.J. Abrams to morph the basic 'plane crashes on an island' idea into the series *Lost* has become without the splendid failure of *Twin Peaks*" (147). I would argue that ABC "allowed" such departures only haltingly, with *Lost*'s fantastical nature only revealing itself when its success was confirmed, and would also question whether *Lost* is quite so "splendid" in its relative failings. *Twin Peaks* may take equivalent liberties with extreme storylines—including psychic abilities, spatiotemporal dislocation, and supernatural forces—but these are counterbalanced by comparable excesses in its soap elements, so we never expect any sense of realism. *Lost*'s multi-purpose plotting—part island adventure, part conspiracy thriller, part melodrama, part metaphysical investigation into the mysteries of human existence—is genre-bending ad nauseum, leaving its audiences well and truly lost in attempting to make sense of it.

In advance of the finale, many fans anticipated a "twist" ending, presuming the entire series would be consigned to the realm of fantasy, either in terms of a dream, a delusion, or some other device; yet *Lost*'s creators repeatedly denied this, with Cuse stating, "What we have said, and will continue to say, is that we will not end the show with a cheat" (Lostpedia, "Debunked Theories"). Lindelof corroborated this statement, asserting, "It's happening in the real world, there are real stakes" (ibid.). Like his earlier statement about its action occurring in a comparable world to ours, he clearly needs a reality check, and having a dead character insist the events on the island were real scarcely imbues this claim with any veracity. Given a premise that rests on gathering individuals from different corners of the globe, reveals their lives to have crisscrossed in a multitude of ways, and finally makes a supernatural being responsible, the show cannot claim any stake in reality. If Lindelof and Cuse were seeking to reassure the network with rational statements of intent, they failed to fool audiences, who identified its metaphysical implications early on. Ultimately, despite claims to the contrary, its creators did end the show on a "cheat"; and although they would no doubt argue that they did so with the best of intentions—to retain an element of surprise—whether it was worth the wait is questionable, leaving *Lost*'s ultimate reputation open to debate. Although some may perceive it as intelligent, well-crafted entertainment which did not treat viewers as idiots by giving us everything on a plate, it could equally be argued that an abundance of interpretations indicates confusion rather than complexity. Invariably, the longer its mysteries were prolonged, the more dissatisfaction seemed inevitable. As past cult shows have indicated—particularly those that refuse categorical answers—the tease has to be deemed worthwhile. *The Prisoner* may have used a great deal of symbolism that puzzled many viewers; *Twin Peaks* may have alienated a degree of its audience, particularly as its second season failed to match its initial promise; and *The X-Files* may have caused frustration in not appearing to go anywhere, but these shows have acquired greater appreciation as the years have passed. How *Lost* will be perceived in years to come is uncertain, for while it may have elicited cult interest as it aired, its ability to engender long-term interest is another matter. Without accompanying promotional material, or the ability to fuel curiosity about what happens next, it must prove itself capable of encouraging ongoing groups of fans to ponder what it was all about—a test of its cult status that it may not necessarily measure up to.

In seeking to align itself with established cult series, *Lost* reworked a number of ideas. Like *The Prisoner*'s Number 6, *Lost*'s survivors are continually tested and find it virtually impossible to escape the strange world they are placed in. The series also bears comparison with *Twin Peaks*, as we have seen, particularly the complex interrelationships between characters, its mix of generic features, and its supernatural mysticism. *The X-Files* is most clearly discernible in its intimated conspiracy, extended plot arc, and narrative enticements, as well as its prolonged mystery. As Porter and Lavery point out, in *Lost*'s numerous enigmas, including its

> Others, polar bears, Monster, and Hatch, we find echoes of the *X-Files*' reliance on its own recurring mysteries: the alien bounty hunter, the black oil, the Cigarette Smoking Man, the Syndicate.... By the end of its run, however, many, if not most, *X-Files* regulars had grown tired of its mysteries without end. Marketing, on TV and in print, constantly promised that our questions would be answered, but they never were, and even more were raised (155).

Lost made similarly false promises, premiering seasons with such taglines as "The truth will be revealed" and "The wait is over"—knowing that if it really were to deliver the goods there would be little incentive to keep watching. However, it arguably built up such a level of expectation that no finale could do it justice, least of all the one supplied—much like Carter's series.

In an interview given early in the series, Lindelof and Cuse claimed to have learned a number of valuable lessons from previous cult shows, stating an intent to avoid repeating *Twin Peaks*' mistake of "postulating new mysteries without answering old ones," or the frustrations generated by *The X-Files* in satisfactorily "sustaining the mythology," while identifying the emphasis on characterization in *Buffy the Vampire Slayer* as a key point they wished to emulate (Jensen 2005). Ironically—and frustratingly—all three lessons were forgotten, with *Lost* succumbing to layers of unresolved enigma, an overly complex mythology that did not bear much scrutiny, and characters that undergo unconvincing transitions. By season five, an "all-change" approach makes Sawyer an eager member of the Dharma community (despite formerly epitomizing a profound loner), and two of the most assertive females on the show—Kate and Juliet—become little more than passive love-interests competing for his affections. Jack's behavior is completely out of character, eclipsing Locke's fanaticism by embracing the mystical; and Ben's turn against Jacob is similarly inconsistent and weakly explained. The final season saw a rapid attempt to make Hurley into a convincing hero, seemingly to surprise audiences, while our understanding of the other characters remains limited. Far from following Whedon's advice and allowing characters to evolve in a credible manner, *Lost*'s makers prioritized novelty over plausibility; and it is both notable and lamentable that while Lindelof and Cuse admitted to being fans of the shows they cite, their insights did not prevent them from making the same mistakes.

Nonetheless, the show managed to forge a remarkable connection with viewers, achieving cult appeal through various means. A place of wonder, far from civilization, provides escapism; a wide cast offers variety; and an overriding meta-arc kept us watching from one season to the next. The series also contains the unresolved sexual tension that has long enticed certain sectors of the audience, as Kate and Jack, although seemingly made for one another, were resolutely kept apart. In addition, it purported to hold greater significance for fans willing to do some digging—by naming several characters after philosophers, referencing key figures in psychology, and even suggesting that Sawyer's reading material was significant to the plot (motivating some viewers to get a copy of everything he read). In turn, corroborating fan investment, the series would routinely incorporate online discussions in lines of dialogue, and even particular scenes. For example, a number of secondary characters exist among the crash survivors; they silently sit around fires or occupy the background of shots, piquing the interest of some online posters. Towards the end of the first season, one such character, Leslie Arzt (Daniel Roebuck), is given a task (moving dynamite) and asks Hurley if he has ever wondered about figures like himself who do not comprise the inner circle of survivors. He remonstrates, "I'm sorry I'm not cool enough to be part of your merry little band of adventurers. I know clique when I see it, I teach high school, pally!" Like a redshirt in *Star Trek*, he dies shortly afterwards; yet by momentarily shining a spotlight on such a character, the show's writers indicate that they have paid attention to fan concerns, even including in-jokes designed for the most hardcore elements of the audience. For example, indicating the factionalism that exists among fans (contra Jenkins' idealized "knowledge communities"), one of the most derided of *Lost*'s fan-groups were the WHISPERERS—a group given to digitally recording whispered dialogue and transcribing it. Few took such efforts seriously, yet season four's finale made a point of showcasing these talents, as Sawyer's final whisper to Kate allowed this group to reveal their expertise (deciphering his request to find his daughter in Albuquerque). It is in such moments that *Lost* proved itself a quintessential cult series, eliciting painstaking attention to detail among fans and revealing makers that paid attention to their following, even as they toyed with them.

Was it little more than a fabulously staged fantasy? Remove all the flashbacks, flashforwards, and flash sideways, concentrate only on action that occurs in the present, and the scantest of plots remains. This is partly why season one provides a host of diversions, transporting us to a crime thriller in Korea (where the henchman woos the boss's daughter), a hospital drama in the U.S. (where a son is torn between loyalty to his father and his duty to uphold the Hippocratic Oath), and an Australian soap (with a pregnant young woman's abandonment by her lover). These narrative departures amalgamate various generic influences, takes us away from the island, and provide a diversity of locations to add interest; yet the lack of events on the island itself would remain a problem in subsequent seasons—which is seemingly why supernatural features intensified, resulting in a somewhat confused identity. Ultimately, although *Lost* strives for metaphorical depth, it fails to provide a coherent allegory; suffers from too little whimsy to be deemed a fulfilling fantasy; has too little exposition to be claimed as SF; lacks the required momentum to serve as a thrilling adventure series; and is insufficiently austere to work as a convincing drama. What might have led to a fascinating study of diverse characters placed in an extreme situation sidesteps the chance to portray them in too negative a light. Instead, *Lost* presents an updated fantasy island on which "visitors" get a chance to reevaluate their lives, making wishes come true—for the pure of heart. As a consequence, Locke's paralysis is healed, and Sun and Jin manage to conceive, despite fertility problems. The island can mend broken marriages, just as it can heal physical injuries; it can overcome the fears of a reluctant single mother and allow a junkie to go cold turkey with a minimum of fuss. And if it takes lives, as well as enriching them, the cameras never get close enough to the graveyard to upset us. Given its symbolism, the attempt to situate *Lost* within a realistic scenario, as its creators initially claimed, invariably works to the detriment of understanding it. The downed passengers of Oceanic 815 each carry emotional baggage, as season one makes clear, and rather than seek to identify a vast conspiracy, it makes more sense to situate *Lost*'s island as an unscheduled stop located somewhere in the Twilight Zone, where passengers can assess where they are heading, both literally and metaphorically. A captured criminal, bound for jail, thus gets the chance to prove she is a good person; a couple having marriage problems have time to work them out; and a young woman intending to give her baby up after its birth falls in love with it instead. As with *The Prisoner*'s Village, *Lost*'s island is best conceived as another realm—and it is only a shame that much of what transpires there (the majority of seasons 2 through 5) seems rather pointless in the end. Lindelof and Cuse ultimately rely a great deal on magic and myth to explain the island's mysteries, making further *Star Wars* references in equating the source of its powers with "the Force," as well as including a touch of *Lord of the Rings* by making the most innocent and hobbit-like of the characters the island's protector. True to form, the finale raised more questions than it provided answers, failing to tie up all the disparate threads and thereby ensuring continued debate. *Lost*'s makers evidently learned enough from past cult shows to retain a level of ambiguity, even if they also left more plot holes than a magic plug could fix. Whether such flaws will undermine its reputation remains to be seen; yet while the frustrated may contend that it will soon be forgotten, it seems more likely that *Lost* will be remembered in a similar vein as *The Prisoner* and *Twin Peaks*—as a show that challenged convention, causing huge speculation (and ultimate controversy) while testing the limits of television drama. Although by no means the first "mystery island" to appear on television, *Lost* showed the premise to be capable of new tricks, involving some inspired experimentation, and enabling a flagging network to get ahead of the game. In retrospect, Braun's magic beans reaped bigger rewards than anyone anticipated, and ABC must have thanked their lucky stars that he had the courage of his convictions.

While it is too early to speculate on *Lost*'s long-term legacy, its immediate impact was demonstrated in the range of telefantasy shows commissioned after its release, many of which were significantly happier to pin their generic colors to the mast, affirming the extent to which *Lost* revolutionized industrial attitudes. Other networks, seeking to emulate its phenomenal success, would more readily develop fantastical ideas, extending the impact *The X-Files* had in the 1990s by helping to ensure telefantasy would no longer be consigned to minimal budgets and marginal networks. One such example was Abrams' next venture into telefantasy. Having developed a number of film projects, including *Cloverfield* (2007), where he took his monster fixation further, as well as directing *Star Trek* (2009), which he worked on with Lindelof, Abrams returned to television with the new SF series *Fringe* (2008–), reportedly being paid $10 million to write and direct its pilot. Interestingly, just prior to its launch, Abrams affirmed that the series would be delivered in a more straightforward manner than either *Alias* or *Lost*, describing it as having the long-term interest of "an overall story and endgame, but also a show that you don't have to watch episodes 1, 2 and 3 to tune in to episode 4" (Brownfield 2008). The comment suggests the critical reaction to *Lost* had been noted, implying an end to complex mythology shows demanding immense audience loyalty and intensive interest. As successful as *Lost* undoubtedly was, it also affirmed the risk factor for continuous series, a fact which a number of subsequent telefantasy series would confirm—with many new shows planned as long-term serial dramas and evidently striving to become "crossover cults"—while failing to find the same reaction. One such example, *Heroes*, developed by NBC a year after *Lost* was launched, may have initially suggested that lightning could strike twice, seemingly confirming telefantasy's new status as blockbuster material; but ultimately proved that mighty heights can lead to great falls, as the next chapter illustrates.

6

Why *Heroes* Failed: The Superpowered Franchise That Fell from Grace

Heroes is the kind of thing that can keep spinning and spinning. There is not an island to get off of, or a time-frame when the world ends.
—Tim Kring

Tim Kring had lofty ambitions for *Heroes* (2006–10), believing that, with an ever-evolving format, the show had the potential for long-term success. However, a promising opening season was followed by a steep decline in ratings, mounting criticism, and eventual cancellation. The show's floundering fortunes serve as a cautionary tale for the industry, one likely to have big ramifications for the genre; and this chapter questions how it got things so badly wrong. Developed by NBC soon after *Lost* was launched, *Heroes* similarly sought to combine cult interest with mainstream appeal, taking advantage of a favorable industrial climate to consolidate telefantasy's newfound popularity. Diverse sources were ransacked for inspiration, and an array of multimedia platforms were used to deliver additional content in its expanded universe, with *Heroes Evolutions*—an interactive investigation of the show's mythology—winning awards for integrating game, graphic novel and mobile phone technologies. However, while such efforts sought to accommodate a post-broadcast era, they could not assure the franchise's future. With ratings dropping from an initial 15 million average to 4 million by its fourth (and last) season, the series proved to be beyond rescue or remedy, its makers having ignored numerous opportunities to correct the show's flaws—proving that even a composite cult cannot ensure success.

Built on a premise that equips ordinary people with extraordinary powers, and lavishly funded by a major network (with an initial budget of $4 million dollars an episode), *Heroes* was scarcely conceivable before *Lost* changed industrial attitudes toward the genre. When NBC approached Kring to develop the series, he could see they were keen to match the success of *Lost* and *24*. Kring has acknowledged the debt *Heroes* owes these precursors, both in exciting network interest in a show of its kind and suggesting what they needed to avoid, asserting:

> *Heroes* couldn't have existed without shows such as *Lost* and *24*. But by coming along after those shows we got to look back at how the audience reacted and avoid some of their pitfalls. One of the big lessons was not to posit an ending. *Heroes* isn't about getting off an island; it does not have a finality to it. So it lends itself to spinning in many different directions [Morgan 2008].

At it turns out, *Heroes* would continually make "pitfalls" of its own, turning viewers off in droves. Far from devising the perfect franchise formula, Kring was forced to admit that making the show was "an imperfect science" (Wylie 2008)—even for someone as experienced as himself.

Kring's career has been closely aligned with the telefantasy genre: writing an episode of *Knight Rider* in 1982; co-creating a series about people with superhuman powers, *Misfits of Science* (1985–6); co-writing the film sequel *Teen Wolf Too* (1987) with former *Heroes* co-executive producer Jeph Loeb; and co-creating *Strange World* (1999–2002), one of the many series that followed *The X-Files* in evaluating paranormal phenomena. He additionally devised the popular drama series *Providence* (1999–2001) and *Crossing Jordan* (2001–7) and it is this mix of SF/cult and mainstream experience that recommended him to NBC in seeking to make a crossover hit of their own—intended as an in-house production, like ABC's *Lost*, designed to make the most of available resources and aiming to draw a similar audience. Essentially, *Heroes* revises the *Misfits of Science* motif, yet with the intent of making the concept work as a popular drama. As Kring has revealed:

> We were going after a mass audience and usually the most genre shows end up finding is just a cult audience that can exist on smaller cable channels. But with a big network like NBC ... we wouldn't have survived with that kind of audience [Wylie 2008].

From the outset, Kring was anxious to avoid curtailing the potential audience, asserting:

> I am very concerned that it not be seen only as a cult show. My fear is that it could be labeled as such and discourage a huge segment of the mainstream audience. I think if a person is watching it just for the genre "cult" aspect they will be disappointed. It just won't lean hard enough in that area for them ... my hope is that everyone can find something they like [Kring, 9thwonders. com, 2005].

The comment reveals a somewhat anachronistic idea of a "cult" show as one likely to have only limited appeal, yet as Benji Wilson articulates, such distinctions have altered. He notes that while *Heroes* was initially dismissed as "cult viewing for boys waving imaginary light-sabers, not quality drama," it forced such preconceptions to be revised:

> With its blend of superhero lore and low-grade mysticism, *Heroes* squarely fits the tradition of "cult" viewing. What no one predicted was the extent to which cult viewing has moved into the mainstream [Wilson 2007].

In fact, far from serving as a random mutation, as Wilson further asserts, "this kind of cult crossover has been edging its way in to prime time for several years," citing *Buffy the Vampire Slayer* as a new kind of cult which "took comic-book themes and motifs and sold them to non-nerds through slick action sequences and even slicker scripts" (ibid). As we have seen, however, *Buffy* received only modest ratings and would scarcely have been conceivable on a major network. *The X-Files* more clearly breached the divide between "cult" and "mainstream" programming by proving that a show with "genre" trappings could attain a mass audience—a feat *Lost* confirmed a decade on, and which *Heroes* clearly aimed to emulate. Despite Kring's stated aversion to the "cult" tag, the series was evidently constructed with cult interest in mind: providing opportunities for audience interaction online, as well as a means of exploring its mythology; pilfering other shows for actors and in-jokes; and using a premise about superheroes that drew from a very particular field of interest. By modeling itself on comics in its premise, look, and story structure, the show aimed at a ready-made "niche" market; and in premiering each season at Comic-Con, a very select audience was chosen—making Kring's reservations about the "genre/cult aspect" somewhat strange. However, while the geek fraternity was tagged as *Heroes*' primary audience, secondary appeal among non-genre fans was needed to boost its ratings, creating divided interests for its makers. While Kring distanced himself from the "genre" aspects, admitting his ignorance about the world of comics, various members of the production team were well-versed in comic lore. Jeph Loeb had an extensive background writing for comics such as DC while fellow co-executive producer, Greg Beeman, was a former graphic novel artist, and both had additionally worked on *Superman* spin-off *Smallville*. Although Kring seemed the odd one out among this group, his lack of familiarity with the genre was considered an asset, with cast member Masi Oka arguing that this helped make the show accessible to mainstream viewers:

> The fact that he's not a comic-book person, I think, is a great thing.... Tim will say, "Hey, I don't get that. What do you mean, this time-travel thing? Can you kind of explain it?" If Tim understands it, America's going to understand it [Boedeker 2007].

For his part, Kring sought to contribute dramatic ballast to the writing by making individual abilities serve a particular function. As David Kushner summarizes:

> Kring started with a character's personal struggles and predicaments and assigned special abilities to suit. A harried single mom gets superstrength. A clock-watching Dilbert type learns to control time. A prison escapee is sud-

denly able to walk through walls. And when Kring's protagonists develop their powers, they don't strap on spandex and capes—they grapple with these strange developments like believable human beings [Kushner 2007].

Kring believed the show had potential for ongoing appeal, asserting, "If one can assume that dealing with their extraordinary abilities is something that these characters will always face then their stories can bend and morph and evolve forever" (9th Wonders.com, 2005). Where the series would fall down is in maintaining any consistency with its characters and a profound lack of continuity—oversights that are particularly notable given that *Heroes* was such a cannily conceived product. Having worked with Damon Lindelof on *Crossing Jordan*, Kring had the benefit of drawing from his experience while creating his new series, admitting, "I bounced everything I could off him" (Boedeker 2007). The debt owed to *Lost* is considerable, as Kring has acknowledged:

> The truth is there is no way that *Heroes* would have been made without *Lost* having paved the way for a large serialized saga. It not only prepared the audience for this kind of storytelling, but the networks as well [9thWonders.com, 2005].

NBC clearly pinned a lot of hope on it, with chief executive Jeff Zucker describing *Heroes* as "a huge asset for the company, hopefully for many years to come" (Boedeker 2007). While Lindelof and Cuse insisted that their mystery island drama could not go on forever, Kring sold *Heroes* as a show that could secure a mass audience for an indefinite period, offering what appeared to be the ideal product, openly branding itself as a similar series to *Lost*. Indeed, a book written soon after season one aired, *Saving the World: A Guide to Heroes* (2007), even includes an opening chapter by David Lavery entitled "Are Our Heroes *Lost*?"—questioning whether the new series simply retreads the same format. It is easy to see why such conjecture occurred, with both shows commissioned by major networks within a few years, and bearing more than a passing resemblance to one another.

Lost and *Heroes* are each big-budget dramas featuring an ensemble cast and high production values. On a narrative level we have good guys pitted against their adversaries, some of whom change "sides" in an effort to confound expectations. A large cast provides a variety of characters to identify with— and ample scope for rivalries and romances. Sinister organizations feature in their respective mythologies and an interest in father/son relations is equally apparent, focusing on questionable paternal role models. A male protagonist is highlighted as the main hero of each series, tasked with protecting others and becoming a better man than his father. Cult interest is fostered by thus reworking ideas popularized in *Star Wars* (as well as other pop cultural references), while impressive sets and an array of subplots aim to encourage broad appeal. An element of the fantastic is central to each premise. *Lost* is set on a strange island which can shift its position, undergo temporal flux, create apparitions, and raise the dead, with inhabitants capable of extraordinary abilities, and a central mystery posed in why seemingly random passengers have been assembled there. In *Heroes*, select figures discover superhuman powers during a solar eclipse (the significance of which remains an enigma), acquiring a common purpose in averting specific catastrophes. Furthermore, a number of similar characters appear in each show, including a handsome and virtuous male lead, with Jack's heroism echoed by Peter Petrelli (Milo Ventimiglia); an attractive female counterpart, with Kate paralleled by Niki/Jessica/Traci (Ali Larter), as well as younger versions offered by Claire (Hayden Panettiere), Elle (Kristen Bell) and Daphne (Brea Grant); drug-addicts that serve a tragi-heroic function, with Charlie's death alerting others of danger, while junkie painter Isaac Mendez (Santiago Cabrera) warns the world in his art; an enigmatic Black man, with the mysterious "Haitian" (Jimmy Jean-Louis) paralleling Mr. Eko; and a comic equivalent to Hurley found in Hiro (Masi Oka) and his sidekick Ando (James Kyson Lee). Further links between each series indicate deliberate cross-referencing, and Lavery even provides a 13-page table of related motifs, including the same scene (young women who survive an autopsy); the same episode title ("Collision, Homecoming" is used in both series); and similar narrative tropes, such as visits to the future and various religious connotations (2007, 17–29). In addition to several poor father figures, both shows feature a tough matriarch with precognitive powers, with Eloise Hawking finding a formidable counterpart in Angela Petrelli (Cristine Rose); and ideas of family, fate and destiny are notable in both shows, contrasting an attempt at metaphysical depth with glossy production values and interactive features to provide contemporary cults with commercial appeal.

However, while *Heroes* openly shares many features with ABC's hit, it would also attempt to avoid perceived problems, such as *Lost*'s attenuated plotting, with Kring asserting that he and his writers had "made a pact with the audience that something is going to happen every week," affirming this was "an absolute direct reaction to the audience frustration over *Lost*" (Boedeker 2007). Storylines were consequently delivered with a faster pace and the action divided into mini-arcs (termed as "volumes") rather than a continuous overriding plot—a move that simply created a different set of problems. Numerous narrative strands were left dangling on the way to each season finale, suggesting only the bare bones had been plotted, and a sense of repetition soon became evident, with each story arc presenting a disaster that must be averted (whether it be preventing an explosion in season one, stopping a deadly virus in season two, thwarting plans to develop a formula for human mutation in season three, and another attempt to prevent mass murder in season four)—calamities that are always foiled in the final moments. Frustratingly, little progression occurs from one season to the next, with writers tending to hit the "re-set button," as many fans noted, removing characters from any sense of normality (or consistency) and thereby reducing any incentive to take the drama seriously.

These problems are particularly disappointing because *Heroes* began so well, winning over detractors with a promising level of sophistication; but successive seasons indicated ever diminishing returns and a general sense of aimlessness. Although the writers' strike of 2007 was widely blamed for disrupting production during the second season and causing the show to lose its way, internal problems were also evident. Loeb, Beeman and fellow writer-producer (and former *Alias* and *Lost* writer) Jesse Alexander were dismissed by NBC in 2008 due to conflicts over the creative direction the series was taking, and celebrated series creator Bryan Fuller, who left the show in 2007 to make *Pushing Daisies*, briefly returned in 2009, rekindling the hopes of many fans that it would recover a sense of purpose. Having begun his career writing for the *Star Trek* spin-offs *Deep Space 9* and *Voyager*, Fuller acquired a cult following in creating offbeat series such as *Wonderfalls* and *Dead Like Me*, and many hoped he could revive *Heroes*' fortunes. Noting problems in the writers' room, arguing that "what was a cohesive group had become divided" (Wilkes 2009), Fuller's apparent role as "consulting producer" was to oversee story and character development, and his comments on the show's failings revealed an affinity with fan criticisms. However, he left the show after only a few months, leaving Kring one of the few original production staff still in place—and the least trusted by fans. With credible characterization and coherent plotting ignored, Kring proved incapable of saving *Heroes*, clearly not taking its problems seriously enough. Although it initially received considerable acclaim, leading one critic to enthuse, "It may well end up surpassing other cult touchstones" (Kushner 2007), *Heroes* would rebut such lofty predictions, falling a long way from its original promise.

The first season encompasses volume one ("Genesis") and introduces key characters—and their powers—as they draw together from various parts of the world to prevent a predicted explosion in New York. Additional threats include potential capture by a mysterious "Company" (later named as Primatech) run by wealthy businessman Daniel Linderman (Malcolm McDowell). He plans to take advantage of the anticipated explosion by asserting greater political power over the American nation—although what he means to do with his captives is unclear. A further danger is posed by serial killer Sylar (Zachary Quinto), who tracks and kills "evolved humans" to acquire their abilities. The season culminates at the Kirby Plaza, where our fledgling heroes manage to prevent disaster. Sylar is apparently killed, yet an empath, Peter Petrelli, serves as the unwitting cause of the explosion, having absorbed the radioactive power of another "special" and proving unable to control this cataclysmic force. His brother, Nathan (Adrian Pasdar), saves the day by using his ability to fly and taking Peter into the sky as he detonates, leaving the fate of the Petrelli brothers unknown as they apparently sacrifice themselves for the greater good.

Season two was intended to feature two further volumes, yet the Writers Strike limited the season to 11 episodes, forcing writers to concentrate on volume two, "Generations." Having united at the end of the first season, the heroes go their separate ways, including the Petrelli brothers, who are shown to have survived the explosion but fallen to Earth in different locations. The source of the heroes' powers is explained as the result of genetic manipulation and traced to 12 individuals who formed the Company—many of whom are revealed to be the heroes' parents. Their successive murders reveal a new villain, and a new disaster is introduced in the form of a genetic disorder known as the "Shanti virus." This attacks a minority of evolved humans, removing any powers before killing the victim, but threatens to become a global pandemic in the future. One of the first to succumb is Sylar—who survives being stabbed at the end of "Genesis" to gain greater prominence in the series. Despite losing his powers, Sylar continues his murderous ways and recovers his abilities at the season's close by stealing a vaccine designed by genetics professor Mohinder Suresh (Sendhil Ramamurphy). Mohinder is one of many lost sons featured in the series, who struggles to avoid emulating his father. However, he opts to work for Primatech to redress mistakes made by Chandra Suresh (Erick Avari), whose research was vital to the Company, thereby following him down the same wayward path by colluding with the same organization. The virus is named after his younger sister, who died as a child, giving Mohinder similar attributes to Fox Mulder. Further allusions to *The X-Files* include parental figures tampering with humanity's future and similar shades of post–Watergate cynicism (with the 12 notably hatching their plans in the 1970s, the same period in which *Lost*'s Dharma Initiative experiment began). For the first three seasons former members of the Company serve as the main antagonist. While Linderman fulfilled this role in the first season, Adam Monroe (David Anders) continues his nihilistic ambitions in the second, intent on using the virus to purge humanity's sins. Adam is revealed to be many centuries old, fostering several lifetimes of cynicism, his extreme beliefs once leading to a period of containment by another member of the group, Kaito Nakamura (George Takei). Now at large, Adam sets about killing the Company's other founders and plans to unleash the deadly virus. He is finally thwarted by Peter after dumbly assisting him for the majority of the season, and Hiro Nakamura, the son of his earlier captor, opts to bury him alive so he can do no further harm.

Season three is divided into two volumes, "Villains" and "Fugitives," the first of which introduces another Company man, Arthur Petrelli (Robert Forster), to take over antagonist duties. The father of the Petrelli clan was presumed dead, but recovers from being poisoned (by his wife Angela) through draining the life-force from the newly escaped Adam. He confirms his villainy by even taking abilities from his own son Peter, leaving him powerless. Having formed another company, Pinehearst, Arthur recruits less ethically inclined "specials" to work for him, aiming to reproduce the original "formula" to create a genetically enhanced army. His abilities—and supreme self-assurance—make him a formidable opponent; yet by this point, apparently to compensate for season two's delayed plotting, characters are rapidly killed off and Arthur is abruptly shot by Sylar before the series makes full use of him. Nathan remains intent on continuing his father's plans, however, naively equating an enhanced army with a souped-up U.N., and uses his new political connections to begin experimentation. Peter is violently opposed to this plan, and acquires unexpected accomplices among his father's recruited "villains," who help destroy the formula, concerned they would no longer be unique if it were used. The volume ends with another narrative about-turn as Nathan abandons the plan to create more evolved humans and opts to contain them instead, securing presidential approval to round up and imprison people with powers for the sake of national security. Having attempted to rework the "supersoldiers" plot from *The X-Files*, Nathan's new agenda makes little sense—other than to reshuffle the deck in advance of the next volume, with little concern for logic or consistency. The finale also shows Primatech burn to the ground with Sylar inside, although few believed his future was in any doubt.

"Fugitives" redraws the battle lines, as evolved humans unite to avoid persecution. The volume begins promisingly with our heroes attempting to lead ordinary lives; yet after escaping detention and subsequently trying to conceal their presence, they fail to behave either like credible people or convincing heroes. After a brief stint as a villain, Nathan has a crisis of conscience, and a mercenary zealot, Danko (Zeljko Ivanek), takes his place, overseeing Guantanamo-style abuses in a holding facility known as "Building 26." Danko heeds the advice of fellow worker Noah Bennet (Jack Coleman—dubbed by fans as "HRG") in using "specials" to find others, and enlists Sylar as a partner (after taking a brief road-trip in search of his father). However, Sylar opts to kill, rather than capture, fugitives, and after acquiring the ability to shape-shift, he frames Danko for his murders and detains him in the facility he once presided over. The finale allows Hiro and Ando to infiltrate the unit, and Nathan returns to Washington to convince the president to revise his policy. A twist ending sees Nathan killed by Sylar, yet the killer is subconsciously manipulated into assuming Nathan's identity. Peter partially recovers his powers, although he can now only assume one ability at a time (rather than the multiple powers he was once capable of), and Hiro's ability to time travel is also curtailed. The finale culminates with a new Company formed, yet how this will differ to Building 26 or the former Primatech remains uncertain, particularly with the sole remaining member of the original 12, Angela Petrelli, in charge. A flashback episode ("1961"), shown late in the season, attempts to humanize her via a traumatic past, but merely provides greater incoherence. We learn the government rounded up mutant humans before (at a secret research base called Coyote Sands) and that a massacre was sparked when Angela abandoned her unstable sister one night. Adolescent escapees, including herself and a young Linderman, subsequently formed the beginnings of the Company (providing a backstory that does not mesh with the history previously given and fails to explain why Primatech subsequently rounded up others like themselves, seemingly continuing the government's work and even hiring the same scientist,

Chandra Suresh). The fact that the new Company's first act is one of deception is equally sinister, using telepath and mind controller Matt Parkman (Greg Grunberg) to manipulate Sylar into staying in Nathan's persona. Angela is divested of her widow's black for the first time, and by dressing her in red (the code for scheming vamps in the series), the narrative suggests that, having previously seen her attempt to deceive Sylar into thinking he is her son, she has finally got what she wants.

The fourth season, aptly named "Redemption," was motivated by a desire to redeem the series' flaws and bring back fans. Kring assured viewers that they did not need to see previous events to make sense of the season, yet an inconsistent narrative meant this had always been the case, and the negation of two seasons left the faithful wondering why they had bothered to keep watching. The attempted reboot had some admirable ideas, particularly in seeking to return the heroes to their normal lives, but the feeling remained that the writers were making it up as they went, and the show's potential, as ever, was frustratingly unfulfilled. Peter goes back to working as a paramedic, using his powers to save lives, and meets a new love interest, yet she merely serves as another damsel in distress; while another new character, a tattooed woman called Lydia (Dawn Olivieri), also amounts to little more than a victim, affirming continued problems for female roles. Matt Parkman returns to life as a policeman, yet far from seeing his abilities used at work, he is ignored throughout most of the season. Claire Bennet (Hayden Panetierre) goes to college and embarks on a lesbian relationship which proves just as cringe-worthy and unconvincing as her heterosexual dalliances. Most promising was the idea of the Sullivan Brothers carnival. Seemingly drawing from the cult HBO series *Carnivàle* and the literary work of Ray Bradbury, its master of ceremonies, Samuel (Robert Knepper), provided an intriguing new character, and the specials that travel with him offered further abilities to explore. Yet while Kring described this community of outsiders as adding "a new wrinkle in the mythology of the show" (Moorhouse 2009), they failed to revitalize the series. Samuel is yet another charismatic villain who is sorely wasted through insubstantial motivation. Initially suggested to be bitter due to a poor upbringing among a family of servants, he is subsequently shown to have been at Coyote Sands as a child (an attempt to create a sustainable mythology) and finally becomes murderously enraged when a love interest jilts him, causing him to plot revenge against "straight" society. Apparently aiming to remind viewers of the first season, the impending calamity is located in New York, where Samuel plans to murder citizens visiting the carnival to force the world to respect his "family." However, the other carnies turn against him, and various established characters unite to thwart him. In as contrived an ending as it gets, Ando remembers his "supercharge" abilities and enables Hiro to teleport thousands, en masse, to safety, while Samuel is confined to the safekeeping of the new Company—an organization we still know virtually nothing about.

The next volume, "Brave New World," was teased at the end of the finale, with Claire jumping from a Ferris wheel and snapping her bones back into place in front of the astonished press—a stunt aiming to inspire intrigue about the world's likely response to the existence of people with special abilities. The tease failed to entice the network, however, and while NBC boss Angela Bromstad praised the show's international sales and brand recognition a year earlier, the decision was made to cancel the series in May 2010. Evidently surprised at not being renewed, Kring's response was to issue a statement ostensibly thanking fans, yet additionally defending his creation:

> Every week more than 45 million TV viewers around the world, as well as millions of social and digital media-based fans, have made *Heroes* one of the five most-watched shows across traditional and digital media screens in the history of television. For NBC, I certainly understand the challenge of creating a business model around a show which arrived precisely as the audience was finding new ways to watch traditional content on multiple screens [Kring, 9th Wonders.com, 2010].

The intent was evidently to excuse the show's poor terrestrial ratings, remind the network of its global and multimedia audience, and suggest that outmoded forms of assessment were being used to appraise the show, yet for many, NBC's decision was long overdue, with *Heroes* continually failing to learn from its mistakes. As numerous fans pointed out, the plot made little sense and characters were never explored adequately, negating features that would make them worth caring about. In Fuller's view, *Heroes* became "Sci-Fi ghetto storytelling—everything ordinary about their lives went out the window" (Bentley), promising, before quitting for a second time, "We'll keep it grounded ... they can have their lives back" (Wilkes, 2009). This echoes Kring's initial claim that "the show can go on forever as long as their lives have normal needs and jobs and relationships" (Boedeker 2007); yet with the same mistakes continuing to be made in the fourth season, the show's sole capacity to surprise consisted of staying on the air as long as it did.

The biggest disappointment for its fans is that *Heroes* promised so much. A premise in which superheroes unite against a dastardly foe might easily have been rendered absurd or juvenile, yet by featuring a range of older characters, and involving the audience in their individual circumstances, the opening season confounded negative expectations. As we got to know each hero we realized their powers compensate for specific lacks in their lives. A self-effacing cop becomes the ultimate crime fighter when he acquires the ability to hear people's thoughts; a high-school student who discovers she is adopted also realizes she is virtually indestructible; and a male nurse, dismissed as a low-achiever by his family, discovers his natural empathy is the most important power imaginable. As Fuller says of this allegorical feature, "One of the great things about the first season is that the metaphor for their abilities was very clear. Those metaphors seem to have gotten complicated in the past two seasons" (Fuller

2008). In fact, they disappeared altogether as the series opted to focus on the powers themselves rather than who wields them. This is contrary to Kring's intentions, having stated at the outset that "*Heroes* is, at its core, a character-based saga. I'm much more fascinated by the personal struggles that these abilities present to the characters" (9thwonders.com, 2005). The intent to emphasize humanity over flashy effects might have given the superhero premise an adult edge, yet as the show took off its writers largely fast-forwarded through the process of its heroes coming to terms with their powers.

Matt Parkman provides a good example of how characterization went astray after the first season. Introduced as an overlooked underdog, his fortunes change when he discovers telepathic abilities, yet these also prove to be a mixed blessing. Initially dismissed as detective material, his career advances with his newfound power, and his marriage problems are allayed as communication improves with his wife Janice (Lisa Lackey). However, the flip-side to this power is also shown when he realizes she has had an affair by "overhearing" a colleague's thoughts. The unhappy consequence of being unable to turn his power off is further demonstrated in a scene at a convenience store when the cacophony of hearing everyone's thoughts causes him to break down. Regrettably, such explorations prove all too rare, and the "personal struggles" attached to powers become sidelined. After season one, relationship difficulties are dispensed with, characters are removed from their ordinary lives, and the plot moves at such a pace that continuity is sacrificed and any measure of depth abandoned altogether. Character investment is consequently made futile, particularly when their treatment is highly erratic, and Parkman is a case in point. Having left his job and pregnant wife at the start of season two, he becomes a doting foster father to a relative stranger (who is packed off to India by the end of the season, never to be seen again). An improbable romance with a younger woman follows in season three (romancing Daphne, with a suggested destiny to marry and start a family), yet she is mortally wounded while performing a heroic deed. With barely a pause, Parkman is swiftly reunited with his wife (and new baby son) and rejoins the police force—seemingly returning to the accessible Everyman he was once suggested as, only to be ignored for the majority of the fourth season.

It was Bryan Fuller's first written episode since returning to *Heroes* ("Cold Snap") which killed Daphne off and reinstated Janice, affirming his promise to return the series to its foundations, and intensifying fan conviction that a trusted series creator had a firm hand on the rudder. Consequently, it caused waves of lamentation when his departure was announced only a few months after rejoining the *Heroes* team. However, there is a danger of overestimating what he could realistically have achieved. Fuller may have the imagination fans admire (consistently highlighting quirkiness over commercialism in his career), yet we might recall that it was his idea to soften Angela up with arguably the most dire episode of the series ("1961")—which not only lacks coherence but oddly seeks to humanize a figure who excelled as an enigma. A more understandable decision was Fuller's insistence on saving Traci Strauss (Ali Larter), asserting that seeing her character change would be more interesting than killing her off, as intended, and thereby initiating the sense of development fans had long craved. However, Traci was yet another character the writers had no idea what to do with; she underwent a series of personality overhauls that left her completely inexplicable by the end of the series. The series' lack of strong female characters was a problem many hoped Fuller might remedy, but both Angela and Traci had little to do in the fourth season, while Claire continued to play the whiny teen seen from the start. In fairness, Fuller's second departure was by no means the sole reason for the show's continued decline, but the comparative lack of fan support given to its creator is a notable indication of profound frustration. While Lindelof and Cuse recouped considerable integrity in standing up to ABC and insisting that *Lost* develop (and end) as they desired, Kring made an increasingly negative impression on viewers, with many fans deeming *Heroes'* initial success to be less attributable to his input as that of his collaborators. Kring was generally labeled a studio hack who came up with a hit concept without knowing what to do with it. To give him his due, helming *Heroes* clearly had its share of challenges: having to steer a multimillion dollar franchise through a problematic writers' strike; managing the scale and expense of a show with an ensemble cast and high production values; and overseeing its various multimedia features. In this last respect, in particular, Kring showed an understanding of the innovations required by the industry; and in anticipating how television must adapt to changing times, he seemed ideally equipped to make a show with a future, arguing:

> When I pitched *Heroes* I knew an important element to getting it on air was how it can incorporate the Internet.... It doesn't take a genius to figure out that things are changing quickly. Production costs are going up. We're losing eye-balls. We have to reach people in other ways [Kushner 2007].

Much as *Lost* placed "clues" to its contorted narrative online, *Heroes* invested heavily in new media technologies. The series benefited from Internet "leaks" prior to its initial broadcast, and established its online presence via i-stories, webisodes, and graphic novels. The website 9thwonders.com provided viewers with a means to exchange their views. Other innovations include graphic novel character "Evs Dropper" sending messages to viewers via text and voicemail, while blogs purportedly posted by series characters also appeared — methods that confirm the active pursuit of a changing audience. As Kring notes:

> The idea is to create a currency for the people who are true fans of the show. A casual viewer may only watch *Heroes* on television. But if viewers go to the other platforms they'll know one more thing about the show than their friends [Morgan 2008].

The comment indicates how much *Heroes* courted "cult interest"; yet viewers need to deem this kind of information-gathering worth their time, and with few mysteries to explore in its mythology—and declining credibility—the show's cult factor was somewhat diminished. Furthermore, irrespective of the way broadcast material is supplemented by other media today, *Heroes* still had to make an impact on television (where ratings and accompanying advertising revenue still matter) and prove that it could attract a primetime audience on a regular basis—which requires fulfilling the basics of good drama: consistent characterization and a rewarding and compelling narrative. Ultimately, it doesn't matter what shiny new ways are offered to interact with fans if continually voiced complaints are not heeded—as Kring should have known. The show may have encountered its share of problems, with the writers' strike delaying plot developments, limited production time between seasons one and two, a reduced budget as ratings dwindled, and the simple burden of sustaining its initial impact, but inattention to detail, a plot that lurches from one idea to the next, incoherent characters, and a pronounced lack of direction are faults that should have been identified and overcome. Like the serial killer at its center, *Heroes* may have seemed intriguing at first, but the more it borrowed from other sources the less interest it yielded, causing some to speculate that it should have confined itself to one season. This is contrary to the pitch Kring promised NBC, however, having designed the series to secure ongoing interest and using a host of methods to maximize its appeal.

Just as *Lost* combined a number of generic elements in tracing the backstories of its characters, *Heroes* merged various scenarios together, with the first season including elements of political drama (following Nathan's campaign to become a senator); horror (in the murders performed by Sylar); conspiracy thriller (via the Company's activities); comedy (with Hiro and Ando providing amusement); and supernatural teen drama (as schoolgirl Claire comes to terms with both her ability and her family, and starts to grow up). Movie and television references additionally played with familiar conventions, continuing the same tendency towards hybridity and intertextuality that has been noted in other series, providing various citations to recognize. Ultimately, with a premise about superheroes, the show could hardly make any claims for originality, yet it was how the concept was (initially) handled that set it apart, setting expectations higher than it was subsequently able to achieve.

Premiering with domestic ratings that were almost comparable to *Lost*, and garnering a huge international response, *Heroes*' appeal can be attributed to various factors, including its innovative design, the suggested complexity of its plot, and its thematic timeliness. It emerged during a dark period in global politics, with a premise that unites people in adversity, and Kring has suggested that it caught a particular mood. As he has argued:

> There's a message of "interconnectivity" that's really powerful in the world right now. This idea that we're all somehow connected for some greater pur-

pose. The idea that there could be people among us, or even ourselves, who could do something about current issues, I think, is a huge part of why the audience is connecting to this show [Naughton 2007, 21].

Although Kring does not specify what he means by "current issues," season one's explosion in New York, and later references to government-endorsed detention camps, clearly refer to 9/11 and its aftermath. A subtext warns against presidents who are really duplicitous murderers and national laws in which fear and hostility hold sway, yet *Heroes* also insists that change is possible and that people can work together to make a difference. The spate of catastrophe scenarios that emerged in U.S. broadcasting post–9/11 suggests a preoccupation with such themes, with shows that transcend national borders in urging us to think about humanity and its prospects. *Battlestar Galactica* (2004–9) may model itself on a 1970s series, yet it updates its plot with contemporary relevance; and in pitching humanity against an enemy that we have (literally) created, the series plays on ideas of infiltration, terrorism, and "insurgency"—with obvious allusions to 9/11. While gritty plotlines recognize our species as flawed, the series also upholds a degree of faith in our representatives (and belief in a higher power), as the survivors of various planets unite in the mission to find the promised land. *Lost* also contains some interesting political overtones in questioning what kind of civilization can be forged in the aftermath of an airplane disaster. Its survivors come from various parts of the world, yet are forced to work together to survive, particularly when Others threaten their group, and although some characters collude with the enemy (and various flaws are exposed), the narrative insists that redemption is possible. *Heroes* unites a similarly mixed group, tasked with protecting the human race, and strives for metaphysical depth in questioning our ability to evolve, as well as repeated discussions of our duality. Voice-overs by Mohinder Suresh recall the kind of cosmic questioning Mulder would often conclude an *X-File* episode with, questioning whether a grand design is at work regarding humanity's fate. This philosophizing gave the show a certain edge during a period of uncertainty, and although the heroes' abilities are shown to be the result of human ambition, rather than divine intervention, the series tends to champion the better side of human nature, even if the struggle to overcome "evil" is a seemingly endless battle. However, while the show initially resembled a heroic saga, Kring's suggested sense of "interconnectivity" is another factor where *Heroes* would disappoint—repeatedly disbanding our heroes and thereby frustrating any sense of common purpose. Political concerns may come to the fore when the U.S. government are framed as villains, incarcerating innocent people (without due process), but if an anti–Bush campaign was covertly waged in the run-up to a general election in the U.S., political considerations appeared to dissipate thereafter.

"Fugitives" makes overt political inferences by outlawing U.S. citizens and clothing "detainees" in orange boiler suits, yet misgivings about contemporary U.S. policy (both at home and abroad) were subsequently sidelined as Danko becomes the principal architect, ousting Nathan, and absolving the president (and his government) from any responsibility in the mistreatment of captives. The volume concludes with the president revoking his earlier mandate, and Nathan's openness about his "special" identity suggests the dawning of a new liberal era (coinciding with the Obama administration taking office). A sense of distrust may be fostered in the finale, when our heroes set up a psychopath to potentially become the next president of the United States (with Sylar feigning Nathan's identity), yet these intriguing possibilities were shelved to make room for another storyline (a continual frustration in *Heroes*). The series' version of Guantanamo was abandoned by the end of the volume, and those in political office granted a handy reprieve. With a carnival operator set up as the villain of the next installment, "Redemption" returned us to comic-book fantasy, leaving the political ideas that were present from the show's outset unfulfilled.

For the most part, political concerns appear to have become sidelined because the show explicitly targeted younger viewers. From what seemed to be an adult take on the superhero premise (with powers that posed their own problems rather than offering simplistic solutions), juvenilia ultimately took precedence, with powers either lost or acquired to further the plot rather than advance our understanding of characters. The lack of emotional impact and limited character development provided little incentive to get involved. Our heroes may change, yet scarcely in a credible way, their actions serving the interests of a fast-moving narrative rather than effective drama; and for all the onward momentum of each season, a degree of stalling was evident. Hence, Peter's potential to become a commanding hero (as anticipated from season one) was continually frustrated by removing his power, his memories, or his confidence—repeatedly failing to assume necessary leadership skills and thus paralleling the show's relative lack of progression. While *Lost*'s characters are largely stuck on an island that prevents them from going anywhere except the past, they at least get the chance to discover new qualities in themselves. *Heroes* ostensibly offers its protagonists a similar opportunity in learning to accommodate and use their powers, yet this was erratic and underdeveloped. The various adult scenarios of the first season are replaced in the second with more adolescent concerns. Many of the Company's founders are revealed to be the flawed parents of our "heroes," leaving their offspring struggling to assert a separate identity. This reworks a key motif in supernatural teen dramas, and the prominence of several *Smallville* staff among the show's initial production team is notable in this regard—yet their subsequent dismissal also affirms a marked uncertainty about the show's aims. Ultimately, while *Heroes* netted 50 percent more viewers in the coveted 18–49 demographic than an average NBC show, finding particular favor among ad-friendly young males (Wilkes 2008), it alienated a growing number of viewers and failed to satisfy on various levels, with budget cuts and reduced special effects limiting the sense of wonder, while poor writing failed to provide any emotional connection to characters. Curiously, for a series designed for long-term investment, *Heroes* treated its characters in an alarmingly cavalier manner—killing many off, forgetting that some exist (such as Claire's younger brother, Lyle [Randall Bentley], and failing to allow anyone to develop realistically. Although it proved itself to be more than a fantasy series commissioned to capitalize on *Lost*'s success—achieving its own style, look, and tone—*Heroes* glossed over necessary details in its execution. Despite borrowing from a variety of sources, and switching moods, locales, and time periods in an effort to retain interest, the factors that would ensure a lasting legacy were oddly overlooked. *Heroes* thus proves the extent to which a higher level of investment in telefantasy (and numerous derivative features) would not necessarily pay dividends, its problems affirming that ticking all the boxes in terms of high production values, fantastic features, hybrid influences, and a degree of self-reference will not compensate for inadequate characterization or plotting.

Diverse "cult" elements were included in the show in an attempt to win favor. Obviously aiming to court the comic sub-culture, *Heroes* incorporates design features that emulate its source material, uses a comic as a key prop (with artist Tim Sale providing the prophetic illustrations created by fictional *9th Wonders* creator Isaac Mendez), and makes various other allusions (such as a cameo by Stan Lee). Interesting casting decisions were evident, such as Seth Green (of *Austin Powers* and *Buffy* fame) playing a nerdy comic shop owner, while other actors associated with cult shows provide the kind of in-joke fans tend to appreciate, with notable cameos from George Takei and Nichelle Nichols (from *Star Trek*) and Christopher Ecclestone (from *Doctor Who*). *Heroes* even goes so far as to borrow an entire character from a cult series, with indestructible blonde school girl Claire obviously referencing *Buffy the Vampire the Slayer*—and potentially aiming to attract some of its fans. However, like Whedon, who has claimed Kitty Pryde—a troubled female character in *The X-Men* comics—to be an influence for *Buffy*, *Heroes* owes its greatest debt to *The X-Men*, with a similar premise in which "mutants" join forces to protect humanity—sometimes from their own "kind." The blockbuster success of *The X-Men* films (Bryan Singer, 2000, 2003, Brett Ratner, 2006) no doubt convinced NBC that a series with a similar premise would be a hit, yet this also created attendant financial demands. High production values were intrinsic to the look of the show (particularly in demonstrating the powers available to characters), featuring beautifully designed sets and stunning special effects, yet at considerable expense, which set up further expectations that successive seasons could not meet. Some early scenes are outstanding artistic achievements, as occurs in season one when Peter Petrelli confronts Sylar for the first time, makes himself invisible, and is surrounded by shards of glass that Sylar mentally raises into the air to detect his position. The effect is the kind of astonishing set-piece many viewers would rave over (with the "trail" left by Daphne's first entrance offering another spectacular example), yet budget cutbacks meant fewer opportunities for spectacle; and with little substance in terms of theme or characterization, declining interest was inevitable.

Although it strove to be a "mainstream cult" series—designed to be appreciated by SF fans without alienating wider audiences—*Heroes* overlooked the basics of good storytelling, which is vital to any show. Even the most casual of viewers seeks a level of satisfaction in return for their attention, which involves characters we can identify with and a plot that amounts to more than a series of stunts and false trails. Although a sense of mystery was created in Primatech's origins, most members of the Company were murdered in the second season, leaving little impetus to learn more about them. The "hook" of knowing how each season's adversary would be defeated also fails to sustain much interest, particularly when we know this outcome to be such a certainty. And with many characters either killed off or insufficiently developed, another reason for watching was lost. *Heroes* may strive to be a mythology show, but without a coherent narrative universe it gave us nothing to believe in and no one to care about. The most interesting figures were either written out or revised beyond recognition, and qualities that made it seem smart disappeared in the face of exasperating inattention to detail. As Joseph Baxter has commented, "When you invest in a character or plot point in *Heroes* it almost never pays any dividends." His advice, as a self-confessed member of the "geek community," was to follow *Lost*'s example more closely:

> Get weird. Let the freak flag fly! Bring back the dead characters, oddball relationships, more time-travel, more alternative universes. "Patriot Act" agitprop is SO 2004, and frankly, people standing on their political soapboxes tend to produce self-indulgent, formulaic fiction.... Instead, go for broke, but be sure that we bring the idea of continuity back, making sure that it all pays off towards the grand scheme of the entire series itself. *Heroes* seemed like it had a larger goal in the first season, but then abandoned it, leaving it wandering aimlessly with lofty, short-term goals and plot points [Baxter 2009].

The desire to see the show make more of its telefantasy potential is a suggestion many would endorse, yet while the carnival offered the opportunity to see a genuine draw of the show—the chance to see new characters and their abilities—this remained limited. As to perceived "agit-prop," we might question whether the abandonment of political allusions was inevitable, with a new government in place. Despite references to 9/11, far from providing a jingoistic hymn to American patriotism in the aftermath of attack, a more nuanced meditation on individuality, difference, and community was seen—appearing to challenge the climate that resulted from the destruction of the World Trade Center. An alternate future shown in the season one episode "Five Years Gone" makes the political point manifest in imagining the consequences of the cataclysmic explosion having occurred, rather than having been averted. Former senator Nathan Petrelli is now president and delivers a commemorative "America Remembers" speech that recalls Linderman's aims of creating unity through grief and hardening resistance to "outsiders." The speech strongly invokes Bush rhetoric, stating, "We've won battles against those who would do us harm," and asserting the need to "preserve our way of life." The satire is wracked up a notch in a later scene when Petrelli arrogantly states, "I'm the leader of the free world—Lord knows how special I am!" before being revealed as the killer he truly is—with Sylar having assumed his form.

Parallel universes and alternate futures have often been used to alert us to diverse possibilities emanating from differing courses of action, and the differing dispositions characters might reveal in contrasting circumstances, and the episode is a stand-out not only because its political ideas are so overt, but because they cannot easily be forgotten, even after the catastrophe is avoided. Within this scenario the formerly virtuous Matt Parkman is now Chief of Homeland Security. He is disillusioned, bitter, and resolved in his hatred toward perceived enemies of the state; while Noah Bennet, formerly occupied with "bagging and tagging" those with powers, smuggles targeted families to safety. It is a frightening future which, the series implies, is never truly avoided, with season three making allusions to Guantanamo, featuring "level 5" prisoners dressed like "detainees" and denied any rights, and a chilling government-endorsed plan to outlaw select citizens. Even without a catastrophe in New York, the ease with which Nathan's proposal is passed suggests that prejudice may not need to be prodded; and although the new fictional president (played by *Star Trek*'s Michael Dorn) revokes the decision, seemingly anticipating a new liberal era, suspicions remain in having a murderer masquerade as ambitious Senator Petrelli. It is consequently a shame the Nathan/Sylar storyline goes nowhere in "Redemption," with Nathan killed off and Sylar redeemed as a hero, thus failing to capitalize on the potential to bring the series in line with its earlier prediction—the kind of clever cross-referencing that would have helped establish its true cult credibility. Commentators such as Baxter may consider the political allusions passé, but in many ways this helped give *Heroes* relevance, drawing on a legacy that includes *The X-Files* and *The Prisoner* in suggesting that politicians cannot be trusted, contending that the threat faced by humanity is global, and affirming that heroes of various nationalities must collaborate.

The diverse nationalities of the "heroes" introduced in the first season not only plugged Kring's ethos of "interconnectivity" but helped establish the show as an international success. While *Lost* was daring in presenting an Iraqi character as a hero in the immediate wake of the Gulf war, as well as a multicultural cast that included British, Australian, African and Korean characters, *Heroes* was similarly inclusive—with characters from India, Japan, Haiti, South America, and the U.K., in addition to the U.S. (where the principal action takes place). The first season interestingly unveils the considerable power held by senior Company man Daniel Linderman over a cross-section of the nation, with three classes represented by three different families under his influence: the Petrellis, an affluent Italian-American family with political ambitions (which Linderman seeks to advance for his own ends); the Bennets, a middle-class WASP household (headed by a man who captures specials for Linderman); and the Sanders family, the disempowered working class, comprised of a jailbird and a stripper (who are equally in thrall to Linderman). D.L. Sanders (Leonard Roberts) is revealed as a fall-guy for Linderman's criminal activities, serving time in jail while "The Man" exploits his family. His powers enable him to flee prison, uniting with estranged wife Niki (Ali Larter) to protect their son, Micah (Noah Gray-Cabey), whose ability to manipulate computers is sought by Linderman, aiming to rig an election and establish Nathan Petrelli as Senator. This complex narrative arc would cause many to look back wistfully and wonder what might have been. In associating villainy with immense corporate power and the ability to manipulate a host of characters' lives, an unsettling conspiracy is suggested. The fact that the least socially powerful of the families fights back adds a radical touch—yet such promise was eclipsed by competing storylines. Linderman dies at the end of the season, Sylar is promoted to top villain, and an explosion becomes the focus of attention rather than Linderman's sinister web of influence. D.L. is killed by Linderman's henchmen after a few appearances, and the writers prove no more successful in developing roles for his family. The second season relocates his wife and son to New Orleans, presenting Micah's cousin, Monica Dawson (Dana Davis), as a beacon of hope in the aftermath of Hurricane Katrina—with powers that allow her to emulate anything she sees on television. However, her heroic role is undermined by crude stereotypes of criminal gang bangers, and the second season ends dismally for the family, with Monica left to die in a blazing building by a gang of thieves who have robbed little Micah of his father's treasured comic collection. Although Niki saves Monica in the final moments of the finale, at her son's behest, she fails to get out before the building collapses, leaving Micah orphaned—and Monica forgotten for the remainder of the series.

Despite an array of interesting characters in an intricately organized narrative, this falls apart with drastic plot changes and characters who amount to little more than caricatures. Hiro may be intended as the ultimate geek fantasy, trading the confines of his office booth to travel in time and space, yet his childish mannerisms (prone to extending his arms in delight and trundling around looking for ways to prove his destiny) made his regression to a ten-year-old in the third season scarcely any different than his usual demeanor. Hiro and sidekick, Ando, were seemingly intended to appeal to the child audience, but they veer from endearing to irritating. The Haitian was a virtually silent, unfathomable tool of the Company who performs a near lobotomy on subjects, removing their memories. Season three expands his role when he dispatches a murderous, sexually abusive brother (who happens to be in charge of a military dictatorship), yet this is chiefly to inspire Nathan's plan of an augmented army, citing various international conflicts he can subsequently involve himself with! Clichés pile up fast in the series, with Latino characters undone by an excess of emotion, and Irish crooks offering further abysmal stereotypes. When the writers got themselves into a blind alley they simply stopped a storyline and removed the figures involved, with frustrating consequences for those watching closely, reducing the desire to pay any heed at all to events.

Premature deaths were still more disappointing, with a tendency to kill off the most interesting characters. Niki, for example, was one of the most intriguing of the original heroes, with a split personality that allows alter ego "Jessica" to appear whenever she is in difficulty. She is first introduced hustling her body via a webcam strip-show, doing so to pay the bills—including a school that will nurture her son's talents. We discover that "Jessica" is what enables Niki to survive as a single mother, both through her sexual confidence and her ability to defend herself, yet this alter ego is assessed as a danger to her sanity. Thanks to Ali Larter's performance, the character has conviction and sympathy; and even if the reason given for her split persona is weak (reworking the *Single White Female* plot of a dead twin her subconscious has resurrected), her conflicted identity creates one of the most interesting characters seen in the show. Nonetheless, after forcing her on a path of redemption that empties her of any interest, the writers turn Niki into a tragic victim. Hospitalized as a dangerous schizoid, and subsequently electing to work for Primatech in return for having her power removed, Niki is diagnosed with the deadly Shanti virus but dies in New Orleans trying to save her niece, underscoring her total powerlessness without Jessica. While ambivalence always adds interest to characters, the show demonizes this aspect of her personality and ultimately kills her off—along with her "better half." By contrast, indicating the skewered sexual politics at work in the series, its resident bogeyman, far from being condemned and killed, effectively steals the show. Sylar is the name used to describe the destructive id motivating mild-mannered watchmaker Gabriel Gray to become a killer. A mother complex is trotted out in his defense midway through season one, and augmented with a bad father in season three. "Villains" indicates potential redemption, as he briefly works for Primatech, recapturing fellow inmates, and a flash-forward of him as a loving father suggests his capacity to change (and potentially revert to being Gabriel). For the most part, however, he is a ruthless killer who goes unpunished despite his obvious villainy, and even graduates to hero status by the end of the fourth season. Jessica has an equivalent parental excuse and only uses violence as a means of defense, yet is condemned all the same.

Claire Bennet—mawkishly referred to by her adopted father Noah as "Claire-Bear"—seemingly epitomizes the show's idea of approved female heroism. Pretty, pouty, and almost entirely passive, she suffers from arrested development for much of the series. Reminiscent of Buffy Summers in her appearance and remarkable ability to heal, her power is first showcased when we see her jump from a crane, apparently attempting to kill herself, only to realize she is cataloguing her abilities on video with a friend, and that this is her "sixth attempt." How she discovered this ability is perplexing, seemingly emanating from self-harm, yet we never really get to know her beyond a troubling devotion to her foster father and a power that is scarcely empowering. Claire may resemble Buffy in her near indestructibility, but she does not have the Slayer's fighting skills; and when a boy at school tries to rape her, as he has other classmates, she is unable to defend herself and is accidentally killed in the attempt (eventually reviving post-autopsy). Her revenge is to crash a car with him inside, knowing he will recover more slowly from his injuries, and assuming he will use the time to reflect on his misdeeds. Designed primarily to be a figure in peril—the "cheerleader" of the series that requires saving—her primary mission is to unite the other heroes in season one, and she has little to do thereafter. A "flash-forward" at the beginning of season three may show a "badass Claire" with heavy black eye-liner and a skintight leather outfit, anticipating a dramatic transition to look forward to, but this was never followed up (much like the alternate versions of Peter and Nikki). "Redemption" sends Claire to college, further mirroring *Buffy* as she explores campus life and embarks on a relationship with her roommate (a plot development seemingly designed to boost ratings rather than offer a genuine exploration of sexuality); and her final scene, jumping from a Ferris wheel before the press in order to "out" fellow freaks (regardless of the consequences), suggests that she has failed to mature at all in the show.

While Claire amounts to little more than eye candy, without much range beyond her one-note "troubled teen" routine, Angela Petrelli provides an interesting contrast. The black-clad matriarch of the Italian-American clan is first presented as a somewhat pitiable figure, shoplifting socks to gain her sons' attention, yet is subsequently portrayed as a seemingly heartless mother, the epitome of the ball-breaking bitch. Late in season two she reveals that she agreed with Adam Monroe's view that "the world needed to be wiped clean," and further establishes her villainy a season later by deceiving Sylar into thinking he is her son—even feeding him a female special so that he can extract her power. However, an attempt is subsequently made to rehabilitate Angela as a hero. Season three provides a flashback to events 18 months earlier ("Villains"), presenting Angela as a downtrodden housewife subjected to regular bouts of amnesia secured by her husband, with the help of the Haitian. Linderman makes her aware of this deception; and as Arthur plots to kill their eldest son (to protect his ambitions), she poisons his supper. Whether she is a villain or hero remains open, yet the flashback suggests we have been misled by her professed indifference to her sons, and implies that she has created a tough persona to protect herself. The subsequent detailing of her family tragedy (in "1961") affirms this, yet the suggestion that she is, at heart, a sock-stealing softie is both unconvincing and unnecessary. In this new version of events, Angela is responsible for originating the Company (despite previously stating Adam Monroe united the group a decade later)—an attempt at mythologizing that produces yet another inconsistency. Angela's power is vaguely described as a Cassandra-like ability to see the future, yet this fails to benefit her (just as a brief acquisition of precognitive powers prevents Parkman from saving Daphne). By "Redemption," her warnings are finally heeded, helping to avoid disaster, yet by this point she is a far less compelling character thanks to some misguided meddling.

Time and again decisions are made about characters that fail to ring true, as is indicated by the attempt to resurrect Niki as Traci in the third season (explained as a cloned triplet). The writers thus attempt to provide Larter with a reboot, yet squander her talents on a character with a so-so power (the ability to freeze and—later—to become water) given little to do. Although she is introduced as a political campaigner who is so devastated by guilt over the fatal consequences of her power that she attempts suicide, she undergoes a series of transformations, resulting in a scheming hustler who is dropped by Nathan after a brief romance and even punched in the face by Hiro, ultimately amounting to little more than a convenient hate figure. Although Fuller vetoed her death—affirming Larter was too good an actress to waste—Traci's subsequent treatment in season four was deplorable, with a scene in her underwear during a girly evening with Claire achieving a new low. Other female characters underscore the apparent difficulty of portraying powerful women without demonizing or belittling them. Maya Herrera (Dania Ramirez) and her brother Alejandro (Shalim Ortiz) are twins from the Dominican Republic who travel to the USA to seek a cure for Maya's power—an ability to kill with her tears—which is particularly unsettling given a temperament that provokes tears at the drop of a hat. Maya undergoes a startling transformation. From the woman first seen demurely dressed in a nun's habit, believing herself to be cursed, she is subsequently clothed in increasingly skimpy outfits, embarks on a rapidly devised romance with Sylar (who attempts to murder her), and later takes up with Mohinder (who also becomes a murderous monster). A deadly female is thus made into a naïve dupe who barely survives two near-death experiences (at the hands of former lovers) prior to being written out.

Many female characters are not so fortunate. A procession of females are killed off (most frequently by Sylar), including Charlie (Charlene Andrews), the waitress with an astonishing memory (later saved by Hiro); the *Nikita*-like Eden (Nora Zehetner), whose telepathic abilities—and shady past—begged to be explored further; and Candice (Missy Peregrym), an illusionist with an ability to conjure vivid fantasies who appeared in various guises in season one, demonstrating mesmerizing potential, but was brutally killed by Sylar at the start of the second series shortly after telling him she saved his life at Kirby Plaza ("Kindred"). The removal of so many powerful females means they never become regular characters, and their abilities are simply given to someone else (if not Sylar then another male character), with Candice's power later explored via Matt's father, Maury Parkman (Alan Blumenfeld). Indeed, one of the most interesting episodes of the series ("Fight or Flight") features the illusions Maury is able to conjure in a brilliantly shot, disorientating psychodrama accomplished in a dazzling directorial turn by Lesli Link Glatter (who also helmed one of the most memorable *Twin Peaks* episodes). The fact that Maury is subsequently killed by Arthur Petrelli while attempting to defend his son (á la *Star Wars*) indicates that male characters are not immune to being killed off, with the writers regularly culling the cast to inject drama, yet tending to lose the most intriguing figures.

We see marriages fail and new romances undertaken, with astonishing rapidity, and characters introduced and dispensed with at an alarming rate— all of which may be good for momentum yet does not provide the character development and emotional realism audiences seek today. Massive plot holes and casual disregard for continuity deter investment, expressing greater interest in astounding viewers than providing any depth. The hasty re-writing of characters and their situations is particularly marked from season two. Nathan's family is abruptly removed from the series and never heard from again. The end to Matt Parkman's marriage is still more unsettling because we saw his relationship with Janice improve, and both seemed overjoyed by her pregnancy at the close of the first season. Nonetheless, the second season opens with his marriage over, and an explanation—that the child wasn't his—only disclosed in passing a few episodes on. Her return two seasons later, and the discovery that the child is, in fact, Matt's, aims to excise two seasons of plotting—including a romance with the tragic Daphne—taking obvious liberties with credibility and further indicating sloppy writing. Although Janice was treated appallingly by Matt, she seemingly bears no ill-feeling, and resembles nothing so much as a manikin by the fourth season. Sandra Bennet (Ashley Crow), Noah's long-suffering wife, had an equally poor storyline. We learn, early in the first series, that Noah regularly wiped her memories by using the mental powers of the Haitian (as Arthur did with Angela). He did so, he claims, to spare her any worry, yet the result is a daffy child-woman who coos over her dog, Mr. Muggles, as if it were a baby and suffers from a facial tic that resembles the aftermath of a stroke. Even when she discovers what has been done to her, Sandra stays loyal to H.R.G., and it is only in the fourth volume, after realizing he is still lying to her, that she files for divorce—a move designed to liberate *his* character rather than hers, continuing a tendency to privilege male characters.

Despite routinely brainwashing her mother, Claire's devotion to H.R.G. seemingly knows no bounds, even when she learns the truth about his job (working as a henchman for the Company), and that former boyfriend West (Nick D'Agosto) was abducted by him as a child. Furthermore, the show problematically supports her unflinching forgiveness, evidently wishing to make a hero out of H.R.G., no matter what atrocities he has committed. His lack of pity about the near-vegetable he turned his wife into scarcely seems to trouble the show's writers, and in a series where bad fathers stack up in numbers that rival *Lost*, H.R.G. appears to be exonerated by his love for his adopted daughter. This is partly achieved by contrasting him with Bob Bishop (Stephen Tobolowsky), who can turn base metal into gold yet seems more intent on turning his girl into an accomplished killer. Thanks to brilliant performances by Tobolowsky as new Company head Bob, and Kristin Bell as his daughter Elle, a crucial dynamic was added to the series. Able to shoot electricity from her hands, we first see Elle overstepping her father's orders by killing a "civilian," and subsequently witness a vulnerable and somewhat unhinged girl, desperate to secure her father's approval. Bob may aim to hone his daughter's killing skills, in a relationship reminiscent of Mayor Wilkins and Faith in *Buffy*, yet his lack of paternal affection is what makes him monstrous—and H.R.G. subverts Elle's loyalties by revealing that Bob would test her with electrical shocks as a child, warping his daughter's development. Season one provided a maternal equivalent to this backstory when Sylar visits his mother and blames her for creating the inadequacy that made him into a murderer—eventually killing her when she turns on him ("The Hard Part"). Season three unites the pair of messed-up offspring, sharing their parental disappointments as they become lovers, despite Bob's death at Sylar's hands. Although Elle shows heroic potential and affirms Sylar's capacity to change, he senselessly kills her while they are on the run together, shocking and disappointing many fans. An annoying younger brother is suggested for Sylar later the same season, sharing similarly psychopathic tendencies and marked antipathy towards women (including his own mother) but he is notably spared, like Sylar's equally abhorrent father, showing a degree of mercy to repellant male figures that he denies his lover, despite the understanding she has shown him, affirming a deep-seated misogyny. H.R.G.'s questionable morality, and poor father figures such as Maury, Arthur and Bob, are all eclipsed by the villainous Sylar, who the writers inordinately focus on, ignoring other plot points in their efforts to keep him onscreen.

For example, a key mystery, set up from the beginning of *Heroes*, is the Company's motivations in creating special powers. An aim to improve the world was seemingly compromised by the contrasting conviction that humanity is not worth saving. Linderman believed destruction would bring unity, while Adam's four hundred years observing humanity convinced him another "flood" was needed to wipe our sins clean—leading to his imprisonment by Kaito Nakamura, the sole member of the group to apologize for their actions. By contrast, Angela defends them, stating, "Our generation mortgaged our souls to protect your interests, show a little respect. Get over your daddy issues and let us be" ("Cautionary Tales"). Whether they truly intended to protect their children or to exploit them is never stated, with the writers seeming uncertain about their purpose and failing to adequately develop the underlying mythology of the series. Although further background to the Company is found in the extended universe (for those who cared to look online), the information largely fails to cohere into anything substantial, much like the series itself.

There are some practical reasons for many such omissions and inconsistencies, with Kring and his cohorts having to devise the show quite rapidly and deliver it on a host of platforms (diverting their attention while spreading the material thin). Many of *Heroes*' discrepancies can be attributed to the sheer scale of production soon after being commissioned, with escalating expectations adding further pressure. Production was so intense that several characters were created *after* auditions (as occurred with *Lost*), and the somewhat ad hoc nature of the planning process is indicated by Kring's admission that the tag-line used to market the series—"save the cheerleader, save the world"—was simply thrown out during a meeting without making any sense (Naughton 21). Events in season two were designed to make the phrase more meaningful, with Claire's blood saving the world from a fatal virus, yet these healing properties were subsequently ignored to preserve a sense of jeopardy. In making Claire the "Catalyst" in season three (the agent needed to activate the genetic formula), her importance is further explained, borrowing from the Dawn/key trope in *Buffy*; yet this was yet another addition that went nowhere. Like *The X-Files* (which ensured the Truth was literally "out there") and *Lost* (which relies so much on the supernatural to fuel its mysteries it loses any connection with reality), *Heroes* created an incoherent mess, initiating developments that jar with audience expectation, characters that either change too radically or not enough, and plot points which are either implausible or repetitive. Unlike *Lost*, destiny is not predetermined, and key changes occur at the whim of the writers, with little ability to predict events—and still less inclination to care.

Abrupt decisions are taken about characters without the pacing or plotting required to explain matters, and the writers frequently perform a "Haitian"-style trick with viewers, aiming to wipe our memories of the past to focus on the present. Regular viewers know something is not right in the resulting discontinuity, yet such tendencies seemingly result from differing writers working on the show who were severely at odds in their intentions, without any real authorial presence on Kring's part (who seems to have left them to their own devices). Perhaps the biggest letdown is the failure to show how characters accommodate their abilities or struggle to cope with more everyday problems, which would add greater emotional resonance to the series. Rather than focus on the problems caused by their powers, complex figures such as Nikki, Maya and Elle are eliminated, wasting their dramatic potential. The Vortex Man, Stephen Canfield (Andre Royo), offers another missed opportunity to assess the premise with intelligence. Categorized as a "level 5" prisoner, he reveals himself to be a decent man who, like season one's Radioactive Man, Ted Sprague (Matthew John-Armstrong), has seen his power destroy his life. Refusing to be used as a killer by H.R.G., he finally uses it on himself. Jeremy

(Mark L. Young) offers a similar example. A misunderstood teen, able to either kill or cure with his touch, he atones for his guilt at accidentally murdering his parents by allowing the police to kill him, dispensing with yet another intriguing character. The pursuit of endless novelty may motivate such exits, allowing room for further "specials" to make their entrance, yet the result is a frustrating succession of protagonists at the expense of effective drama.

It is seemingly to invite emotional investment that difficult family relations are prominent. Some characters have "daddy issues," as Angela pithily puts it; some have mother complexes; and many either fail to live up to their parents' expectations or are otherwise traumatized by them. Niki blames her father for her sister's death—which leaves her with schizophrenic symptoms. Elle is deeply affecting as a little girl figure, desperately craving her father's approval, and subsequently transferring her affections to the man that killed him in a vain desire to see the best in Sylar—which is as touching as it is tragic. Mohinder and Matt experience paternal rifts that can never be healed, once their fathers are killed, yet emulate their flaws, with Mohinder compromising his integrity prior to removal from the series, and Matt, on one interesting occasion, causing Angela to have a nosebleed as he tries to force thoughts from her mind, prompting her to point out that he is no different than his father, Nathan proves that he is party to the same genetic flaws in pledging to continue his father's aims of creating an augmented army, and is even willing to kill his brother to realize this ambition—before the writers opt to reshuffle the deck again. However, while we are meant to forget their quarrel and move on, their conflict exposes a fundamental inconsistency. Is Nathan wrong in desiring to reproduce the formula, particularly as the series has attested that the human race needs people with special powers? We may see figures abuse their powers, but many more use them for good, which seemingly condones the Company's actions (in genetically creating abilities); but the series leaves their reason for doing so (and subsequent actions) frustratingly unclear.

For the most part, rather than provide a coherent narrative, the chief aim seemed to be in surprising viewers with continuous twists, seeking to create fabled "water cooler moments." As a younger demographic became a more explicit focus, adult concerns were excised, along with the majority of older characters, leaving us with an array of childlike women and boyish men acting out comic fantasies. *Heroes* may have evolved to meet the needs of the network, but it fundamentally misfired, having the pace of an action series without the depth or consistency of characterization that make for a gripping drama. Although the series set itself apart by emulating a comic in its look and premise, it failed to provide a credible fictional world or protagonists we could identify with. While comics allow for such sketchiness, with inferred events requiring the reader to fill in the gaps, television series are expected to provide more than the minimum to tell an effective story. It is all very well to have continued variation in mood and setting, comic childlike characters to please younger viewers, and darker touches like a ruthless serial killer who slices skulls open, but *Heroes* badly needed a sense of purpose and effective characterization. As one blogger tellingly commented:

> I'm no longer feeling invested in this series at all.... *Heroes* characters are just sloppy and inconsistent as hell. They switch sides any time the writers want them to. They gain and lose powers on a whim. If a character can go anywhere, do anything, who really cares what they eventually do? [Delucci 2008].

Prior to its cancellation, entire message boards were dedicated to complaining about the series, resulting in an online community of "haters" stating their continued disappointment and lamenting how far *Heroes* had declined from the intelligence of season one. Time will tell whether it is likely to be recalled as anything more than an expensive flop, yet it is doubtful it can redeem itself in retrospect—even if Kring manages to get a 2-hour movie to wrap it up, as sought. Genuine cult interest requires complex characters and narrative details that develop logically from one season to the next in order to be considered a worthwhile investment (both on an emotional and intellectual level), all of which was conspicuously absent from the show. Although some effort was made to inscribe cult appeal, with features designed for a "knowing" audience, such strategies reveal only the most superficial understanding of what constitutes a cult. When Christopher Ecclestone introduces himself by saying, "I'm the invisible man. I'm Claude Rains" ("The Fix"), those familiar with the classic film version of Wells' story will recognize the allusion, while *Doctor Who* fans get a chance to see the ninth doctor in another milieu, augmenting the postmodern referencing we have come to expect from cult shows. By the same token, when Noah Bennet urges a couple to try the cherry pie in a diner scene ("The Hard Part"), *Twin Peaks* is deliberately invoked. Some in-jokes are more obvious, such as when Hiro, a self-confessed *Star Trek* fan, meets with his father, and we recognize the actor as George Takei, who played Lt. Hikaru Sulu in the original *Star Trek* series. Such referencing suggests more than a gag for the geeks, it attempts to situate the series among an established lineage of shows it clearly hoped to emulate.

Whether it will be equally revered and recognized in years to come is unlikely, yet in many ways *Heroes* found global appeal by reiterating a similar dictum to *Star Trek*—affirming that people can become extraordinary and work together for the common good. A hymn to humanity's potential was posited, creating a saga in which the ability to fly or heal are only as important as the ends they serve. Villains may epitomize the worst of humanity, yet our heroes shone a beacon of hope (like the eclipse logo used in the show), defying the nihilism that characterizes the majority of cult telefantasy shows appraised in this study. *The Prisoner* presents a community where camaraderie is made impossible through surveillance and social coercion, while *Twin Peaks* residents are under continual threat from internal rivalries and demonic forces. *The X-*

Files underscores a similar fatalism, with protagonists incapable of achieving a degree of personal happiness in their lives, much less eliciting change in the wider world. *Buffy* came along and changed all the rules, allowing its long-suffering hero to emerge triumphant, while *Lost* also sought to reassure, in its own way, by presenting an ideal community capable of restoring a metaphoric paradise. *Heroes* invests more overtly in old-fashioned feel-good optimism, providing heroes that triumph over disaster (and poor parental role models), even as they are condemned to repeat the same scenario each season. However, despite endeavoring to be a crowd pleaser, it failed to sustain interest, irrespective of the vast potential and enviable resources at its disposal.

If *Buffy* was the little show that could, *Heroes* may well be recalled as the big show that couldn't, despite network backing and a seemingly winning formula. An attendant irony lies in the fact that although the show made the most of its multimedia potential, these same technologies were perceived as a cause of declining ratings, encouraging fans to watch through other forums and thus obscuring its true appeal. Kring blamed the increased use of DVRs and streamed episodes for lower Nielsen ratings, contending that viewers were opting to see *Heroes* in alternative formats (Hinman 2008), and he made a similar point when the show was cancelled two years later. This highlights a problem likely to affect any contemporary series, with broadcast ratings serving as the central measure of a show's success, which is clearly unfair to those watched via other media (as is increasingly likely). However, it was not simply the case that *Heroes* lost terrestrial viewers because they moved to digital media, as Kring sought to argue. Many simply abandoned the show due to its failure to remedy mistakes and reward fan loyalty by paying equivalent attention to details—and Kring's denial on this score confirms that the series had no chance of improving. Ultimately, the real test for *Heroes* is whether there is an audience for it in the future—the yardstick of a true cult series and one it seems unlikely to measure up to. Long after a show has ended, a new life can be found via DVDs and the Internet. Fans will continue to discuss specific episodes, pore over details, speculate on characters and events, and perhaps extend them through their own fiction. The continued interest generated around the shows discussed in this book proves how persistent such devotion can be. Whether it is the ideology or iconography of *The Prisoner*, the quirkiness of *Twin Peaks*, the memorable monsters featured in the classic episodes of *The X-Files*, or the continued capacity for surprises wrought by *Buffy*, a series can survive long after its cancellation; and in some cases, it can even be resurrected. The next chapter focuses on two such shows, *Doctor Who* and *Star Trek*, which have become the longest-running telefantasy franchises of all time. While Kring had these in mind in his plans for *Heroes*, stating, "You only hope to have that kind of success and longevity" (Morgan 2008), he wrongly believed continual evolution was the principal factor required, negating the other elements needed to give a show staying power—including listening to fans.

7

Doctor Who and *Star Trek*: Twenty-First Century Reboots

This chapter brings the study of telefantasy full circle by evaluating two of the most enduring cult series, *Doctor Who* (1963–) and *Star Trek* (1966–), contrasting their premises, recalling their production histories, and assessing their likely futures. Although both have become globally successful franchises, they have struggled to attract continued interest, faced with increased commercial pressure, changing tastes, and the perennial dilemma of providing new variations on established themes without deviating too drastically from expectations. In attempting to explain their remarkable longevity, critics have outlined several factors, including their ability to inspire differing levels of interest and continued innovation around a central conceit. Henry Jenkins and John Tulloch assert that a capacity to attract (and reward) multiple forms of interest is fundamental to their appeal, with Tulloch noting that "like *Star Trek*, *Doctor Who* clearly constitutes itself to position several different audiences" (1995, 59). James Chapman affirms that a major draw for *Doctor Who* is the "flexibility of its format in exploring a wide range of narrative possibilities and genre templates" (2006, 3), while Catherine Johnson commends *Star Trek*'s ability to fulfill "the dual demands of story latitude and audience identification, offering a wide range of different stories within one format" (2005, 82). Both shows have clearly benefited from a concept that enables narrative diversity within a familiar framework. Emerging at a time when television SF consisted of anthology shows or brief serials, the utilization of a continuous series format (featuring the same characters and basic premise) played a crucial role in fostering audience engagement, while SF's expansive narrative potential enabled a variety of stories to be told—factors that would help *Doctor Who* and *Star Trek* defy the odds by surviving, in one form or another, for the better part of four decades. With five-year runs the standard aim for most series (providing the optimum number of episodes for syndication), and many failing to last this long, these franchises are notable exceptions to the rule in managing to survive so long, albeit with varying fortunes. In assessing their attempts to reinvent themselves for the twenty-first century, evident tensions are discernible in attempting to balance familiarity and variety, and in their mutual need to attract new interest without alienating the existing fan base.

Doctor Who and *Star Trek* are each iconic SF shows. Not only have they attracted an intense fan following, they also signify a huge commodity for their respective corporations, with vast franchises evolving to reap the rewards of their popularity. Nonetheless, although they are now considered to be quintessential cult hits, success was by no means assured, with both series taking a remarkable leap of faith at the time of their inception. Originating on either side of the Atlantic within a few years of one another, each show pushed the boundaries of broadcasting in developing long-form telefantasy, using regular characters to create familiarity while SF tropes generated a multitude of plot ideas. A new take was thus provided on the action-adventure format, with satirical or allegorical themes creating additional intellectual appeal, taking telefantasy to a hitherto unexplored realm. A great deal of SF and fantasy was aimed at a juvenile male audience in the early years of television, often made by individuals unfamiliar with the genre and led by false perceptions about who it would interest. Headway was made by key innovators who believed that a wider audience existed for fantastic material, and that quality drama could be delivered without resorting to cliché. *Doctor Who* and *Star Trek* each emanated from a shared belief on the part of their makers in SF's potential; and while their early effects may appear a little creaky by today's standards, their lengthy histories testify to an enduring quality that has given them genuine landmark status. While both shows began as risky ventures—and had a tumultuous history in which they experienced poor scheduling slots, declining ratings, and eventual cancellation—they have since become globally successful franchises, proving, through continually reinventing themselves, that longevity is achievable, even in a medium that tends to be very transitory. Carefully crafted fictional universes have been developed in each show, populated by a variety of species, planets, and recurring characters. Equally significantly, viewers have played an active role in their construction: writing fan fiction, organizing campaigns to save them, keeping their spirit alive when networks had given them up for dead, and sometimes playing a direct part in their creation. Indeed, while Whovians and Trekkers have gained notoriety as the most devoted of fans, some have also taken a professional role in production, a development that indicates the increasingly complex relationship between a cult text, its makers, and its audience.

Critical assessments of fan interest in popular television tend to invoke a "David and Goliath" template in which lowly fans fight industrial Titans to keep their favorite shows on the air, battling copyright restrictions to discuss episodes online or to defend their right to make ancillary products of their own, such as drawings, stories, or other creative enterprises. Henry Jenkins' evaluation of the fan as "textual poacher" champions the perceived underdog in a vastly unequal battle, arguing that "fandom originates, at least in part, as a response to the relative powerlessness of the consumer in relation to powerful institutions of cultural production and circulation" (Jenkins 1992, 278). While audiences are said to take what they need from popular texts, Jenkins notes that undue power remains with broadcasters, as is demonstrated by their ability to alter or cancel a show, despite fan protests. More recently, however, he has shifted his position, as the relationship between audience and industry is itself perceived to have shifted in today's "convergence culture"—a situation in which feedback is readily sought from viewers and media products shaped accordingly (Jenkins 2006). This assertion may seem somewhat idealistic, yet greater interaction between the industry and audience is increasingly apparent, together with greater willingness among industry personnel to admit fannish sympathies. The emergence of the fan-producer is key in this regard, holding the promise of brokering fan interests through their mutual appreciation of a beloved show and their presumed ability to represent shared concerns. However, this does not preclude upsetting fans on occasion, with the creative ownership of shows remaining a highly contested area. This is particularly so in the case of series which have existed for over forty years, having attained an established fan base that is keen to protect its investment, prone to voice disgruntlement in noting any changes (or perceived wrong turns), and ready to target those deemed responsible.

When self-confessed fan Russell T. Davies became involved in revising *Doctor Who* in 2005, he was swiftly championed by fans for reviving a beloved show; yet detraction soon mounted against him, proving how quickly the tide of popular approval can turn. After Davies stepped down as head writer and executive producer in 2009, the BBC took the unusual decision to "rest" the show for a year, taking *Who* off the air—bar a few one-off "specials"—with a 21-month gap between seasons 4 and 5. This coincided with a new actor chosen to play the lead character, the announcement of fan favorite Steven Moffat taking over as head writer, and a number of changes among the production staff—decisions seemingly aimed to stall any hints of franchise fatigue and effectively start again. While the periodic replacement of producers and head writers is a familiar part of *Doctor Who*'s production history, taking a year off appears to have been a shrewd attempt to avoid being taken for granted. Series 5 returned in April 2010 with a new theme tune, a new cast and crew, a redesigned set, HD-compatible shooting style, and a limited run of only 13 episodes. An interactive game version, The Adventure Games, was launched online, and a seasonal story arc was set up to maintain audience interest until the denouement—ideas adopted by contemporary U.S. cult series, which affirm the show's attempt to continually reinvent itself. However, despite these measures and a great deal of prior anticipation, the season saw a decline in its former ratings and elicited grumblings of discontent about poorly plotted stories and limited character development—affirming that achieving (and, more importantly, maintaining) cult success is a continual challenge. Like Davies, Moffat was a long-term fan of the show, and has credited his childhood love of *Doctor Who* for inspiring him to work in television, yet while this personal investment would help endear them to fans, it has not saved either Davies or Moffat from criticism, eliciting, if anything, still greater disappointment for making perceived mistakes.

Star Trek makes an interesting contrast, with its own share of reboots and revivals over the years, the most successful of which was the first revised series, *Star Trek: The Next Generation* (1987–1994). A host of spin-offs followed, with the franchise staying on the air for eighteen successive years, only to conclude dismally with *Enterprise* (2001–5). This final spin-off sought to radically reboot the franchise; yet in displaying an appalling lack of understanding by executive producers Rick Berman and Brannon Braga, it adversely affected it instead. Neither individual had been a fan of the original series, which was a poor recommendation in helming a prequel series; but an additional problem was that both mistakenly thought they could rewrite the show's mythology in a bid to attract new fans—a move that left them alienating the established cohort. By the time they realized the error of their ways (when long-term fan Manny Coto took charge in the fourth season), it was too late to avoid cancellation, and many wondered if this was the end for *Trek*. After a four-year hiatus, continued appeal was proven when Paramount commissioned an eleventh film, *Star Trek* (2009), featuring the original series' crew (played by younger actors), using *Lost*'s creative team to secure a cult cachet, and combining narrative elements that give a nod to the existing fan base while also aiming to appeal to non–Trekkers. The film was a huge hit, leading to two sequels planned (at the time of writing) and prompting discussions about a potential new series—proving that, like *Doctor Who*, the franchise cannot easily be written off. Fan approval of these latest incarnations may remain tentative, but a strategy of continued evolution is how they have survived thus far (and is an evident necessity if they are to have any kind of future). It is in eliciting new interest while remaining "true" to their established identities that they face their biggest dilemma, having to redesign themselves in a bid to survive while also remaining recognizable.

When they each began they had novelty on their side, originating at a time when serious SF was relatively untested. In the U.K., the BBC's *Quatermass* serials (1953, 1955, 1958–9) and Nigel Kneale's adaptation of *1984* (1954) broached sobering concerns about science and the power of the state. In the U.S., CBS oversaw two landmark anthology series—*Alfred Hitchcock Presents* (1955–62), offering assorted tales of mystery, suspense, and occasional horror; and Rod Serling's *The Twilight Zone* (1959–64), providing viewers with well-crafted dramas, an element of whimsy, and something to think about. Serling's show was born from frustration at continued interference with his writing, complaining that "by the time it's seen on the home screen, all the message has been squeezed out of it" (Gerani 36). By utilizing a genre the censors generally overlooked, he was able to create television drama where the message remained intact, and gave the world of telefantasy its first masterpiece. *Doctor Who* and *Star Trek* would similarly seek to explore the genre's imaginative intellectual function, using SF scenarios to extrapolate fantastical events on Earth, or speculate about the existence of other worlds, species and social systems. In doing so they would provide compelling drama that frequently aimed to provoke consideration, questioned specific values and beliefs, and promoted ideals that struck a chord with audiences.

Travels in time and space serve as the central trope in each series, offering excitement, escapism, and a sense of variety that would play an important part in attracting viewers, yet their underlying optimism is equally significant in understanding their appeal. Although conflicts regularly arise, an orderly narrative universe is presented in each show, and order is generally restored by the end of each story. *Doctor Who* features an alien Time Lord from Gallifrey, known as "the Doctor," who wanders the galaxy in a time and space machine (the TARDIS) and overcomes oppression wherever he finds it. *Star Trek* is similarly "progressive" in its own way. A multinational crew of quasi-military explorers cruise unknown sectors of the galaxy in a vast spaceship, and while they often evade an official policy of non-interference by intervening in the concerns of other (less developed) species, they do so under the rubric of spreading democracy and liberation. At the time of their inception there was an inspirational quality to these ideals, with characters daring to act, despite risk of censure, armed with the conviction that they are morally right. This ideological commitment would attract a growing number of fans, suggesting that exploitation can be overcome, and tolerance and understanding attained, securing an audience that crosses gender, age, and even national boundaries by providing an essentially optimistic message. They have proven to be inspirational on a meta-textual level also—in the fan response they have generated (which has been integral to their ongoing success) and in affirming SF's compatibility with long-form television (simply by surviving so long). As their respective histories indicate, both franchises relied on key figures who were keen to test the audience with untried material, networks willing to endorse such experiments, and viewers prepared to protest when their shows were threatened (and who would continue to demonstrate their interest even after they went off the air). As time has passed, a second generation of executive producers and show-runners has been required to implement change and attract new audiences—while retaining the approval of established fans—no mean feat by any stretch of the imagination and a continual challenge for both franchises.

Doctor Who has the distinction of being the longest-running SF series of all time, an achievement which can partly be explained by its numerous franchise features, including a format that enables generic flexibility (vital to enabling variety and prolonging audience interest) and in being created by a network that was able to release a range of affiliated material (widening its market and increasing revenue). It also made a virtue out of necessity when original lead actor William Hartnell was forced to retire due to ill health in 1966. A peculiar physiological feature for Time Lords (aside from having two hearts) is the ability to physically "regenerate" twelve times, allowing the Doctor to alter his appearance (and elements of his personality) via new performers every few years, enabling the series to retain an element of freshness (and also attract younger audiences as increasingly more youthful actors have been cast in the role). From its beginning, the series was devised with popularity in mind, explicitly aiming to be a hit show designed to foster regular viewing. Since the advent of commercial rival ITV in 1955, the BBC had to compete for viewers and sought to retain interest through smart scheduling. *Doctor Who* was designed as a "loyalty show" created to fill a gap in the BBC's Saturday evening schedule, fitting between *Grandstand* (providing sports coverage for the week) and *Jukebox Jury* (a pop music show). This was clearly a challenge—aiming to retain the attention of older males that made up the typical sporting audience at the time, as well as appealing to the youth audience who were about to tune in to watch "their" show—and it is by endeavoring to span such a diverse audience that the series incorporated different modes of appeal, the result of considerable research.

Although Sidney Newman is often credited as its creator, *Doctor Who* originated in 1962, a year prior to Newman joining the BBC. Eric Maschwitz, the Head of Light Entertainment, sought to test the feasibility of an SF series, and successive reports were compiled by Donald Bull, Alice Frick, and John Braybon, who surveyed a range of British SF literature and drew up a list of potential themes. Various novels were evaluated as prospective adaptations, with the time travel story *Guardians of Time*, by Poul Anderson, considered particularly promising. These plans were further developed in March 1963 when the Head of Serials, Donald Wilson, asked Braybon, Frick and Cecil "Bunny" Webber to devise a continuous serial that would include a variety of stories, feature recurring characters, and last at least 52 weeks. The aim was to ensure that the gap between the BBC's two hit shows was appropriately filled to avoid audiences switching over to their commercial rival. *Doctor Who* was thus conceived via a practice known as "hammocking"—placing a new show between two established hits to maintain network loyalty. The following month Newman took up his position as Head of Drama at the BBC, transferring from the U.K.'s independent television company, ABC, where he had worked on the prestigious anthology drama *Armchair Theatre*. While Newman officially commissioned *Doctor Who*, Braybon, Frick and Webber had already hammered out its basic concept via several meetings with Wilson, who suggested a machine "not only for going forward and backward in time, but into space," as well as establishing the four main characters (Chapman 2006, 18). Newman's main contribution to the series was in providing its title, affirming that no BEMs (Bug Eyed Monsters) should feature (a point Braybon and Frick had already recommended), and appointing relative newcomer Verity Lambert as its executive producer. A family audience was sought, with a cast intended to appeal to both male and female viewers of diverse ages. An older male character was devised to provide "mystery," a male and female schoolteacher were intended to play the heroes, and a teenager was added for younger viewers to identify with. As events transpired, the mysterious older man — originally conceived as a means of transporting the heroes to new worlds and time-periods — would become the show's hero instead, a figure revealed to be from another world who lends an important sense of mystique. Virtually from the outset, established rules were broken, with Lambert opting to defy the "no BEMs" rule with the show's second story, "The Daleks," a tale about a species that have mechanically adapted to survive. This decision would introduce the Doctor's most fascinating enemy and turn the series into a national sensation. The show subsequently earned an average of 12 million viewers, and the Daleks became recurring villains. BBC Enterprises was created to license their image for various merchandising endeavors, and over the next few years two feature films (released by Amicus Films) made the most of ensuing "Dalekmania." Monstrous antagonists would subsequently appear throughout the series, leading Kim Newman to assert that "it is impossible to overestimate the importance of the Daleks to *Doctor Who*. If the series had remained faithful to Sidney Newman's 'no monsters' decree, it would have lasted a year or two" (Newman 2005, 28). While the claim is interesting, monsters are not the sole reason for the show's success, with continuous flexibility playing a vital role in enabling continued interest.

Webber had advised, in a memo drafted in 1963, that writers should "avoid the limitations of any label and use the best in any style or category as it suits us"—and this advice has been faithfully followed ever since (*Doctor Who* BBC Archive). The series has incorporated a range of styles and influences, including, as Newman summarizes, "the blood-and-thunder Gothicism of Hammer horror, panto humour, conspiracy thriller, studio-bound fantasia, social satire ... deliberate and unintentional camp, even ambitious philosophising" (Newman, 3). New actors playing the Doctor, and a series of companions accompanying him on his travels, additionally provide a crucial sense of variety, alongside differing production teams. *Doctor Who* would alter with each story, each actor in the starring role, and via different producers and script editors, with successive "eras" including Jon Pertwee's Earthbound years as an advisor to the military organization UNIT (in which Barry Letts and Terrance Dicks included allegorical resonances in their stories); the controversies of Tom Baker's time (shifting from the Gothic tendencies of Philip Hinchcliffe and Robert Holmes to the parodic interests of Graham Williams' period as producer—particularly when Douglas Adams became script editor), and an ensuing period in which successive Doctors became increasingly less popular, stories lacked originality, and the same old monsters were endlessly recycled. The series eventually became hampered by too little investment, growing criticism over content, increasingly unfavorable time-slots, and a series of unsympathetic producers. BBC Controller Michael Grade suspended the series in 1985, during which time a protest single was released by the popular tabloid *The Sun*, and fans campaigned for the show's return. When season 23 was eventually aired a year later, it had the innovation of an overarching storyline for the entire season and another new lead (with Sylvester McCoy replacing Colin Baker), changes which failed to prevent its eventual cancellation in 1989 by new Controller of BBC 1, Jonathan Powell.

After this the only opportunity viewers had to see the series on television consisted of comic sketches in the annual BBC fundraiser *Children in Need*, yet fan interest was maintained via a magazine, a comic, a *Big Audio* cassette series, four "webcasts" screened between 2001 and 2003, and a series of novels published by Virgin Publishing entitled *The New Adventures of Doctor Who*. The latter included stories by Russell T. Davies, Paul Cornell, and Mark Gatiss—who would all contribute to the revised series, yet not before an abortive attempt to repackage the franchise for the U.S. market. Rumors that Steven Spielberg was interested in reviving *Doctor Who* were partly corroborated in 1995 when former Amblin producer Philip Segal entered a co-production agreement with the BBC. A feature length film, *Doctor Who* (Geoffrey Sax, 1996)—unofficially titled *Enemy Within*—served as the intended pilot and introduced Paul McGann as the eighth Doctor. Created jointly by BBC Worldwide, Universal Television, and the Fox Network, the tele-movie featured an American setting, improved special effects, and an emphasis on action. Indicating an anticipated breadth of appeal, the Doctor acquires two companions—an adolescent boy and a female physician (with whom the Doctor shares an uncharacteristic kiss)—yet there are also some nice gestures for fans, such as when the newly regenerated Doctor looks for a costume and holds up Tom Baker's iconic multicolored scarf, or offers a policeman a jelly-baby. The plot also introduced a major new detail, with the Doctor claiming to be "half-human" on his mother's side. While this may have been meant as a joke, humanizing the Doctor would become paramount in updating the series for a new generation, and the detail has entered the mythology. The film failed to secure the level of appeal Fox were looking for, attracting 5.5 million viewers in the U.S. (although it secured 9 million in the U.K.), and the planned series was stalled, as were any further developments as protracted wrangles over ownership ensued.

It was only after full copyright reverted to the BBC that they could consider sole investment in a new series, prompted by the success of the "webcasts" (featuring Richard E. Grant) and the conviction of several well-placed individuals. Although Russell T. Davies tends to be credited with returning the

Doctor to our screens, Chapman asserts that this was "due entirely to the fact that the generation of executives at the BBC in the early 2000s included a number of dedicated 'Whovians' who had grown up with *Doctor Who*"—including BBC 1 Controller Lorraine Heggessey, producer Phil Collinson, and Head of Drama at BBC Wales, Julie Gardner, who became co-executive producer of the revised series (Chapman, 186–7). Industry professionals with fan enthusiasm may have helped revive the series, but the BBC's ability to lure a writer of Davies' esteem was also undoubtedly crucial. The acclaimed drama *Queer as Folk* (1999–2000) secured his reputation as a popular and critically admired dramatist, and it was his agreement to serve as head writer which ultimately convinced the BBC that *Doctor Who* could be successfully revised. After a fifteen-year hiatus the series resumed production in 2005, with a new TARDIS, a new cast, and new production staff, as Davies assembled a team of equally dedicated enthusiasts to overhaul the show for the 21st century.

Aware of the need for adequate investment, Davies managed to secure a considerable budget (averaging £1m per episode); and in overseeing an array of merchandise, as well as two spin-off series, he built up a multimedia empire around the franchise. With Davies at the helm, *Doctor Who* would return to Earth, particularly the U.K., a decision he explained with the oft repeated assertion that viewers were not interested in "Planet Zog." Contentious as this claim might be, a desire for accessibility would also motivate him to give the Doctor greater human interest, providing a back-story designed to elicit sympathy. Christopher Ecclestone played the role with brooding intensity, explained as the result of losing his home world in the catastrophic Time War—a battle with the Daleks that ended both civilizations. Season one also introduced new companion Rose Tyler (Billie Piper), who provided the human "anchor" for the series, characterized by curiosity and compassion. A level of intimacy between the pair would further bring our alien down to earth, with Rose frequently upbraiding the Doctor when he failed to behave in a recognizably "human" way. This made him a character we could get closer to, in contrast to the somewhat aloof figure he had been in the past—at the expense of reducing his former enigma.

The format for the series also altered, extending each episode from 25 to 45 minutes, and replacing serialized stories (told over a number of installments) with self-contained episodes or two-parters, allowing a faster pace. Retaining a level of continuity with the established series, famous actors made regular guest appearances, and satirical self-reflexive elements (present in the Graham Williams era) were also apparent. Several storylines question media power, including "The Idiot's Lantern," starring Maureen Lipman as a terrifying manifestation of "Auntie Beeb," stealing the audience's identity; a future elaboration of a media-ted world ("The Long Game") in which Simon Pegg plays a maniacal "Editor" working with an alien entity to manipulate humanity; and its follow-up, "Bad Wolf," in which extreme versions of U.K. game shows kill the losers. Allusions to fan culture were also made, veering from comic to caustic incarnations, from Rose googling "blue box" in her hunt for the Doctor and finding a considerable fan base online, to "Love & Monsters" (written by Russell T. Davies), starring Peter Kay as the Absorbaloff—a monstrous depiction of avaricious fandom literally living off other people.

While in-jokes and allusions provide greater topicality and humor, various means were used to make the series (and its lead character) culturally relevant to British audiences. The aim of transforming our resident alien into a naturalized citizen began with past Doctors having a fondness for tea, British confectionary, or an ability to play cricket; and the new version expresses an interest in the British soap opera *Eastenders* and a fondness for chips, making him so familiar as to potentially remove his most fascinating feature (with little revealed about the Doctor, despite over 900 years of existence, until now). Inspiration was drawn from other cult hits, with Davies citing *Buffy* as the main model for the show (Chapman, 185), and its influence can be seen in numerous references to popular culture, the mix of humor and pathos, seasonal story arcs (with "bad wolf" referencing *Buffy*'s "Big Bad"), and the impossible love between an older man with a dark past and the young girl that falls for him. The fact the Doctor reciprocates these feelings is seemingly designed to interest the "shipper" contingent of the audience, yet feels very wrong, not only because Rose is only a few years older than the granddaughter that first accompanied him in the original series, but because a "rule" is broken regarding the Doctor's relationship with companions (even if the pair don't act on their feelings).

While the old guard grumbled about such changes, the revised series met its brief in staying true enough to the original to please most fans, while additionally attracting new recruits, with ratings averaging 6 to 9 million viewers in its opening season. It also generated palpable excitement in the media. When Ecclestone departed the series after season one, reluctant to be typecast, many wondered if it could survive without him, yet David Tennant stepped in and made the role his own. Rose left at the end of the second season, and trainee doctor Martha Jones (Freema Agyeman) assumed the role of new companion for season three. She was sorely underused, however, as unrequited love for the Doctor remained her defining characteristic. The Doctor experiences several thwarted romances, adding pathos and poignancy, yet contrasting episodes undercut these melodramatic features. The show occasionally tips a wink at audiences, threatening to remove the "fourth wall" by referencing the cult interest that surrounds the Doctor, as well as moments where viewers are explicitly hailed. In "The Shakespeare Code," for example, when the Bard expresses an interest in both sexes, David Tennant almost looks directly at the camera to exclaim, "22 academics just punched the air"—amusingly alluding to genuine claims that have been made about the playwright, as well as suggesting that depicted events are real and will be cited by Shakespeare scholars as such.

An interest in sexuality was a discernible subtext during the Davies era, which a number of fans criticized. A scene in the season finale of the third season, "Last of the Timelords" (written by Davies), in which the Doctor cradles his old nemesis, a dying Master (John Simms), in his arms, is one such instance where a subtext seemed evident, leading some to speculate that the Doctor was being turned into a gay icon—a claim fuelled by the fact that spin-off series *Torchwood* (2006–) openly mined such themes. Whether or not such detractions influenced his decision to pursue other projects, it is a sad irony that Davies' last season as head writer would also be the most effective. A new companion, Donna Noble (Catherine Tate), provided the Doctor's most interesting counterpart through her assertiveness and intelligence, as well as her humor. Like Mulder and Scully (before things got slushy), they work effectively together without any romantic interests, making Donna much more his equal than her predecessors. As Davies commented of her role in the behind-the-scenes documentary *Doctor Who Confidential*, "She's there to undercut the Doctor, take the wind out of his sails, which is exactly what she's there to do." Although Donna was another little-girl-lost, a temp from Chiswick (as she describes herself) who regards herself as "nothing special," she was, in fact, an extraordinary female character. The fourth season was the most interesting, in many respects, thanks to her contribution, with Tate (previously best known as a comedienne) proving herself to be a surprisingly accomplished actress.

The fourth season took some interesting gambits, such as "Midnight"— arguably Davies' finest story, as well as his most cynical—which dismantles the mystique surrounding the Doctor in terrifyingly prosaic fashion. He takes a pleasure cruise (away from the relative safety of the TARDIS and the support of his companion) and is almost killed by fellow space tourists when their ship comes under attack. Humans (the race this man from Gallifrey has taken such an interest in) reveal themselves to be petty, bigoted, selfish and merciless— not the ideal the series has sought to champion—and if the story shows the Doctor's confidence reduced by an extraordinary degree, our estimation of humanity diminishes accordingly, departing from the show's usual optimism. Determinedly ending on a high note, "Journey's End" unites various characters from the franchise, including Rose, Martha, and the lead characters from the spin-off series *Torchwood* and *The Sarah Jane Adventures* (2007–). Davros (the creator of the Daleks) is the Big Bad, plotting to destroy the universe so the Daleks can reign supreme. Taking a cheeky liberty with creative license, Davies showed the Doctor partly regenerate in order to allow two Doctors in the finale, with a "copy" incorporating some of Donna's DNA. This helps defeat Davros and grants Rose a humanized version of the Doctor to grow old with in an alternate universe, enabling the fulfillment of a romance that has been fostered since the first series. Donna has a more tragic finale—one that sees her absorb the Time Lord's mind and save the universe, only to have all memory of her travels with the Doctor deleted to save her life (reworking *Angel*'s

"I Will Remember You"). She ultimately returns to the mundane suburban existence she tried so hard to escape from. Lamentably, the brilliance of the "Doctor-Donna" hybrid, a quick-thinking human with a Time Lord's mind, is impossible to sustain. We are only allowed a brief glimpse of a female Doctor via this narrative cheat before she experiences meltdown, and the explanation given—that the human mind is not advanced enough to possess a Time Lord's knowledge—reiterates his fundamental alien-ness at the very last moment. In Davies' very last story, a stand-alone special, "The End of Time," the rules are again broken when the tenth Doctor is given a protracted death to enable him to bid farewell to several key figures encountered in the revised series. His last battle is against the "evil" president of Gallifrey—who has secretly existed in a "timelock" and is ultimately banished (with the rest of his kind) to "the void"—a gesture Davies seemingly devised to allay the Doctor's guilt over their downfall, thereby removing his contributions to the series to make room for his successor.

The appointment of Steven Moffat as head writer and executive producer for the fifth season was highly anticipated, as he had written some of the most memorable episodes of the revised series, many of which had won Hugos, as well as other critical accolades. His celebrated debut, "The Empty Child/The Doctor Dances," set during the Blitz in London, is fun and frightening in equal measure, announcing Moffat's dual concern to extend our knowledge of the Doctor (quietly empathizing with an old man who states the war has cost him his family) while giving the child audience new monsters to delight in. His second story, "The Girl in the Fireplace," skillfully bridges the interests of a cross-section of the audience by jumping forward in time from a little girl afraid of clockwork men (who sees the Doctor as a hero) to the young Madame de Pompadour he falls in love with and finally loses when space, time, and mortality out-maneuver his attempts to be with her. It is in combining moving adult drama with scary monsters that appeared to be Moffat's forte, making him seem the ideal show-runner for the franchise; and his appointment suggests fan responses had been noted, with many calling for him to replace Davies for some time. However, no sooner had he achieved this position than the backlash began. Even before the season commenced, Moffat became the focus of fan concerns after choosing (alongside new executive producer Piers Wegener) the youngest actor ever to take the lead role—twenty-seven-year-old Matt Smith. The decision may have been partly derived from the need to find an actor willing to commit to the role for a number of years (particularly given the limited number of "lives" the Doctor has left), yet it also seemed motivated by a desire to target a young audience, with Moffat's labeling of *Doctor Who* as a children's show provoking further concern among fans. Those who'd hoped for a return to the Hinchcliffe/Holmes era, on the strength of Moffat's prior contributions, would be disappointed by the result. Accompanied by an equally youthful companion, Amy Pond (Karen Gillan), later joined by her fiancé and eventual husband, Rory Williams (Arthur Darvil), with storylines that trade scares for silliness and seem primarily aimed at children, there was little indication of Moffat's past writing, much to the dismay of his fans. While Moffat has rightly contended that "change is part of *Doctor Who*'s formula" (Anders, 2008), this comes with the risk of alienating the old guard, and although Matt Smith would prove doubters wrong, with a demeanor that suggests an ancient alien far more than his immediate predecessors, this was badly let down by an annoying companion and somewhat lackluster stories.

The resulting disappointment was keenly felt because Moffat had been held in such esteem. The revised series (under Davies' charge) had made the mistake of over-relying on old villains, with the Daleks over-used, the Cybermen vs. Dalek story disappointingly realized, and the return of the Master another wasted opportunity. By contrast, episodes where new "monsters" were conceived — whether it be children with gas-masks for faces or flesh-eating bugs that hide in the shadows — were far more successful, and the fact that Moffat devised the most memorable of these testifies to his imaginative prowess, including the terrifying "angels" featured in "Blink"—an episode in which the Doctor was virtually absent throughout and a "fan" figure saves the day (a heroic representation that stands in marked contrast to Davies' monstrous Absorbaloff). Sally Sparrow (Carey Mulligan) acquires a sense of purpose when she loses her friend and sets out to uncover what is happening with time. An Easter egg on a series of DVDs contains a message from the Doctor (attracting the interest of an obsessed fandom). In acquiring the information needed to defeat the menace, as well as saving the Doctor at some point in the future, Sally fulfils a popular fan fantasy, and Moffat even inserts a joke about the size of the TARDIS windows — aimed directly at complainants on the Outpost Gallifrey website (legendary, prior to its closure, for such pedantry), winning points from hardcore fans by paying them amused attention. Gestures of this kind may once have endeared him, but Moffat is now directly in the line of fire, having inherited not only a carefully constructed empire, but one of the most devoted (and demanding) of audiences.

While Russell T. Davies has taken his share of flak, his role in revising the series should not be underestimated, evidently adoring the show while also understanding the need to manufacture and market *Doctor Who* as a "product." As he asserts:

> When I think of something like *Doctor Who* I'm not ashamed of those words because much as I love it — and I think *Doctor Who* can be as intelligent, as witty, and as profound as any other drama — it *is* a whacking great big science fiction entertainment show, and it's *designed* to be watched by millions of people, and it's *designed* to have merchandise, and it's *designed* to be shown all over the world. You know, you can't be that precious about it [Davies 2008].

It is this approach that enabled the series to become a viable business proposition, as well as reinstating a beloved cultural icon; and the fact that it took an avid fan—in the right place at the right time—to bring the series back on the air should not be ignored, as he provided the insider knowledge that would earn the approval of established viewers (albeit with grumblings of discontent subsequently voiced). Davies oversaw the extension of the franchise via two spin-off shows, explained as a pragmatic decision to "get more product" and cater to different niches, breaking down the franchise as being "very carefully designed as *Doctor Who* in the middle, as the family show *Sarah Jane* for children, [and] *Torchwood* for adults. They're very very different shows, all nonetheless feeding into each other in a very sort of complicated way" (Davies 2008).

Torchwood, the version "for adults," which Davies remains involved with, had the opportunity to experiment the most and has also seen some pronounced changes. Created by Davies, with Chris Chibnall as co-producer and head writer, it borrows heavily from other series without having a solid identity of its own. The premise might best be described as "*The X-Files* in Cardiff," focusing on aliens infiltrating the Welsh capital and the taskforce that polices them. The Torchwood Institute is a covert facility that works, as the title sequence tells us, "outside the government, beyond the police." First referenced in season one of the revised *Doctor Who*, in which the Torchwood Institute was introduced in the 19th century, its flamboyant lead was first introduced in Moffat's debut story, "The Empty Child." Situating its base in Cardiff is explained by the fact that this is the location of a space-time "rift"—a cosmic equivalent of the Hellmouth in *Buffy* from which alien life-forms routinely emerge. The first series aired on digital channel BBC 3, which is principally aimed at a youth audience, and achieved the channel's highest ratings in 2006, peaking at 2.8 million during the initial season. Co-produced with a Canadian company, *Torchwood* has broadcast in Canada, Australia, and New Zealand, and was one of the biggest hits for BBC America when it premiered in September 2007, attracting an audience of almost half a million viewers. The show has been extended in audio book, magazine and novel form, endeavoring to be a franchise in its own right, yet has found itself floundering. The Torchwood team was initially made up of five principal characters: Captain Jack Harkness (John Barrowman), an immortal alien haunted by a mysterious past, and Ianto Jones (Gareth David-Lloyd) who serves as his love interest, coffee maker, and technical support. Gwen Cooper (Eve Myles) is a former policewoman newly recruited into the organization, who serves as the equivalent of the Doctor's companion in providing the human anchor. Reminiscent of *Star Trek: The Next Generation*'s Deanna Troy (Marina Sirtis), she is distinguished by her compassion for others (and even shares a similar storyline in which she is impregnated by an alien). Techno-nerd Toshiko Sato (Naoko Mori) bears more than a little resemblance to early incarnations of *Buffy*'s Willow Rosenberg: brilliant but insecure, and suffering from unrequited love for her colleague, Owen Harper (Burn Gorman), who is sexist, arrogant, and easily the least likeable of the team. Everyone, bar Ianto, is consumed by narcissism or neurosis, providing scant reason to get involved, and the premise proves equally disappointing. Far from aiming to better understand the different life-forms encountered, the series uses its post-watershed timeslot to extend greater interest in alternative sexualities. The mystery of Jack's identity is so prolonged it becomes a bore, alongside various references made to his sexual proclivity. An episode in which an old flame returns, played by James Marsters (Spike in *Buffy*), is cringe-worthy in its contrivance, revealing little beyond Jack's immense vanity as he cruelly points out how his ex has aged. Seemingly cast to appeal to straight women and gay men, John Barrowman's good looks fail to conceal the fact that he is out of his depth in the acting stakes, and his character lacks effective leadership skills, as well as any compassion (notably unmoved by Owen's attempt to deal with returning from the dead in season two, for example, despite his own immortality). A weak backstory involving a lost brother parallels the parent series via the "tortured alien" routine and sums up the main flaw of the series in its lack of originality. If *Doctor Who* is designed for the family audience, and thus unable to discuss sexual relations, *Torchwood* clearly aims to compensate; but it fails to convince in its attempt at edgy SF. Aware of the need to shake up the format, season two culminated in killing off all the characters, bar Jack, Gwen and Ianto, who returned in a five-part miniseries entitled "Children of Earth," screened over one week in the summer of 2009. The BBC made the interesting gesture of placing it in a primetime slot on BBC 1, where it proved to be a surprising success. An evident throwback to the *Quatermass* serials, its premise of aliens in cahoots with the government was written by Russell T. Davies and provides a bitter tale of corrupt politicians lying to their electorate.

The prime minister agrees to sacrifice a percentage of the world's children to maintain peace with an alien species, the 456. An apparatchik carries out the deal—only to have his own children placed on the list of victims, and slaughters his family to spare them. Captain Jack parallels the politico's narrative journey, having handed over a dozen children in 1965—a history that destroys any vestige of heroism in this already problematic figure and places his team in the government's firing line. Outlawed by a government that orders their deaths (to conceal their prior pact), the three surviving Torchwood members get inside information from an improbably well-placed temp in the cabinet, yet fail to appease the invaders, leaving Ianto senselessly killed and an unthinkable resolution. *Torchwood*'s divergence from *Doctor Who* is confirmed in the concluding installment. A video message by Gwen asserts their dire need of the Doctor, and Jack's manifest difference is indicated in the bleakest of finales: sacrificing his own grandson to kill the aliens and save Earth. The fact that we have only just been introduced to his secret family, as well as Ianto's sister, adds to the frustration of finally being given something to get invested in only to see it demolished. After a compelling first half, the plot excessively demonizes the government (who opt to make the best of things by sacrificing children from low achieving schools), while the alien interest in using children as a narcotic is too absurd for words. As an adult SF show, *Torchwood* had a remit to be dark and challenging, yet ending with Ianto's death, and that of an innocent young boy, was a devastating conclusion; and the impending birth of Gwen's first child offers little hope. Gaining an average of 5.8 million viewers over the week, "Children of Earth" found a sizable audience, but seemingly offered little incentive to watch future installments of the series, with Jack's gesture confirming his utter alien-ness in too unsavory a fashion to champion him—even if we might wonder what the Doctor would have done in his place. If "Midnight" was disturbing in its all too believable assessment of human fallibility, "Children of Earth" is outlandishly plotted, politically confused, and utterly contemptible in murdering an innocent child to foster sympathy for Jack, who self-pityingly exits the planet after his "sacrifice." Nonetheless, despite fan protests at the dark turn taken by the miniseries—particularly in killing off Ianto, its ratings proved sufficient to inspire a new season, relocating *Torchwood* to the U.S. for its fourth season, with Russell T. Davies at its helm, *Buffy* and *BSG* alumni Jane Espenson recruited as a writer, and additional funding provided by premium cable channel, Starz; although whether this revamp will ensure its success remains to be seen.

If *Torchwood* exemplifies the problems that result when a spin-off takes too divergent a path from its parent show, *Enterprise* was equally at odds with *Star Trek*'s narrative universe. Admittedly, Berman and Braga had the difficulty of upholding the vision initiated by original series creator Gene Roddenberry while providing sufficient dramatic interest for a contemporary audience. However, an additional problem was that the executive producers didn't seem to care about the show, its fans, or the legacy it drew upon, despite their prior involvement in the franchise. While the series aimed to emulate the sense of adventure aligned with the original series, it allowed radical deviations from the *Trek* universe, including duplicitous Vulcans overseeing humanity's first steps into space. Far from providing an interesting take on perceived events, such changes merely infuriated fans. *Enterprise* flouted the liberal tenets built up since the original series, and by the time its executive producers realized their mistake and explicitly targeted established fans by drawing connections with the original series, cancellation loomed. Its fate signals the comparative strictures faced by those seeking to expand the *Star Trek* universe, with the franchise having a limited degree of creative license compared to *Doctor Who*. Indeed, while *Doctor Who* was created by committee, and changed with each head writer and executive producer (with considerable variation over its narrative history), *Star Trek*'s fictional universe was carefully mapped out by Roddenberry, and the films, series and additional material that make up the "canon" have stayed true to his vision, allowing little room for deviation. Braga may have aimed to create a new version for a younger generation—pitching *Enter-*

prise as "not your father's *Star Trek*"—yet the fact he had never been a fan of the original series explains a great deal about his dismissive attitude toward continuity (Hark 2008, 136, 148). Berman's part is more difficult to understand, as he was personally mentored by Gene Roddenberry on the "rules" of *Star Trek* and vowed never to break them. *Enterprise* proved the exception, dramatically departing from Roddenberry's rules and scarcely resembling a *Trek* product as a result, proving how closely the show is tied to its creator.

Since his death in 1991, various commentators have criticized Roddenberry, intent on knocking the "Great Bird of the Galaxy" from his lofty position as the visionary creator of a beloved show; but while he may not have been as virtuous—in person—as his aspirations for humanity, his vision of the future has inspired countless fans. Contributing staff, such as D.C. Fontana, Bob Justman and Gene L. Coon, may have played an integral part in developing the series, yet Roddenberry created *Star Trek*, investing it with his ideals and affirming a faith in our potential to improve, which is integral to the franchise's popularity. Although it began production in 1966, Roddenberry first conceived *Star Trek* in 1960, a few years prior to *Doctor Who*, developing it after the police series he was working on—*The Lieutenant*—was cancelled. The juvenile tendencies of rampaging monsters in television SF convinced him the genre was not fulfilling its potential. Like *Twilight Zone* creator Rod Serling, Roddenberry wanted to make a series that had something to say and was keen to break through television's censorship barrier to achieve this. *The Making of Star Trek*, written by Stephen E. Whitfield in collaboration with Roddenberry, provides some insight into its creator's motives, using SF tropes as a "Trojan horse" in which to place ideas. As Whitfield puts it:

> By using science fiction yarns in far-off planets he was certain he could disguise the fact that he was actually talking about politics, sex, economics, the stupidity of war, and half a hundred other subjects usually prohibited on television [Whitfield 1968, 21–22].

Roddenberry was interested in SF's ability to make people think, and keen to prove that "adult science fiction" could be made which would secure mass appeal if it "adhered to the proven rules of drama, [providing] a cast of continuing characters, and a familiar home base from which to operate" (Whitfield, 37). If *Doctor Who* was the product of exhaustive fieldwork by a group of researchers, *Star Trek* was devised by one man eager to prove that the format for hit westerns and cop-shows could equally be used for a weekly SF series. In 1964 he signed a 3-year contract to make pilots at Desilu Studios and used the opportunity to pitch his idea. It was rejected by CBS, who had just commissioned *Lost in Space* (1965–8), yet NBC vice president, Mort Wiener, serves among the many mavericks that have peppered the history of cult telefantasy in deciding to back a hunch. Wiener even made the unprecedented move of seeking a second pilot when the first failed to convince fellow executives, who voiced hesitance about its "cerebral" plot, eroticism, the satanic appearance of alien officer Lieutenant Spock (Leonard Nimoy), and a rational female character placed second-in-command—the last concern being due to doubts about Majel Barrett's performance, according to Justman and Solow (*Inside Star Trek* 1996, 60). Another story was developed as a second pilot, and Barrett was demoted to the part of love-struck nurse Christine Chapel, but Roddenberry insisted that Spock's alien-ness was vital to the show and insisted on retaining his pointy ears. NBC duly commissioned a series, and the Starship *Enterprise* began her mission.

Star Trek's premise combined variety and familiarity. A five-year journey through space offered escapism and adventure, while recurring characters gave viewers someone to identify with—in sufficient number to provide wide-ranging appeal. Roddenberry also conceived two concepts to overcome budgetary problems: the "transporter," which enabled an "away team" crew to "beam down" to any planet instantaneously (dispensing with costly landing scenes); and the mission's particular interest in "M-class planets"—those similar to our own conditions on Earth—explaining the humanoid appearance of their inhabitants. This last detail would reduce expenditure on make-up and costumes, allowing actors to be easily recognized in guest appearances, and also provide the series with an important allegorical quality—enabling an exploration of contrasting societies and value systems. Much of *Star Trek*'s appeal lies in this feature, together with its avowedly utopian vision of the future. The series affirms that we will improve (once technology eradicates material need), and a united world can then focus on learning about others (and "liberating" them, on occasion). In Roddenberry's vision, enlightenment is achieved by the 23rd century, freeing humanity to travel the universe. Like the lead in *Doctor Who*, described by one fan as "the ultimate and most eminent of all democrats" (Tulloch and Jenkins 1995, 115), Captain James T. Kirk (William Shatner) is distinguished by compassion and empathy for others. Both men have a strong sense of morality and justice, which motivates them to intervene in planetary problems, and although reprimands are made (at times) for such involvement, they achieve heroic status by fighting against tyranny and persecution. The Doctor may be a renegade—having stolen his TARDIS and fled his home world rather than lead an official state-approved mission, like Kirk—yet exploration, and liberation, are mutual concerns for both men (and both series), with a willingness to take direct action that was particularly appealing in the 1960s.

Nonetheless, their histories dramatically diverge in the shape each franchise took. While *Doctor Who* was on the air for twenty-six years prior to its cancellation, *Star Trek* barely survived three. Public outcry from *Who* fans during the first attempt at cancellation in 1985 led to a stay of execution for another four years, while *Star Trek* was under threat from the start. Its first episode aired on September 8, 1966, to disappointing ratings, and by December the threat of cancellation loomed. At Roddenberry's behest, support was shown by Harlan Ellison, Frank Herbert, and other noted SF writers, who sought to convince executives that, despite low Nielsen ratings, the show was a worthy exploration of ideas—advancing its status as a quality television series. When cancellation continued to dog the second season, two prominent fans, Bjo and John Trimble, initiated a huge campaign (with encouragement from Roddenberry), culminating in thousands of letters sent to NBC. The network agreed to another season but dropped the budget and kept shifting the timeslot. Midway through its third season rumors of cancellation spread again, attracting huge public protest. In addition to letters sent to NBC, students marched in protest and a group delivered a petition to the Burbank office. On the East Coast, picketers marched up and down Rockefeller Plaza, carrying placards and handing out leaflets and bumper stickers. On Friday, March 1, 1968, NBC made an unprecedented "on-air" announcement to reassure viewers the series would continue. As Whitfield puts it:

> The "Save Star Trek" campaign, which culminated in NBC's announcement, must surely rank as the most phenomenal expression of viewer opinion ever recorded in the annals of television. It must also serve as a graphic reminder to the networks that people like to believe they have a voice in affairs that concern them, and will express that voice, sometimes in staggering proportion [Whitfield, 395].

Phenomenal as this campaign was, the network's inclination to listen to fans proved short-lived. The timeslot was rescheduled again, this time for 10 P.M. on a Friday night, yet *Star Trek* was abruptly cancelled before reaching the end of the season. Despite clear evidence that a dedicated audience had invested in the show—and the public commitment made to those fans—the network reneged on their agreement. Uncertain about its likely future at the time of writing, Whitfield maintains that:

> The starship launched by Roddenberry, and manned by an extraordinary crew, will not depart the scene without leaving a few ripples in its wake. *Star Trek* has proved that it really does matter to the viewer what he sees on television. Contrary to what the networks may believe, people do care about television programming. And they do not at all mind learning while being entertained.... The response to *Star Trek*'s message is irrefutable proof of the totally inaccurate network concept of the viewer as a clod [Whitfield, 401–2].

The series acquired a growing audience when new parent company Paramount sold its syndication rights in 1969. It proved particularly popular after the moon landing, and demand for merchandise helped build up the franchise. Conventions, and impressive syndication ratings, inspired Paramount to create an animated series in 1972, and a live action series, provisionally titled *Phase II*, was intended to be launched in 1977. Instead, a feature film, *Star Trek: The Motion Picture* (1979), was released, aiming to capitalize on the success of *Star Wars* (1977) and *Close Encounters* (1977). Good box office returns for this film and its sequels, *The Wrath of Khan* (1982), *The Search for Spock* (1984), and particularly *The Voyage Home* (1986), led to the eventual creation of a new series, *Star Trek: The Next Generation* (1987–94). Set 78 years ahead of the original series, with a new crew and ship, it would take audiences further forward in Starfleet history, retaining Roddenberry as executive producer. The same utopian vision remained, with greater liberalism indicated by the fact that a Klingon—a race previously depicted as villainous—serves onboard the new Enterprise, as well as an android. (A resident "alien" would feature in further spin-offs in the franchise, in an inversion of the human companions provided in *Doctor Who*.) The new captain also provided an interesting contrast to Kirk, with Jean-Luc Picard (Patrick Stewart) offering a more democratic style of leadership, with a greater emphasis on learning and diplomacy. Just as *Doctor Who* ranged from stories set in different historical periods on Earth to alien planets, *TNG* made the most of a bigger budget and more advanced special effects to provide a variety of scenarios. The "holodeck" facilities, for instance, enabled a means of switching genres, recreating the literary worlds of Sherlock Holmes, pulp westerns and detective novels (or anywhere else the computer could generate), allowing new sets and storylines, in addition to the various planets visited. The spin-off was a ratings success, surviving seven seasons and winning a number of awards. Roddenberry's failing health had forced him to rely on Paramount executive Rick Berman during production, a figure who was previously unfamiliar with *Star Trek* yet became Roddenberry's successor after his death, playing a key role in developing ensuing series.

Star Trek's continuing mission would start to stall in attempting to remain true to Roddenberry's vision, while allowing sufficient scope for dramatic creativity. *Deep Space Nine* (1993–9) was set on a space station, paralleling *Babylon 5* (1993–9), jointly run by Starfleet Commander Benjamin Sisko (Avery Brooks) and his Bajoran second-in-command, Major Kira Nerys (Nana Visitor). The premise provided a number of political intrigues, with the Cardassians serving as fascistic foes; and although some argued that it veered too far from the optimistic future envisaged by Roddenberry, and was too limited in scope, others admired its willingness to question Federation policies. *Voyager* (1995–2001) was an attempt to straddle both camps, placing its crew in the unknown Delta Quadrant with a female captain, Kathryn Janeway (Kate Mulgrew), in charge. It reprised the original series' mission of exploring new worlds and civilizations, while additionally addressing the factionalism posited in *DS9*. Dissent had started to appear in the *Star Trek* universe from the latter end of *TNG* in the form of the Maquis, a resistance group working against the Federation, with some very legitimate grievances against them; and by including members of this group among its crew, *Voyager* promised greater complexity. The premise features Janeway pursuing a Maquis ship across a rift in space, and subsequently having to join forces with its crew when both ships are stranded in space. Unfortunately, instant deference is secured from her counterpart, Commander Chakotay (Robert Beltran), and former rebels don their enemy's uniform (and adhere to their chain of command) within the space of the pilot, settling their differences for the greater good. This was the same message promoted in the original series; but while it may have been inspirational at a time of cold war politics and civil protest, it would appear increasingly incongruous (even facile) at the close of the 20th century.

The spin-offs each came to an end. The Deep Space 9 space station was finally handed to Bajoran rule, and the Starship *Voyager* eventually came home. The fact that the lost ship was retrieved due to the actions of a recurring character—a figure who clearly resembled a "fan" in the depth of his imagination and devotion—suggested the audience were being directly acknowledged. Like Sally Sparrow in "Blink," diagnostic engineer Lt. Reg Barclay (Dwight Schultz) recalls a specific kind of fan-produced story in which an ordinary person (known as the "Mary Sue") is inserted into the text and granted heroic status. Barclay first appeared in *TNG* as an unlikely officer distinguished by a lack of confidence and an active imagination. Although prone to "holodiction"—over-investing in the ship's holodeck facilities rather than socializing with others—he would become crucial in getting *Voyager* home when his fixation with the ship (and virtuoso technical abilities) conceive a means of communicating with them—reinvigorating a mission that had been abandoned by Starfleet command. Telefantasy writers have increasingly acknowledged fans in this way, including the Lone Gunmen in *The X-Files*, their more youthful equivalents—the nerds Jonathan, Andrew and Warren—in *Buffy*, and the aforementioned Sally Sparrow in *Doctor Who*, and fans have taken a keen interest in all these suggested stand-ins. Reg Barclay also secured a degree of adoration, with websites created in tribute to him; and in seeming to commend fan commitment via this character, the franchise provided a fitting finale. However, Paramount's desire to extend the franchise, coupled with Berman and Braga's conviction there were further seams to mine, resulted in *Enterprise*.

Aiming to try something new, they opted for a premise set 10 years before Kirk and crew began their mission; yet the idea of a prequel seemed to tarnish the memory of the original series, and it further infuriated fans by paying insufficient attention to the established universe. Eschewing the franchise's usual liberalism, an unreconstructed male captain is placed in charge, with Captain Jonathan Archer (Scott Bakula, of *Quantum Leap* fame) lacking the tolerance associated with former command figures. A female Vulcan, as second-in-command, had the promise of fulfilling Roddenberry's original plans for a female Number One, yet T'Pol (Jolene Blalock) fulfils much the same function as *Voyager*'s Borg pin-up, 7 of 9 (Jeri Ryan)—who was similarly devised by Berman and Braga to titillate male viewers—representing another frosty female in clingy clothes who needs to be thawed out. Compounding such problematic characterizations, the Vulcans—generally much admired in *Trek* mythology—are accused of thwarting humanity's development rather than advancing it, oddly demonizing a race formerly cast as mentors. The show's looks also flouted continuity, and in its set design, as well as being shot in digital video, it simply didn't look right for the period in which it was set. Finally, in anticipating "our" Enterprise crew and their voyages, the entire premise seemed to be a redundant exercise.

Low ratings prompted the producers to look at the most successful of the *Star Trek* films, *First Contact* (1996), for inspiration, and in season three they fabricated a new enemy, the Xindi, in a season-long arc in which Earth comes under attack. In being renewed for a fourth season, *Enterprise* exceeded the lifespan of the original series, yet this would prove to be its last. Long-term fan Manny Coto was promoted to co-executive producer status, becoming the series' show-runner for the final season, and a more concerted effort was made to tie concepts to the established mythology, such as exploring the origins of the parallel universe seen in "Mirror, Mirror," and providing an explanation for the disappearance of Klingon cranial ridges. Despite appreciative feedback from fans, these changes were too belated. UPN cancelled the series on February 2, 2005, and although a "Save Enterprise" campaign was launched, they remained resolved in their decision. Despite having the opportunity for closure denied the original series, which ended awkwardly with the histrionic and misogynistic "Turnabout Intruder," *Enterprise* caused an outcry when its finale, "These are the Voyages..." (written by Berman and Braga), wasted the opportunity to segue into the original series and framed the entire series as a holodeck program viewed by *TNG* characters Deanna Troi and Will Riker (Jonathan Frakes), dismissing the entire *Enterprise* series from the official mythology (and thus reiterating the view of many fans).

It is partly in response to the disappointments of *Enterprise* that fan-created films based on *Star Trek* started to proliferate, with increasingly affordable digital cameras enabling fans to make series of their own and distribute them on the net. Online series gained particular prominence as the official franchise declined, suggesting that if Paramount failed to give fans what they want, they would simply create it for themselves. By reclaiming the series in this way, fan films and webisodes reiterate a long history of fan fiction; yet some of these products would not only blur traditional boundaries between consumer and producer, but between amateur and professional endeavors. The most prominent of such web-series is *Star Trek: New Voyages* (subsequently re-titled *Star Trek: Phase II*), which has run since 2004. James Cawley used blueprints from the original series (and his earnings as an Elvis impersonator) to recreate the *Enterprise* bridge in his garage, collaborating with fellow fan Jack Marshall in making a series, with the aim of completing the original series' five-year mission (with Cawley playing Kirk). Significantly, members of the original cast have become involved, including Walter Koenig reprising his role as Pavel Chekov in an episode written by D.C. Fontana ("To Serve All My Days"), while "World Enough and Time" stars George Takei as Hikaru Sulu and was nominated for a Hugo. In addition, official writers and production crew have lent their services for nothing (including Ron D. Moore), contributing to the series' reputation as a more authentic continuation of Roddenberry's ideal than *Enterprise* (with premiere episodes proving more popular). These activities indicate an important development in the history of telefantasy, with the Internet providing not simply a means by which networks interact with audiences, but through which fans can share increasingly professional products with one another. Admittedly, online series do not enjoy the same facilities as a dedicated studio and rarely produce more than one webisode per year. In order to remain within copyright restrictions they must also be non-commercial (unable to recoup production expenses, which at $45,000 an episode for *New Voyages* is a considerable sum); yet money-making was never the point of fan fiction, but an aim to contribute to a shared fictional world, and in this sense they remain very interesting. Justin Everett regards *New Voyages* as "the reclamation of *Star Trek* by its fan base (which must now be redefined to contain many former Trek professionals)" (Geraghty 2007, 195)—a statement which affirms how former distinctions have altered. Making this point explicit, Tim Russ (*Voyager*'s Tuvok) opted to mark *Star Trek*'s 40th anniversary by directing the digital miniseries *Of Gods and Men*, starring a number of actors involved in the franchise and intended as a "gift to the fans," while the official response, with no series in production, was to ignore the landmark date.

Such endeavors illustrate the role fans have played in shaping a favored text. They can do so directly by assuming creative roles within the industry, such as Davies and Moffat, while Cawley and Marshall indicate the ability for those outside the industry to produce quality texts of their own (with the aid of professionals inspired by their project). *Doctor Who* and *Star Trek* are each stories of reinvention, with fan dedication enabling them to survive and often pointing them in the right direction when they have lost their way. Indeed, it seems scarcely coincidental that Paramount's decision to reboot the *Star Trek* franchise should emulate *New Voyages* so closely in opting to recreate the original series—even if the resulting film also seeks to appeal to a non–*Trek* audience. In choosing J.J. Abrams to direct the new film, with Damon Lindelof as producer, a cast that includes Zachary Quinto (Sylar from *Heroes*) as Spock, and a guest appearance from Leonard Nimoy, its cult appeal is strong, yet various non-canonical departures also occur. With an established timeline posing obvious problems for creativity, particularly in placing known characters in a realistic sense of jeopardy, its writers, Roberto Orci and Alex Kurtzman, used a hokey time-travel plot to posit an alternative timeline, sidestepping forty-odd years of mythology. The gamble paid off, with *Star Trek* more than doubling *First Contact*'s earnings in its opening weekend, playing on a mix of nostalgia and action that nods to established fans while additionally drawing new audiences in. A Romulan baddie uses a time-travel device to screw up the past, leaving Kirk to grow up without a father, and we see how a tearaway Kirk turns his fortunes around at Starfleet. As one critic summarized the plot, this is "*Star Trek*: The Early Years" (Bradshaw 2009), telling a story that had not yet been told: how Kirk meets his crew and makes an astonishing career ascent from a rebellious cadet to captain of the *Enterprise*. Orci and Kurtzman have asserted that an infusion of *Star Wars* was needed to make the premise more accessible, and this can be seen in Kirk's farmboy origins, the ice planet sequence arbitrarily placed in the film, and the fact that women are relegated to mothers and love interests. Uhura (Zoe Haldana) is no longer stuck behind a console, but basically plays Leia—a seemingly feisty female whose main purpose is to serve as the token woman in a "boys own" adventure, the added twist being that she is revealed as Spock's lover. The fact that Spock enters into such a relationship proves that the *Trek* we knew has been radically revised, with a half–Vulcan who is now more in touch with his human side than his previous incarnation (like the revised Doctor), unencumbered by the former need to please his father, and without the conflict that made him so dramatically interesting—which may serve the interests of populism but is precisely the kind of departure many fans dreaded.

While assurances were given during production that the franchise would be respected, Abrams has since dismissed the original series as a "silly campy thing," stating, "I was trying to make a movie, not trying to make a *Trek* movie" (Rose 2009). Orci and Kurtzman have similarly expressed limited appreciation for the franchise, despite claiming to be fans, with Kurtzman describing *Star Trek* as "a naval battle set in space" and contending that "you cannot honestly expect ... a 12-year-old boy to walk into a theater and sit through two hours of very slow naval battle. It's just not going to work" (SciFi Wire 2009). The statement is illuminating not only due to the questionable understanding of *Star Trek* made by professed admirers, but because it confirms that pleasing fans was not their main concern. Their remit was seemingly to turn the franchise into a summer blockbuster, and they evidently succeeded on this score; but for those of us who are not 12-year-old boys, who perhaps desired more than facile plotting, non-stop action, and amusing one-liners, the result is both a disappointment and a worry. Appealing as it is to see a young cast at the outset of their adventures (rather than the ponderous assessments of mortality offered by the aging crews of other *Star Trek* films), the result is a noisy, effects-driven actioner without a shred of substance. One admiring reviewer noted the lack of plot, but praised Abrams' flair for action, concluding that "*Star Trek* used to be smarter. But it was never this fast, fresh, and exciting" (Cocker 2009). With narrative scope to do as they please for the sequel, Orci and Kurtzman have been studying tie-in novels for inspiration, and have promised to canvas fan opinion—gestures that affirm a reluctance to upset the established fan base, even if they are clearly not the main market sought. Former *Trek* alumni have commended Abrams' *Star Trek* as a necessary departure, including Ron D. Moore, while Bryan Fuller has declared his interest in making a series set in the same universe. A slicker version of *New Voyages* may thus be heralded, the ultimate in industrial co-optation, with shades of *Star Wars* added to try and please old fans and newcomers alike.

The aim to win over new fans is understandable. After all, if either franchise is to have a future it must clearly encourage new viewers, yet how *Doctor Who* and *Star Trek* can find the size of audience needed to support them, while retaining their original identity, is where the quandary lies. While it is easy to see why *Doctor Who* is currently aiming to attract younger viewers, fans seeking greater adult drama cannot help but feel ousted, as well as a little nostalgic for Davies' reign (with some fans already calling for his return). Though the gung-ho reboot of the *Star Trek* franchise may have appeased most fans, it threatens to provide little more than a parody of *Trek*. The perils of a crossover cult are thus underwritten—with the irony that, by endeavoring to widen interest, they risk losing an integral part of themselves. It is difficult to predict what the future for each franchise will be, yet while they remain profitable, networks are unlikely to abandon them (even if some fans feel tempted to), particularly with so much material to draw upon.

Each franchise has deployed a number of strategies to ensure longevity, with time and space travel allowing expansive settings and storylines, taking us beyond our solar system, into the distant past, or to the far future. *Doctor Who*'s regular cast changes may have derived from the need to accommodate actors wishing to leave the series, but it has become a crucial means of eliciting new interest, with spin-off series diversifying the audience through specific niches. *Star Trek* has also reinvented its format via spin-offs, each providing a different take on the same theme and offering a similarly optimistic message about virtuous Starfleet officers working for a (generally) benign Federation of Planets. The same tendencies are notable in the *Who*niverse, opting to highlight humanity's most positive traits, with any signs of corruption exposed and overcome. As might be expected from their comparable histories and concerns, both franchises share similar characters also, with *Star Trek*'s Borg (a cyborg species intent on universal rule) previously anticipated via *Doctor Who*'s Daleks and Cybermen, while the Q Continuum are akin to the representation of Gallifreyans as a powerful yet austere species (with Q [John de Lancie] comparable to the trickster Time Lord known as the Meddling Monk). The revised *Doctor Who* also draws upon *Star Trek*, as well as referencing other U.S. cult shows such as *Buffy* and *The X-Files*, which is partly attributable to writers paying homage to related telefantasy series, as well as seeking transatlantic appeal (with the U.S. and U.K. frequently serving as one another's secondary market). The revised *Doctor Who* includes notable U.S. touches, such as the teaser trailer at the end of each episode, a faster pace, more mobile camerawork, and much greater sentiment than previously seen. Chapman claims the show has implicitly modeled itself on "American Quality Television" in terms of "self-consciousness, visual stylishness" and being "closely associated with creative writer-producers" (Chapman 2006, 185). Nonetheless, while more Americanized tastes are intimated, *Doctor Who* remains a quintessential "British" show, albeit one the BBC has turned into a global brand (selling well in a variety of countries and proving among their most lucrative products). Clearly, its writers will need to think of a way to prolong the Doctor's life, with only two regenerations remaining, yet fans are unlikely to object to changing this rule for the sake of prolonging the show—particularly in a series that broke them from the outset.

As to their respective achievements, perhaps their most significant feature is that both franchises have proven SF's breadth of appeal beyond the male adolescent stereotype that tended to dog the genre. *Doctor Who* has attracted an increased number of female fans, partly through casting younger, more attractive Doctors, as well as including some interesting female figures. Although companions have comprised a number of "screamers," strong female characters have also featured throughout its history, from the "savage" Leela (Louise Jameson)—anticipating warriors such as Xena and Buffy—to female Time Lords the Rani (Kate O'Mara) and Romana (Mary Tamm/Lalla Ward). Tough female leaders have also appeared in the revised series, such as Professor River Song (Alex Kingston) and the inestimable Captain Adelaide Brooke (Lindsay Duncan), although the frequency with which female heroism is proven by self-sacrifice remains disconcerting. By contrast, female *Star Trek* fans have been visible since the original series, despite the relatively limited roles given to female crew members, Lt. Penda Uhura and Nurse Christine Chapel. Female "trekkers" were subsequently rewarded with high profile characters in later series, such as Major Kira (Nana Visitor) and Captain Janeway (Kate Mulgrew), as well as intriguing figures such as Ro Laren (Michelle Forbes). However, female roles have significantly deteriorated in the franchise, with 7 of 9 and T'Pol clearly intended as eye candy for the boys, while the new *Star Trek* film relegates female roles to background figures. Despite disproving the cliché that SF primarily appeals to an adolescent male market, these are worrying signs of retrenchment, particularly with a 12-year-old boy perceived as the ideal market for the film. *Doctor Who*'s latest incarnation also appears to target young boys over female viewers, and although Moffat bridled when asked at a writers' conference how long it would be before a 14-year-old boy was cast in the role of the Doctor, the point is clear, with the series at risk of disenfranchising female audiences (and its current female companion proving less than inspiring).

Providing something for everyone has never been easy, but a continued concern, particularly in skewing material towards a younger audience, is whether both franchises will continue to discuss serious matters. *Doctor Who* has voiced an array of issues, from environmental disaster and industrial unrest to satirical features questioning media power, joking about WMDs at Westminster, or revealing politicians to be duplicitous aliens who are full of wind. *Star Trek* has also commented on issues such as war, as well as countering various forms of prejudice, albeit with specific limitations. When fan campaign "the Gaylaxians" petitioned *Star Trek* to provide a regular gay crew member, they secured Roddenberry's support, yet Paramount vetoed the idea, claiming such a move would upset parents (Tulloch and Jenkins 1995, 237–265; Reeves-Stevens 1997, 89). The BBC had no such qualms, and Russell T. Davies was able to go where no SF show-runner had gone before in placing the openly bisexual Jack Harkness in the lead role of *Torchwood*. It is only a shame the character is so immensely flawed, and that the eminently more likeable Ianto was killed off. Davies's ability to promote greater diversity was seemingly proven in the strong fan reaction to Ianto, a regular gay character with the evident makings of a popular hero, making his death somewhat inexplicable. Ironically, despite taking the opportunity, in helming *Doctor Who*, to push at given boundaries, Davies was heavily criticized by fans for misusing the franchise for his own agenda, and it is interesting to note that Moffat has since focused on reinstating the show as "family viewing." Although an interesting satirical moment featured in the Moffat-scripted episode "The Beast Below"—making some notable comments, coming up to the U.K.'s general election, about the choice to either "protest" or "forget"—for the most part the new season played it very safe, leaving little to interest adult viewers. While it may be cynical to suggest that the show has been dumbed down in order to sell more child-friendly merchandise, this may not be altogether inaccurate.

In terms of narrative scope, *Doctor Who* has the advantage of much greater flexibility than *Star Trek*, situated in a narrative universe that is vaguely drawn, with little established continuity, providing a host of opportunities to fill in details (such as the Doctor's past). By contrast, up until the recent reboot, *Star Trek* appeared to have little room to maneuver, with a timeline that can be traced from Earth's first Warp speed flight to key events centuries in the future; and the franchise was additionally hamstrung by the need to ensure that Roddenberry's ideal remained unsullied. The *Lost* crew's take on the show is thus an understandable and perhaps welcome deviation. As one commentator argues, "The time-travel plot neatly side-steps all that hazardous Trek lore—and sets up a fresh blank future in a parallel reality" (Rose 2009); yet whether further installments will repeat its success, after its initial kitsch appeal, remains to be seen. Whatever the future holds for either franchise, their inherent optimism is likely to be preserved, upholding the best of human qualities within a liberal-humanist ethos. These ideals may look a little simplistic today, particularly compared to edgier material set in more complex narrative universes, but the appeal of both franchises is deeply invested in their intrinsic reassurance, affirming that certain ideals are eternal, whatever else may change.

The long-term success of both shows proves that some concepts really can stand the test of time, yet neither show can afford to be complacent. The revised *Doctor Who* may seem keener at exciting children than producing satisfying adult drama; but the franchise's survival relies on its continued ability to attract a diverse audience, and it thus seems likely to keep morphing to suit its surroundings, borrowing from other sources to create continued interest. As Moffat notes, "*Doctor Who* has always been eclectic and kleptomaniac. You start grabbing bits of shows. *Doctor Who* switches shows all the time" (Anders 2008). *Star Trek* has proved equally mutable, with the last film providing a new lease on life by infusing features from *Star Wars*. Die-hard fans may dislike such innovations, but they are often the first to note if a show has gone stale, necessitating that those involved in production perpetually innovate while also taking heed of the potential diversity of responses. After all, for every fan that welcomed changes in the new *Doctor Who*, there were those who wanted everything back the way it was, from the old TARDIS (and its windows!) to the serial format, indicating the kind of conservatism that has dogged *Star Trek* also.

Doctor Who and *Star Trek* survived cancellation thanks to fan interest, yet the incentive for their revival is also grounded in practical considerations—as it was in the beginning—in aiming to create a hit. If anything, the stakes have increased today, with both franchises having to secure new viewers without alienating the established audience. Neither *Doctor Who* nor *Star Trek* have consistently achieved this task, but they serve as important landmarks in the history of the telefantasy series, with an apparent stake in its future. They have shown that telefantasy can be a big draw, particularly when a feel-good factor is achieved through disasters avoided, enemies thwarted, and new insight gained, with heroes who are immune to corruption and the prospect of a better breed of humans to follow us—remaining distinctly old-fashioned in giving us something to believe in. Even as dangerous flaws such as greed, vanity and ambition are highlighted, humans are still deemed to be worth saving (even from themselves). Both franchises reiterate the sense of optimism they began with: confirming that no master plan can destroy mankind—no matter how advanced the adversary may be—and that good people can always make a difference. Fans have played a prominent role in the survival of both shows, particularly via their viewing and spending habits, their feedback, and their creative endeavors, causing the industry to take note of cult television's potential, although *Enterprise* and *Torchwood* also prove that fans may still be ignored, and that show-runners are all too capable of mishandling a concept.

In questioning whether the *Trek* franchise has become outmoded, long-term fan Ina Rae Hark insists that its "essential components are neither obsolescent nor fatiguing, but timeless," particularly in its repeated concern to promote compassion and freedom (Geraghty 2008, 57), ideals that *Doctor Who* similarly endorses. As we have seen, many telefantasy series do not share the same optimism, including darker visions where heroic figures are shown to be corrupt, demonic forces cannot be destroyed, plans for alien colonization are approved by government officials, and good seems incapable of triumphing over evil. These other possibilities may be infinitely more cynical, yet they have also intrigued audiences via narratives prepared to challenge the idea of an ordered universe and an essentially benign self. In recent times, as reality has become more conflicted and uncertain, fantastic television appears to have become imbued with similar ideals to those seen in *Doctor Who* and *Star Trek*, aiming to uphold a sense of kinship and camaraderie, to test humanity's virtue in the face of adversity, and signaling a continued desire for meaning and hope, affirming the continued legacy—and relevance—of the two longest-running telefantasy shows to date.

Conclusion

As the preceding chapters attest, telefantasy is one of the most dynamic and diverse of genres, incorporating a range of influences, originating a host of ideas, and undergoing various changes in style, subject matter, and audience reaction over its history. Where it was once considered to be of relatively limited interest, its changing fortunes have been pronounced, with select shows achieving extraordinary popular appeal and critical recognition. Many of the series discussed in this book serve as landmarks in television, earning Baftas and Emmys and accompanying industrial esteem, proving the genre's affinity with "quality TV" in offering challenging and innovative material, and resulting in a proliferation of similar output. Surprising successes have paved the way for future formats, creating distinct subgenres, such as the paranormal detective series, the supernatural teen drama, and other hybrid concoctions. Such shows have moved from the margins to the mainstream in terms of their perceived audience, and from niche programming to primetime slots on the major networks. This remarkable transition can be attributed to several factors, including the genre's ability to attract "prestige" viewers (those most desired by advertisers), narrative flexibility (enabling a variety of storylines), and potential intersections with a range of media forms (of particular interest to multimedia corporations wishing to make the most of their assets, extend their revenue, and attract audiences moving away from traditional television formats). Given these features—and the ratings certain shows have achieved—it is easy to see why the industry has revised its preconceptions about fantastic television, with all the major networks having invested in "genre" shows in recent years. However, such investment comes at a cost, and there is evidence to suggest the boom years are about to go bust.

A number of high-profile shows have significantly underperformed, resulting in abrupt cancellations and an apparent industry rethink. Although new telefantasy ventures have continued testing the waters, genre fans are growing accustomed to shows being pulled. Superhero themed series that emerged after *Heroes*—NBC's *The Cape* and ABC's *No Ordinary Family*—were cancelled after one season. Jesse Alexander's post catastrophe drama, *Day One*, was shot by NBC, only to be shelved, while the network's long-haul gambit, *The Event* (2010-11), a conspiracy drama about aliens living among us (which executives declared would replace *Lost* and *24*) failed to secure a second season due to declining ratings. ABC's similarly themed *V* (2009-11) received equally tentative treatment, confined to a restricted run in its second season before also being cancelled. TNT's newly commissioned *Falling Skies* (2011)—which deals with the aftermath of alien invasion—may attest to telefantasy's increasingly derivative nature in reworking familiar themes, yet such tendencies also invite us to question whether network interest—and the pursuit of mainstream popularity—ultimately benefits the genre. *Lost* may have revitalized industry attitudes towards fantastic material, encouraging big-budget investment in new genre shows, yet inflated expectations tend to coincide with minimal risks, resulting in increasingly formulaic productions, a discernible strategy of aiming to emulate the latest hits, and little scope for innovation. Although telefantasy has enjoyed an apparent golden age due to the level of investment made, the flipside to such prominence is an increasingly apparent desire to transform the genre into a populist vehicle designed to churn out a succession of variations on established themes—far removed from the experimental and unorthodox examples it once proved capable of. Commercial success may have granted a higher profile for new telefantasy series, yet it is arguably in flying "under the radar" that telefantasy is best able to provide the most compelling and insightful ideas. What appears to be a wane of network interest is therefore not necessarily to be mourned, and may enable the genre to find some interesting new directions, out of the spotlight, particularly given a proclivity towards continual reinvention—as this study attests.

Although the term remains relatively rare, I have been keen to label the shows assessed as examples of telefantasy because their generic identity is often obscured or elided in critical discussions but is deemed fundamental to understanding the exceptional qualities possessed by the genre. The fantastic links all the series discussed, and is the crucial component that allows them to depart from convention and flout expectation, situating their stories within a "heightened reality" in which virtually anything can happen. This element of novelty and wonder is a key part of telefantasy's appeal, expanding the usual parameters of possibility to elicit audience curiosity, and enabling shows to attain cult status when a sufficiently complex and compelling narrative universe is provided. Longstanding series such as *Doctor Who* and *Star Trek* have proven themselves to have enduring cult appeal; yet, as I have argued, *The Prisoner* serves as a more immediate precursor to the cult telefantasy shows we see today, by dint of its visual detail and narrative intricacy, its ongoing mysteries, and the intensity of engagement fostered among fans—pioneering strategies that would find their way into many subsequent shows. *Twin Peaks* and *The X-Files* would similarly use elements of the fantastic to propel the imagination and provide enigmas for the audience to speculate on, drawing a wider audience to telefantasy than had hitherto been established. By utilizing stylish production values and an innovative approach to genre, these shows would inspire new hybrid constructions, initiating variations on the quirky community and paranormal detective series that are still in evidence today, just as *Buffy* would serve as a precursor to the numerous supernatural dramas that have followed— from female-led paranormal investigations to vampire romances. Partly due to the impact of these examples, growing critical acclaim and increasing academic interest has helped elevate the genre's reputation; yet its improved industrial status is equally attributable to the commercial success garnered by specific shows, particularly the phenomenal ratings achieved by *Lost*—signaling a watershed in telefantasy's history.

Although its makers were initially forced to downplay its generic identity, indicating the stigma telefantasy has long labored under, *Lost* would subvert negative perceptions by reaching double figures in the Nielsens, securing high DVD sales, and becoming a global hit—affirming that big-budget telefantasy could be big business, and proving that cult appeal did not necessarily conflict with commercial success. A number of earlier shows had indicated as much, with *The X-Files* helping Fox become a major network (as well as influencing them to invest in further telefantasy shows), and *Buffy* proving equally vital in securing a brand identity for the WB and UPN (fostering a mutual interest in creating supernatural dramas that their successor, the CW, has continued to this day). In a similar vein, *Lost* would provide a much-needed hit for ABC and instigate new interest in the genre's potential, affirming the dramatic transition telefantasy has undergone. From relegation to poor scheduling slots and relative dismissal, the networks began to take telefantasy seriously, realizing its ability to deliver what a changing industry needs: the ability to incorporate a range of influences to offer broad appeal; narrative strategies that provoke intense engagement (including narrative "clues" to spot and puzzles to work out); and a ready affinity in being transposed to various media forms. Factor in its propensity to showcase new technologies, its affinity with the coveted youth audience, the potential to sustain long-term interest via narrative twists, and the incentive for fans to purchase ancillary material such as games and DVDs, and we have what appears to be a winning formula, creating a post–*Lost* flurry of commissions. However, given the conspicuous disappointment of *Heroes* and a number of new shows which were swiftly axed, we have good reason to question what went wrong.

One simple answer is that the increased interest taken in telefantasy has come at a price, with pressure to find the next big hit at odds with indulging innovation. Network investment has generally resulted in shows that recycle familiar tropes (ensemble cast, inter-relationships, and in-jokes) and rework established themes (post-catastrophe scenarios, metaphysical questions about fate, mysteries to entice viewers over successive installments), with many new productions obviously attempting to become the next *Lost*—and finding audiences less than enthused. The pursuit of the "franchise factor" (shows with the potential to be exploited in various media, narrative features that offer an excuse to showcase spectacle, and the ability to generate crossover appeal) has clearly influenced the commissioning of new series, yet a higher weight of expectation poses additional pressure, with *Heroes* aptly illustrating the danger of overlooking the basics in the scramble to create a hit multimedia franchise. *FlashForward* (2009) was similarly designed through reverse engineering to generate a similar response to *Lost*, but it failed to meet its brief. Rapidly commissioned by ABC to fill *Lost*'s place, it combined an ensemble drama with a tenuous SF premise, had a narrative that questions fate and destiny, and an ambition to last for at least 5 years; yet ratings fell from 10 to 5 million in a troubled first season, resulting in cancellation. A host of locations, a conspiracy at work, and numerous twists failed to maintain audience interest, and its hokey conceit—a device enabling the world to briefly fall asleep (and inexplicably glimpse their future)—created a "tease" that simply wasn't deemed worthwhile. *Defying Gravity* (2009) provides another example of an SF show intended for mass consumption, reworking the same components of relationship drama and cosmic destiny while failing to yield sufficient interest. A group of astronauts travel together through the solar system, guided by an alien artifact and overseen by shady officials on Earth with secret links to extraterrestrials. Flashbacks among the crew aim to provide intrigue and intimacy, yet the show was cancelled as ratings dwindled long before the intended journey was complete.

The swift demise of series designed for long-term success indicates the need to rethink what constitutes a hit formula. Even established series have found it hard to retain network interest as ratings have dipped, with *Medium* and *Ghost Whisperer* both abruptly cancelled by CBS, despite each series averaging 7.7 million viewers in their last seasons. Although these shows proved that a sizable female audience is keen to follow supernatural drama with a female lead (particularly if some soapy features are included) their cancellation suggests a somewhat dismissive attitude towards such fans. Indeed, we might recall that a new variation on a similar theme, *Eastwick* (2009), was swiftly pulled when ratings fell below 5 million, affirming that familiar tropes cannot guarantee success—or at least not the level of success desired by the industry. ABC cancelled the show after only two months, despite positive critical reaction and a big proportion of female viewers, pulling the show from the schedules in a similar vein to their equally short-lived *Happy Town*, forcing fans to go online or buy the DVD to find closure. New commissions such as *Teen Wolf* and a drama about a super-empowered teen, *The Nine Lives of Chloe King*, affirm that a youth demographic is being prioritized, with obvious pragmatic incentives, yet how long any such ventures last remains uncertain in what are clearly tough times for television. Although dwindling fortunes have prompted networks to take chances on telefantasy (as was proven by *Twin Peaks* and

Lost), expensive production costs (typically $1 million plus per episode) have fueled industrial reservations towards the genre, uncertain whether such expenditure will be recouped. Telefantasy shows with continuous storylines are also becoming negatively regarded by the industry, as serialized narratives often deter casual viewers from tuning in (while committed viewers will acquire DVDs or downloads rather than wait for syndicated re-runs). The downside to creating shows with cult appeal is thus evidenced. While an avid following offers some appeal to investors, ratings still need to be high enough to yield necessary advertising revenue, which is why the crossover cult has been pursued, aiming to attract a "mainstream" audience as well as "genre" fans, yet resulting in an uneasy mix that is clearly difficult to get right.

That is not to say this quest will not continue, particularly given the numbers secured by *Lost*. As former ABC Entertainment president Stephen McPherson has stated:

> Nothing can replace *Lost*. We're looking for something unique and innovative and exceptional, because that's what grabs viewers and ignites their passion and makes them want more. That's why *Lost* worked—no one had seen anything like it and it promised a lot. So we're not focused on finding "the next *Lost*." We're looking for the next great, groundbreaking, game-changing idea [Rice 2010].

What McPherson neglects to mention is that the executives behind this groundbreaking game-changer were fired before its pilot was even aired, including his predecessor. Far from signaling an industry that is conducive to creativity, *Lost* was a surprise hit that was scarcely allowed—only to be cynically exploited once the network realized what they had. Furthermore, while it certainly "promised a lot," it failed to deliver on expectations, and an unsought aspect of its legacy may well be in provoking considerable wariness among viewers at being led along in the same way. As to its impact on the industry, although the show was undoubtedly a game-changer, particularly in reinstating network interest in telefantasy, the result has not necessarily been positive, with most shows launched in its wake faring badly. *Lost*'s phenomenal success was a hard act to follow, setting expectations unnaturally high, with unhappy consequences for McPherson (himself fired as ABC fell back to pre–*Lost* status), as well as negatively impacting upon new genre shows.

Excessive expectation is partly responsible for the number of recent telefantasy shows that have failed to last beyond their first season, with the major networks aiming for overly ambitious ratings, allowing limited opportunity for a series to find an audience, and preferring to pull the plug if it is not an immediate big hitter (generally deeming anything below the 5 million mark not worth persevering with). Niche channels such as Syfy and the CW may once have had relatively modest requirements in determining a show's viability, but this seems to be changing, with the CW's cancellation of long-running hit *Smallville*, and SyFy's axing of *Stargate Universe* (despite a five year arc planned) signaling a reluctance to extend existing formulas if the returns prove insufficient. By contrast, we might consider the success of *Warehouse 13* (2009–) and its implications. Providing a variation on *The X-Files* in combining episodic paranormal investigations with the longer-term intrigue of a potential relationship between its leads, the series prioritizes fun and adventure and has earned the SyFy channel's highest ever ratings, suggesting a worrying trend for things to come. Challenging, innovative and (heaven forbid) unsettling telefantasy—the kind that poses questions beyond narrative teases—is in danger of becoming obsolete in a climate where the majors want big hits (based on past performers), and smaller networks and cable channels may settle for a smaller share of the audience but also appear reluctant to take risks, with funding requirements that still make them answerable to commercial sponsors.

Nonetheless, surprises are still possible, as was proven by Syfy's *Battlestar Galactica*. Although executives complained about its dark tone and low ratings (averaging 1.4 million after its opening season), it was allowed considerable creative freedom and lauded as a pioneering SF series. *BSG* would attract only a small audience, despite its potential to be a crossover cult (with its ensemble cast, an emphasis on inter-relationships, impressive effects, and continued intrigue in its central premise—guessing the identity of cyborg infiltrators among the remnants of humanity, a question which extends beyond simple "tease TV" in broaching philosophical and political concerns). The show consolidates many features found in preceding cult series, including the radicalism of *The Prisoner*, the trippiness of *Twin Peaks* in its visions and visual flourishes, the camaraderie and social relevance once tackled in *Star Trek*, and the metaphysical speculation offered by *Lost*; while prominent female characters upped the ante on *Buffy*—at least initially. The pronounced loss of ratings after its first season can be attributed to several factors. Aside from the fact that many viewers opted to watch it in forms not counted by the Nielsens, there was a decline in quality as the series progressed, with narrative leaps that emulated the sporadic jumps across space routinely made when the show's fleet found themselves in trouble. However, for all its flaws, even as much of it was clearly made up as they went, the series affirms that challenging and beautifully wrought telefantasy was still possible—even if it did not manage to sustain its quality or achieve a sizeable audience. A prequel series, *Caprica* (2010), was created with the aim of achieving greater accessibility and appeal, reflecting the new concerns of the rebranded Syfy channel, which has been eager to dilute its focus on the genre (even including wrestling and reality television shows in its schedules) in a bid for higher ratings. However, the series was cancelled after one season due to disappointing ratings, and although another attempted *BSG* spin-off, *Blood and Chrome*, is about to be launched, its prospects are equally contingent upon securing sufficient viewers. Given such developments, even on a network designed to foster new forays in telefantasy, genre fans have good reason to be concerned, with the likelihood of similarly edgy adult shows (beyond the risqué contrivances of *True Blood*) appearing increasingly unlikely.

Dollhouse may have sought to fulfill this aim, defended by its creator as a means of exploring adult fantasies and relationships, yet its unsavory premise deterred many viewers from watching. Given its marked incoherence, *Dollhouse* appears to have been created by Whedon simply to give his friends and family some work. The series was developed for Fox, alongside a number of other genre shows, in an interesting attempt to curry favor with fans by airing these new commissions with limited commercials on scheduled "sci-fi nights" to enhance the viewing experience (and encourage viewer loyalty). However, Fox swiftly deemed the exercise too costly to continue and further engendered distrust by demanding detrimental changes to their new shows, including shifting them to poor timeslots prior to cancellation (as occurred with *The Sarah Connor Chronicles* and *Dollhouse*). While *Fringe* has (thus far) survived, seemingly fulfilling the network ideal in combining an episodic structure that allows casual viewers to jump on at any point while additionally giving cult fans deeper intrigues to explore, initial ratings of 10 to 12 million halved after a change in its time-slot, affirming Fox's continued failure to learn from past mistakes.

More widely, notable changes are afoot. Aware that hits are hard to sustain over a longer term, and hit by difficult financial times, networks have devised new strategies, such as reducing the number of episodes made, confining themselves to single-season dramas, or creating miniseries (with the opportunity to extend them if the response proves favorable). The continuous series is thus becoming increasingly outmoded—with huge ramifications for cult television. While the extra time enabled by successive seasons enables the narrative intricacy prized by fans, this may not pay sufficient dividends for sponsors, particularly if casual viewers are deterred. A cult audience may provide intense commitment to shows, yet this will not necessarily make them economically viable. As Lynette Rice has put it, "Passion doesn't translate into dollars." She cites *Fringe* executive producer Jeff Pinkner in hoping a means is found to take fan interests into account, asserting:

> Something that I have learned is that having a limited audience, but an audience that cares deeply and passionately, is not necessarily a bad thing. What's important is that the networks and the studios figure out a business model where they can keep shows like that on the air. A lot of the best human, emotional character storytelling comes within the context of these larger-than-life stories [Rice 2010].

It is in placing "character storytelling" within "larger-than-life stories" that telefantasy has transcended its former reputation as escapist or abstract, securing critical acclaim, fan commitment, and, on occasion, the kind of appeal that has made the genre seem to be a lucrative commercial gambit. However, the attempt to secure mass popularity has also resulted in disappointments such as *Heroes*, *FlashForward* and *Defying Gravity*. Dumb, derivative, and defying any measure of credibility, these shows might well have been the shape of things to come for telefantasy—aiming at mass appeal, reworking established formats, and seemingly designed by committee—and their cancellation thus provides an odd sense of relief in hopefully deterring other expensive mistakes. As these examples indicate, many innovations in previous telefantasy have been incorporated in new productions for the crassest of reasons: blending genres to attract a cross-section of viewers, adding fantastical motifs simply to propel the action and provide intrigue, and utilizing stylistic features to divert attention from gaping plot holes and overused ideas. Such failures affirm that traits once associated with "quality" do not necessarily create a good show, and reiterate that a hit, much less a cult hit, requires a great deal more.

It would be nice to think that genuine innovation and originality are still possible, and that telefantasy is certain of a future as extensive and inspiring as its past. Series such as *The Prisoner* and *Twin Peaks* may have frustrated the majority of the audience when they first aired, but they inaugurated an important legacy in refusing to pander to audiences, taking chances with unconventional approaches, admitting their status as media products, and drawing on other texts to remind viewers of their artifice. Combining generic signifiers and subverting expectation, they raised the bar not only for telefantasy, but television in general, incorporating traits later identified as quintessentially postmodern—particularly in their use of parody and self-reflexivity—ideas which would resurface in a variety of later series yet invariably lose their impact through over-use. Far from encouraging audiences to question the degree to which we are consumers of media culture, intertextual allusions arguably do little more than celebrate this fact; and if exposing the "fourth wall" was once a radical device aimed at encouraging "distanciation" and fostering accompanying cynicism, it has increasingly been used simply as an amusing in-joke. Techniques that once unsettled audiences have thus become conventions, and former markers of "quality" no longer have the exclusive cache they once did.

That is not to say that the examples we have looked at simply aimed to push the boundaries of broadcasting. Telefantasy faces the same practical considerations as any television production—needing to develop ideas that will sustain audience interest—and the case studies assessed each found innovative ways to achieve this. As offbeat and extraordinary as they were, their primary aim was to keep viewers enthralled, deploying narrative strategies designed to ensure their survival. Number 6 was thus condemned to repeat the same futile bid for escape to extend *The Prisoner*'s commerciality as much as its allegory, while BOB could never be apprehended because he was, in essence, a phantasmagoric entity created to perpetuate *Twin Peaks*' surreal soap. By the same token, the conspiracy hinted at in *The X-Files* could never be exposed—as Carter and Fox were well aware—as this would undermine the series' raison d'etre. *Buffy* placed its protagonist in a similar existential plight, tasked with battling demons to fulfill her Slayer duties, as well as the show's requirements, and only granting her a reprieve when it ended. *Lost* took Tease TV to a new level, playing games with time and a succession of narrative departures to sustain its premise, and craftily getting viewers to fill in its narrative blanks. Common features among these shows include their stylistic innovations, a tendency toward generic slippage, a marked sense of playfulness, and continually deferring resolution to encourage involvement and keep each series going. Such strategies evolved from pragmatic considerations (a bid to remain on air), and have been carefully noted and replicated largely to pursue the same ends. As we have seen, however, audiences can quickly tire of a concept, any changes made may not necessarily be approved, and securing continued interest remains as challenging as ever, causing the industry to question if this goal is worth pursuing.

The decision to opt for shorter seasons is but one of the changes affecting telefantasy, a trend that originated as a consequence of the Writers Strike of 2008 (to compensate for lost ratings and advertising revenue) and which seems likely to continue. Many perceive shorter seasons to be an advantage, with the task of making a series with an average 22 episodes per season generally considered antithetical to maintaining quality. As Tim Kring has asserted:

> Serialised TV dramas are extremely challenging to make and to watch. They take commitment from an audience. I think the way for them to survive is for them to be something rare and something special. You do this by not being on the air all of the time and by having fewer episodes [Morgan 2008].

His wish was granted for *Heroes*' last season, with fewer episodes (and the series' eventual cancellation) justified as a cost-cutting measure. This follows a wider industry trend aiming to limit seasons and create greater variation in the schedules to test new shows. The former model, demanding 100 episodes (around 5 full-length seasons) before a series was deemed suitable for syndication, appears to be undergoing significant revision, partly as a consequence of notable changes. Sales for second runs can now occur prior to a show ending (the rights to *Buffy* were sold to cable channel *FX* in its second year). And with seasonal DVD sales providing revenue during production, there are indications of a new strategy at work, with broadcasters motivated by a desire to exploit audience interest when it is at its most intense, rather than aiming to create long-haul shows where interest is likely to peter out and new fans are discouraged. However, while limited runs may prove to be beneficial in reducing the practical demands faced by creative teams, a preference for standalone episodes and less serialization will also potentially eradicate cumulative narratives and complex characters, undermining cult appeal.

If intelligent and innovative shows are to have a future, a number of changes need to occur, including an industrial willingness to pay attention to fan interests and moderate expectations about audience size. Crossover cult series may appear to offer the best of both worlds, but they arguably dilute material to such an extent the fantastic is often used simply as a gimmick.

While some examples can attain mainstream success, telefantasy largely appeals to a core audience, a group that may not guarantee double figures domestically, but have a significant global presence and should not be overlooked. Where genre fans once relied entirely on network scheduling decisions, they can now buy series on DVD (minus ads and with various "extras" included) and may wait for a show to be made available in this way rather than watching it on television. Additionally, the Internet and PVRs enable greater flexibility in when they choose to watch a given series. New media technologies have thus revolutionized access to material, yet also pose specific problems. Those time-shifting their viewing by recording shows may now be incorporated in the Nielsens (in a relatively recent move), yet many who watch a show on DVD or online cannot be properly measured, providing problems for gauging accurate ratings. In addition, savvy viewers who avoid ads on the Internet have caused consternation by undermining the industry's relationship with sponsors, with Fox accusing users who found a way to filter ads on downloaded series of "theft," illustrating notable problems for a post-broadcast era to contend with. While we are likely to see further online investment, shows will be difficult to police, particularly given sites which illicitly share material. The consequences are likely to damage consumer interests the most, with illegal downloads adversely affecting the revenue made on shows and thus potentially hindering future production, and it remains to be seen how such problems are to be overcome.

Telefantasy shows were among the first to be made available online, enabling notable innovations, such as alternate reality games and webisodes, to promote audience interest and extend fictional universes. However, far from using the Internet simply to immerse themselves in texts or provide free marketing for the networks, fans have become adept consumers online, exchanging criticism as well as appraising the likely fate of their favorite shows through sites like digital spy, bythenumbers.com and E!Online. While executives may aim to think like fans, in designing shows with cult appeal, it seems fans have learned to think like executives in gauging the sustainability of a favorite show. A notable wariness about network decisions has resulted from the fact that series cancellations continue to occur, with fan protests rendered futile if ratings remain relatively modest, reiterating a continued imbalance of power. As series creators grow frustrated with network demands, and telefantasy fans turn away from mass market series, we may have alternative options opening up, including a situation where series are launched online and purchased directly by viewers. Forays such as Whedon's horror musical *Doctor Horrible's Sing-alongblog* (2008), partly influenced by *Star Trek* webseries *New Voyages* (aka *Phase II*), suggest notable moves in this direction. However, while Whedon and Cawley were able to privately fund their projects, the main obstacle for any new production lies in securing adequate investment, as well as creative freedom, while trying to ensure that material finds sufficient returns, even with the risk of being illicitly shared.

Just as cinema needed to find new ways to attract an audience in the face of competition from television, broadcasters have had to adapt to survive a multimedia environment by incorporating new media forms, rationalizing their output, and attempting to secure as wide an audience as possible. While cult telefantasy series have proven able to attract a diverse following, networks increasingly appear to prioritize the younger viewers most coveted by advertisers. Even companies that don't rely on commercial revenue, such as the BBC, are replicating these tendencies (as the youthful new lead of *Doctor Who* illustrates); while the pursuit of a younger fan base is further indicated by the fact that the target market for the rebooted *Star Trek* film was perceived as a "12-year-old-boy," irrespective of the established audience. A desire to appeal to adolescents has considerable implications for content, and the emphasis on male characters in ensemble shows like *Lost* and *Heroes* further indicates a worrying reversal of the gains made by *The X-Files* and *Buffy*, with female characters relatively sidelined in these series. While we have also seen telefantasy series primarily aimed at a female audience, these either consist of vampire romances (where female leads play second fiddle to vampire lovers) or supernatural soaps such as *Ghost Whisperer* and *Medium* (where they balance family life with acting as spooky social workers), evidencing continued use of stereotypes, even in a genre that should be most conducive to experimentation. An industrial urge at replication and recycling is likely to continue, impairing the chances of genuine innovation—without eliminating it altogether. As this study attests (and the range of shows in the appendix affirm), while the genre has produced a number of variations on established themes, it has also created standout shows with continued potential to surprise, even in less than ideal conditions.

Contemporary telefantasy faces a number of tricky challenges. New shows must have sufficient intrigue to entice audiences—without being overly complex—while established shows must seek to satisfy the old guard, as well as welcome new recruits. All must look good on today's high definition televisions, yet equally impress on laptops and mobile phones, and satisfy a diversity of viewers (as well as executives) on a number of competing demands. The pursuit of the franchise factor is perhaps the biggest hazard facing telefantasy—implying that only shows with major corporate investment and content deemed appropriate to be extended in multiple platforms are likely to be commissioned—yet an equivalent concern is that networks may decide the possibilities have been exhausted (for the time being) and find another genre to mass produce, leaving telefantasy to cable shows and the Internet, where they may potentially have greater freedom to try out new ideas yet will not necessarily benefit from the investment and marketing they require. Given a situation where shows are either cancelled before they have a chance to reveal their potential, or spun out way past their remit, the prospects of a good quality telefantasy show being produced—one which allows its production team adequate creative freedom, is funded, scheduled and marketed appropriately, and which satisfies its audience from beginning to end—relies as much on chance and good fortune as much as it ever did; yet the hope of finding a series worthy of emotional and intellectual investment remains a big draw for a significant number of viewers. Although the genre's future remains uncertain, the shows assessed in this study are likely to continue wielding their influence on a new generation of prospective writers and show runners, reiterating the same tendencies noted throughout this study. As Janet Staiger notes, "The programs watched by today's youth will likely serve as the touchstones for their experiences as they move into their roles as cultural producers" (Staiger 173). Given the genre's extraordinary capacity to enthrall, experiment, and adjust itself to differing media, cult telefantasy is sure to play a part in the shape of things to come. Even as the genre is likely to face numerous challenges and take many forms, telefantasy's ability to amuse, inform, and astound audiences will ensure its survival—in one shape or another.

An A to Z of Telefantasy Series

The following offers a brief description of the series discussed in this book, as well as notable precursors, antecedents, and interesting kin. While by no means comprehensive, the selection indicates the various formats included in the category of "telefantasy," and provides an understanding of influential themes and cycles. Examples of telefantasy may include an SF element—using tropes such as future or alternate worlds, time travel, extraterrestrial life, or other extrapolations based on rational possibility—or lean toward a supernatural premise, including the occult, humans with special powers, and phenomena given a mystical rather than scientific explanation. Far from neatly falling into either category, some series may possess elements of each. I also include comedic variants to illustrate the variety of forms the term may encompass. Feature films and other adaptations of these series are not included.

Information is cited in the following order: country of origin, production companies/network(s) responsible for original transmission, and production dates. Abbreviations are as follows: ABC—American Broadcasting Company; AMC—American Movie Classics; BBC—British Broadcasting Corporation; CBS—Columbia Broadcasting System; HBO—Home Box Office; ITC—Incorporated Television Company; ITV—Independent Television; NBC—National Broadcasting Company; UPN—United Paramount Network; The WB—Warner Bros. Television Network; "ms"—miniseries.

The Addams Family (U.S., Filmways/ABC, 1964–66)
Based on the cartoons of *New Yorker* illustrator Charles Addams, this sitcom places a family of ghouls in a contemporary suburban setting, finding its fun in subverting conventional ideas of normality. It was made at the same time as CBS's uncannily similar sitcom *The Munsters* and became an unexpected hit. Variations on the motif of strange characters in suburbia include aliens in series such as *My Favorite Martian* and *Third Rock from the Sun*, while the likes of *Buffy*, *Roswell* and

Reaper explore "being different" from an adolescent perspective, providing drama as well as humor.

Alfred Hitchcock Presents (U.S., Revue Studios/Shamley Productions/Universal TV/CBS, 1955–62)

This was one of the first anthology shows, as well as one of the earliest contributions to telefantasy, with the legendary director introducing tales with horror and thriller motifs. The extent of its influence lies in the fact that it was name-checked by the writers of *Fringe*.

Alias (U.S., Touchstone Television/Bad Robot Productions/ABC, 2001–6)

Created by J.J. Abrams, this genre-bending "spy-fi" show features a female double agent caught in a web of intrigue and who incurs memory loss. The extremely convoluted storyline, elements of time travel, and the idea of fate would be reused in *Lost*, while *Dollhouse* also borrows a number of its ideas.

Alien Nation (U.S., Kenneth Jonson Productions/Twentieth Century–Fox Film Corporation, 1989–90)

Aliens on Earth, with a subtext on the immigrant experience in the U.S., provides a variation on the buddy-cop formula as a cynical L.A. cop works with an idealistic Tenctonese partner to solve crime. Despite winning awards, it was cancelled after one season, with 5 tele-movies later released.

Amazing Stories (U.S., Amblin Entertainment/Universal TV/NBC, 1985–7)

Steven Spielberg's anthology show was inspired by *The Twilight Zone* and used original contributor Richard Matheson as a creative consultant, boasting high production values, a top cast, and various acclaimed directors in assorted SF, fantasy and horror tales.

American Gothic (U.S., CBS/Renaissance Pictures/Universal TV/CBS Television, 1995–6)

Gothic conventions are reworked in a small southern U.S. town, Trinity, where evil is at large, a dysfunctional family is central, and supernatural phenomena occur.

Angel (U.S., Mutant Enemy Inc./Kuzui Enterprises/Sandollar Television/20th Century–Fox Television/David Greenwalt Productions/The WB Network, Chum Television (1999–2004)

This spin-off of *Buffy the Vampire Slayer*, in which Buffy's ex, a reformed vampire, heads a paranormal detective agency, reworks the format of *Forever Knight* and would influence later series on a similar theme such as *Blood Ties* and *Moonlight*.

Armchair Mystery Theatre (U.K., ABC, 1960–65)

This variant of the conventional anthology drama *Armchair Theatre* (1956) features stories that lean further toward suspense, thriller and horror, clearly influenced by *Alfred Hitchcock Presents*.

Babylon 5 (U.S., Babylonian Productions/Warner Bros. Television, 1993–99)

J. Michael Straczynski's epic space opera set a number of precedents for contemporary cult shows, particularly in a plot-arc extending over 5 years. Interspecies conflict creates the drama in an ambitious narrative filled with surprises. *Deep Space Nine* offers an interesting counterpart.

Batman (U.S., 20th Century–Fox Television/Greenway Production/ABC, 1966–8)

This is a camp comic adaptation featuring the "Caped Crusader" fighting crime in fantastical Gotham City with his trusty sidekick Robin. Intended for children, the tone is much lighter than the later film franchise, anticipating the likes of *Hercules*, *Buffy*, and *Reaper* in sending itself up.

Battlestar Galactica (U.S., Glen A. Larson Productions/Universal TV/ABC, 1978–9)

Written and produced by Glen A. Larson, the series was unsuccessfully sued by George Lucas as a *Star Wars* rip-off, yet deviates considerably in charting the remnants of humanity, pursued by the "evil" Cylons, on a quest to find a mythical planet called Earth. In response to fan protest at its cancellation, a short-lived spin-off, *Galactica 80*, set on present-day Earth, was produced, only to be cancelled after a few episodes, leaving two decades until a revival.

Battlestar Galactica (U.S., BSkyB/NBC Universal television/R & D TV/Stanford Pictures/Universal Media Studios/The Sci-Fi Channel, 2004–9)

Richard Hatch, who played Captain Apollo in the original series, initiated ideas for a revival by producing a trailer, *Battlestar Galactica: The Second Coming*, in 1999, set 20 years later. Tom DeSanto and Bryan Singer announced plans for a new series in 2001, but it was former *Star Trek* writer/producer Ronald D. Moore and David Eick behind the rebirth, creating a miniseries in 2003 and an eventual series. The result is far more complex than the original, with Cylons so human in appearance and attitude that they cannot be easily detected—or demonized. The narrative journey ultimately divided fans with a baffling and inconclusive finale. Attempts to continue its legacy include the short-lived *Caprica* (2010), and another prequel series, *Blood and Chrome* (2011), which details the first Cylon war.

Being Human (U.K., Touchpaper Television/BBC (2008–)

A supernatural teen drama featuring a werewolf, vampire and ghost, which has earned a surprising cult following, inspiring a U.S. version.

Bewitched (U.S., Ashmont Productions/Screen Gems Television/Sidney Sheldon Productions/ABC, 1964–72)

Comedy fantasy in which a young witch endeavors to be a good suburban housewife and tries to keep her meddling mother from upsetting her new husband. As with *I Dream of Jeannie*, the laughs come in the difficulties that ensue. Created at the same time as *The Addams Family* and *The Munsters*, it created a subgenre dubbed the "magic-com." A similar juxtaposition of fantasy and suburbia would be reworked in series such as *Buffy*, *Reaper*, *Roswell*, and other scenarios where extraordinary people are placed in ordinary settings.

The Bionic Woman (U.S., Harve Bennett Productions/Universal TV/ABC, 1976–1977, NBC, 1977–8)

This spin-off of *The Six Million Dollar Man* centers on Jaime Sommers (Lindsay Wagner), who formerly appeared as a love-interest for Steve Austin (Lee Majors) before popular interest gave her a series of her own. In featuring a woman of exceptional strength, it might be compared to *Wonder Woman*, as well as anticipating *Xena* and *Buffy*. The show also pioneered the series "crossover," as Wagner and Majors appeared in one another's shows—an idea later repeated by *The X-*

Files/Millennium/Lone Gunmen, *Buffy/Angel*, and *Torchwood/the revised Dr. Who*. The relatively rare phenomenon of moving from one network to another was later emulated by *Wonder Woman*, *Buffy*, and *Medium*.

Bionic Woman (U.S., NBC Universal Television/Universal Media Studios/NBC, 2007–8)

In this updating of the original series a young woman, Jaime Sommers (Michelle Ryan), is recruited by mysterious government agency, BIRKUT, which involves her in a serious accident in order to rebuild her, using her enhanced physical skills to counter threats to the U.S. With a little sister to look after and super strength, there are evident shades of *Buffy*, yet Jaime is much happier working for her version of the Initiative. The series was cancelled after one season.

Blake's 7 (U.K., BBC, 1978–81)

Terry Nation's gritty space opera follows a group of rebels battling against the oppressive Federation, and was a huge hit in its day. The ruthless female villain Servalan (Jacqueline Pierce) led many to see the series as an allegory of Thatcherism; yet despite a stirring theme of resistance, its bloodbath finale was memorably bleak, suggesting complicity and self-interest will triumph over any altruistic ideals. Its continued cult appeal is proven by the fact that it has since been extended in several radio episodes, voiced by the original cast.

Blood Ties (U.S., Insight Film Studios/Chum Television/Lifetime Television/Living TV, 2006–8)

Crossing *Buffy* with *Angel*, and based on a series of novels by Tanya Huff, this supernatural detective series features a female cop, a vampire love interest, and a goth research assistant, and was understandably cancelled after its second season.

Buffy the Vampire Slayer (U.S., 20th Century–Fox Television/Mutant Enemy/Kuzui Enterprises/San1dollar Television/The WB Television Network, UPN, 1997–2003)

Unto every generation a television series is born that serves as a cultural touchstone and is enthusiastically embraced. This story of a teenager gifted with good looks, sharp humor, and remarkable fighting skills (and whose home town is perched precariously above a demonic underworld) mixed it up in its assorted references and moods, and reaped the rewards. Its success may have seemed as improbable as its hero's name, but its ability to surprise lasted 7 seasons, and it has since been endlessly mined by later shows.

The Burning Zone (U.S., Universal TV/UPN, 1996–7)

A group of scientists, appointed by the government, investigate potential biological disasters, yet have another agenda: to track an organization known as "The Dawn" who aim to rid the planet of humans—a premise that bears obvious comparison to *The X-Files*.

Caprica (U.S., David Eick Productions/Universal Media Studios/Syfy, 2010)

This prequel series, spinning off from *Battlestar Galactica* and set 58 years earlier, prior to the unification of the 12 colonies, explores ethnic divides and prejudice, as well as the background to Cylon slavery.

Carnivale (U.S., HBO, 2003–5)

A traveling show during the Depression is the setting for a world of magic and intrigue, strange forces and mystical overtones. Though it was created by Danial Knauf, *Battlestar Galactica*'s Ronald D. Moore worked as show-runner prior to its abrupt cancellation. The fourth season of *Heroes* borrows obvious motifs.

Charmed (U.S., Spelling Television/Northshore Productions Inc./Paramount Pictures/The WB/Viacom, 1998–2006)

Three sisters share Wiccan powers and have various battles with demons, as well as boyfriend problems. The fact this outlasted *Buffy* is perhaps its most curious aspect.

Crusade (U.S., Babylonian Productions/Turner Network Television /Turner Network Television, 1999)

J. Michael Straczynski tried to remove his name from this spin-off of *Babylon 5*, which probably says enough.

Dark Angel (U.S., 20th Century–Fox Television/Cameron Productions/The Fox Network, 2000–2)

A genetically enhanced female tries to survive a *Terminator*-style future, created by James Cameron.

Dark Shadows (U.S., Dan Curtis Productions Inc./ABC, 1966–71)

A Gothic soap opera, created after *The Addams Family* and *The Munsters*, which played its scenario as melodrama rather than comedy, featuring a large extended family that includes a vampire and his henchman. An attempted revival in 1991 lasted only 12 episodes, yet elements resurface in later series, with the frustrated romance between female character, Angelique, and "reluctant vampire" Barnabas, reappearing in *Buffy*.

Dark Skies (U.S., Bryce Zabel Productions/Columbia Pictures Television, 1996–7)

Exploring similar territory to *The X-Files*, with an interest in aliens and government cover-ups, *Dark Skies* features a male and female lead who have two missions: fighting the alien group known as "the Hive" and avoiding the government agency "the Majestic-12."

Dead Like Me (U.S., DLM Productions/John Masius Productions/MGM Television/Showtime Networks, 2003–4)

A college drop-out dies when she is hit on the head by the toilet seat of fallen space station Mir, and is recruited as a grim reaper; yet she also needs to hold down a job in the "real" world. The plot was recycled, with a male lead, for the more successful *Reaper*. Bryan Fuller would subsequently make similarly quirky ventures *Wonderfalls* and *Pushing Daisies*.

Defying Gravity (CAN, Canadian Television/Defying Gravity Productions/Edelstein Company/Fox Television Studios/Omni Film Productions/Pro Sieben Entertainment/Space/BBC/CTV/ABC, 2009)

Pitched as "*Gray's Anatomy* in space," this attempts to combine soap and space opera on a 6-year mission that failed to last the distance, canceled by ABC after a few episodes.

Demons (U.K., Shine/ITV, 2009)

The last member of the Van Helsing dynasty discovers his destiny and fights various monsters in another variant of the supernatural teen drama. An aim to marry *Buffy* with *Urban Gothic* is hamstrung by a low budget, muted fear factor, and general cheesiness.

Doctor Who (U.K., BBC, 1963–)

The premise is a space-ship able to travel in time and space, piloted by a mysterious man from another planet, accompanied by an assortment of companions. Together they explore various worlds and overcome a number of inter-species conflicts and perils. The longest-running SF series of all time was cancelled after 26 years and then revamped a few years later, becoming a globally successful franchise with two spin-off series.

The classic series (1963–1989). From William Hartnell to Sylvestor McCoy, 7 actors took the lead role in the original series, surviving the transition to color, various cast changes, and the contrasting concerns of different producers before poor scheduling and increased criticism finally led to its cancellation.

The revised series (2005–). After an attempt to rekindle interest with a film in 1996, full copyright finally reverted to the BBC, and a new series was commissioned, with Russell T. Davies as head writer. Updating the show for a modern generation, and with effects that were no longer risible, new interest was successfully secured, with Stephen Moffat taking Davies' role in 2010.

Torchwood (2006–9, BBC Wales/Canadian Broadcasting Corporation/BBC/ BBC and 2011, BBC Wales/BBC World Wide/Starz). Captain Jack Harkness (John Barrowman) a roguish alien (of ambivalent sexuality) from the future, heads a facility with a similar premise to *The X-Files* in investigating alien life-forms (while the series additionally draws a great deal from *Buffy*). A fourth season, "Miracle Day," relocates the action from Cardiff to LA, adding an American cast and using cable channel Starz as host, a move that cements its transatlantic influences.

The Sarah Jane Adventures (2007–11). A former companion, Sarah Jane Smith (Elizabeth Sladen), returned in a touching episode in the revised series and was subsequently given a spin-off aimed at children, in which she investigates paranormal phenomena with her young son. The series ended with Sladen's untimely death.

Dollhouse (U.S., Sandollar/Mutant Enemy/The Fox Network, 2009–2010)

Conceived by *Buffy* creator Joss Whedon, *Dollhouse*'s premise focuses on agents who have their memories wiped after each assignment and return to the HQ that gives the show its title. Eliza Dushku plays "Echo," a manipulated "doll" who gradually rediscovers her identity (see *Alias*).

Earth: Final Conflict (U.S., Alliance Atlantic Communications/Atlantis Films Ltd./BBS/CTV/Chum Television/Polygram Filmed Entertainment/Roddenberry Productions/Kirschner Productions/TMG/Tribune Entertainment/Baton Broadcasting Incorporated (BBS)/Canadian Television/Chum Television, 1997–2002)

Based on a pilot scripted by Gene Roddenberry, the series' setting is Earth in the early 21st century, chronicling events following the arrival of a mysterious species, the Taelons, who aim to take over their host planet.

Eastwick (U.S., Bonanza Productions/Warner Bros. Television/ABC, 2009)
This adaptation of John Updike's book *The Witches of Eastwick* (1984) features three women who acquire magic powers in a New England town. ABC cancelled the series after two months, despite notable interest from female viewers, in a situation comparable to *Joan of Arcadia*.

Eerie, Indiana (U.S., Cosgrove/Meurer Productions/Hearst Entertainment Productions/Unreality/NBC, 1991–2)
Produced in the wake of *Twin Peaks*, the series is set in a strange U.S. town where two young boys investigate various phenomena, from aliens and ghosts to time warps and alternate realities. Cancelled after one season, a spin-off, *Eeerie, Indiana: The Other Dimension*, was trialed in 1998, yet failed to compare.

The Event (U.S., Steve Stark Productions/Universal Media Studios/NBC, 2010–11)
A conspiracy drama featuring aliens on Earth, detained on arrival in 1945, and ensuing conflict in their relations with humans. After a mid-season hiatus failed to stem declining interest the series was axed.

Fantasy Island (U.S., Columbia Pictures Television/Spelling-Goldberg Productions/ABC, 1978–84)
A spin-off of *Love Boat*, the premise is an island where visitors can travel to any time and have their wishes granted by a wealthy philanthropist. *Lost* would play on a similar theme yet also require its recipients to prove their worth.

Farscape (U.S., Jim Hensen Productions/9 Network/Hallmark Entertainment/Jim Hensen Television/Nine Film and Television Pty. Ltd./The Sc-Fi Channel, 1999–2003)
A disparate crew travel through space, led by an astronaut who (like Buck Rogers) has been propelled forward in time. Although muppet characters made it difficult to take seriously, innovations include ongoing story arcs and a cult franchise has since emerged, with a magazine and Internet "webisodes" devoted to it.

Firefly (U.S., Mutant Enemy/20th Century–Fox Television/The Fox Television Network, 2004)
Joss Whedon's follow-up to *Buffy* features another extraordinary young woman (played by Summer Glau) but sets her adventures in space, with a crew of renegades. After its quick cancellation (much to fan disappointment), the film *Serenity* was made in 2005 to show them Whedon's appreciation.

FlashForward (U.S., HBO Entertainment/ABC Studios/Phantom Four Films/ABC 2009–10)
Evidently attempting to replace *Lost*, this series involved similar issues of fate and coincidence, combining elements of a police procedural and hospital drama with a hokey SF premise, only to be cancelled abruptly after its first season.

Forever Knight (CAN/GER/U.S., Paragon Entertainment Corporation/TMG/USA Network/Columbia TriStar Domestic Television, 1989–96)
An 800-year-old vampire seeks redemption by working to solve crimes with

a female detective. A precursor to *Angel*, and the first series to tap the vampire market, *Forever Knight*'s cancellation was announced several times yet staved off by fan protest.

4400 (U.S., Renegade 83/American Zoetrope/Viacom Productions/Paramount Network Television/CBS Paramount Network Television/4400 Productions/Sky Television, 2004–7)

Dubbed by *Zoo* magazine as "*The X-Files* for a new generation," the series' premise follows 4400 abductees who are returned to Earth at the same time.

Freaky Links (U.S., Haxan Films, 20th Century–Fox Television/Regency Television/The Fox Network, 2000–2001)

A premise that explores strange phenomena on the Internet, updating *The X-Files* for a new generation.

Fringe (U.S., Bad Robot/Fringe Element Films/Warner Bros. Television/20th Century–Fox Television, 2008–)

Co-created by *Alias* and *Lost* man J.J. Abrams, and drawing from influences including *Alfred Hitchcock Presents*, *Amazing Stories*, *The Twilight Zone* and *The X-Files*, *Fringe* is a paranormal detective show in which a female FBI agent works with a father and son team attempting to rationalize unexplained phenomena, uncovering a conspiracy along the way.

Garth Merenghi's Dark Place (U.K., Avalon Television/Channel 4, 2004)

Drawing on various sources, including *Kingdom Hospital*, and frequently pausing the action to allow its cast to comment on the production, this is postmodern horror comedy at its best.

Ghost Whisperer (U.S., ABC Studios/CBS Paramount Network Television/CBS Productions/Sander/Moses Productions/Touchstone Television/CBS, 2005–2010)

Jennifer Love Hewitt appears in another variant of the supernaturally gifted female detective series (alongside *Tru Calling* and *Medium*), using her abilities to contact the dead to bring closure to their souls—and families.

Hammer House of Horror (U.K., Cinema Arts International/Chips Productions/Hammer Film Productions Ltd./ITC/ITV, 1980)

As the title implies, horror is the key theme, yet its contemporary setting provides the chill, whether it be a werewolf clan ("Children of the Full Moon"), voodoo dolls that kill ("Charlie Boy"), or haunted houses ("The House That Bled to Death"). The series suggests the supernatural still exists in the modern world and will usually win out.

Happy Town (U.S., Space Floor/ABC Studios/ABC, 2010)

This is a child kidnapping mystery in a quirky small town, harking back to *Twin Peaks*, with a touch of fantasy hinted at in the fabled "Magic Man." A rushed finale was placed online to appease fans after the series' abrupt cancellation.

Harsh Realm (U.S., 20th Century–Fox Television/Ten Thirteen Production/Fox Television, 1999)

Chris Carter's short-lived cyberpunk series, based on a comic of the same name, has characters trapped inside a virtual reality program. Poor ratings led to it being pulled after only 3 episodes aired.

Hercules: The Legendary Journeys (U.S., MCA Television/Universal, 1995–9)
Important mainly because of its tongue-in-cheek humor, the series conflates historical fantasy with contemporary satire, and lead to the spin-off *Xena: Warrior Princess*.

Heroes (U.S., NBC Universal Television/Tailwind Productions/NBC, 2006–2010)
Human mutation is the theme in a series which unites people with different powers who work to avoid seasonal catastrophes. An intended meta-arc (investigating how they acquired these powers) stalled early—along with the show's popularity.

Hex (U.K., Shine/Sony Pictures Television International/BSkyB, Sky One 2004–5)
This British take on the supernatural teen drama aimed for the same audience as *Buffy* and *Charmed*. Cassie Hughes is a misfit at a private boarding school who battles evil with her ghostly roommate, using telekinetic powers to fend off the "Big Bad"—a fallen angel intent on impregnating her.

The Hitchhiker's Guide to the Galaxy (U.K., BBC, 1981)
This SF spoof, written by Douglas Adams, mocked the conventions of the genre, using a literal deus ex machina ("The Infinite Improbability Device") to propel events, employing surreal comedy, and pioneering computer graphics.

I Dream of Jeannie (U.S., Screen Gems Television/Sidney Sheldon Productions/CBS, 1965–70)
Alongside *Bewitched*, this piece of whimsy about a supernaturally gifted woman and her relationship with an ordinary man would serve as an early precedent for the likes of *Buffy*, *Sabrina*, and *Charmed*.

The Incredible Hulk (U.S., Marvel Productions/Universal TV/CBS, 1978–82)
This comic book premise, adapted for television, has a scientist's experiments with gamma radiation leading him to transform "whenever he is angry or frustrated" into a furious, muscle-bound green ogre. The *Jekyll and Hyde* concept of man's inner struggle over his id is given a positive spin as Dr. Bruce Banner travels across the U.S., using his "ability" for good. Later films would lose the human angle in their emphasis on CGI.

The Invaders (U.S., Quinn Martin productions/ABC, 1967–8)
Architect David Vincent (Roy Thinnes) stumbles on an alien invasion plot and attempts to convince others not to be deceived by their human appearance (the stiff little finger is the giveaway). The second season found his mission less lonely, with a group called "The Believers." Cancelled without resolution, the series would spawn a four-hour miniseries in 1995, and countless variations on a similar theme, including *V*, *Earth: Final Conflict*, *The X-Files* and *Invasion*.

Invasion (U.S., Warner Bros. Television/Shaun Cassidy Productions/ABC, 2005)
This short-lived series on aliens taking over humans in a small southeast American town was hampered by the fact that a hurricane explains their arrival (an unfortunate plot detail in the year of Katrina), as well as its creeping pace.

What the aliens wanted was never explained, although a lack of emotion in those they take over suggests unfavorable prospects.

Invasion: Earth (U.K./U.S., BBC/The Sci-Fi Channel, 1998) (ms)

An Anglo-American cast feature in this ambitious project, expensive by BBC standards for the time, yet insufficient to deliver the effects required for an epic story of a small band of soldiers battling aliens in the Scottish highlands.

Jericho (U.S., CBS Paramount Network Television/Junction Entertainment/CBS, 2006–8)

Set in the wake of a nuclear attack on the U.S., the series focuses on the small Midwestern town of Jericho, Kansas. In a similar vein to *Survivors*, the premise explores the relative fragility of civilization amid scarcity and fear. It also bears comparison to other post–9/11 series, such as *Lost*, *Heroes* and *Battlestar Galactica*, and interestingly suggests the U.S. government secretly nuked its own citizens to manipulate national outrage. A huge fan campaign failed to prevent cancellation.

Joan of Arcadia (U.S., Sony Pictures Television/CBS Productions/Deborah Hall Production/CBS, 2003–5)

A teenager acts as a conduit for God, performing various good deeds in a popular fantasy drama that was cancelled when ratings dipped from 10 to 8 million—seemingly because its main audience was found to be women with an average age of 53. CBS replaced it with *Ghost Whisperer*.

Kingdom Hospital (U.S., Touchstone/Sony Pictures Television/ABC, 2004)

This creation of maverick Danish director Lars Von Trier was inspired in part by *Twin Peaks*, and subsequently teased in *Garth Merenghi's Dark Place*.

Kolchak the Night Stalker (U.S., Francy Productions/Universal TV/ABC, 1974–5)

Initiated by two television movies about a reporter encountering various supernatural beings (released in 1971 and 1973), the series explored the possibilities of monsters in modern America, inspiring *The X-Files*.

Land of the Giants (U.S., 20th Century–Fox Television/Irwin Allen Productions/ABC, 1968–70)

This Irwin Allen–produced series is about a spaceship crew that becomes stranded among giants, updating *Gulliver's Travels*, with a similar hint at satire.

Land of the Lost (U.S., Sid and Marty Krofft Television Productions/NBC, 1974–6)

Another variant on *Lost in Space*, *Land of the Lost* is about a family who find themselves in a prehistoric world after falling through a crack in time while camping near the Colorado River. An updated version was created in 1991.

The League of Gentlemen (U.K., BBC 2, 1999–2002)

Too dark to properly be called a sitcom, *The League of Gentlemen* weaves various horror elements throughout its odd community of Royston Vasey—a Northern U.K. variant of *Twin Peaks*. Residents include such "monsters" as David, the hideous offspring of an incestuous relationship; Papa Lazarou, the bogeyman who comes with the circus and steals wives; Hilary Bryce, the local butcher with a sideline in human flesh; and Herr Lipp, who buries alive a young victim of his aberrant lust in his own front garden. Its writers have cited *The Wicker Man* as a key influence, and it similarly explores the sinister secrets of an insular community, yet also succeeds in making us care about its characters.

Lexx (CAN/GER, Salter Street Films International TiMe Film-und TV-Producktions GmbH/Chum Television/Silverlight Ltd./VIP Babelsberger Filmproduktion GmbH & Co. KG/Vif Babelsberger Filmproduktion GmbH & Co. Erste KG/Chum Television, 1997–2002)

A group of renegades flee from tyranny in a powerful spaceship in a premise that sounds similar to *Blake's 7* yet is a comic space adventure in a similar mold to *Red Dwarf*, *Hyperdrive*, and *The Hitchhiker's Guide to the Galaxy*.

Lois and Clark: The New Adventures of Superman (U.S., December 3rd Productions/Gangbuster Films Inc./Lorimar Television/Roundelay/Warner Bros. Television, 1993–7)

The series explores the romance between the "Man of Steel" and his love interest, Lois Lane, as she gradually discovers her colleague's true identity. A further spin-off, aimed at younger viewers, subsequently followed with *Smallville*.

The Lone Gunmen (U.S., 20th Century–Fox Television/Millennium Canadian Productions Ltd./Ten Thirteen Productions/The Fox Network, 2001)

This comic spin-off of *The X-Files* follows the antics of minor characters Byers, Frohike and Langly, three writers for the underground conspiracy-based newsletter *The Lone Gunman*, as they attempt to confirm their suspicions about U.S. surveillance and state corruption. Though it amusingly counterbalanced the drama of the parent series, *The Lone Gunmen* failed to emulate its success.

Lost (U.S., ABC Studios/Touchstone Television/Bad Robot/MotionStar Entertainment/ABC, 2005–10)

Devised by a studio executive as a reality-based show, the concept was refined by J.J. Abrams and Damon Lindelof with a greater leaning toward fantasy (with countless citations of cult shows, including *Twin Peaks*). Crashed airplane passengers, stranded on an island, realize they have improbable connections to one another, which are slowly unraveled over successive seasons.

Lost in Space (U.S., 20th Century–Fox Television/CBS Television/Irwin Allen Productions/Jodi Productions Inc./Space Productions/Van Bernard Productions/CBS, 1965–8)

The Swiss Family Robinson transferred to space in this light hearted entertainment that follows an American family stranded on a spaceship with a dodgy scientist and a handy robot.

The Lost Room (U.S., Lions Gate Films/Lionsgate Productions/BSkyB/The Sci-Fi Channel, 2006)

A policeman discovers a key that takes him, via any door, into a strange motel room. The premise is reminiscent of the Red Room in *Twin Peaks*, creating a supernatural detective series in which the policeman's quest similarly becomes very personal.

Medium (U.S., CBS Paramount Network Television/Gramnet Productions/Paramount Network Television/Picturemaker Productions/NBC, 2005–2009, CBS, 2009–2011)

Patricia Arquette stars as a psychic mum who converses with the dead to solve various crimes (see *Tru Calling* and *Ghost Whisperer*). CBS purchased it when NBC lost interest, only to cancel the series when the seventh season dipped from 8.4 to 7.7 million viewers.

Millennium (U.S., Ten Thirteen Productions/20th Century–Fox Television/The Fox Network, 1996–9)

Chris Carter's series about ex–FBI profiler, Frank Black (Lance Henriksen), shared *The X-Files* interest in conspiracy theory but focused largely on murder investigations, with a more adult edge. Black would later appear in the 7th-season *X-Files* episode "Millennium."

Misfits of Science (U.S., USI Universal Television/NBC, 1985–6)

Created by Tim Kring, this series about a group of humans with special abilities would serve as an interesting precursor to *Heroes*.

Mission Galactica (U.S., Glen A. Larson Productions/Universal TV, 1978)

A spin-off of the original series *Battlestar Galactica* detailing the Cylon attack.

Moonlight (U.S., Silver Pictures Television/Warner Bros. Television/CBS, 2007)

Another series aiming to fill the hole left by *Buffy* and *Angel*—with a vampire detective.

The Munsters (U.S., Kayro-Vue Productions/CBS, 1964–66)

Following a similar premise as *The Addams Family*, CBS made the most of their connections with Universal with a series that featured a Frankenstein-like father, a wolf-boy son, and a surprisingly normal-looking blonde niece.

Mutant X (U.S., Fireworks Entertainment/Tribune Entertainment/Marvel Studios/Mutant X Productions Ltd./CanWest Global Television Network, 2001–4)

A fugitive geneticist and four of his "creations" search for others of their kind while attempting to evade capture by a government agent. The human evolution theme bears some comparison to *Heroes*.

My Favorite Martian (U.S., CBS Television/John Chertok Television Productions/CBS, 1963–6)

This "magic-com" hit in which a Martian holes up in a bachelor's apartment while fixing his flying saucer mines laughs from the curiosity their "odd" relationship arouses. *Mork and Mindy* offers a variation on a similar theme, while *Third Rock from the Sun* explores our definitions of normality via its alien "family." A film version, with Christopher Lloyd as the alien, was released in 1999.

Mysterious Island (CAN/NZ, Atlantis Films Limited/The Fremantle Corporation/Tasman Film & Television Ltd./The Family Channel, 1995)

Based on a Jules Verne novel, the story centers on a group of Confederate soldiers who become stranded, with a captured prisoner, on an island, encountering Captain Nemo, hostile natives, and strange beasts. It is perhaps most notable in the concerns it shares with *Lost*. A great film preceded the series in 1961, with monsters courtesy of Ray Haryhausen, and a poor tele-movie version was made in 2005.

Mysterious Ways (CAN/U.S., Crescent Entertainment/Lions Gate Television/Paxson Entertainment/Canadian Television, Columbia TriStar Domestic Television, 2000)

In yet another variant on *The X-Files*, an obsessive anthropologist investigates "miracles," accompanied by a skeptical female psychiatrist. This was aimed more explicitly at a "family" audience, with religious concerns that might be compared to *Touched by an Angel*.

Night Gallery (aka *Rod Serling's Night Gallery*, U.S., Universal TV/NBC, 1970–3)

The anthology show with which Serling followed *The Twilight Zone* was more horror-based, and granted many young directors like Steven Spielberg their debuts.

Nineteen Eighty-Four (U.K., BBC, 1954)

Broadcast live, this legendary adaptation of George Orwell's dystopia has a particular irony in being made by the corporation that inspired Orwell's indictment against propaganda and totalitarianism. Its hero, Winston Smith, working for the Ministry of Truth, begins to realize how corrupt the prevailing system is, and how insidious his own role is within it. While the series was not preserved, its themes have endured in telefantasy, and Smith lives on in every rebel that has featured in the genre, including Number 6, Fox Mulder, and Buffy Summers, all of whom, in asking questions and refusing to tow the line, share his heroic legacy.

Northern Exposure (U.S., Universal TV/Cine-Nevada Productions/CBS, 1990–5)

The quirky Alaskan community of Cicely is not simply a variation on *Twin Peaks* but an inversion of it, with goodwill and acceptance among its oddball residents, and a sense of warmth in contrast to its frozen landscapes. The longer lifespan of this series might be explained by the greater appeal of a place that recruits a doctor from the outside world, rather than a detective; and the secrets uncovered by our grouchy lead, Dr. Joel Fleischman, are mostly pleasant surprises.

One Step Beyond (U.S., ABC Films/Joseph L. Schenck Enterprises/ABC, 1959–61)

Made at the same time as *The Twilight Zone*, and interestingly pre-dating *The X-Files*, this series takes a pseudo-realistic approach, investigating different phenomena, such as ESP, premonition, and fire-starting, and claiming each analysis to be based on authenticated cases.

Outcasts (U.K., Kudos Film and Television/BBC, 2010) (ms)

Set in 2040, humans settling a new planet are troubled by the consequence of their genetic experiments, borrowing obvious elements from *Battlestar Galactica* in theme, without any of its style.

The Outer Limits (U.S., Daystar Productions/United Artists Television/Villa di Stefano/ABC, 1963–5)

An unabashed attempt to emulate *The Twilight Zone*, Leslie Stevens' anthology series is let down by an hour long format, crude special effects, and endless variations on alien/Cold War parables. Lacking the resonance or range of its predecessor, this is a pale imitation in every respect. A modern version was briefly aired in 1995.

Perversions of Science (U.S., Chum Television/Home Box Office Home Video/ HBO, 1997)

This anthology series produced by Robert Zemeckis and Joel Silver offered stories that took their inspiration from *Weird Science* magazine, including the usual mix of tropes such as time travel and human mutation.

Picket Fences (U.S., 20th Century–Fox Television/CBS Television/David E. Kelley Productions/Nina Saxon Film Design/CBS, 1992–6)

Another variation on *Twin Peaks*, this series focuses on bizarre events and residents in the town of Rome, Wisconsin.

Point Pleasant (U.S., 20th Century–Fox Television/Adelstein-Parouse Productions/The Fox Network, 2005)

In this supernatural drama a young woman is found on a beach, suffering from amnesia, and taken in by the town doctor. Tensions emerge as she learns about her supernatural origins in the town and exhibits strange powers. Romantic entanglements add soapy strains to a curious mix of *Buffy* and other supernatural teen series, with elements of *Twin Peaks* in her discovery, and shades of J-horror.

Poltergeist: The Legacy (CAN/U.S., PMP Productions/Showtime Networks/Trilogy Entertainment Group/Showtime Networks, 1996–9)

The series premise has more apparent links to *The X-Files* than the *Poltergeist* films, featuring members of the Legacy Group battling various monsters and supernatural villains.

Prey (U.S., Edelson Productions/Lars Thorwald Inc./Warner Bros. Television/ ABC, 1998)

Superhuman mutations take Darwin's theory about the survival of the fittest literally and attempt to take over the world. Offering some hope amid dismal prospects, one such mutant elects to side with ordinary mortals and fights his "own" kind. The series was cancelled after only 13 episodes, leaving matters unresolved. *Heroes* follows a similar premise yet resets the odds in humanity's favor, with the majority of mutants battling to save mankind against the villainous minority aiming to wipe it out.

Primeval (U.K., Impossible Pictures/BBC Worldwide/Watch/ProSieben/ITV, 2006–)

The Lost World meets *Land of the Lost* as a time-traveling team encounter dinosaurs.

The Prisoner (U.K., Everyman Films/ITC/ITV, 1968)

An allegorical series in which an unnamed protagonist repeatedly attempts to escape a strange seaside resort where sinister forces use high-tech surveillance techniques to keep the population acquiescent. The series would broach themes that remain the subject of much discussion and continued relevance, and has been referenced by numerous series and films.

The Prisoner (U.K./U.S., AMC Granada International/ITV Productions/AMC, 2009) (ms)

Following years of rumor and speculation, an updated version was finally created, remolding the premise with new themes and much less interest.

Probe (U.S., MCA Television/ABC, 1988)

An interesting precursor to *The X-Files*, co-created by Isaac Asimov, the series follows an eccentric scientist as he investigates unusual crimes, assisted by his secretary. It fell victim to a Writers Strike and was cancelled after only 7 episodes.

Project UFO (U.S., Mark VII Ltd./Worldvision/NBC, 1978–9)

In a manner similar to *One Step Beyond*, this series adopted a realistic approach. Alleged UFO sightings are the theme, referencing the American Air Force's actual investigation into such sightings, "Project Blue Book," in its opening sequence, and claiming to base each case on a reported sighting, anticipating the myth-arc of *The X-Files*.

PSI Factor: Chronicles of the Paranormal (CAN, Alliance Atlantis Communications/Atlantis Films Limited/First Television/Paranormal Productions/CanWest Global Communications, 1996–2000)

Another series which attempts to ground its content in fact, this claimed to be inspired by the real-life Office of Scientific Investigation and Research. Essentially another foray into *X-Files* territory, studying paranormal phenomena, its fictional status was confirmed in being hosted by former *Ghostbuster* Dan Akroyd.

Pushing Daisies (U.S., Jinks/Cohen Company/Living Dead Guy Productions/Warner Bros. Television/ABC, 2007–8)

Owing much to Jean-Pierre Jeunet's *Amelie* in its color scheme, café setting, voice-over narration, and sweet oddness, this comic fantasy by Bryan Fuller secured his status as an off-beat series creator. The premise features a man who can both kill and revive with his touch, and the problems this creates when a childhood sweetheart is brought back to life. Working together to solve a series of murders, after briefly reviving the deceased, a touching tension is created with the pair never able to touch. The series ended when ABC asked Fuller to make the show more grounded in reality(!).

Quantum Leap (U.S., Belisarius Productions/Universal TV/NBC, 1989–93)

Dr. Sam Beckett (Scott Bakula) travels back in time, leaping into other people's bodies at a critical juncture in their lives, advised by a holographic sidekick.

Quatermass (U.K., BBC/Euston Films/BBC/Thames Television, 1953–1979)

Written by Nigel Kneale, this quartet of serialized stories was the first telefantasy franchise. It began with *The Quatermass Experiment* (BBC, 1953), in which rocket scientist Professor Bernard Quatermass oversees a manned space mission and witnesses the returning astronaut's transformation into a monster. A film version by Hammer followed in 1955, and a second series, *Quatermass II* (BBC, 1955), further explored the possibility of alien invasion. Presaging themes that were hailed as subversive in the meta-arc of *The X-Files* 40 years later, aliens have already begun colonization and taken human form, and our hero must overcome a political cover-up to defeat them. A third series, *Quatermass and the Pit* (BBC, 1958–9), followed. Workmen excavate a strange craft in London, and the Professor learns that aliens existed on Earth long before humans, and are still capable of wielding a supernatural influence over us—a finale so frightening a female viewer apparently dropped dead while doing her ironing. The fourth and final series appeared in 1979, simply titled *Quatermass*, and was made by Euston Films (and aired on ITV), as the BBC were reluctant to pick up the bill. Following previous events, society is now on the brink of collapse. A disillusioned Quatermass no longer works for the government but attempts to dissuade groups of young people from congregating at ancient monuments, looking to aliens for salvation.

Randall and Hopkirk, Deceased (U.K., ITC/ITV, 1969–71)
   This whimsical series is based on the investigative partnership between a mortal and a ghost, who provides insight from "the other side." In conferring with the dead to solve crimes it can be seen as a forerunner of the fantasy comedy *Pushing Daisies*, as well as paranormal detective series such as *Medium*, *Tru Calling* and *Ghost Whisperer*. The series was re-made by Working Title in 2000 yet failed to stir much interest.

The Ray Bradbury Theatre (CAN, Alberta Filmworks/Atlantis Films Limited/Ellipse Programme/Granada Television/Showtime Networks/Showtime Networks, 1985–92)
   This series was written, produced and hosted by Ray Bradbury, one of the most prolific writers of SF and fantasy.

Reaper (U.S., ABC Studios/The Mark Gordon Company/Reaper Productions/Touchstone Television/CW Television Network/ABC, 2007–)
   Working as an employee at the Workbench hardware store, underachieving Sam gets a contract on his 18th birthday and starts moonlighting as a reaper for the Devil, capturing escaped souls, with a little help from his friends. A male version of *Dead Like Me*, this also parallels *Buffy* in focusing on the tribulations of emerging adulthood, alongside fighting demons.

Roswell (aka *Roswell High*) (U.S., 20th Century–Fox Television/Jason Katims Productions/Regency Television/The WB, UPN, 1999–2002)
   A high school drama in which alien teenagers try to fit in with their classmates, this is "*The X-Files* meets *Buffy*," as well as a variation on *Smallville*.

Sabrina the Teenage Witch (U.S., ABC/Hartbreak Films/Viacom/Finishing the Hat/ABC, The WB, 1996–2003)
   Predating *Buffy* and *Charmed*, *Sabrina* features a similar concept as that seen in the U.K. children's series *The Worst Witch*, focusing on a trainee witch who struggles to cast spells successfully, as well as deal with the difficulties of growing up. Some feature films were also released.

Sanctuary (U.S., The Sci Fi Channel/The Sci-Fi Channel, 2007–)
   This series about a group of scientists investigating "monsters" started life as an 8-part webisode series and was later turned by the Sci-Fi Channel into a popular television show. The premise bears some similarity to the *Dr. Who* spin-off *Torchwood*.

The Six Million Dollar Man (U.S., Harve Bennett Productions/Silverton Productions Inc./Universal TV/ABC, 1974–8)
   NASA test pilot Steve Austin receives devastating injuries during a crash, and is rebuilt with revolutionary technology funded by the U.S. government. He fights aliens, terrorists, and even Bigfoot, yet the series was only saved from can-

cellation when a love interest was added in the form of Jaime Sommers, later heading her own series, *The Bionic Woman*.

Sliders (U.S., St. Clare Entertainment/Studios USA Television/Universal TV/The Fox Network, 1995–2000)
  Parallel universes are explored in inventive fashion, placing our protagonists in a range of scenarios that rework various SF possibilities, eventually returning home again.

Smallville (U.S., Tollin Robbins Productions/Millar Gough Ink/Warner Bros. Television/Warner Bros. Pictures/DC Comics/Smallville3 Films/Smallville Films/The WB, CW Television Network, 2001–2011)
  Spinning off from an earlier spin-off of the *Superman* franchise, *Lois and Clark*, this series takes us further back in time. Set in a small town in Illinois in the early 1960s, it follows an adolescent Clark Kent and Lex Luthor at high school in another supernatural teen drama.

Space: Above and Beyond (U.S., 20th Century–Fox Television/Fox Television Network/Hard Eight Pictures/The Fox Network, 1995–6)
  It is 2063, humans are at war with another race, and a group of space marines fight to save Earth. *X-Files* writer-producers Glen Morgan and James Wong were behind this, and various cast members from the show made guest appearances, none of which could prevent abrupt cancellation without closure.

Special Unit 2 (U.S., Paramount Television/Rego Park/UPN, Chum Television, 2001)
  Another short-lived supernatural detective series taking obvious inspiration from *The X-Files*, *Special Unit 2* centers on a Chicago-based taskforce set up within the police department to cope with various mythological monsters. The female officer recruited to the team also anticipates a strategy used in *Torchwood* and *Fringe*.

Star Trek (U.S., 1966–)
  Pitched as "*Wagon Train* to the stars," this exploration of space, and humanity's potential, would become one of the most successful franchises in SF television history, leading to four spin-off series and eleven films so far.
  The original series (U.S., Desilu Productions/Norway Corporation/Paramount Television/NBC, 1966–9). Created by Gene Roddenberry, the original series follows Captain Kirk and his crew on a five-year mission "to explore new worlds and new civilizations." Episodes broached themes about racial conflict, war, and the importance of "democracy."
  The Next Generation (U.S., Paramount Television/Paramount Pictures, 1987–1994). Also created by Roddenberry, *The Next Generation* sees a more liberal intent invested in this revised series, with a Klingon Starfleet officer onboard the new *Enterprise*, a less gung-ho style of leadership, and a caring counselor. Oddly, this seems more dated than the "classic" series, despite broader themes.
  Deep Space Nine (U.S., Paramount Television/Paramount Pictures, 1993–9). Created by Rick Berman and Michael Piller, *Deep Space Nine* has a space station as the setting, much like *Babylon 5*, while a conflict between Cardassians and Bajo-

rans is the main theme, with Starfleet crew serving as a peace-keeping force overseeing a difficult situation, which some have linked to the Middle East.

Voyager (Paramount Television/UPN/UPN, 1995–2001). Created by Rick Berman, Michael Piller and Jeri Taylor, Homer's *Odyssey* is the basis behind the show's premise, in which a Federation spaceship becomes stranded in an unknown region of the galaxy, delaying their ability to get home. With the crew joining forces with a dissident group, the Maquis, the series showed that adversity and conflict can be overcome—perhaps too easily for contemporary tastes.

Enterprise (Braga Productions/Paramount Network Television Productions/Paramount Television/Rick Berman Productions/UPN, 2001–5). Created by Rick Berman and Brannon Braga, this controversial spin-off returns to the earliest days of warp flight. Set ten years ahead of events depicted in *the original series*, it aims to capture the same sense of discovery, but has a vastly different feel and was hated by many fans.

Stargate SG1 (CAN/U.S., Sony Pictures Television/Double Secret Productions/Gekko Film Corp./Kawoosh! Productions IX/Kawoosh! Productions VII/MGM Worldwide Television Productions Inc./Stargate SG-1 Production II Inc./Showtime Networks, The Sci-Fi Channel, MGM Domestic Television Distribution, 1997–2007)

In this spin-off of the hit film *Stargate*, various new worlds are explored in a premise similar to that of the original *Star Trek*. A further spin-off followed in *Stargate Atlantis*.

Stargate Atlantis (U.S., Sony Pictures Television/Acme Shark/MGM Television/Pegasus Productions/The Sci-Fi Channel, 2004–2009)

A spin-off of a spin-off, going underwater rather than outer space, this revives the ancient myth of Atlantis.

Stargate Universe (U.S., MGM Television/The Sci-Fi Channel/The Sci-Fi Channel, 2009–2011)

Yet another spin-off from the *Stargate* franchise, which appeared to model itself on the revised *Battlestar Galactica*, without earing the same critical plaudits.

Strange World (U.S., 20th Century–Fox Television/Teakwood Lane/The Sci-Fi Channel, 1999)

In this series created by Howard Gordon, executive producer for *The X-Files*, and *Heroes* creator Tim Kring, a Gulf War veteran works as a special investigator with the army, uncovering covert scientific experiments such as cloning and genetic engineering.

Supernatural (U.S., Warner Bros. Television/Wonderland Sound and Vision/Kripke Enterprises Scrap Metal and Entertainment/Supernatural Films/Warner Bros. Pictures/The WB, CW Television Network, 2005–)

Combining elements of *The X-Files* and *Buffy*, this series follows two brothers, Sam and Dean Winchester, as they travel across the USA, encountering witches, demons, and other supernatural phenomena, as well as fighting their own demonic inheritance.

Survivors (U.K., BBC, 1975–77)
  This bleak Terry Nation vehicle is about the dismal prospects for humanity after a deadly virus is unleashed, questioning the fragility of civilization. The BBC remade it as a miniseries, broadcast in 2008, with a further installment aired in 2009, and its plot threads have since been left dangling.

Taken (U.S., DreamWorks Television/The Sci-Fi Channel, 2002) (ms)
  Steven Spielberg returns to an obvious interest in a series about abductees, pushing at metaphysical issues in charting how abduction affects the lives of three families over successive generations, reworking the same mythology as *The X-Files* via alien-human hybrids, with events said to be based on actual abductee accounts.

Tales of the Unexpected (U.K., Anglia Television/ITV, 1979–1988)
  An anthology show in the same mold as *Alfred Hitchcock Presents*, this originated with Roald Dahl's short stories but subsequently included the work of various writers. The main theme was tales with a twist, some of which made an outright departure into the fantastical, including a story about a "bee baby" reared on royal jelly, and a device that keeps a tyrannical husband's brain alive to enable his widow to exact revenge. It remains memorable in refusing to provide viewers with a happy ending.

Terminator: The Sarah Connor Chronicles (U.S., C-2 Pictures/Warner Bros. Television/Fox Television, 2008–9)
  The film *Terminator 3: Rise of the Machines* informed us that Sarah Connor died from leukemia, yet this spin-off allows her to live by jumping forward in time. Set a few years ahead of *T2: Judgment Day*, she works with her son John to stop Skynet's development, as well as evading terminators on their trail. They are helped by one of their own, Cameron, with a mission to protect John. Its potential wavered in the second season, along with ratings, leading to cancellation, concluding with John Connor transported into the future.

Third Rock from the Sun (U.S., Carsey-Werner Company/YBYL Productions/NBC, 1996–2001)
  The oddball Solomon family are aliens on an exploratory mission, reworking the same premise as *My Favorite Martian* as they attempt to understand human identity and values. In using the family unit as their cover, the traditional sitcom is toyed with, while the series questions various belief systems. Inter-textuality is also wittily shown in casting William Shatner as "The Big Giant Head," who occasionally appears to debrief them, referencing the Orc figure in *Mork and Mindy*, as well as *Star Trek*.

The Time Tunnel (U.S., ABC/20th Century–Fox Television/Irwin Allen Production/Kent Productions Inc./ABC, 1966–7)
  Irwin Allen's follow-up to *Lost in Space* features two scientists, lost in time, who visit famous historical events, serving as the precursor to *Quantum Leap* and *Sliders*.

The Tomorrow People (U.K., ITV, 1973–9)
  Created as a rival to the BBC's *Doctor Who*, this series featured a group of young adults with psychic powers who battle various aliens and villainous humans

from their secret base in London, and also serve as humanity's emissaries in space. It was recreated for the Nickelodeon channel in the early 1990s.

Total Recall 2070 (CAN/GER/U.S., Alliance Atlantis Communications/Poly-Gram Television/Pro 7/Screenventures XXXVI Productions/TEAM Communications/Showtime Networks, 1999)

Despite its title, the series bears more relation to *Blade Runner* than Verhoeven's film. A human detective and his android partner strive to fight crime and maintain a coherent sense of reality in a future where mega-corporations use disorienting technologies to maintain social control. This distillation of Philip K Dick's main literary themes provides a bleak vision of the future—which may explain its brief survival.

Touched by an Angel (U.S., CBS Productions/Caroline Productions/Moon Water Productions/CBS, 1994–2003)

This family fantasy is about a trio of angels dispatched to Earth to help mortals in difficulty.

The Triangle (U.S., Bad Hat Harry Productions/BBC/Electric Entertainment/Uncharted Territory GmbH/The Sci-Fi Channel, 2005) (ms)

In this three-part miniseries based on the myth of the Bermuda triangle, a millionaire shipping owner enlists various crew members to solve the mystery, while the U.S. Navy is shown to be involved in a cover-up. Elements of *Lost*, particularly the island's mysterious location, touch on similar concerns.

Tru Calling (U.S., "Oh That Gus!" Inc./20th Century–Fox Television/Fox Television Network/Millennium Canadian Productions Ltd./Original Television/Tru Calling Productions/The Fox Network, 2003–5)

Rejecting the chance to lead a spin-off of *Buffy* based on Faith, Eliza Dushku opted to star in this supernatural detective series instead, playing a mortuary attendant who can relive the last day of the victim's life and thus solve the mystery of their death. *Medium* and *Ghost Whisperer* followed in its wake.

True Blood (U.S., Your Face Goes Here Entertainment/HBO/HBO, 2008–)

Created by *Six Feet Under*'s Alan Ball, and based on a book series by Charlaine Harris, this show focuses on a telepathic barmaid romanced by a vampire in the small southern town of Bon Temps, Louisiana, where explicit references to sex and drugs offer a more adult take on *Buffy*.

The Twilight Zone (U.S., Cayuga Productions/CBS, 1959–64)

This anthology series, devised by Rod Serling, arguably set a benchmark for telefantasy that subsequent series have still to equal, using the relative freedoms of the genre to fascinate, move, horrify, and, above all, make us think. Serling followed it with the more horror-based anthology show *Night Gallery* (1970–72) and tragically died a few years later. A new version of *The Twilight Zone* (1985–9) began a decade after his demise, with Harlan Ellison as creative consultant, yet despite some interesting ideas this did not have the same period charm as the original series, which continues to wield its influence on various examples of TV and film.

Twin Peaks (U.S., Lynch-Frost Productions/Spelling Entertainment/Twin Peaks Productions Inc./ABC, 1990–91)

Surreal is the adjective that immediately comes to mind in describing this one-off series set in a small town in the Pacific Northwest, which belies its apparent ordinariness as mystical forces, spirits, and dream-worlds combine to create a bizarre challenge to television drama, laying down a gauntlet for any series that followed in terms of challenging expectations.

UFO (U.K., Century 21 Television/ITC/ITV, 1970–3)
This was the first venture into a live action show for "supermarionation" pioneer Gerry Anderson, broaching the disturbing prospect of aliens kidnapping humans and harvesting them for body parts. The Vidiians, a species in *Star Trek: Voyager*, would reprise a similarly grim idea, yet were sympathetically presented in typically liberal fashion; while the idea of alien/human hybrids, often posited in alien mythology as an attempt to explain abduction, would become part of the meta-arc of *The X-Files*.

Ultraviolet (U.K., World Productions/Channel 4 Television, The Sci-Fi Channel, 1998) (ms)
Another part of *Buffy*'s legacy, this miniseries featured a vampire hunt set in modern-day Britain. Despite being optioned by Fox as a series, it was abandoned after the pilot.

Urban Gothic (U.K., Blackjack Productions/Columbia Tri-Star Television/Golden Square Pictures/Channel 5, 2000–1)
An anthology series about the supernatural, set in London, this cult hit comprises 13 tales that range from vampires and alien-infested supermarkets to East End gangsters returning from the grave. *Demons* resurrects a similar premise with the "last of the Van Helsings" fighting various monsters in London.

V (U.S., Warner Bros. Television/NBC, 1983–5) (ms)
Written and directed by Kenneth Johnson, this intelligent treatment of the invasion theme consists of aliens that come to Earth, promising to bring prosperity, yet are found to have sinister intent. An allegory of the rise of fascism, it would spawn more action-oriented additions via *V: The Final Battle* (1984) and *V: The Series* (1984–5).

V (U.S.) The Scott Peters Company/HD Films/Warner Bros. Television/Visitors Films/ABC (2009-11)
This revised series reprises the idea of benign aliens that turn out to be duplicitous invaders, with some pundits perceiving it as a satirical comment on the election pledges of the Obama administration! Fans of the original miniseries generally view the remake as a disappointment, and ABC seemingly concurred.

The Vampire Diaries (U.S., Alloy Entertainment/CB Television/Outerbanks Entertainment/Warner Bros. Television/CW Television Network, 2009–)
Primed to cash in on the teen vampire trend rekindled by the hit film *Twilight*, this is based on a book series by L.J. Smith and features a teenager caught in a love triangle with two vampire brothers. Executive production by *Dawson's Creek* creator Kevin Williamson indicates another supernatural teen drama emerging from *Buffy*'s legacy.

Vampire High (CAN, Les Productions La Fete Inc./Microtainment/YTV, 2001)
A school with, yes, you guessed it!

The Visitor (U.S., 20th Century–Fox Television/Centropolis Television/CanWest Global Communications, 1997)
Roland Emmerich and Dean Devlin began their career descent with this series about an abductee returning to Earth 50 years after his disappearance. Evidently aiming to catch the same wave as other series following *The X-Files*, and potentially influencing *Taken* and *4400*, its protagonist's mission is to steer Earth away from a path of destruction, while evading pursuit by government agents and the aliens that abducted him. It was cancelled halfway through its first year.

Warehouse 13 (U.S., Universal Cable Productions/Universal Media Studios/Syfy, 2009–)
Co-created by Jane Espenson, this continues the legacy of *The X-Files*, as an immense hangar serves as a repository for a number of strange artifacts with supernatural powers—overseen by a boffin and two special agents.

Wild Palms (U.S., ABC/Greengrass Productions/Ixtlan Corporation/ABC, 1993)
This Oliver Stone–produced series elaborates on his conspiracy interests and owes an obvious debt to *Twin Peaks* in its oddball soap elements and other touches. In near-future L.A. a major television company attempts to manipulate minds with a technology called "The New Reality" projecting three-dimensional images into living rooms around the country. The cyberpunk theme was further signaled with a cameo by William Gibson, and various film directors were involved as guest directors.

Wolf Lake (U.S., Big Ticket Television/CBS Productions/Cherry Pie Productions/CBS, Chum Television, UPN, 2001–2)
Set in the Pacific Northwest, this thriller from *Carnivale* creator Daniel Knauf explores what happens when werewolves overtake a small Seattle suburb.

Wonder Woman (U.S., Bruce Lansbury Productions/DC Comics/Douglas S. Cramer Company/Warner Bros. Television/ABC, 1976–6, CBS, 1976–8)
Originating in DC comics, the lead character, Diana Prince (played by former Miss World Lynda Carter), was intended as an Amazon princess fighting crime in a revealing costume, which she transforms into with a memorable spin. Although intended to amuse, and perhaps even ridicule "women's lib," the series would prove, alongside *The Bionic Woman*, that women could take the lead in a show, paving the way for the likes of *Xena* and *Buffy*. An updated version was piloted by NBC in 2011, but rejected as a series, partly due to negative fan response online.

Wonderfalls (U.S./CAN, Living Dead Guy Productions/Millennium Canadian Productions/Regency Television/Twentieth Century–Fox Film Corporation/Walking Bud Productions/Fox Network, 2004)
Co-created by Bryan Fuller, this story about a modern Joan of Arc was nominated for a Television Critics Award as an outstanding new program yet canceled by Fox after airing 4 episodes. In deference to its fans, the full series was released on DVD. (See *Joan of Arcadia*.)

The X-Files (U.S., Ten Thirteen Productions/20th Century–Fox Television/Fox Television, 1993–2002)

Two FBI agents examine paranormal phenomena and alien encounters, with a meta-arc which implies the government has routinely misled the public about alien existence in the most sinister of cover-ups. Past influences can be traced from *Quatermass* to *The Invaders*, and its legacy extends to shows such as *Supernatural*, *Torchwood* and *Fringe*.

Xena: Warrior Princess (U.S., MCA Television Entertainment Inc./Renaissance Pictures/Studios USA Television/Universal Television, 1995–2001)

A spin-off of *Hercules*, this had a similar tendency to laugh at its own ridiculousness, and to undercut its historical setting with a contemporary sensibility. It would inspire a host of series via such humor, and its tough female protagonist serves as an important precursor to *Buffy* (similarly attracting a wide female fan base).

Bibliography

Abrams J.J. (2006). *TV Guide*, July 24–30, 2006, available at www.theunmutual.co.uk/newsarchive203.htm.
Adalian, Josef (2007). "Lost Set for Three More Years: ABC Hit Expires in 2010." *Variety.com*, May 6, 2007, http://www.variety.com/article/VR1117964371.html?categoryid=14&cs=1.
alt.tv.twin-peaks. Available at http://twinpeaks.org/faqtop.htm (includes newsgroup discussion with Harley Peyton).
Anders, Charlie Jane (2008). "Exclusive Interview with *Doctor Who*'s Steven Moffat." io9.com, July 24, 2008, http://io9.com.5028464/exclusive-interview-with-doctor-whos-steven-moffat.
Armstrong, Mark (2001). "UPN Smacks Down Bid for Buffy." *E! Online*, March 22, 2001, http://uk.eonline.com/on/au/shows/chelsea/chuy/b41349_upn_smacks_down_bid_buffy.html.
ATC correspondent (1968). "A Plain Man's Guide to *The Prisoner*." Distributed in 1968, reprinted in *The Prisoner Poses a Question to the World*, a collection of articles and clippings compiled by Six of One—The Prisoner Appreciation Society, p. 18. Hastings: World Gallery, 1981.
Bacon-Smith, Camille (1992). *Enterprising Women: Television Fandom and the Creation of Popular Myth*. Philadelphia: University of Pennsylvania Press.
Baxter, Joseph (2009). "*Heroes* Gets Slimmed Down for Next Season: Will It Help?" April 27, 2009, http://g4tv.com/thefeed/blog/post/695041/Heroes-Gets-Slimmed-Down-For-Next-Season-Will-It-Help.html.
Berman, Gail (2002). "*Buffy the Vampire Slayer*—Television with a Bite." Season 6 DVD, *The Complete Buffy Box Set*, 20th Century–Fox Television.
Bignell, Jonathan (2005). "Space for 'Quality': Negotiating with the Daleks." In *Popular Television Drama: Critical Perspectives*, edited by Jonathan Bignell and Stephen Lacey. Manchester University Press.
Bignell, Jonathan, and Stephen Lacey (eds.) (2005). *Popular Television Drama: Critical Perspectives*. Manchester University Press.
_____ (2005). "Quality and the 'Other' Drama" (editor's introduction). In *Popular Television Drama: Critical Perspectives*, edited by Jonathan Bignell and Stephen Lacey. Manchester University Press.
Billsun, Ann (2005). *Buffy the Vampire Slayer*. BFI TV Classics Series, London: BFI.
Boedeker, Hal (2007). "Big Hero at NBC: Series Creator Kring Deftly Guides *Heroes*." *The Orlando Sentinel*, January 22, 2007, http://blogs.kansascity.com/tvbarn/2007/11/big-hero-at-nbc.html.

Bould, Mark (2005). "This Is the Modern World: *The Prisoner*, Authorship and Allegory." In *Popular Television Drama: Critical Perspectives*, edited by Jonathan Bignell and Stephen Lacey. Manchester University Press.
Brownfield, Paul (2001). "Fangs Bared Over Buffy." April 23, 2001, http://articles.latimes.com/2001/apr/23/entertainment/ca-54460.
Brownfield, Robin (2008). "Abrams: 'Fringe' Not Just Another 'The X-Files.'" *SciFiWire*, July 15, 2008, http://www.airlockalpha.com/node/5216.
Buck, Michelle (2009). Online interview about *The Prisoner*, http://player.canalplus.fr/II/254295.
Caldwell, John Thornton (1995). *Televisuality: Style, Crisis and Authority in American Television*. New Brunswick, NJ: Rutgers University Press.
Carraze, Alain, and Helen Oswald (1990). *The Prisoner: A Televisionary Masterpiece*. London: Virgin Press.
Chapman, James (2002). *Saints and Avengers: British Adventure Series of the1960s*. London: I.B. Tauris.
_____ (2006). *Inside the Tardis: The Worlds of Doctor Who*. London: I.B. Tauris.
Clover, Carol (1992). *Men, Women and Chainsaws: Gender in the Modern Horror Film*. London: BFI.
Cox, David (2008). "Why the New *X-Files* Film Is a Misunderstood but Compelling Tract for Our Times," guardian.co.uk, August 4, 2008.
Craig, Olga (2005). "The Man Who Discovered *Lost*—and Found Himself Out of a Job," *Timesonline*, August 13, 2005.
Creeber, Glen (ed.) (2001). *The Television Genre Book*. London: BFI.
_____ (2004). *Serial Television: Big Drama on the Small Screen*. London: BFI.
Cuse, Carlton (2009). "'Lost' Masterminds Carlton Cuse and Damen Lindelof Drop Hints About How ABC Hit Drama Will End," http://www.sundaymercury.net/entertainment-news/celebrity-news/2009/06/02/lost-masterminds-carlton-cuse-and-damen-lindelof-dop-hints-about-how-abc-hit-drama-will-end-66331-23767193/.
Davenport, Randi (1993). "The Knowing Spectator of *Twin Peaks*: Culture, Feminism and Family Violence," *Literature/Film Quarterly* 21, no. 4 (1993): 264.
Davies, Russell T. (2008). Interview with Mark Lawson, BBC 4, trx. March 2008.
Davis, Anthony (1968). "Patrick McGoohan Talks..." *TV Times*, January 1968, reprinted in *The Prisoner Who Poses a Question to the World*, compiled by Six of One—The Prisoner Appreciation Society, p. 24. Hastings: World Gallery, 1981.
Dean, Jodi (1998). *Aliens in America: Conspiracy Cultures from Outer Space to Cyberspace*. Ithaca, NY: Cornell University Press.
Delucci, Theresa (2008). Posted December 19, 2008, 12:48 P.M., http://www.Tor.com/index.php?option=com_content&view=blog&ID=10656.
Doctor Who BBC archive material, http://www.bbc.co.uk/archive/doctorwho/docs/DR6401-4.txt.
Dyer, James (2008). "*Star Trek*: Back to the Future," *Empire* 234: The Sci-Fi Issue (December 2008).
E!Online (2009). "Matthew Fox on *Lost*'s Last Season," reported in *SFX* on June 11, 2009, http://www.SFX.co.uk/page/sfx?entry=matthew_fox_on_Lost's_last_season.html.
EW.com (2007). "ABC Chiefs Say TV Show *Lost* Will End in 2010," http://www.ew.com/ew/article/0,,20008549,00.html.
Fane-Saunders, Kilmeny (ed.) (2001). *Radio Times Guide to Science Fiction*. London: BBC Worldwide.
Fenn, Sherilyn (2007). Commentary in "Into the Night: Creating Season Two," Special Features Disc, *Twin Peaks Gold Box Set*, 2007.
Ferren, Mick (1977). "I Am Not a Number, I Am a Free Man," review of *The Prisoner*, *NME*, 1977, reprinted in *The Prisoner Who Poses a Question to the World*, compiled

by Six of One—The Prisoner Appreciation Society, p. 37. Hastings: World Gallery, 1981.
Feur, Jane, Paul Kerr and Tise Vahimagii (eds.) (1984). *MTM— "Quality Television."* London: BFI.
Fiske, John (1989). *Understanding Popular Culture.* London: Routledge.
Freedman, Eric (2005). "Television, Horror and Everyday Life in *Buffy the Vampire Slayer.*" In *The Contemporary Television Series*, edited by Michael Hammond and Lucy Mazdon. Edinburgh University Press.
Frost, Mark (2002). Online interview with Luke Ford at http://www.lukeford.net/profiles/profiles/mark_frost.htm.
Fuller, Bryan (2008). http://primetime.unrealitytv.co.uk/bryan-fuller-slams-heroes-villians/ (retrieved January 5, 2008).
Geraghty, Lincoln (ed.) (2007). *The Influence of Star Trek on Television, Film and Culture.* Jefferson, NC: McFarland.
Gerani, Gary (1977). *Fantastic Television: A Pictorial History of Sci-Fi, the Unusual and the Fantastic.* New York: Harmony Books.
Gilbert, Gerard (2007). "No Escape for Sky: The Curse of *The Prisoner,*" September 25, 2007, http://www.independent.co.uk/news/media/no-escape-for-sky-the-curse-of-the-prisoner-403470.html.
Gilbert, Matthew (2004). "Getting 'Lost': Show Pursues TV's Most Elusive Genre—Mythology. Or Maybe That's Not It at All," *Globe Staff*, October 27, 2004, http://www.losttvforum.com/forum/archive/index.php/t-722.html (accessed February 13, 2009).
Golden, Christopher, and Nancy Holder (1998). Buffy the Vampire Slayer: *The Watchers Guide.* New York: Pocket Books.
Goldman, Eric (2007). "How Will *Lost* End? Co-Creator/Executive Producer Damon Lindelof Talks About the Future of the Show and When He Thinks It Might End," January 16, 2007, http://uk.tv.ign.com/articles/755/755527p1.html.
Greenwald, Jeff (1999). *Future Perfect: How* Star Trek *Conquered Planet Earth.* New York: Viking.
Gregory, Chris (1997). *Be Seeing You: Decoding the Prisoner.* Luton, Bedfordshire, UK: University of Luton Press.
_____ (2000). Star Trek: *Parallel Narratives.* London: Macmillan.
Hammond, Michael, and Lucy Mazdon (eds.) (2005). *The Contemporary Television Series.* Edinburgh University Press.
Hark, Ina Rae (2008). *Star Trek* (BFI TV Classics). Basingstoke: Palgrave Macmillan.
Harrison T., S. Projansky, K. Ono, and E. Helford (eds.) (1996). *Enterprise Zones: Critical Positions on Star Trek.* Oxford: Westview Press.
Headlam, Bruce (1995). "Closing the X-Files," reprinted from *Saturday Night Magazine*, December 1995, http://www.mjq.net/xfiles/satnite.htm.
Hibberd, James (2010). "*Lost* Producers Come Full Circle in Final Season," *Hollywood Reporter*, January 6, 2010, reported in Reuters, http://in.reuters.com/article/idINTRE6050HX20100106.
Hills, Matt (2002). *Fan Cultures.* London: Routledge.
_____ (2005). "Cult TV, Quality and the Role of the Episode/Programme Guide." In *The Contemporary Television Series*, edited by Michael Hammond and Lucy Mazdon. Edinburgh University Press.
Hilton, Beth (2007). "Stars Want 'X-Files' Love Scene Dropped," December 17, 2007, http://www.digitalspy.co.uk/cult.
Hinman, Michael (2008). "Tim Kring Apologizes for 'Mangled Quote,'" November 23, 2008, http://www.syfyportal.com/news425602.html.
Hora, Max (1989). *The Prisoner of Portmeirion.* Published by Six of One—The Prisoner Appreciation Society (n.p.).

Hume, Kathryn (1984). *Fantasy and Mimesis: Responses to Reality in Western Literature.* London: Methuen.
Ivan-Zadeh, Larushka (2008). "Chris Carter's Mystery Tour de Force," July 27, 2008, http://www.metro.co.uk/metrolife/films/article.html?in_article_id=235997&in_page_id =27&in_a_source=.
Jackson, Kevin (1992). "Higher Peaks in View: The Man Who Wrote *Twin Peaks* Has Plans to Get Weirder," interview with Mark Frost, August 22, 1992, http://www.independent.co.uk/arts-entertainment/higher-peaks-in-view-the-man-who-wrote-twin-peaks-has-plans-to-get-weirder-mark-frost-talked-to-kevin-jackson-about-sherlock-and-warlocks-1541807.html.
Jackson, Rosemary (1981). *Fantasy: The Literature of Subversion.* London: Methuen.
James, Meg (2006). "Buffy Fight May Have Slain Two Networks on the Edge," January 26, 2006, http://articles.latimes.com/2006/jan/29/business/fi-buffy29.
Jancovich, Mark, and James Lyons (eds.) (2003). *Quality Popular Television: Cult TV, the Industry and Fans.* London: BFI.
Jefferies, Mark (2009). "Prisoner Who Could Never Escape His Past," *Daily Mirror,* January 15, 2009.
Jenkins, Henry (1991). "*Star Trek* Rerun, Reread, Rewritten: Fan Writing as Textual Poaching." In *Close Encounters: Film, Feminism and Science Fiction,* edited by C. Penley, E. Lyon, L. Spigel and Janet Bergstrom (eds.), 172–202. Minneapolis: University of Minnesota Press.
_____ (1992). *Textual Poachers: Television Fans and Participatory Culture.* London: Routledge.
_____ (1995). "Do You Enjoy Making the Rest of Us Feel Stupid?": alt.tv.twinpeaks, the Trickster Author and Viewer Mastery." In *Full of Secrets: Critical Approaches to* Twin Peaks, edited by David Lavery, 51–69. Detroit: Wayne State University.
_____ (2003). "Interactive Audiences? The 'Collective Intelligence' of Media Fans," [WWW document] URL http://web.mit.edu/cms/People/henry3/collective%20intelligence.html.
_____ (2004). "The Cultural Logic of Media Convergence," *International Journal of Cultural Studies* 7, no. 1 (2004): 33–43.
_____ (2006). *Fans, Bloggers, and Games: Exploring Participatory Culture.* New York: New York University Press.
_____ (2006). "On Convergence Culture," e-mail interview Monday, August 14, 2006, available at http://www.bigshinything.com/henry-jenkins-on-convergence-culture.
_____ (2008). *Convergence Culture: Where Old and New Media Collide, Revised Edition.* New York: New York University Press.
Jenkins, Henry, and John Tulloch (1995). *Science Fiction Audiences: Watching* Doctor Who *and* Star Trek. London: Routledge.
Jensen, Jeff (2005). "What to Do: Lessons from Cult TV Shows—*Lost*'s Executive Producers Talk About What Should Be Done on Watercooler Shows," April 11, 2005, http://www.ew.com/ew/article/0,,1046376,00.html.
_____ (2007). "David Lynch: Climbing the Peaks," http://www.ew.com/ew/article/0,,20 154190_3,00.html.
Johnson, Catherine (2001). Review of *The X-Files, the Television Genre Book,* edited by Glen Creeber. London: BFI.
_____ (2005). "Quality Cult Television: *The X-Files* and Television History." In *The Contemporary Television Series,* edited by Michael Hammond and Lucy Mazdon. Edinburgh University Press.
_____ (2005). *Telefantasy.* London: BFI.
Jones, Sara Gwenllian (2003). "Web Wars: Resistance, Online Fandom and Studio Censorship." In *Quality Popular Television: Cult TV, the Industry and Fans,* edited by Mark Jancovich and James Lyons. London: BFI.

_____ (2010). *Television, Cult and the Fantastic.* London: Hodder Education.
Jones, Sara Gwenllian, and Roberta Perason (eds.) (2004). *Cult Television.* Minneapolis: University of Minnesota Press.
Kaveney, Roz (ed.) (2002). *Reading the Vampire Slayer: An Unofficial Critical Companion to Buffy and Angel.* London: Tauris Parke.
Kellner, Douglas (1995). *Cultural Studies, Identity and Politics: Between the Modern and the Postmodern.* London: Routledge.
King, Stephen (2005). "*Lost*'s Soul," *Entertainment Weekly,* posted September 2, 2005, published in no. 838–839 (September 9, 2005), http://www.ew.com/ew/article/0,,1100 673,00.html.
Kirby, Jonathan (2007). "Not Just a Fluke: How Darin Morgan Saved *The X-Files*," October 29, 2007, http://www.beyondthesea.it/news.asp?id=339.
Koga, Jeff. "Symbols/Motifs in the 'Twin Peaks' Universe, Version 10!!!" 6600koga@ucsbu xa.ucsb.edu. Kring, Tim (2005). http://www.tv.com/tim-kring/person/22510/biogra phy.html.
_____ (2005). "*Heroes* Origins: An Interview with Tim Kring by Damon Lindelof," http://www.9thwonders.com/interviews/tim.php.
Kushner, David (2007). "Behind the Scenes with *Heroes* Creator Tim Kring and 'Hiro,' Masi Oka," *Wired Magazine,* April 13, 2007, http://www.wired.com/entertainment/hol lywood/news/2007/04/magkring.
Lavery, David (ed.) (1995). *Full of Secrets: Critical Approaches to Twin Peaks.* Detroit: Wayne State University.
Lavery David, Angela Hague and Marla Cartwright (eds.) (1996). *Deny All Knowledge: Reading* The X-Files. London: Faber and Faber.
Lavery, David, and Angela Porter (2006). *Unlocking the Meaning of* Lost*: An Unauthorized Guide.* Naperville, IL: Sourcebooks.
Lavery, David, and Lynette Porter (2008). *Lost's Buried Treasures.* Naperville, IL: Sourcebooks.
Lavery, David, Lynette Porter and Hillary Robson (2007). *Saving the World: A Guide to* Heroes. Toronto: ECW Press.
Lewis, Lisa A. (ed.) (1992). *The Adoring Audience: Fan Culture and Popular Media.* London: Routledge.
Lindelof, Damon (2010). Television Critics Association Press Tour, 2010, reported in *Total Sci-Fi Online,* 2010, http://totalscifionline.com/news/4504-michael-and-libby-return-to-lost-s-final-season.
Littleton, Cynthia (2008). "Tim Kring Refocuses *Heroes*," *Daily Variety,* November 3, 2008, http://www.variety.com/article/VR1117995212.html?categoryid=14&cs=1.
Lostpedia. Debunked Theories, http://lostpedia.wikia.com/wiki/Purgatory_(debunked_the ory).
Lowry Brian (1995). *The Truth Is Out There: The Official Guide to The X-Files.* London: HarperCollins.
_____ (1996). *Trust No One: The Official Third Season Guide to The X-Files.* London: HarperCollins.
Lynch, David (2005). *Lynch on Lynch, Revised Edition* (ed. by Chris Rodley). Faber and Faber.
_____ (2007). "A Slice of Lynch," DVD special feature, *Twin Peaks Gold Box Edition,* 2007.
Lynch, Jennifer (1990). *The Secret Diary of Laura Palmer.* London: Penguin Books.
Lyttle, John (1996). "Do We Need *The X-Files*?" May 6, 1996, http://www.independent. co.uk/life-style/do-we-need-the-x-files-1345935.html.
Mann, Doug (1998). "Truth, *The X-Files* and the Postmodern Condition," first published in the *Mid-Atlantic Almanack* Vol. 7 (1998), reprinted at http://home.comcast.net/~ crapsonline/Library/xfiles.html.

Mann, Peter (1999). *The Slayer Files: A Completely and Utterly Unauthorised Guide to* Buffy the Vampire Slayer. Hertfordshire, Herts, UK: Pocket Essentials.

Markstein, George (1984). Channel 4 documentary, *The Prisoner File*, broadcast to coincide with screening of *The Prisoner*, available at http://www.the-prisoner6.freeserve.co.uk/markstein.htm.

Mason, M.S. (2002). "*The X-Files*: Case Closed," *Christian Science Monitor*, http://www.csmonitor.com/2002/0517/p13s02-altv.html.

McCabe, Janet, and Kim Akass (eds.) (2007). *Quality TV: Contemporary American Television and Beyond*. London: IB Tauris.

McGoohan, Patrick (1976). "From the Village to Watergate." In *The Great Television Series*, author unknown, reprinted in *The Prisoner Who Poses a Question to the World*, a collection of articles and clippings compiled by Six of One—The Prisoner Appreciation Society, p. 20. Hastings: World Gallery, 1981.

_____ (1977). Interview with *New York Daily News*, August, 22, 1977, reprinted in *The Prisoner Who Poses a Question to the World*, a collection of articles and clippings compiled by Six of One—The Prisoner Appreciation Society, p. 45. Hastings: World Gallery, 1981.

McPherson, Stephen (2007). Quoted in *Metro.co.uk*, "TV Producers Set End Date for *Lost*," May 7, 2007, http://www.metro.co.uk/fame/article.html?in_article_id=48129&in_page_id=7.

Moorhouse, Drusilla (2009). "Did *Heroes* Redeem Itself at Comic-Con?" July 25, 2009, http://uk.eonline.com/uberblog/watch_with_kristin/b135138_did_heroes_redeem_itself_comic-con.html.

Morgan, Clive (2008). "*Heroes*: Want to Make a Hot Drama? Then Start with a Myth," August 2008, http://www.telegraph.co.uk/culture/tvandradio/3558941/Heroes-Want-to-make-a-hit-drama-Start-with-a-myth.html.

NBC Universal Media Village (2006). "*Heroes* Debut Paces NBC's Second Monday Win of the New Season," September 26, 2006 (accessed January 5, 2008).

Newman, Kim (2005). *Doctor Who*, BFI TV Classics Series. London: BFI.

Nicholson, Lee Ann (ed.) (1996). Star Trek*: 30 Years, Radio Times Official Collector's Edition*. London: BBC Worldwide Publishing.

Nordyke, Kimberley (2006). "AMC Captures Prisoner for '08." *Hollywood Reporter*, December 19, 2006, http://www.hollywoodreporter.com/hr/content_display/television/news/e3i2d2333041a2e6510bc11fb5c368d642b.

Nussbaum, Emily (2006). "Revenge of the Niche: 'Netlets' like the WB and UPN Weren't a Failed Experiment. They Were Simply Ahead of Their Time," February 5, 2006, http://nymag.com/arts/tv/features/15710/.

O'Brien, Daniel (2000). *SF: UK—How British Science Fiction Changed the World*. London: Reynolds & Hearn.

Odell, Colin, and Michelle Le Blanc (2007). *David Lynch*. Harpenden, Herts, UK: Kamera Books.

O'Hare, Kate (2001). "Bullies, Battles and Buffy," March 22, 2001, Zap2it.com, reproduced at http://www.slayage.com/news/archived/010325-bullies.html.

Older, Jon (1981). "Patrick McGoohan—The Prisoner," original date of article unknown, reprinted in *The Prisoner Who Poses a Question to the World*, a collection of articles and clippings compiled by Six of One—The Prisoner Appreciation Society, p. 108. Hastings: World Gallery, 1981.

Page, Adrian (2001). Review of *The Prisoner*. In *The Television Genre Book*, edited by Glen Creeber. London: BFI.

Palgut, Tim (2003). *The Prisoner: The Village Files*. London: Titan Press.

Patterson, John (2008). "The Truth Is Back Here." *The Guardian*, July 25, 2008, shttp://www.guardian.co.uk/film/2008/jul/25/sciencefictionandfantasy.

Patterson, Troy, and Jeff Jensen (1990). "Our Town: An Interview with the Makers of *Twin Peaks*." *Entertainment Weekly* Special Edition, Spring 1990, updated posting 2000 (www.glastonburygrove.net/texts/magazines/ourtown/pdf).
Pearson, Roberta (2005). "The Writer/Producer in American Television." In *The Contemporary Television Series*, edited by Michael Hammond and Lucy Mazdon, 11–26. Edinburgh University Press.
Petrie, Douglas (2001). Interview in "Season 3 Overview," featurette on Season 3 DVD, *The Complete BuffyBox Set*, 20th Century–Fox Television.
Pilkington, Mark (2008). "I Want to Believe: FT Interviews *X-Files* Creators, http://www.forteantimes.com/reviews/films/1326/ft_interviews_xfiles_creators.html.
PMA online (2007). "TV Producers Set End Date for *Lost*," May 7, 2007, http://www.pma-online.co.uk/lost.htm.
Porter, Rick (2009). "AMC's *Prisoner* Doesn't Want to Copy the Original," January 8, 2009, http://blog.zap2it.com/frominsidethebox/2009/01/amcs-prisoner-d.html.
Pringle, David (1996). *The Ultimate Encyclopaedia of Science Fiction*. London: Carlton.
Rakoff, Ian (1999). *Inside* The Prisoner *and Radical Television and Film in the 1960s*. London: Batsford Press.
Reeves, Jimmie L., Mark C. Rogers and Michael M. Epstein (1995). "Rewriting Popularity: The Cult Files." In *Deny All Knowledge: Reading the X-Files*, edited by David Lavery, Angela Hague and Marla Cartwright. London: Faber and Faber.
_____ (2007). "Quality Control: *The Daily Show*, the Peabody, and Brand Discipline." In *Quality TV: Contemporary American Television and Beyond*, edited by Janet McCabe and Kim Akass. London: IB Tauris.
Reynolds, Simon (2008). "Interview with Chris Carter and David Duchovny," July 31, 2008, 17:12 BST, http://www.digitalspy.co.uk/movies/a117523/david-duchovny-chris-carter-x-files.html.
Rhodes, Jesse (2008). "Q&A: Chris Carter of *The X-Files*," July 17, 2008, http://www.smithsonianmag.com/arts-culture/qa-chris-carter.html.
Rice, Lynette (2001). "Slayer It Ain't So: EW Reports on the Chilling Effects the Outcome May Have on Network TV," March 23, 2001, http://www.ew.com/ew/article/0,,92414,00.html.
_____ (2007). "The Endgame? 'Lost' Producers, Carlton Cuse and Damon Lindelof, Say Talks Are Underway About a Series Finale." *Entertainment Weekly*, January 14, 2007, http://www.ew.com/ew/article/0,,20008549,00.html.
_____ (2010). "*Lost*: Networks Search for a Successor." *Hollywood Insider*, March 26, 2010, http://www.ew.com/ew/article/0,,20356866,00.html.
Richards, Thomas (1997). *Star Trek in Myth and Legend*. London: Orion Books.
Roberts, Robin (1999). *Sexual Generations: Star Trek the Next Generation and Gender*. Chicago: University of Illinois Press.
Rodley, Chris (ed.) (2005). "Suddenly My House Became a Tree of Sores: A Tale of *Twin Peaks*." In *Lynch on Lynch*, revised edition. London: Faber and Faber.
Rose, Steve (2009). "J.J. Abrams: I Never Got *Star Trek*." *The Guardian* online, May 7, 2009, http://www.guardian.co.uk/film/2009/may/07/jj-abrams-interview-star-trek.
Roush, Mark (2003). "Buffy 101: Studying the Slayer," DVD extra, *The Complete BTVS*, 2003.
Salem, Rob (2003). "The Season to Talk to Dead People," *Thestar.com*, transcribed in Whedon.info, August 25, 2003, http://www.whedon.info/article.php3?id_article=1319&img=.
Short, Sue (2005). "Countering the Counter-Culture: *The Prisoner* and the Sixties." In *British Science Fiction Television: A Hitchhiker's Guide*, edited by Peter Wright and John Cook. London: IB Tauris.
_____ (2006). "Fighting Demons: Buffy, Faith, Willow and the Forces of Good and Evil."

In *Misfit Sisters: Screen Horror as Female Rites of Passage*. New York: Palgrave Macmillan.

____ (2008). "*Star Trek*—the Franchise! Poachers, Pirates and Paramount." In *The Influence of Star Trek on Television, Film and Culture*, edited by Lincoln Geraghty. Jefferson, NC: McFarland.

Six of One—The Prisoner Appreciation Society (1981). *The Prisoner Who Poses a Question to the World*, a compilation of articles and clippings. Hastings: World Gallery.

Solow, Herbert F., and Robert H. Justman (1996). *Inside Star Trek: The Real Story*. Pocket Books.

Staiger, Janet (2000). *Blockbuster TV: Must-See Sitcoms in the Network Era*. London: Manchester University Press.

Sullivan, Michael Patrick (2004). "Interview with Joss Whedon," www.ogo.com/channels/filmtv/features/firefly/josswhedon.asp, accessed February 8, 2004. Cited in Roberta Pearson's "The Writer/Producer in American Television." In *The Contemporary Television Series*, edited by Michael Hammond and Lucy Mazdon, p. 21. Edinburgh University Press, 2005.

Surette, Tim (2009). "Joss Whedon Is Back in Control of the *Dollhouse*," September, 17, 2009, *TV.com*, http://www.tv.com/story/18134.html?ref_story_id=18134&ref_type=1101&ref_name=story&tag=content;main.

Tanswell, Adam (2009). "A Q&A with Team Darlton," January 23, 2009, http://www.forum.digitalspy.co.uk/tv/a143979/a-qa-with-team-darlton.html.

Thompson, Robert J. (1997). *Television's Second Golden Age: From* Hill Street Blues *to* ER. New York: Syracuse University Press.

____ (2007). Preface to *Quality TV: Contemporary American Television and Beyond*. Edited by Janet McCabe and Kim Akass. London: IB Tauris.

Todorov, Tzvetan (1975). *The Fantastic: A Structural Approach to a Literary Genre*, translated by Richard Howard. Ithaca, NY: Cornell University Press.

Troyer, Warner (1977). "Interview with Patrick McGoohan," for TVOntario (TVO), available at http:geocities.com/SunsetStrip/4589/troyer.html, accessed April 7, 1999.

Tucker, Ken (1990). *Twin Peaks* review. In *Entertainment Weekly*, 1990, http://www.ew.com/ew/article/0,,317112,00.html.

Turner, Graeme (2001). "Genre, Hybridity and Mutation." In *The Television Genre Book*, edited by Glen Creeber. London: BFI.

____ (2001). "The Uses and Limitations of Genre." In *The Television Genre Book*, edited by Glen Creeber. London: BFI.

Variety (2007). "TV Producers Set End-Date for *Lost*," May 7, 2007, available at http://www.lost-tv.co.uk/news/Lost_will_end_in_2010/4/.

Vaz, Mark Cotter (2005). *The Lost Chronicles: The Official Companion Book*. London: Transworld Publishers.

Wheatley, Helen (2006). *Gothic Television*. Manchester University Press.

Whedon, Joss (1999). Interview in "Welcome to the Hellmouth Interview," featurette on Season 1 DVD, *The Complete Buffy Box Set*, 20th Century–Fox Television.

____ (2002). Interview in "*Buffy the Vampire Slayer*—Television with a Bite," featurette on Season 6 DVD, *The Complete Buffy Box Set*, 20th Century–Fox Television.

____ (2002). Interview extract from NPR *Fresh Air*, November 8, 2002, available at http://www.whedonverse.co.uk/#/jossquote4/4535285927.

____ (2002). Interview in "The Story of Season 5," featurette on Season 5 DVD, *The Complete Buffy Box Set*, 20th Century–Fox Television.

____ (2003). Interview in "The Last Sundown," featurette on Season 7 DVD, *The Complete Buffy Box Set*, 20th Century–Fox Television.

Whitfield, Stephen E., and Gene Roddenberry (1968). *The Making of Star Trek*. New York: Ballantine Books.

Wilcox, Rhonda and David Lavery (eds.) (2002). *Fighting the Forces: What's at Stake in* Buffy the Vampire Slayer? Lanham, MD: Rowman Littlefield.
Wilkes, Neil (2005). "*Lost* Creators Have Mysteries Worked Out," January 25, 2005, http://www.digitalspy.co.uk/ustv/news/a18692/lost-creators-have-mysteries-worked-out.html
____ (2007). "Q&A: Sky One Head Richard Woolfe," August 24, 2007, http://www.digitalspy.co.uk/broadcasting/news/a73571/qa-sky-one-head-richard-woolfe.html.
____ (2008). "U.S. Ratings Update: *Heroes* and *Prison Break*," October 8, 2008, http://www.digitalspy.co.uktv/a132087/us-ratings-update-heroes—prison-break.html.
Williams, Linda Ruth (2005). "*Twin Peaks*, David Lynch and the Serial-Thriller Soap." In *The Contemporary Television Series*, edited by Michael Hammond and Lucy Mazdon. Edinburgh University Press.
Wilson, Benji (2007). "*Heroes*: Why We've Fallen for the Nerds." *Telegraph* online, August 1, 2007, http://www.telegraph.co.uk/culture/tvandradio/3666869/Heroes-Why-weve-fallen-for-the-nerds.html.
Wylie, Ian (2008). "Backstage at the Baftas: *Heroes*," http://blogs.manchestereveningnews.co.uk/ianwylie/2008/04/backstage_at_the_baftas_heroes.html.
Zimmerman, Howard (1978). "*The Prisoner*." *Starlog*, first published January 1978, reprinted in *The Prisoner Who Poses a Question to the World*, a collection of articles and clippings compiled by Six of One—The Prisoner Appreciation Society, pp. 53–4. Hastings: World Gallery, 1981.

Index

Abrams, J.J. 1, 3, 26, 81, 108, 111, 124, 137, 188, 189
Addams Family 207–8, 209
Adventures of Brisco County, Jr. 63
Alexander, Jesse 111, 143, 195
Alfred Hitchcock Presents 169, 208, 214, 225
Alias 1, 3, 8, 18, 26, 105, 111, 129, 137, 208, 212
Alien Nation 208
All the President's Men (Alan Pakula, 1978) 77
Alt.tv.twin-peaks 48
Alt.tv.x-files 77
Amazing Stories 208, 214
American Gothic 53, 208
Angel 88, 93, 97, 101–2, 176–7, 208, 210, 214
Armchair Mystery Theatre 208

Babylon 5 208–9, 223
Band of Brothers 53
Batman (series) 209
Battlestar Galactica (original series) 209, 218
Battlestar Galactica (revised series) 4, 7, 151, 200, 209, 216
Baxter, Joseph 154, 155
The Beach (book) 130
Beeman, Greg 140, 143
Berman, Rick 169, 181, 182, 185, 186, 187
Bewitched 209, 215
Billsun, Anne 101
Bionic Woman (original series) 88, 209, 223, 228
Bionic Woman (revised series) 104, 210
Blake's 7 210

Blood and Chrome 200
Blood Ties 102, 208, 210
Blue Velvet (David Lynch, 1986) 36, 40, 45, 90
Bones 81
Bould, Mark 23, 31
The *Bourne* Trilogy (Doug Liman, 2002; Paul Greengrass, 2004 and 2007) 32
Boys from Brazil (Franklin J. Schaffner, 1978) 77
Braga, Brannon 169, 181, 182, 186, 187
Braun, Lloyd 110, 111, 112, 113, 128
Buffy the Vampire Slayer (Fran Rubel Kuzui, 1992) 85
Buffy the Vampire Slayer (series) 1, 4, 10, 11, 25, 47, 82–3, 84–107, 109, 125, 134, 140, 153, 157–8, 161, 162, 165, 175, 179, 186, 190, 196, 197, 200, 202, 203, 205, 207, 209, 210, 211, 212, 215, 220, 222, 224, 226, 229
Burk, Brian 111
Burning Zone 80, 210

Caldwell, John 7, 34
Campbell, Joseph 95
The Cape 195
Caprica 200, 209, 210
Carnivale 146, 211
Carter, Chris 55, 56, 57, 58, 59, 60, 63, 64, 65, 66, 70, 73, 75, 77, 78, 82, 123
Cawley, James 187, 188, 204
Chapman, James 23, 25, 166, 174, 190–1
Charmed 103, 211, 215
Chase, David 53
Close Encounters of the Third Kind (Steven Spielberg, 1977) 65, 184
Clover, Carol 96

Coma (Michael Crichton, 1978) 77
Coto, Manny 169, 187
Crossing Jordan 111, 139, 141
Crusade 211
Cube (Vincenzo Natali, 1997) 31
Cuse, Carlton 63, 111, 120, 122, 123, 124, 128, 133, 134, 135, 141, 149

Danger Man 16, 18, 19
Dark Angel 211
Dark City (Alex Proyas, 1998) 31
Dark Shadows (original series) 211
Dark Skies 81, 211
Davies, Russell T. 104, 168, 173–4, 176, 177, 178–9, 180, 181, 188, 190, 192, 212
Day One 196
Dead Like Me 103, 143, 211, 222
Defying Gravity 198, 201, 211–2
Demons 212
Desperate Housewives 53
Doctor Horrible's Sing-alongblog 204
Doctor Who (franchise) 1, 4, 8, 11, 14, 165, 166–9, 170, 181, 183, 190, 191, 192, 193, 194, 196, 212; original series 171–3, 191, 212; revised series 3, 27, 84, 104, 153, 164, 173–9, 180, 190, 191, 204, 210, 212; *Sarah Jane Adventures* 176, 179, 212; *Torchwood* 176, 179–81, 208, 210, 212, 229
Doctor Who (Geoffrey Sax, 1996) 173, 212
Dollhouse 105, 201, 208, 212

Earth: Final Conflict 212–3
Eastwick 104, 198, 213
Eerie, Indiana 213
Eick, David 209
Eraserhead (David Lynch, 1978) 36
Espenson, Jane 87, 181, 212, 228
E.T.: The Extra-Terrestrial (Steven Spielberg, 1983) 64, 65
The Event 81, 196, 213

Falling Skies 196
Fantasy Island 129, 213
Farscape 213
Ferren, Mick 25
Fight Club (David Fincher, 1999) 32
Fight the Future (Rob Bowman, 1998) 71
Firefly 104–5, 213
FlashForward 198, 201, 213
Forever Knight 101, 213–4

4400 81, 214
Freaky Links 81, 214
Fringe 81, 137, 201, 208, 214, 229
Frost, Mark 26, 33, 36, 38, 39, 40, 45, 48, 50, 53
Fuller, Bryan 53, 103, 143, 147–8, 149, 159, 189–90, 211
Fury, David 125, 128

Gallagher, Bill 30
Garth Merenghi's Dark Place 214, 216
Gerani, Gary 59
Ghost Whisperer 103, 198, 205, 214, 216, 218, 222, 226
Glatter, Lesli Link 160
Grade, Lew 16, 19, 26, 28, 31
Greenwalt, David 106
Gregory, Chris 31

Hammer House of Horror 214
Happy Town 54, 198, 214
Harsh Realm 56, 214
Headlam, Bruce 57
Hercules: The Legendary Journeys 209, 214
Heroes 1, 4, 7, 11, 47, 58, 72, 81, 84, 104, 138–65, 197, 198, 201, 203, 205, 211, 215, 216, 218, 220
Hex 102, 215
Hill Street Blues 7, 34, 36
Hills, Matt 2, 4, 6,
Hitchhikers Guide to the Galaxy 215
Hume, Kathryn 11

I Dream of Jeannie 209, 215
I Want to Believe (2008 film) 56, 79–80
The Incredible Hulk 215
The Invaders 63, 215, 229
Invasion 81, 215
Invasion: Earth 216
Invitation to Love 46
The Island (book) 130
Island of Dr. Moreau (book) 130

Jackson, Rosemary 11
James, Meg 106
Jenkins, Henry 4, 38, 48, 49, 101, 110, 131, 135, 166, 167–8
Jericho 28, 81, 216
Joan of Arcadia 82, 213, 216, 228
Johnson, Catherine 4, 5, 9, 59, 166
Jones, Sara Gwenllian 2, 9

Kellner, Jamie 93
King, Stephen 58
Kingdom Hospital 53, 214, 216
Kitty Pryde 96, 153
Kneale, Nigel 63, 169
Knight Rider 139
Kolchak the Night Stalker 59, 81, 216
Kring, Tim 60, 111, 138, 139, 140, 141, 143, 147, 148, 149, 150–1, 162, 203
Kurtzman, Alex 81, 188, 189
Kushner, David 140–1, 143

Land of the Giants 216
Land of the Lost 216, 220
Lavery, David 4, 51, 117–8, 128, 133, 134, 141, 142
League of Gentlemen 216–7
Leiber, Jeffrey 110–11
Lexx 217
Lindelof, Damon 3, 53, 111, 122, 123, 124, 128, 132, 133, 134, 135, 137, 141, 149, 188
Loeb, Jeff 139, 140, 143
Lois and Clark: The New Adventures of Superman 217
The Lone Gunmen 56, 73, 210, 217
Lord of the Flies (book) 130
Lord of the Rings 136
Lost 1, 2, 3, 4, 5, 7, 8, 10, 11, 18, 25, 26, 28, 49, 58, 60, 63, 78, 82, 100, 107, 108–37, 138, 139, 140, 141–2, 149, 150, 151, 152, 153, 155, 161, 162, 165, 169, 196, 197, 198, 199, 200, 202, 205, 208, 213, 216, 217, 218
Lost in Space x, 216, 217
Lost Room 217
Lost World 220
Lynch, David 25, 33, 35, 36, 38, 43, 44, 45, 47, 48, 49, 52, 53, 57

Mack, John 65
Marathon Man (John Schlesinger, 1976) 77
Markstein, George 16, 18, 22–23, 24, 29, 31
Marshall, Jack 187, 188
Mary Tyler Moore Show 34
M*A*S*H 34
Matrix (Larry and Andy Wachowski, 1999) 32
McGoohan, Patrick 13, 14, 15, 16, 17, 18, 21, 22, 26, 29, 30, 31, 48, 51

McPherson, Stephen 112, 199, 124
Medium 103, 198, 205, 210, 214, 217–8, 222, 226
Millennium 56, 60, 70, 88, 210, 218
Misfits of Science 139, 218
Mission Galactica 218
Moffat, Stephen 168, 169, 177–8, 188, 192, 193, 212
Moonlight 102, 208, 218
Moonlighting 34, 74
Moore, Ron D. 188, 189, 209, 211
Morgan, Darin 60, 68, 70, 71, 78
Mork and Mindy 218, 225
Mulholland Drive (David Lynch, 2001) 53
The Munsters 207, 209, 218
Mutant X 218
My Favorite Martian 207, 218, 225
Mysterious Island (book) 130
Mysterious Island (series) 218
Mysterious Ways 80, 219

Newman, Kim 172
Newman, Sidney 171, 172
Night Gallery 219
9/11 28, 81, 151, 154, 216
Nine Lives of Chloe King 195, 198
Nineteen Eighty-Four 219
No Ordinary Family 195
Northern Exposure 53, 219
Nussbaum, Emily 105, 107

On the Air 53
One Step Beyond 219
Orci, Roberto 81, 188, 189
The Outer Limits 219

Page, Adrian 20, 24, 76
Pearson, Roberta 34, 87–8
Perversions of Science 220
Petrie, Douglas 101
Peyton, Harley 38, 51–52
Picket Fences 53, 220
Pinkner, Jeff 111
Point Pleasant 220
Poltergeist: The Legacy 220
Porter, Lynnette 117–8, 128, 133, 134
Prey 220
Primeval 220
The Prisoner (miniseries) 3, 13, 27–31, 220
The Prisoner (series) 1, 2, 4, 8, 10, 11, 13–

32, 33, 34, 35, 38, 39, 40, 41, 43, 48, 51, 52, 53, 54, 56, 58, 60, 73, 76, 86, 88, 95, 99, 105, 117, 125, 126, 134, 136, 137, 155, 164, 165, 196, 200, 202, 220
Probe 221
Project Blue Book 47, 61, 64, 221
Project UFO 63-64, 221
Providence 139
PSI Factor: Chronicles of the Paranormal 80, 221
Pushing Daisies 103, 143, 211, 221

Quantum Leap x, 221, 225
Quatermass 63, 169, 180, 229

Randall and Hopkirk, Deceased 222
Ray Bradbury Theatre 222
Reaper 54, 103, 208, 209, 211, 222
Reeves, Rogers and Epstein 2
Rice, Lynette 201
Roddenberry, Gene 181, 182, 183, 184, 185, 188, 192, 212
Roswell (series) 103, 207, 209, 222
Roswell incident 64, 65, 67, 76

Sabrina the Teenage Witch 103, 215, 222
Sanctuary 222
Sarah Connor Chronicles aka *Terminator: The Sarah Connor Chronicles* 104, 201
Secret Agent see *Danger Man*
Serling, Rod 169, 182
Silence of the Lambs (Jonathan Demme, 1990) 62, 77
Six Million Dollar Man 36, 88, 209, 222-3
Six of One 14, 27
Sliders 223, 225
Smallville 103, 106, 140, 152, 199, 222, 223
Space: Above and Beyond 60, 223
Special Unit 2 81, 223
Staiger, Janet 205-6
Star Trek: franchise 1, 4, 11, 14, 165, 166-7, 169, 170, 190, 191, 192, 193, 194, 196, 200; original series 129, 135, 153, 164, 182-4, 223
Star Trek (JJ Abrams, 2009) 3, 30, 137, 169, 188-9, 205
Star Trek: Deep Space Nine 143, 185, 186, 209, 223-4
Star Trek: Enterprise 169, 181-2, 186-7, 188, 224

Star Trek: The Motion Picture (Robert Wise, 1979) 184
Star Trek: New Voyages (webseries aka *Star Trek: Phase II*) 187-8, 190, 204
Star Trek: The Next Generation 169, 179, 185, 187, 223
Star Trek: Of Gods and Men (mini-series) 188
Star Trek: Voyager 143, 185-6, 224, 227
Star Trek II: The Wrath of Khan (Nicholas Meyer, 1982) 185
Star Trek III: The Search for Spock (Leonard Nimoy, 1984) 185
Star Trek IV: The Voyage Home (Leonard Nimoy, 1986) 185
Star Trek VIII: First Contact (1996) 187, 188
Star Wars 111, 132, 136, 141, 160, 184, 189, 190, 193, 209
Stargate Atlantis 224
Stargate SG1 224
Stargate Universe 199, 224
Strange World 60, 80, 139, 224
Strieber, Whitley 65
Supernatural 82, 103, 106, 199, 224, 229
Survivors 225

Taken 81, 225
Tales of the Unexpected 225
Terminator: The Sarah Connor Chronicles 225
The Thing (John Carpenter, 1982) 77
Third Rock from the Sun 207, 218, 225
Thirtysomething 34
Thompson, Robert J. 6, 7-8, 34, 53
Time Tunnel 225
Todorov, Tzvetan 10, 63
Tomorrow People 225-6
Total Recall 2070 226
Touched by an Angel 82, 219, 226
The Triangle 226
Troup, Gary 125, 126
Tru Calling 103, 214, 218, 222, 226
True Blood 102, 200, 226
The Truman Show (Peter Weir, 1998) 28, 31
Tulloch, John 166
24 139, 195
Twilight Zone 68, 136, 169-70, 182, 208, 214, 219, 226
Twin Peaks 1, 2, 4, 8, 9, 10, 11, 18, 25, 33-54, 56, 57, 58, 60, 61, 64, 66, 67, 68, 73,

76, 77, 86, 88, 95–6, 98, 99, 100, 109,
110, 112, 114, 125, 126, 129, 130, 133,
134, 137, 160, 164, 165, 196, 198, 200,
202, 213, 216, 217, 220, 226–7
Twin Peaks: Fire Walk with Me (David
Lynch, 1992) 39, 52

UFO 63, 227
Ultraviolet 227
Urban Gothic 212, 227

V 81, 196, 227
Valenzetti Equation 126
Vampire Diaries 102, 106, 228
Vampire High 102, 227
Videodrome (David Lynch, 1983) 31
The Visitor 81, 228

Waiting for Godot (play) 20
Warehouse 13 81, 200, 228
Wheatley, Helen 51, 53
Whedon, Joss 26, 53, 84, 86, 87, 88–9,
91, 92, 93, 95, 99, 104–5, 135, 153, 200,
204, 212

Whitfield, Stephen E. 182, 184
Wild at Heart (David Lynch, 1990) 38
Wild Palms 53, 228
Williams, Linda Ruth 44–45
Wilson, Benji 3, 11, 139–40
Wolf Lake 228
Wonder Woman (new series) 105, 195, 198
Wonder Woman (original series) 209, 210,
228
Wonderfalls 103, 143, 211, 228

The X-Files (series) 1, 2, 4, 7, 8, 10, 11, 18,
25, 52, 54, 55–83, 86, 88, 89, 92, 96,
97, 98, 99–100, 109, 123, 124, 134, 139,
140, 144, 145, 151, 155, 162, 164–5, 186,
190, 196, 197, 199, 202, 205, 209–10,
211, 212, 213, 214, 216, 219, 221, 224,
225, 227, 228, 229; *Fight the Future*
(Rob Bowman, 1998) 71; *I Want to Believe* (2008 film) 56, 79–80
X-Men (comics) 96
X-Men (films) 153
Xena: Warrior Princess 209, 214, 229

www.ingramcontent.com/pod-product-compliance
Ingram Content Group UK Ltd.
Pitfield, Milton Keynes, MK11 3LW, UK
UKHW041937140426
5217IPUK00014B/531